The Individualization of War

The Individualization of War

Rights, Liability, and Accountability in Contemporary Armed Conflict

Edited by
JENNIFER WELSH
DAPO AKANDE
AND
DAVID RODIN

Great Clarendon Street, Oxford, OX2 6DP,
United Kingdom

Oxford University Press is a department of the University of Oxford.
It furthers the University's objective of excellence in research, scholarship,
and education by publishing worldwide. Oxford is a registered trade mark of
Oxford University Press in the UK and in certain other countries

© The Editors and Contributors 2023

The moral rights of the authors have been asserted

All rights reserved. No part of this publication may be reproduced, stored in
a retrieval system, or transmitted, in any form or by any means, without the
prior permission in writing of Oxford University Press, or as expressly permitted
by law, by licence or under terms agreed with the appropriate reprographics
rights organization. Enquiries concerning reproduction outside the scope of the
above should be sent to the Rights Department, Oxford University Press, at the
address above

You must not circulate this work in any other form
and you must impose this same condition on any acquirer

Published in the United States of America by Oxford University Press
198 Madison Avenue, New York, NY 10016, United States of America

British Library Cataloguing in Publication Data

Data available

Library of Congress Control Number: 2023932531

ISBN 978–0–19–287220–3

DOI: 10.1093/oso/9780192872203.001.0001

Printed and bound by
CPI Group (UK) Ltd, Croydon, CR0 4YY

Links to third party websites are provided by Oxford in good faith and
for information only. Oxford disclaims any responsibility for the materials
contained in any third party website referenced in this work.

Acknowledgements

This book is a cornerstone of a long and fruitful collaboration between the three co-editors, who in 2008 founded the Oxford Institute for Ethics, Law and Armed Conflict (ELAC). In 2013, that collaboration was deepened and broadened by the award of a European Research Council Advanced Grant (340956) to pursue research on the phenomenon that we call the 'individualization of war' (IOW). We thank Oxford colleagues Stephen Whitefield and Andrew Hurrell, who provided comments on a (very) rough version of the original proposal to the ERC and encouraged us in the application process. We also thank the ERC itself for the financial support to dream, convene, and experiment, and for its willingness to bet on a project that combined international relations, law, and moral philosophy.

The IOW project, which ran from 2014 to 2019, gathered together a talented interdisciplinary team of researchers at various stages of their careers, who participated at different points along the way. We would like to thank each of them here for the energy, wisdom, and creativity they dedicated to understanding individualization and exploring its effects: Lars Christie, Alexandre Skander Galand, Emanuela Gillard, Yuna Han, Rebecca Mignot-Mahdavi, Helen McDermott, Emily Paddon Rhoads, Graham Parsons, Ruben Reike, Heather Roff, Hugo Slim, Rebecca Sutton, and Maja Spanu. The European University Institute in Florence served as the main research hub for IOW, with the University of Oxford as a partner institution. We extend our deep appreciation to the Research Support team at EUI, led by Serena Scarselli, who assisted us in managing a large team, with multiple events, streams of work, and fieldwork trips. We also thank the wonderful coordinators who supported both Jennifer Welsh as Principal Investigator and the broader team – Martina Selmi and Claudia Fanti. As the inaugural coordinator, Martina was particularly instrumental in ensuring that our gatherings in Florence were not only productive, but also full of laughter and wonderful Tuscan cuisine.

The IOW project also benefited from a set of friendly commentators who joined us at our team meetings and provided both further inspiration and – in some cases – useful correction. We extend our gratitude first and foremost to Gabriella Blum, who shared our fascination with individualization and steered us in productive directions early on. We also thank two former senior officials of the UN Secretariat, Alvaro de Soto and Jean-Marie Guéhenno, who sharpened our understanding of individualization's complex effects, and scholars Scott Sagan and Ben Valentino, who encouraged our embrace of interdisciplinary analysis.

The research and reflection that features in this book, and particularly our conceptualization of individualization as centred on protection, liability, and accountability, were shaped through a variety of events and workshops that were sponsored by the IOW project. They include: the annual ELAC workshops on the ethics of war held in 2015 (at the Stockholm Centre for the Ethics of War and Peace), 2016 (at the EUI), and 2017 (at the University of Oslo's Concept Lab); the workshop on Protection, Peacekeeping and Individualization (held at Columbia University in 2015); the workshops on International Law and the Crime of Aggression (hosted by Oxford in 2016) and on The International Criminal Court in Active Armed Conflicts (held at the EUI in 2016); the 2017 and 2018 Transatlantic Workshops on International Law; the Expert Workshop on Sanctions in 2017 (hosted by the EUI); the conference on The Ethics of Stabilization and Security (organized in collaboration with the Armed Forces Chaplaincy Centre at the UK Defence Academy in 2018); the workshop on Protecting Populations and Regulating Armed Force in Mexico (co-hosted with CIDE in Mexico City in 2018); and the IOW Practitioner Engagement Workshop (held in collaboration with the US Military Academy, Westpoint, in 2019). We thank the many participants and presenters in these events, who included not only leading scholars from the fields of law, moral philosophy, and political science, but also many practitioners from international organizations, humanitarian organizations, and national governments and militaries. Collaboration with policymakers grappling with individualization was one of the core objectives of the IOW project and we are grateful for the in-depth conversations with practitioners that these events facilitated. We also extend our gratitude to the co-sponsors and hosts of these gatherings for their willingness to support our ongoing research.

The papers on which this edited volume is based were first discussed at the IOW conference at the EUI in June 2018. We extend huge thanks to our stellar (and patient) team of contributing authors, who engaged with our project's conceptual framework and pushed our thinking about individualization, often in critical ways. We would also like to thank the discussants and participants who enriched this meeting in Florence: Ziv Bohrer, Sarah Cleveland, Janina Dill, Helen Frowe, Claus Kress, David Luban, Marko Milanovic, Scott Shapiro, and Nina Tannenwald. We would also like to thank Christopher Daase, Cecile Fabre, Amos Guiora, Yagil Levy, Jeff McMahan, and Cheyney Ryan for their support of, and input into, the IOW project.

This volume has been long in the making, as is the case with many edited books. The world around us has changed in ways that are challenging some of the forces driving individualization. We would like to thank our research assistant in the final phase, Daniel Theriault of McGill University, and our editor at OUP, Dominic Byatt, who enthusiastically took on the book. Most of all, we extend thanks to our families for their steadfast support of our work and for tolerating the many distractions that the IOW project and this edited book created.

Jennifer Welsh, Dapo Akande, and David Rodin
April 2023

Contents

List of Contributors   ix

Introduction: Understanding Individualization   1
Jennifer Welsh, Dapo Akande, and David Rodin

PART I. EXTENDING INDIVIDUALIZATION IN THE ETHICS AND LAW OF ARMED CONFLICT

1. After War and Peace   41
   Adil Ahmad Haque

2. The Direct Rights of Individuals in the International Law of Armed Conflict   58
   Anne Peters

3. The Supererogatory Moral Risks of Military Service   89
   Bradley Jay Strawser

PART II. RETHINKING INDIVIDUALIZATION: PHILOSOPHICAL AND PSYCHOLOGICAL PERSPECTIVES

4. Collective Values in Just and Unjust Wars   117
   Victor Tadros

5. Situationism and the Individualization of Responsibility in War   135
   Benjamin Valentino

PART III. THE CONSEQUENCES OF INDIVIDUALIZATION

6. The Individualization of IHL Rules through Criminalization for War Crimes: Some (Un)Intended Consequences   163
   Paola Gaeta and *Abhimanyu George Jain*

7. Tensions between the Pursuit of Criminal Accountability and Other International Policy Agendas in Situations of Armed Conflict   187
   Sarah M.H. Nouwen

viii CONTENTS

8. Two Decades of Civilian Protection Mandates for United
Nations Peacekeepers 220
Paul D. Williams

PART IV. BEYOND FORMAL ARMED CONFLICT

9. Individualization and Collectivization in Contexts of
Organized Criminal Violence: The Case of Mexico's War
on Organized Crime 247
Pablo Kalmanovitz and *Miriam Bradley*

Index 270

List of Contributors

Dapo Akande is Professor of Public International Law at the University of Oxford and a Member of the United Nations International Law Commission. He has served on the editorial boards of several leading international law journals including the *American Journal of International Law*, the *European Journal of International Law* and the *African Journal of International and Comparative Law*. He is one of the authors of the *Oppenheim's International Law: The United Nations* (2017, OUP) which was awarded the Certificate of Merit by the American Society of International Law, and an editor of the *Oxford Guide to International Humanitarian Law* (2020, OUP). He has acted as advocate, counsel or adviser in cases before international tribunals, including the International Court of Justice, the International Tribunal for the Law of the Sea, the European Court of Human Rights, the International Criminal Court and the World Trade Organization panels. He has also acted as a consultant/advisor in cases in national courts, including the UK Supreme Court, and regularly provides advice on international law issues to states, international organizations and civil society organizations.

Miriam Bradley is a Senior Lecturer in the Humanitarian and Conflict Response Institute at the University of Manchester. She was previously Associate Professor at the Institut Barcelona d'Estudis Internacionals and has also held research and teaching positions at the Geneva Graduate Institute, University College London, the University of Oxford, and Oxford Brookes University. Her research focuses on international responses to conflict, violence, and migration, and she is the author of *The Politics and Everyday Practice of International Humanitarianism* (OUP, 2023) and *Protecting Civilians in War* (OUP, 2016). She is currently a member of the editorial board of the *Journal of Humanitarian Affairs*.

Paola Gaeta is Professor of International Law at the Graduate Institute of International and Development Studies. She is also a member of the Editorial Board of the *Journal of International Criminal Justice* and of the *International Spectator* (formerly *The Italian Journal of International Affairs*). Previously, Professor Gaeta was Director of the Geneva Academy (2007–2014) with Professor Andrew Clapham, where she directed the LLM in International Humanitarian Law and Human Rights, Adjunct Professor at the University L. Bocconi (Milan) (2015–2018), Adjunct Professor at the Graduate Institute of International and Development Studies (2010–2015) and Professor of International Criminal Law at the University of Geneva (2007–2015). From 1998 to 2007, she was consecutively Assistant Professor, Associate Professor and Professor of International Law at the University of Florence. Professor Gaeta is a leading expert on international criminal law and international criminal courts and tribunals and has published widely on these issues. Her research interests focus on international criminal law, particularly with regard to topics more closely related to general issues of public international law and exposed to cross-fertilization by international human rights law and international humanitarian law.

X LIST OF CONTRIBUTORS

Abhimanyu George Jain is a legal adviser at the International Committee of the Red Cross (ICRC). He is admitted to the practice of law in India and England and Wales, and has previously worked as a management consultant (McKinsey & Co), corporate lawyer (Norton Rose Fulbright LLP), counsel (to India) for investment disputes, and lecturer of international law (National Law School of India University). His co-authored chapter in this volume was finalised before he started working at the ICRC, and the opinions presented in the chapter do not necessarily reflect the views or positions of the ICRC.

Adil Ahmad Haque is Professor of Law and Judge Jon O. Newman Scholar at Rutgers Law School. Professor Haque's scholarship focuses on the international law of armed conflict and the philosophy of international law. His first book, *Law and Morality at War* was the subject of a symposium in *Ethics*, a review essay in the *European Journal of International Law*, and several reviews in leading journals. His work has been cited by the European Court of Human Rights and by the United Nations Special Rapporteur on extrajudicial, summary, or arbitrary executions in her report on the use of armed drones for targeted killing. Professor Haque is also frequently quoted by the media, including by *The New York Times*, *The Washington Post*, *The Guardian*, and *The Economist*.

Pablo Kalmanovitz is professor in the Department of International Studies at the *Instituto Tecnológico Autónomo de México* (ITAM) in Mexico City. Previously he was professor at the *Centro de Investigación y Docencia Económicas* (CIDE) in Mexico, the Universidad de los Andes in Bogotá, postdoctoral fellow at Yale University and the European University Institute, and has been visiting scholar at Freie Universität in Berlin, McGill University, and the University of Ulster in Belfast. His research focuses on normative aspects of organized violence, in particular the international regulation of armed force, on which he has published numerous articles and book chapters. He is general editor of the Yearbook of International Humanitarian Law and his book *The Laws of War in International Thought* was published by Oxford University Press in 2020.

Sarah Nouwen is Professor of International Law at the European University Institute. She is on leave from the University of Cambridge, where she is a Professor in Public International Law and a Fellow of Pembroke College and was for many years a Co-Deputy Director of the Lauterpacht Centre for International Law. She is also an Editor-in-Chief of the *European Journal of International Law*. Prior to assuming her lectureship at Cambridge in 2012, she worked in international diplomacy: at the Netherlands mission to the United Nations, at the Netherlands Ministry of Foreign Affairs in The Hague, at the Netherlands Embassy in Khartoum, and as a Senior Legal Advisor to the African Union High Level Implementation Panel in Sudan. She also served as a consultant for the UK Department of International Development in Darfur.

Anne Peters is Director at the Max Planck Institute for Comparative Public Law and International Law in Heidelberg, a professor at Heidelberg, Freie Universität Berlin, and Basel, and a L. Bates Lea Global Law Professor at the University of Michigan. She was a member of the Venice Commission (2011–15), served as the President of the European Society of International Law (2010–12), and as the President of the German Society of International

Law (2019-2023). She is a member of the Permanent Court of Arbitration and an associate member of the Institut de Droit International. She holds an honorary doctorate of the University of Lausanne.

David Rodin is the Founder and Chair of Principia Advisory and Senior Fellow at the Carnegie Council for Ethics and International Affairs. A former co-director of the Oxford Institute for Ethics, Law and Armed Conflict, he has published broadly on the ethics of war and human rights, including *War and Self-Defense* (OUP 2002), which was awarded the American Philosophical Association Sharp Prize. He is a recipient of the European Prize for Military Ethics and the Presidential Medal of the Republic of France, and he was honoured by the World Economic Forum as a 'Young Global Leader', recognising the most distinguished young leaders in all fields below the age of 40. As Chair of Principia he advises some of the world's largest commercial and non-governmental organisations on ethics, conduct, and culture.

Bradley J. Strawser is Associate Professor of Philosophy in the Defense Analysis Department at the Naval Postgraduate School in Monterey, CA. He has published in such peer-reviewed journals as *Analysis, Ethical Theory and Moral Practice, Philosophia, Journal of Military Ethics, Public Affairs Quarterly, Journal of Human Rights*, and *Epoché*. Dr Strawser has published books with Oxford University Press, Palgrave Macmillan, Martinus Nijhoff Publishers, and Routledge. He has also written widely in popular media such as *The New York Times, The Guardian*, 3 Quarks Daily, among other places, and has appeared on various NPR affiliates, the BBC World Service, and other media outlets. In addition, Dr Strawser is the Founder and CEO of Compass Ethics, an organizational ethics consultancy where he regularly advises senior leadership of Fortune 500 Companies on issues of ethical risk, improving ethical culture, and successful ethical outcomes.

Victor Tadros is Professor of Criminal Law and Legal Theory at the University of Warwick. Prior to joining Warwick in 2006, he held lectureships at the University of Aberdeen and the University of Edinburgh, and in the fall of 2015, was Carter Visiting Professor of General Jurisprudence at Harvard Law School. From 2010 to 2013, Professor Tadros held an AHRC Research Grant, with Antony Duff, Lindsay Farmer, Sandra Marshall, and Massimo Renzo, to work on criminalization. He also held a Leverhulme Major Research Fellowship from 2014 to 2018, and was elected as Fellow of the British Academy in 2018. Professor Tadros is an Associate Editor at *Ethics*.

Benjamin Valentino is Professor of Government at Dartmouth College and Chair of the Department of Government. His research interests include the causes and consequences of violent conflict and American foreign and security policies. At Dartmouth he teaches courses on international relations, international security, American foreign policy, the causes and prevention of genocide and serves as co-director the Government Department Honors Program. He is also the faculty coordinator for the War and Peace Studies Program at Dartmouth's Dickey Center for International Understanding. His work has appeared in outlets such as *The New York Times, The Wall Street Journal, Foreign Affairs, The American Political Science Review, Security Studies, International Organization, Public Opinion Quarterly, World Politics*, and *The Journal of Politics*.

xii LIST OF CONTRIBUTORS

Jennifer M. Welsh is the Canada 150 Research Chair in Global Governance and Security at McGill University and Director of the Centre for International Peace and Security Studies. She was previously Chair in International Relations at the European University Institute and Professor in International Relations at the University of Oxford, where she co-founded the Oxford Institute for Ethics, Law and Armed Conflict. From 2013-2016, she served as the Special Adviser to the UN Secretary General, Ban Ki-moon, on the Responsibility to Protect. She has published several books and articles on the ethics and politics of armed conflict, the 'responsibility to protect', humanitarian action and civilian protection, the UN Security Council, and Canadian foreign policy. Her 2016 book, *The Return of History: Conflict, Geopolitics and Migration in the 21st Century,* was based on her CBC Massey Lectures. Prof. Welsh is a member of the Internally Displaced Persons Protection Expert Group, established by UNHCR and the Global Protection Cluster, and sits on the Advisory Boards of the Global Centre for the Responsibility to Protect and the Auschwitz Institute for Peace and Reconciliation. In 2021, she was elected an International Honorary Member of the American Academy of Arts and Sciences and in 2022 became a Fellow of the Royal Society of Canada.

Paul D. Williams is Professor of International Affairs in the Elliott School of International Affairs at the George Washington University where he directs the MA program in Security Policy Studies. His research focuses on the politics and effectiveness of contemporary peace operations, the dynamics of warfare in Africa, and emerging security threats. His books include *Understanding Peacekeeping* (Polity Press, 3rd edition, 2021); *Fighting for Peace in Somalia: A history and analysis of the African Union Mission (AMISOM), 2007-2017* (Oxford University Press, 2018); *War and Conflict in Africa* (Polity Press, 2nd edition, 2016); and (ed.), *The Oxford Handbook of United Nations Peacekeeping Operations* (Oxford University Press, 2015).

Introduction

Understanding Individualization

Jennifer Welsh, Dapo Akande, and David Rodin

The rights and responsibilities of the individual are at the centre of today's armed conflicts in a way that they have never been before. This process of 'individualization',[1] which challenges the primacy of the sovereign state, has two main drivers. The first are powerful normative developments related to human rights, which have elevated human-centric (vs state-centric) conceptions of security[2] and which have spawned new kinds of wars and peacekeeping missions, and a new class of international crimes.[3] The second are dramatic technological and strategic developments that can both empower individuals as military actors, and enable either the targeting or protection of particular individuals.[4]

The individualization of war forces us to confront the status of individuals in at least three different capacities: (1) as subject to violence but deserving of protection; (2) as liable to harm because of their responsibility for attacks on others; and (3) as agents who can be held accountable for the perpetration of crimes committed in the course of conflict. These three domains served as the organizing framework for a large-scale, interdisciplinary research project (funded by the European Research Council) which we co-directed, and for a gathering of leading thinkers from the fields of international relations, political science, and moral philosophy, who we encouraged to engage with the phenomenon of individualization. Their reflections and arguments further our understanding of not only how individualization is manifest in contemporary armed conflict—in theory and

---

[1] Gabriella Blum, 'The Individualization of War: From War to Policing in the Regulations of Armed Conflicts', in Austin Sarat, Lawrence Douglas, and Martha M. Umphrey (eds), *Law and War* (Redwood City, CA: Stanford University Press, 2014), p. 52; Jennifer M. Welsh, 'Humanitarian Actors and International Political Theory', in Chris Brown and Robyn Eckersley (eds), *The Oxford Handbook of International Political Theory* (Oxford: Oxford University Press, 2018); and Jennifer M. Welsh, 'The Individualization of War: Defining a Research Programme', *Annals of the Fondazione Luigi Einaudi 53*, no. 1 (2019), pp. 9–28.

[2] Matthew Weinert, *Making Human: World Order and Global Governance of Human Dignity* (Ann Arbor: University of Michigan Press, 2015).

[3] Ruti G. Teitel, *Humanity's Law* (New York: Oxford University Press, 2011); Thomas G. Weiss, *Humanitarian Intervention* (Malden, MA: Polity, 2nd ed., 2012); and Kathryn Sikkink, *The Justice Cascade* (New York: W. W. Norton, 2011).

[4] P. W. Singer, *Wired for War* (New York: Penguin Books, 2009); and Michael L. Gross, *Moral Dilemmas of Modern War* (Cambridge: Cambridge University Press, 2010).

Jennifer Welsh, Dapo Akande, and David Rodin, *Introduction*. In: *The Individualization of War*. Edited by: Jennifer Welsh, Dapo Akande, and David Rodin, Oxford University Press. © Jennifer Welsh, Dapo Akande, and David Rodin (2023).
DOI: 10.1093/oso/9780192872203.003.0001

2 INTRODUCTION: UNDERSTANDING INDIVIDUALIZATION

in practice—but also what challenges it poses for today's scholars and practitioners. Our collective research also integrates the currently segregated scholarship on individualization in moral philosophy, international law, and international relations, recognizing that—with some notable exceptions[5]—analysis of individualization has proceeded largely in separate streams, without recognition of the important links between law, morality, and politics that constitute the day-to-day reality for policy actors.

Our analysis of individualization starts from the assumption that while the human rights norms underpinning many aspects of individualization may be normatively desirable in themselves and enjoy relatively strong support, efforts to operationalize norms related to individual protection, liability to harm, and accountability are placing enormous strain on the actors and institutions most actively engaged in contemporary armed conflict: the governments and armed forces of states; international security organizations; and humanitarian agencies. More specifically, individualization is giving rise to a set of ethical, legal, and political dilemmas that are confounding contemporary policymakers and, in some cases, weakening the legitimacy of national, international, and non-governmental institutions.

For example, in the realm of protection, the UN Security Council remains caught between its state-centric constitution, which has traditionally demanded the even-handed treatment of parties to a conflict, and the recognition of its responsibility to protect individuals—illustrated in the contrast between the relative speed with which the Council was able to act in Libya in 2011, compared with its later failure to reach a consensus on how to respond to documented crimes against humanity in Syria. In the UN's most extensive peacekeeping mission in history, in the Democratic Republic of Congo, peacekeepers have faced agonizing strategic and operational dilemmas over how to fulfil their civilian protection mandate, which requires addressing atrocities perpetrated by either state or non-state actors, while at the same time avoiding criticism that might alienate the government of former President Kabila, whose consent has been critical to their continued presence (and which was eventually withdrawn).

Turning to the domain of harm, we see that Unmanned Aerial Vehicles (UAVs or 'drones') have seemingly offered state leaders and national militaries opportunities to target lethal force more precisely against a specific individual who poses a grave threat, thereby minimizing both collateral damage and the loss of their own personnel. Indeed, some moral philosophers have argued that there is an imperative to employ these more precise weapons.[6] On the other hand, the use of lethal force

---

[5] Larry May, *Crimes Against Humanity: A Normative Account* (Cambridge: CUP, 2005); Teitel, *Humanity's Law* (2011); Francessca Lessa and Leigh A. Payne (eds), *Amnesty in the Age of Human Rights Accountability* (Cambridge: CUP, 2012).

[6] Bradley J. Strawser, 'Moral Predators: The Duty to Employ Uninhabited Aerial Vehicles', *Journal of Military Ethics 9*, no. 4 (2010), pp. 342–368.

by the executive branch of governments, without judicial or legislative oversight, has called into question fundamental protections of a liberal-democratic society and arguably weakens some of the restraints embedded in Just War principles such as 'last resort'.[7] Moreover, other actors have also increasingly come to use these 'precision tools' of war, with uncertain and destabilizing effects on the both the nature of conflict and the rules that seek to govern it.

In the case of accountability, diplomatic actors continue to face a dilemma between pursuing criminal action against individual perpetrators (as they did in Libya in 2011), which can close off options for negotiation that might bring a more rapid end to conflict and civilian suffering, or privileging conflict resolution strategies that deny justice to some victims of international crimes and contradict rhetorical commitments about 'ending impunity'. Contemporary legal practices associated with accountability also place humanitarian agencies in a deeply uncomfortable position, since they are closer to the crimes of war than most other institutions and could potentially provide evidence in criminal proceedings. To give such evidence, however, could make their personnel the targets of violence or—as in the case of the International Criminal Court's investigations in Darfur in 2005–6—*persona non grata*, thereby rendering it impossible for them to continue to protect civilians on the ground.

These seemingly discrete dilemmas are all underpinned by a tension between the privileged moral and legal claims of individuals (and the technological changes that often enable them), and the more traditional ones of sovereign states. Methodologically, the project on which this volume draws entertains alternatives to the traditionally dominant, state-centric paradigm for the analysis and regulation of armed conflict in the disciplines of international relations, international law, and moral philosophy.[8] At the same time, we recognize that a great deal of existing literature on individualization is inherently progressivist. In international relations, for example, prominent scholars have posited that the commitment to individual human rights is now firmly embedded in norms and law, and that the most pressing task ahead is to design a better strategy and stronger institutions to ensure compliance with that commitment.[9] In moral philosophy, scholars mounting 'Revisionist' challenges to modern Just War theory[10] argue that while

---

[7] Jennifer M. Welsh, 'The Morality of 'Drone Warfare' in David Cortright, Rachel Fairhurst, and Kristen Wall (eds), *Drones and the Future of Armed Conflict: Ethical, Legal and Strategic Implications* (Chicago: Chicago University Press, 2015).

[8] Michael Walzer, *Just and Unjust Wars* (New York: Basic Books, 4th ed., 2006); and A. J. Coates, *The Ethics of War* (Manchester: Manchester University Press, 1997).

[9] Sikkink, *The Justice Cascade* (2011); and Thomas Risse, Stephen C. Ropp, and Kathryn Sikkink, *The Persistent Power of Human Rights* (Cambridge: CUP, 2013).

[10] Jeff McMahan, *Killing in War* (Oxford: OUP, 2009); David Rodin, *War and Self-Defense* (Oxford: OUP, 2002); Cécile Fabre, *Cosmopolitan War* (Oxford: OUP, 2012); and Helen Frowe, *Defensive Killing* (Oxford: OUP, 2014).

4 INTRODUCTION: UNDERSTANDING INDIVIDUALIZATION

the current law of armed conflict is often incompatible with an ethics of war based on individual human rights, this disjuncture between law and morality is not sustainable—even if there are strong prudential reasons for maintaining it. And in international law, some analysts argue that individual human rights and accountability have transformed states' conceptions of their rights and responsibilities, and the relationship between the state and the individual.[11]

In this volume, we acknowledge that both in practice and in scholarship, individualization is not always held to be an unmitigated 'good'. Analysts have noted the potential for individualization to create problematic forms of asymmetry, in which only the powerful (most notably Western states) have the advanced means to 'individualize' protection, liability, and accountability and in which the reciprocal obligations of IHL are weakened.[12] Individualization has also been accompanied by double standards and hypocrisy: some of the loudest calls for respect for individual human rights come from those whose drone strikes lead to excessive civilian casualties.[13] At a more fundamental level, some have expressed deep unease with the way that individualization can work to transform war itself, either by depoliticizing conflict and delegitimizing particular actors[14] or by broadening the geographical reach of the battlefield.[15] Relatedly, critical theorists have taken issue with the methodological individualism that underpins recent ethical theorizing about armed conflict, arguing that it not only oversimplifies the nature of war, by depicting it as the aggregate of individual actions or decisions,[16] but also constructs a problematic and partial account of moral agency that 'reproduces existing privilege' and reflects a 'parochial historical imagination'.[17]

Given our core interest in analysing how individualization is manifest in the study and practice of armed conflict, and the tensions to which it gives rise, we do not explicitly engage with or in critical theorizing. Nonetheless, some of our contributing authors openly question the argument that individuals, or individualist values, should dominate the ethics, law, or politics of armed conflict, expanding on earlier observations about how the imperative to protect civilians or hold individual leaders accountable can conflict with other powerful norms,

---

[11] Teitel, *Humanity's Law* (2011); Antonio Cassese, *International Criminal Law* (Oxford: OUP, 2nd ed., 2008); and Mark A. Drumbl, *Atrocity, Punishment, and International Law* (Cambridge: CUP, 2007).

[12] Adam Roberts, 'The Principle of Equal Application of the Laws of War', in David Rodin and Henry Shue (eds), *Just and Unjust Warriors: The Legal and Moral Status of Soldiers* (Oxford: OUP, 2008).

[13] For further discussion of how hypocrisy and double standards has fueled the backlash against human rights, see Anne Peters, 'The Importance of Having Rights', *ZaöRV 81* (2021), pp. 7–22; and Stephen Hopgood, *The Endtimes of Human Rights* (Ithaca, NY: Cornell University Press, 2013).

[14] Eliav Lieblich, 'The Humanization of *Jus Ad Bellum*: Prospects and Perils', *European Journal of International Law 32*, no. 2 (2021), pp. 579–612.

[15] Derek Gregory, 'The Everywhere War', *The Geographical Journal 177*, no. 3 (2011), pp. 238–250.

[16] Maya Zehfuss, *War and the Politics of Ethics* (Oxford: OUP, 2018).

[17] Kimberly Hutchings, 'From Just War Theory to Ethico-Political Pacifism', *Critical Studies on Security 7*, no. 3 (2019a), pp. 191–198, at p. 195. See also Kimberly Hutchings, 'Cosmopolitan Just War and Coloniality', in Duncan Bell (ed), *Empire, Race and Global Justice* (Cambridge: CUP, 2019b).

such as non-intervention, impartiality, or the peaceful resolution of disputes.[18] We also elaborate on how the implications of individualization have become evident within national governments, as well as within international and non-governmental organizations, as they seek to navigate a new ethical and legal terrain. Humanitarian agencies, for example, experience profound disagreements within their own organizations over whether and how to cooperate with Western governments pursuing protection and accountability.[19] Concerns about individualization feature too in the evolution and contestation of the principle of the 'responsibility to protect', particularly in the discourse of practice of states that seek to emphasize the primary responsibility of national governments to protect their own populations and to downplay the remedial responsibilities of the international community.[20] Finally, non-Western states often point to the uncomfortable reality that the operationalization of norms related to individualization is often directed solely at countries in the Global South—manifest in the fact that humanitarian interventions have yet to occur in developed countries (with the exception of the former Yugoslavia) and that the criminal cases pursued by the International Criminal Court have related primarily to African countries.

More broadly, scholars and policymakers have pointed to a series of trends that are undermining the human rights advances that help to fuel key aspects of individualization. The international order has been experiencing a profound structural shift, which gives increased power to states such Xi Jinping's China and Vladimir Putin's Russia, both of which have openly challenged human rights and accountability norms and have promoted more 'Westphalian' conceptions of sovereignty.[21] Russia and China have exerted their own sovereignty by crushing dissent and secessionist stirrings at home and attempting to extend their power and jurisdiction over other self-determining communities. But they have also supported other regimes—including in Syria and the Philippines—to reassert sovereign control and limit external interference. Elsewhere, the nationalist-populist revolt in Western democracies has targeted human rights institutions as well as the global economic system in which they are embedded. For his part, former US President Trump did little to stem the tide against globalization and liberal

---

[18] Andrew Hurrell, *On Global Order* (Oxford: OUP, 2007); Brad R. Roth, *Sovereign Equality and Moral Disagreement* (New York: Oxford University Press, 2011); and Jean L. Cohen, *Globalization and Sovereignty* (Cambridge: CUP, 2012).

[19] Antonio Donini, *The Golden Fleece* (Boulder, CO: Kumarian Press, 2012); and Claire Magone, Michael Neumann, and Fabrice Weissman (eds), *Humanitarian Negotiations Revealed: The MSF Experience* (New York, NY: Columbia University Press, 2012).

[20] Jennifer Welsh, 'Norm Robustness and the Responsibility to Protect', *Journal of Global Security Studies* 4, no. 1 (2019), pp. 53–72.

[21] Roland Paris, 'The Right to Dominate: How Old Ideas About Sovereignty Pose New Challenges for World Order, *International Organization* 74, no. 3 (2020), pp. 453–489. Paris also argues that circulating within the discourse of major powers like China and Russia is the return of older, non-Westphalian conceptions of sovereignty that emphasize the power of rulers to act outside the constraints of formal rules and institutions—what is sometimes referred to as 'extra-legal sovereignty'.

6 INTRODUCTION: UNDERSTANDING INDIVIDUALIZATION

internationalism, preferring instead the rhetoric of 'America first' and rejecting what he has disparagingly referred to as the ideology of 'globalism'.

All of these forces, it has been suggested, are challenging post-Westphalian visions of a shared global order and 'giving way to an era of resurgent sovereignty'.[22] Within this context, there is greater momentum behind the argument that individuals should be subsumed morally and politically *into* the state in times of war,[23] rather than made a specific focus of norms or law related to armed conflict. Even long-standing principles of international humanitarian law are now routinely under attack, including by liberal democracies—whether through their own actions or those of their proxy fighters. Not only are legal rules being violated, but actors are increasingly questioning the standing of and rationale for such rules. Indeed, the legal advisor for the International Committee of the Red Cross (ICRC) has warned against creating a vicious cycle, in which not respecting the laws of war becomes the 'new normal' as states and armed groups 'seek to justify their violations as inevitable and realistic behaviour in armed conflict'.[24]

These critiques and forms of push-back therefore cast doubt on linear, teleological models of normative change, and call for an approach that both accepts and analyses the potential for ongoing contestation of individualization and the norm conflict that it can entail.[25] In other words, we do not assume that efforts to operationalize individual rights, liability, or accountability in the context of war necessarily fix the meaning of norms associated with individualization, or ends the debate about either their desirability or applicability in particular cases. An appreciation of the reality of contestation not only enriches our study of the dilemmas associated with individualization, but also requires us to look beyond 'technical' solutions, such as better coordination or more resources, for ways to address them. They also suggest that the trajectory of individualization remains unclear—a theme we return to later.

In the rest of this Introduction, we further elucidate our concept of individualization, and how it challenges more traditional collective entities and values; identify some of the tensions to which it gives rise and how they are being resolved; and posit the different ways in which individualization is (currently) being contested. We conclude by providing an overview of the subsequent chapters, in which

---

[22] Sebastian Strangio, 'Welcome to the Post-Human Rights World', *Foreign Policy*, 7 March 2017.

[23] We thank Tony Lang for this particular phrasing of the contemporary push-back against individualization.

[24] Helen Durham, 'Atrocities in conflict mean we need the Geneva Conventions more than ever', *The Guardian*, 5 May 2016.

[25] For a discussion of norm conflict in the fields of international relations and international law, see, for example, Antje Wiener, 'Enacting Meaning-In-Use: Qualitative Research on Norms and International Relations', *Review of International Studies 35*, no. 1 (2009), pp. 175–193; and Marko Milanovic, 'Norm Conflict in International Law: Whither Human Rights?', *Duke Journal of Comparative & International Law 20*, no. 1 (2010), pp. 69–132.

international lawyers, philosophers, and political scientists further engage with the potential and limitations of the individualization of war.

1. Conceptualizing Individualization

In its most general form, individualization is a process in which individuals, rather than collectives, increase in salience—both empirically and normatively. To arrive at a more specific definition for use in the context of armed conflict, there are two distinctions that are central to analysis and normative assessment.

The first is the distinction between an *agent* (actor) and a *subject*[26] (acted upon):

a. Individualization is the process in which the agency of individuals, rather than of collective actors, increases in importance in the causes, conduct, and consequences[27] of war.

b. Individualization is the process in which the effects on individual, rather than collective, subjects increase in importance in the causes, conduct, and consequences of war.

The second is the distinction between the role that individuals play in *explanations* and *normative assessments* of the phenomenon of war:

c. Individualization is the process in which individual agents and subjects play an increasingly important role in our descriptions and explanations of the causes, conduct, and consequences of war.

d. Individualization is the process in which individual agents and subjects play an increasingly important in role in our normative assessment of the causes, conduct, and consequences of war (where normative assessment entails assessing reasons for action including ethical, legal, and strategic reasons for action).

1.1 The Domains of Individualization: Protection, Harm, and Accountability

By integrating these two aspects, we define individualization *as a process in which individuals (both as agents and as subjects) increase in importance compared with*

---

[26] We acknowledge that in legal analysis a 'subject' is usually deemed to have legal personality, which suggests that the term 'object' would be more appropriate here. However, given our interdisciplinary analysis, we prefer the term 'subject' as a means of acknowledging how individuals can be affected and empowered by changes in armed conflict, even if such changes do not confer legal personality.

[27] By consequences, we are primarily referring to responses to conflict (such as reparations or criminal justice).

8 INTRODUCTION: UNDERSTANDING INDIVIDUALIZATION

collective entities for the purposes of explaining and normatively assessing the causes, conduct, and consequences of war. We further suggest that individualization in the context of war forces us to confront the status of individuals in at least three different domains: (1) as subject to violence but deserving of protection (given their individual right to life); (2) as liable to harm because of their responsibility for attacks on or threats posed to others; and (3) as agents who can be held accountable for the perpetration of crimes committed in the course of conflict. The process of individualization can thus be conceived as affecting the ways in which individuals are protected in war, and the bases under which—and ways in which—they can be legitimately harmed or held to account for their actions.

The first major aspect of individualization is the move to make the individual—and his or her rights—one of the central reasons or causes for engaging in armed conflict (what is referred to in Just War literature as *jus ad bellum*). Whereas conflicts in previous centuries were primarily about the gain of territory or resources, defence of the state against attack, or—in exceptional cases—the rescue of minority groups in neighbouring states, many contemporary conflicts have as one of their central and explicit purposes the protection of individuals' security. The NATO-led action in Libya in 2011 was one highly visible manifestation of this trend, but the practice stretches back to the significant shifts in UN Security Council practice in the early decades of the post–Cold War period, which enabled the United Nations to broaden its definition of what constitutes a threat to international peace and security, and to the endorsement by UN member states in 2005 of the principle of the 'responsibility to protect'.[28]

In addition to justifying the use of force, the protection of civilians has transformed the practice of peacekeeping. Beginning with the conflict in Sierra Leone in 1999, the UN Security Council routinely began to include civilian protection in peacekeeping mandates, calling on member states' contingents to respond to and prevent extreme violations of human rights. Hence, while during the Cold War era, peacekeepers practised a more passive kind of impartiality, in which they were beholden to the wishes of the parties to a conflict, contemporary peacekeepers have been expected and mandated to be robust and assertive, by penalizing infractions against the peace process or broader international norms and principles. Today's blue helmets are now being tasked with roles akin to those of police officers and 'expected to search for, and then side with, the victims' of violence.[29]

---

[28] Jennifer M. Welsh, 'The Security Council and Humanitarian Intervention', in Vaughan Lowe et al. (eds), *The United Nations Security Council and War: The Evolution of Thought and Practice since 1945* (Oxford: OUP, 2008), pp. 535–562.

[29] Emily Paddon Rhoads, *Taking Sides: Impartiality and the Future of the United Nations* (Oxford: OUP, 2016), p. 66, at p. 1. For a discussion of the development, evolution, and interrelationship between the norms of protection of civilians and responsibility to protect, see Emily Paddon Rhoads and Jennifer M. Welsh, 'Close Cousins in Protection: The Evolution of Two Norms', *International Affairs 95*, no. 3 (2019), pp. 597–717.

The second key dimension of individualization concerns the ways in which individuals can legitimately be subjected to harm—such as lethal force or detention—in the context of armed conflict. Analysis here has focused particularly on the move to both establish and act upon individual liability, rather than conflict status, in the conduct of armed conflict (what is commonly referred to as the domain of *jus in bello* rules). Modern Just War theory and the contemporary law of armed conflict assert that principles of liability and immunity derive from a person's status or membership in a particular group: combatants or non-combatants.[30] But a powerful stream within moral philosophy—Just War Revisionism—has challenged this status-based approach to the ethics of war using the framework of individual human rights.[31] If all persons have rights, and if important rights such as the right to life can only be lost or forfeited on the basis of some responsible action of the right-bearer him or herself, then it seems to follow that liability can only be established by examining the particular circumstances of individual actors within a conflict.

There are three important implications of this logic. First, human rights premises raise the question of which combatants are liable to be targeted in armed conflict—thereby challenging the Traditional Just War position of the 'moral equality of soldiers'.[32] According to the Revisionists, rights-bearing individuals can only become liable to lethal violence when they are responsible for inflicting grave unjust harm on others. This conclusion suggests that 'just combatants' (those fighting a morally or legally justified war) are not liable to be intentionally targeted; individual soldiers are only liable if they are fighting in a war that is illegal or unjust.[33] A position in favour of asymmetrical rights and responsibilities also has dramatic implications for how the practice of military establishments would need to be configured, as exemplified by the Rules of Engagement of UK forces in Afghanistan, which permitted engaging the enemy only if it posed an imminent threat to others.

In addition, individualization has implications for the status of civilians in war, who have long enjoyed protected status under the legal and moral principle of distinction. But some philosophers have begun to argue that certain non-combatants (such as the leaders of so-called rogue regimes or terrorist organizations) can be liable to intentional attack if they are responsible for sufficiently grave unjust

---

[30] Walzer, *Just and Unjust Wars* (2006).

[31] See McMahan, *Killing in War* (2009); Rodin, *War and Self-Defense* (2002); Frowe, *Defensive Killing* (2014); and Fabre, *Cosmopolitan War* (2012). For further discussion of the features of Traditional and Revisionist Just War theory, see Seth Lazar, 'Just War Theory: Revisionists Versus Traditionalists', *Annual Review of Political Science* 20, no. 1 (2017), pp. 37–54. For more on debate over how attention to individual rights affects our moral assessment of the use of force in self-defense, see Cecil Fabre and Seth Lazar (eds), *The Morality of Defensive War* (Oxford: OUP, 2014).

[32] Walzer, *Just and Unjust Wars* (2006).

[33] For various philosophical formulations of this argument, see McMahan, *Killing in War* (2009); Frowe, *Defensive Killing* (2014); and Fabre, *Cosmopolitan War* (2012). For further discussion of the debate over the morality of the use of force in self-defense, see Cecil Fabre and Seth Lazar (eds), *The Morality of Defensive War* (Oxford: OUP, 2014).

10 INTRODUCTION: UNDERSTANDING INDIVIDUALIZATION

threats against others.[34] At the same time, technological advances—as described above—have enabled states to operationalize individual liability, particularly as part of counterterrorism operations, through the use of remotely controlled UAVs.

The final implication of Revisionism relates to how, if at all, the tenets of individual liability to attack can be compatible with current or modestly amended interpretations of international humanitarian law.[35] While some critics maintain that the circumstances of war are so unique, and so devastating, that war must be regulated by its own form of morality and law,[36] human rights principles are already intersecting with—and in some cases challenging—the nature and scope of the law of armed conflict. Legal analysis of the increasing 'co-application' of international human rights law (IHRL) and international humanitarian law (IHL)[37] is based not only on reference to and application of IHRL to conflict situations by courts and treaty bodies,[38] but also on more normative arguments that warring parties must be accountable for how they treat rights-bearing individuals in the context of armed conflict and that the more traditional 'status-based' determination of who can be killed or detained violates core rights.[39]

Attempts to give effect to the norms and laws regulating armed conflict have traditionally focused on the imposition of obligations on states and state-like actors. Over the course of the last century, however, specific obligations have been imposed directly on individuals (as either leaders or soldiers), breaches of which give rise to accountability for criminal acts undertaken during the course of war. This third and final domain of individualization culminated in the 1998

---

[34] McMahan, *Killing in War* (2009); Gross, *Moral Dilemmas of Modern War* (2010); and Fabre, *Cosmopolitan War* (2012). For further discussion of potential civilian liability, see Helen Frowe, 'Intervening Agency and Civilian Liability', *Criminal Law and Philosophy* (2022). doi: 10.1007/s11572-020-09555-4.

[35] Seth Lazar, 'The Morality and Law of War', in Andrei Marmor (ed), *The Routledge Companion to the Philosophy of Law* (New York: Routledge, 2012), pp. 364–379; and Jeff McMahan, 'Laws of War' in S. Besson and J. Tasioulas (eds), *The Philosophy of International Law* (New York: OUP, 2010), pp. 493–510.

[36] Janina Dill, 'Towards a Moral Division of Labour Between International Humanitarian Law and International Human Rights Law during the Conduct of Hostilities', in Z. Bohrer, J. Dill, and H. Duffy (eds), *Laws Applicable to Warfare* (Cambridge: CUP, 2020), pp. 197–265.

[37] Daragh Murray et al. (eds), *Practitioners' Guide to Human Rights Law in Armed Conflict* (Oxford: OUP, 2016).

[38] Helen Duffy, 'Trials and Tribulations: Co-application of International Humanitarian Law and Human Rights Law in the Age of Adjudication', in Z. Bohrer, J. Dill, and H. Duffy (eds), *Laws Applicable to Warfare* (Cambridge: CUP, 2020), pp. 15–105. For further discussion of the relationship between IHRL and IHL, see Cordula Droege, 'The Interplay between International Humanitarian Law and International Human Rights Law in Situations of Armed Conflict', *Israel Law Review*, 40 (2007), pp. 310–355; Noam Lubell, 'Parallel Application of International Humanitarian Law and International Human Rights Law: An Examination of the Debate', *Israel Law Review 40* (2007), pp. 648–660; Alexander Orakhelashvili, 'The Interaction between Human Rights and Humanitarian Law', *European Journal of International Law 19* (2008), pp. 161–182; Christian Tomuschat, 'Human Rights and International Humanitarian Law', *European Journal of International Law 21* (2010), pp. 15–23; Orna Ben-Naftali (ed), *International Humanitarian Law and International Human Rights Law* (Oxford: OUP, 2011).

[39] Guglielmo Verdirame, 'Human Rights in Wartime', *European Human Rights Law Review 6* (2008), pp. 689–705; and Anne Peters, *Beyond Human Rights: The Legal Status of the Individual in International Law* (Cambridge: CUP, 2014).

Rome Statute creating the International Criminal Court (ICC). There are two main challenges that this aspect of individualization poses for existing mechanisms for preventing, managing, and resolving armed conflicts, and for existing principles of international law.

The first set of challenges arises from the ICC's status as a permanent court, with universal jurisdiction that can activate investigations of individuals independent of the consent of states. Consequently, recent decades have witnessed the increased engagement of the Court in ongoing armed conflicts as well as the threat of prosecution as a 'tool' of coercive diplomacy in situations where atrocity crimes have been committed or are imminent. Although these powers of the ICC enhance the prospects for accountability, they have had a number of further (in some cases unintended) consequences and raise important theoretical and practical questions about the relationship between peace and justice.[40] Furthermore, there are significant issues with using criminal justice instrumentally as part of international diplomacy, including: the possibility that these strategies potentially destabilize existing mechanisms for resolving conflicts peacefully and challenge the United Nations' traditional approach to treating conflict parties even-handedly;[41] and the increased role for domestic, as opposed to international, courts in the prosecution of international crimes or in the making of decisions on questions of war and peace.[42] As a result of this latter development, domestic courts are being called upon to assess the legality of acts of foreign governments, which has a direct impact on the international relations of the state within which that court is located.

The second set of issues arising from the quest for accountability relate to the Kampala Amendments to the Statute of the ICC to provide for jurisdiction over the crime of aggression, which came into force in 2017.[43] Though the criminalization of aggression seeks individual accountability, it may also require or involve establishing *state* responsibility for the initiation of unlawful wars, thereby raising questions about whether the ICC can operate in the same way when it exercises jurisdiction over aggression as it does with regard to other international crimes.

---

[40] For analysis of the impact of the ICC's pursuit of accountability in the context of conflict, see Sarah Nouwen, 'The International Criminal Court: A Peacebuilder in Africa?', in D. Curtis and G.A. Dzinesa (eds), *Peacebuilding, Power and Politics in Africa* (Athens: Ohio University Press, 2012); Patrick S. Wegner, *The International Criminal Court in Ongoing Intrastate Conflicts: Navigating the Peace-Justice Divide* (Cambridge: CUP, 2015); Mark Kersten, *Justice in Conflict: The Effects of the International Criminal Court's Interventions on Ending Wars and Building Peace* (Oxford: OUP, 2016); and Phil Clark, *Distant Justice: The Impact of the International Criminal Court on African Politics* (Cambridge: CUP, 2018).

[41] For discussion of how the pursuit of accountability by the ICC can affect UN peace operations, see Thomas Buitelaar and Gisela Hirschmann, 'Criminal Accountability at What Cost? Norm conflict, peace operations, and the International Criminal Court', *European Journal of International Relations* 27, no. 2 (2021), pp. 548–571.

[42] Dapo Akande and Sangeeta Shah, 'Immunities of State Officials, International Crimes, and Foreign Domestic Courts', *European Journal of International Law 21*, no. 4 (2010), pp. 815–852.

[43] For analysis and debate on the criminalization of aggression and its different effects, see the Special Symposium, 'The Crime of Aggression before the International Criminal Court', *European Journal of International Law 29*, no. 3 (2018).

12 INTRODUCTION: UNDERSTANDING INDIVIDUALIZATION

What is more, the jurisdiction granted to the ICC is seen by some to undermine the historically central role of the Security Council as the body designated in the UN Charter with the power to determine whether aggression has taken place.[44] Finally, although the criminalization of aggression can be viewed as a further step in the individualization of war, the definition of aggression enshrined at Kampala arguably inhibits attempts to use force for humanitarian or protection purposes, as such uses of force may be construed as being in violation of the new prohibition.[45]

This latter possibility suggests that analysts need to attend to potential incompatibilities between the fulfilment of the three strands of individualization we identify here. However, there are other forms of normative argumentation relating to the crime of aggression that extend and deepen our understanding of individual human rights and bring the streams closer together. Though aggression has long been conceived as a violation of state sovereignty, it has also come to be seen as a particular 'species' of crimes against humanity, given its unleashing of unjustified killing and humanitarian suffering.[46] Most normative and legal accounts of the crime of aggression rightly focus their concern on the rights of civilians and soldiers in the state that is attacked.[47] One recent line of inquiry, which draws on the 2018 adoption of the Human Rights Committee of its General Comment (no. 36),[48] analyses how interpreting aggression through the lens of international human rights law breaks with the traditional view that *jus ad bellum* is wholly an interstate matter. Aggression would not only be deemed to violate the rules of *jus ad bellum*, but the killings it entails would also necessarily be violations of the right to life, *even in cases* where these killings would be lawful under the rules of *jus in bello*.[49]

Some legal and normative theorists have adopted an even more radical interpretation of the relevance of individual human rights, by drawing attention to the ways in which both civilians and combatants in the attacking state are put in harm's way by that state's decision to commit aggression.[50] In this case, it is argued, the

---

[44] For discussion of the institutional effects of the ICC's jurisdiction on the UN Security Council, see Sean D. Murphy, 'The Crime of Aggression at the International Criminal Court', in Marc Weller (ed), *The Oxford Handbook of the Use of Force in International Law* (Oxford: OUP, 2015).

[45] Beth Van Schaack, 'The Crime of Aggression and Humanitarian Intervention on Behalf of Women', *International Criminal Law Review 11*, no. 3 (2011), pp. 477–493.

[46] See for example, Tom Dannenbaum, 'Why Have We Criminalized Aggressive War?', *Yale Law Journal 126*, no. 5 (2017); pp. 1242–1318; and Frédéric Mégret, 'What Is the Specific Evil of Aggression?' (28 March 2012). Available at: SSRN: https://ssrn.com/abstract=2546732 or http://dx.doi.org/10.2139/ssrn.2546732

[47] Dannenbaum, 'Why Have We Criminalized Aggressive War?' (2017); and *The Crime of Aggression, Humanity, and the Soldier* (Cambridge: CUP, 2018).

[48] United Nations Human Rights Committee, General Comment no. 36 (2018) on Article 6 of the International Covenant on Civil and Political Rights, on the Right to Life (GC 36). UN doc. CCPR/C/GC/36, 30 October 2018.

[49] Lieblich, 'The Humanization of *Jus Ad Bellum*' (2021).

[50] Frédéric Mégret and Chiara Redaelli, 'The Crime of Aggression as a Violation of the Rights of One's Own Population', *Journal of the Use of Force in International Law 9*, no. 1 (2022), pp. 99–127. Lieblich also hints at this possibility in his discussion of how a state's failure to reasonably attempt

competition that has developed between IHL and IHRL largely evaporates, as the focus is not on the extra-territorial application of human rights law but rather on the relationship between a state and its own population, where human rights law is most comfortable and relevant.[51] With respect to civilians, the voluntary waging of aggressive war by a state would entail a failure to fulfil its human rights obligations to protect its population from harm—including harm from war. But the violation of rights could also extend to soldiers, whose lives are usually viewed as 'expendable' in the pursuit of war.[52] While legal proceedings have already acknowledged that a state can violate the human rights of soldiers by exposing them to unnecessary risk on the battlefield[53]—which amounts to an *in bello* reading of soldiers' rights—this further application of human rights would extend to the realm of *ad bellum*, claiming that soldiers' rights can be violated when they are deployed for illegal ends.[54] By conceiving of aggression as a form of *self*-harm,[55] this account focuses on the responsibility of sovereign states to protect all individual persons within their jurisdiction, and therefore strengthens the prohibition of war in ways that connect domestic and international law.

2. Individualization as a Process

If individualization is conceived as a process, the logic underpinning it is one of 'from-to': there are collectives that are becoming less central as individuals become more prominent. In the context of war, we can conceive of at least four kinds of collectives that are under challenge. Once again, however, the examples below illustrate that this process is not necessarily linear. The subsequent chapters will reveal that there remains strong evidence for the continued influence of forms of collective authority, agency, and subjectivity both in the theory and in the practice of armed conflict.

2.1 Sovereign States

In each of the domains of individualization we identified above, activities that were once directed at or concerned with the behaviour of sovereign states are experiencing an increased role for individuals (as either agents or subjects). In the realm of liability to harm, for example, we have witnessed uses of force which are aimed

---

to resolve disputes peacefully could amount to a violation of the duty to ensure the right to life of its people. See 'The Humanization of *Jus Ad Bellum*' (2021), at pp. 606–611.

[51] Mégret and Redaelli, 'The Crime of Aggression', p. 109.
[52] Ibid., p. 116.
[53] See, for example, Smith and others v. Ministry of Defence, 18 June 2013, UK Supreme Court 41.
[54] Mégret and Redaelli, 'The Crime of Aggression', p. 117.
[55] Ibid., p. 101. Emphasis added.

14 INTRODUCTION: UNDERSTANDING INDIVIDUALIZATION

not at the sovereign state per se, but rather at those individuals deemed particularly responsible for threats posed to others (through practices of targeted killing).

Similarly, the field of international justice has undergone a shift from what Kathryn Sikkink calls the 'state accountability model',[56] in which the state as a whole was held accountable for human rights violations or the commission of crimes and was expected to remedy the situation (frequently through reparations), toward an 'individual accountability model', in which particular individuals (though often in certain roles) are held criminally responsible. In the state-centric model, the actual individuals committing, ordering, or planning international criminal acts are beyond reach (as entailed by the principle of head of state immunity). In the individual-centric model, the possibility of directly establishing criminal responsibility for individuals without the mediation of the domestic judiciary poses a challenge to the sovereign authority of the state. We can also see individualization transforming the nature of the target of violence, from a broader concept of 'society' or 'oppressed group', to the individual victim. Even if victims are in reality members of important collectives and are often targeted on the basis of a connection to a particular collective (such as a religious or ethnic group), they are sometimes understood within international criminal justice as discrete individuals—with names, faces, and rights. One of the noteworthy aspects of the International Criminal Court, for example, is that it allows for the direct participation of victims in criminal proceedings—whereas in the earlier ad hoc tribunals victims were legally relevant only as witnesses.[57]

At the same time, however, both the architecture and the practice of international criminal justice requires active and ongoing cooperation from states and their representatives in order to achieve accountability for those individuals who are alleged to have committed international crimes.[58] Similarly, while prosecutors and judges at the ICC claim to give voice to victims and to represent their interests, there are limits to the degree to which victims' identities are truly represented. Indeed, some legal scholars contend that the manner in which victims are represented in ICC trials leads not only to a narrowing of victimhood—through its categorization of who is legally relevant—but also to the creation of an abstract entity—The Victim—that transcends the actual experiences and identities of the individual victims of international crimes.[59]

---

[56] Sikkink, *The Justice Cascade* (2011).

[57] Claude Jorda and Jerôme de Hemptinne, 'The Status and Role of the Victim', in A. Cassesse, P. Gaeta, and J.R.W.D. Jones (eds), *The Rome Statute of the International Criminal Court: A Commentary* (Oxford: Oxford University Press, 2002), pp. 1378–1388.

[58] See, for example, Bruce Broomhall, *International Justice and the International Criminal Court: Between Sovereignty and the Rule of Law* (Oxford: OUP, 2004).

[59] Sara Kendall and Sarah Nouwen, 'Representational Practices at the International Criminal Court: The Gap Between Juridified and Abstract Victimhood', *Law and Contemporary Problems 76* (2014), pp. 235–262.

2.2 Combatants and Non-Combatants

Individualization's impact has also extended to international humanitarian law (IHL), where there has been a growing emphasis on the individual in addition to the collective actors—combatants and non-combatants—that have traditionally featured in treaties and conventions regulating armed conflict. While IHL was one of the first areas of public international law to limit states' scope of action in order to grant protection to individuals, this was framed not in terms of individual rights, but rather in terms of prohibitions on what parties to armed conflict were entitled to do, or of their obligations towards particular groups of people (for example, the wounded and sick, or the civilian population in occupied territories).

Over the past two decades, however, the interplay between international human rights law and international humanitarian law has resulted in greater attention paid to individuals. This is particularly so on the combatant side, through—as we noted earlier—the legal recognition given to an individual soldier or detainee's rights. The European Court of Human Rights' evolving (and expanding) interpretation of its jurisdiction[60] has made it difficult for a state party to the European Convention on Human Rights to deny that it owes obligations to its military personnel, wherever they are located. Similarly, efforts by the Council of Europe to ensure military officials are afforded human rights have added to the pressure to acknowledge the relevance of rights claims and arguments.

Individualization of this kind is also prominent within the ethics of war,[61] through challenges to Michael Walzer's concept of the 'moral equality of soldiers'[62] (discussed above), and through philosophical attempts to distinguish among non-combatants some of which (controversially) may be more liable to attack.[63] More generally, Revisionist Just War theory is sceptical of the idea that collectives in war can be proper units of moral responsibility in any basic sense; as a moral matter, a person's liability to attack must be derived from her own choices and actions, and not merely from the group to which she belongs. Finally, it is worth noting that—despite what legal or ethical principles might prescribe—the unpacking of the non-combatant category is a 'real-world' practice. In various conflict settings,

---

[60] One example is with respect to fair trial rights in military courts. See *Findlay v. The United Kingdom*, 110/1995/616/706, Council of Europe: European Court of Human Rights, 25 February 1997.
The extent to which domestic courts recognize states' human rights obligations toward members of their armed forces varies across jurisdictions. In rendering its judgment in 2013 in the case of Smith and others v. Ministry of Defence, the UK Supreme Court held that deceased soldiers were under the UK's jurisdiction for the purposes of Article 2 of the European Convention on Human Rights at the time of their deaths (on duty, in Iraq). See UKSC 41, op. cit. US courts, by contrast, have generally resisted the extraterritorial application of human rights law in conflict settings.

[61] Janina Dill, 'Just War Theory in Times of Individual Rights', in Chris Brown and Robin Eckersley (eds), *The Oxford Handbook of International Political Theory* (Oxford: OUP, 2018).

[62] Christian Barry and Lars Christie, 'The Moral Equality of Combatants', in Seth Lazar and Helen Frowe (eds), *The Oxford Handbook of Ethics of War* (Oxford: OUP, 2018), pp. 339–357.

[63] Frowe, 'Intervening Agency and Civilian Liability' (2022).

16 INTRODUCTION: UNDERSTANDING INDIVIDUALIZATION

actors on the ground recognize different degrees of 'civilianness' and, in the case of some humanitarian organizations, engage in competition to claim a special type of civilian status.[64]

2.3 Conflict Parties

In non-international armed conflicts, the relevant collective entities have traditionally been 'warring parties'. After 1949, IHL expanded its imposition of obligations (and rights) to include organized armed groups, although the treaty rules applicable are more limited than those applying to states engaged in international armed conflict. It is also important to note that the precise nature and scope of such organized armed groups' obligations, and their interplay with those of states, are not completely settled as matters of law (particularly with respect to responsibilities for meeting the needs of civilians under the effective control of such groups). For our purposes here, the question is less about the legal obligations of entities which are not sovereign states, and more about whether *particular members* of those non-state entities can incur obligations and be held accountable for their violation. One significant move in this direction is the growing practice, reflected in Security Council Resolution 2178, of identifying the individual 'foreign terrorist fighter', rather than the 'organized armed group', as the key subject of policy and legal regulation. The provisions of Resolution 2178 are notable in that they are addressed specifically to individuals and prohibit them not only from engaging in terrorist acts but also from forging identity papers or from travelling to combat zones where terrorist groups are active.[65] The resolution also blurs definitions of terrorism and armed conflict, thereby creating ambiguity about the status of legal regimes and potentially undermining the equality of parties within an armed conflict.

Within international criminal justice, the move to hold individuals accountable for core international crimes has also shifted the focus of political and legal discourse away from conflict parties, towards the acts of particular individuals. For example, during the Security Council debate in May 2014 which discussed the referral of the situation in Syria to the ICC, then US permanent representative to the UN, Samantha Power, stated that 'the representative of Syria and perhaps of Russia may suggest that the draft resolution voted on today was biased, and I agree. It was biased in the direction of establishing facts and tilted in the direction of a peace that comes from holding accountable individuals, not entire groups,

---

[64] Rebecca Sutton, *The Humanitarian Civilian: How the Idea of Distinction Circulates Within and Beyond International Humanitarian Law* (Oxford: OUP, 2021).

[65] Anne Peters, 'Security Council Resolution 2178 (2014): The "Foreign Terrorist Fighter" as an International Legal Person', EJILtalk! Available at: https://www.ejiltalk.org/security-council-resolution-2178-2014-the-foreign-terrorist-fighter-as-an-international-legal-person-part-i/

such as the Alawites, Sunnis, or Kurds.'[66] What is more, developments in international criminal law—particularly the broadening of the scope of the crimes against humanity and war crimes to include acts committed in non-international armed conflicts—have enabled the establishment of individual criminal responsibility not only for leaders or representatives of states but also for individual members of non-state armed groups.[67] These steps, along with others, have helped to address what was previously an imbalance in the impunity enjoyed by non-state and state actors. It is now the gravity of the crime, rather than the requirement of statehood, that has become crucial—at least theoretically[68]—for criminal accountability.

2.4 State Consent

In addition to these collective entities, we can identify core collective *values* that underpin the traditional regulation and assessment of the causes and conduct of war, and which are being significantly affected by individualization. A prominent example is the consent of states, which can be conceptualized as a kind of 'proxy' for the self-determination and sovereignty of peoples and which serves as a crucial source of positive law. State consent has long operated as an important principle in the practice and regulation of armed conflict, as well as a precondition for the deployment of UN peacekeeping operations. Similarly, consent is a bedrock principle in the legal framework regulating humanitarian relief operations (in which humanitarian actors can only 'offer' assistance and require the prior consent of the state in order to operate).

As a result of individualization, however, the value of state consent is arguably being eroded, or in some cases counterbalanced, by imperatives to protect individual human rights. This logic is perhaps most visible in arguments in the debate over the legitimacy of humanitarian intervention.[69] The prevailing consensus is that while Security Council authorized action for humanitarian purposes is legal, the use of force by a state or group of states outside of the UN Charter

---

[66] UN doc. S/PV.7180, 22 May 2014.

[67] William Schabas, 'Punishment of Non-State actors in Non-International Armed Conflict', *Fordham International Law Journal 26*, no. 4 (2002), pp. 907–933.

[68] In practice, aspects of the imbalance remain, as national governments have proven willing to cooperate with criminal justice mechanisms when they involve arrest warrants against non-state actors, but are less so when these warrants pertain to state officials. We thank Sarah Nouwen for pointing out this continuing discrepancy.

[69] We define humanitarian intervention as 'the use of force by a state (or group of states acting together) aimed at preventing or ending a humanitarian catastrophe affecting individuals other than its own citizens, without the permission of the state within whose territory force is applied.' See International Law Association, *Final Report on Aggression and the Use of Force* (2018), p. 20. Available at: https://www.ila-hq.org/images/ILA/DraftReports/DraftReport_UseOfForce.pdf

18   INTRODUCTION: UNDERSTANDING INDIVIDUALIZATION

framework—what is known in international law as 'unilateral humanitarian intervention'[70]—does not pass the hurdle of legality.[71] Nonetheless, some states and legal commentators continue to argue that in exceptional cases the nature and scale of humanitarian or human rights crises justify forms of coercive military action (i.e., without the consent of the target state) that do not conform to the exceptions to the prohibition on the use of force explicitly set out in the Charter. In August 2013, in relation to the Syrian government's alleged use of chemical weapons, the British government asserted that 'a legal basis [to use force was] ... available, under the doctrine of humanitarian intervention [subject to certain conditions].'[72] It followed up with a similar argument in April 2018, justifying its involvement in the coalition air strikes as protecting the Syrian population from further attacks.[73]

The status and meaning of consent have also been debated in other contexts. Turning to peacekeeping, the United Nations has claimed since the 2000 Brahimi Report that its operations will no longer be constrained by the injunction to ensure the continued consent of all parties in situations of imminent threat to vulnerable civilians.[74] With respect to the legal rules governing humanitarian relief in armed conflict, legal attempts to interpret what amounts to the 'arbitrary withholding of consent' by states to offers to provide humanitarian assistance have drawn on international human rights law.[75] More controversially, some legal scholars have argued that in response to such an arbitrary withholding of consent, international agencies would be entitled to engage in unauthorized and cross-border deliveries of humanitarian relief.[76]

Finally, within the domain of accountability, the shift in the locus of responsibility under international law from states to individuals calls into question the

---

[70] This term refers to a use of force that does not have Security Council authorization. Thus, the use of the word 'unilateral' does not mean that a state is acting alone. States can act collectively, but unilaterally, if they act without the Council's imprimatur.

[71] For a review of legal opinion, see Vaughan Lowe and Antonios Tzanakopoulos, 'Humanitarian Intervention', in Rudiger Wolfrum (ed), *The Max Planck Encyclopedia of Public International Law* (Oxford: OUPS, 2012), Available at: https://papers.ssrn.com/sol3/papers.cfm?abstract_id=1701560; and Nigel Rodley, 'Humanitarian Intervention', in Marc Weller (ed), *The Oxford Handbook on the Use of Force in International Law* (Oxford: OUP, 2015), pp. 775–776.

[72] Prime Minister's Office, 'Chemical Weapon use by Syrian Regime: UK Government Legal Position', Policy Paper, 29 August 2013. Available at: www.gov.uk/government/publications/chemical-weapon-use-by-syrian-regime-uk-government-legal-position/chemical-weapon-use-by-syrian-regime-uk-government-legal-position-html-version. The Danish government published an opinion arguing along the same lines. See 'General Principled Considerations on the Legal Basis for a Possible Military Operation in Syria', UPN Alm.del Bilag, 30 August 2013. Available at: www.ft.dk/samling/20121/almdel/upn/bilag/298/1276299/index.htm.

[73] See, for example, the statement of British diplomats at the emergency session of the Security Council. UN Doc. S/Pv.8233, 14 April 2018.

[74] Paddon Rhoads, *Taking Sides* (2016).

[75] Dapo Akande and Emanuela-Chiara Gillard, 'Arbitrary Withholding of Consent to Humanitarian Relief Operations in Armed Conflict', *International Law Studies* 92 (2016), p. 483.

[76] Payam Akhavan et al., *Open Letter to the UN on Humanitarian Aid*, 28 April 2014. Available at: https://www.ibanet.org/Article/NewDetail.aspx?ArticleUid=73b714fb-cb63-4ae7-bbaf-76947ab8cac6

relevance of state consent when asserting international criminal jurisdiction.[77] Some scholars have described the Rome Conference creating the ICC as a quasi-legislative process, in which—by a non-unanimous vote—the Statute asserts, on behalf of the international community, prescriptive jurisdiction beyond its states parties.[78] Others, however, contest this view of the source of the ICC's authority, and maintain that state consent remains a significant value in international criminal justice[79]—one that has been reasserted through the process to amend the Rome Statute to define the crime of aggression and new war crimes. This more recent history underscores the ICC's founding in a multilateral treaty, and, by extension, its consent-based 'jurisdictional scheme'.[80]

2.5 State Responsibility

The notion that states—as distinct from individuals—can be assigned responsibility for certain actions or held responsible for violations of certain rules and norms has been a prominent feature of modern international law and politics.[81] It is this logic that has informed various sanctions regimes, claims for debt repayment or reparations, or calls for official apologies for historic wrongdoings. The 2001 adoption of the Draft Articles on the Responsibility of States for Internationally Wrongful Acts[82] has significantly advanced, through both codification and progressive development, the legal rules regarding when a state obligation has been breached and the legal consequences of that violation. Rather than asserting that states, like individuals, are moral agents that can be held responsible, the Draft Articles develop a 'functional' theory of state responsibility, in which states, as legal persons, act *through* their agents and representatives who perform state functions.[83]

---

[77] Gerry Simpson, 'Men and Abstract Entities: Individual Responsibility and Collective Guilt in International Criminal Law', in Andre Nollkaemper and Harman van der Wilt (eds), *System Criminality in International Law* (Cambridge: CUP, 2009), pp. 69–100.

[78] Alexandre Skander Galand, 'The Nature of the Rome Statute of the International Criminal Court (and its Amended Jurisdictional Scheme', *Journal of International Criminal Justice* 17, no. 5 (2019), pp. 933–956.

[79] Dapo Akande, 'Prosecuting Aggression: The Consent Problem and the Role of the Security Council', *Oxford Legal Research Paper Series*, Paper No. 10/2011.

[80] Galand, 'The Nature of the Rome Statute' (2019), at p. 950.

[81] For one recent attempt to theorize state responsibility and apply it to these different practices, see Sean Fleming, *Leviathan on a Leash: A Theory of State Responsibility* (Princeton: Princeton University Press, 2020).

[82] *Draft Articles on the Responsibility of States for Internationally Wrongful Acts*, Report of the International Law Commission on the Work of its Fifty-third Session, UN GAOR. UN doc. A/56/10 (2001).

[83] On the contrast between an 'agential' and 'functional' theory of state responsibility, see Fleming, *Leviathan on Leash*, pp. 32–34. Proponents of the agential approach include Peter French, *Collective and Corporate Responsibility* (New York: Columbia University Press, 1984); and Toni Erskine, 'Assigning Responsibility to Institutional Moral Agents: The Case of States and Quasi-States', *Ethics & International Affairs* 15, no. 2 (2001), pp. 67–85. For more on the functional approach to conceiving

20   INTRODUCTION: UNDERSTANDING INDIVIDUALIZATION

Beyond the legal sphere, however, the theory and practice of state responsibility has also had its detractors, particularly among philosophers and normative theorists who worry about the potential for harming individuals in the process of punishing states.[84] This concern has been particularly prevalent with respect to economic sanctions,[85] which in the past two decades have become much more targeted, or 'individualized', in order to direct punitive action at those deemed most responsible for wrongdoing.[86] The significant steps taken in international criminal law, beginning with the Nuremberg and Tokyo trails, are also part of the broader effort to individualize responsibility for state acts.

But although individual criminal accountability for actions undertaken during armed conflict is one of the most notable normative and legal developments associated with the individualization of war, the notion of state responsibility remains an important part of efforts to prevent and punish international crimes such as genocide. For example, in the Bosnia v. Serbia case before the International Court of Justice, the question of state responsibility—in this case, relating to Serbia's failure to prevent the genocide in Srebrenica—was central to the interpretation of the provisions of the Genocide Convention as extending beyond a state's obligation to prevent and punish genocidal acts occurring within its own territory, to the duty of neighbouring states to use means at their disposal to deter those suspected of preparing genocide.[87] Legal scholars have demonstrated that state responsibility and individual responsibility can in fact work side by side—as opposed to the latter supplanting the former.[88] For their part, some normative theorists have suggested that individual responsibility should not and cannot supplant state responsibility, since state officials lack sufficient resources to pay reparations for large-scale wrongdoing and that states remain the main bearers of treaty obligations.[89]

---

of state responsibility, see James Crawford, *State Responsibility: The General Part* (Cambridge: CUP, 2013).

[84] Toni Erskine, 'Kicking Bodies and Damning Souls: The Danger of Harming "Innocent" Individuals while Punishing "Delinquent" States', *Ethics & International Affairs* 24, no. 3 (2010), pp. 261–285; and Anna Stilz, 'Collective Responsibility and the State', *Journal of Political Philosophy* 19, no. 2 (2011), pp. 190–208.

[85] See, for example, Joy Gordon's analysis of the sanctions imposed on Iraq from 1990 to 2003, following the first Guld War. *Invisible War: The United States and the Iraq Sanctions* (Cambridge, MA: Harvard University Press, 2010.

[86] Arne Tostensen and Beate Bull, 'Are Smart Sanctions Feasible?', *World Politics* 54, no. 3 (2002), pp. 373–403; and Daniel Drezner, 'Sanctions Sometimes Smart: Targeted Sanctions in Theory and Practice', *International Studies Review* 13, no. 1 (2011), pp. 96–108.

[87] International Court of Justice, Case Concerning the Application of the Convention on the Prevention and Punishment of the Crime of Genocide (Bosnia and Herzegovina v. Serbia and Montenegro). General List, no. 91, 26 February 2007. For further discussion of the ICJ's jurisprudence on genocide, see Anthony F. Lang, Jr., 'Punishing Genocide: A Critical Reading of the International Court of Justice', in Tracy Isaacs and Richard Vernon (eds), *Accountability for Collective Wrongdoings* (Cambridge: CUP, 2011).

[88] André Nolkaemper, 'Concurrence between Individual Responsibility and State Responsibility in International Law', *International and Comparative Law Quarterly* 52, no. 3 (2003), pp. 615–640.

[89] Fleming, *Leviathan on a Leash*, p. 179.

3. Tensions Arising from Individualization

We began this introductory chapter by pointing to the possible tensions, or dilemmas, that the individualization of war poses for key actors engaged in or associated with armed conflict. These tensions can be roughly divided into three main types, all of which feature in subsequent chapters by our contributors.

The first set of tensions arises at the normative level such that it appears conceptually or normatively impossible to fully realize two important values. A prominent example is the tension between maintaining impartiality in peacekeeping operations and punishing one party to a conflict for infringement of human rights. A further example is the tension within Traditional Just War theory that arises when a war that is considered unjust from a *jus ad bellum* perspective (i.e., fought for unjust cause), but that is conducted justly from a *jus in bello* perspective (i.e., adhering to the rules of right conduct). In this case the war would be considered unjust in totality, even if the individual acts of soldiers that together constitute the war are considered just.

A second set of tensions associated with the individualization of war exists at a practical level. Here, there are two possibilities. First, tensions can arise from practical attempts to achieve or operationalize two important values, due to intrinsic and unavoidable facts about the world. One example is the often-noted tension between the achievement of peace (between conflict parties) and justice (to address crimes committed in war) given the political nature of conflict resolution. But there are also tensions confronting practical attempts to achieve or operationalize values that are due to more contingent facts about the world. A case in point would be the difficulty of achieving humanitarian objectives with armed forces and strategic doctrines that are tailored to large-scale counterforce operations; another would be the financial constraints on wide-ranging protection mandates in peacekeeping operations and the political reluctance of troop-contributing countries to use robust force to protect civilians.

And finally, there are tensions that arise between different manifestations and domains of individualization—or what we might conceive as 'cross-cutting' tensions. One illustration, hinted at the outset of this Introduction, is the dilemma facing humanitarian actors who may be requested to provide assistance to mechanisms established to bring accountability for violations of international criminal law or international human rights law (such as international and national tribunals, commissions of inquiry, or the imposition of targeted sanctions), while at the same time ensuring continued access to individual civilians in need.[90] Although humanitarians frequently have valuable first-hand information on

---

[90] Sara Kendall and Sarah Nouwen, 'International Criminal Justice and Humanitarianism', in K.J. Heller, F. Mégret, S.Nouwen, J. Ohlin, and D. Robinson (eds), *The Oxford Handbook of International Criminal Law* (Oxford: OUP, 2020).

violations or are in direct contact with affected communities, the sharing of such information with accountability mechanisms risks undermining their operations and, in some cases, putting their staff and beneficiaries at risk. Another case of cross-cutting tensions emerges with respect to the doctrine of so-called command responsibility, which on the one hand has been created to further individual accountability for the perpetration of atrocity crimes but which on the other hand seeks to protect victims of armed conflict. Here, there is a tension between designing a model of command responsibility that ensures that commanders will act to prevent subordinates from committing war crimes against civilians, or punish them for doing so, while retaining respect for the fundamental rights of the commander (in particular, his right not be punished for an act in which he did not participate).[91] Similarly, analysis of the connection between the International Criminal Court and the principle of the 'responsibility to protect' has shown that the relationship between the pursuit of accountability and the pursuit of protection is not always one of 'win–win'. In the cases of Darfur and Libya, the Security Council's use of its referral power to the ICC to address impunity and protect populations from atrocity crimes not only failed to meet these objectives, but also arguably had the effect of weakening the ICC by exposing the limitations of its enforcement powers.[92]

4. Resolving the Tensions from Individualization: A Spectrum of Approaches

How (if at all) can the tensions arising from individualization be resolved? What strategies are the actors engaged in armed conflict currently adopting to address them? We conceive of a spectrum of approaches ranging from, at one end, a principled and general attempt to integrate two sets of important values, to more ad hoc strategies that respond with a particular, context-specific solution to tensions that emanate from individualization. In between these two extremes would sit various forms of reconciliation and institutional adaptation, which enable actors to reduce the frequency and severity of the tensions arising from individualization (if not completely eliminate them).

---

[91] Alexandre Skander Galand, 'Bemba and the Individualization of War: Reconciling Command Responsibility under Article 28 of Rome Statute with Individual Criminal Responsibility', *International Criminal Law Review 20*, no. 4 (2020), pp. 669–700.

[92] Ruben Reike, 'Book Review Essay: The International Criminal Court and its Effects on Active Armed Conflict', *Journal of Intervention and Statebuilding 11*, no. 4 (2017), pp. 555–559.

4.1 Reconceptualization

The first approach for addressing the tensions arising from individualization pursues the reconceptualization of a normative terrain, such that one value or norm is consistently prioritized over another. An illustration from the domain of protection is the notion of 'sovereignty as responsibility': the doctrine which claims that state sovereignty, while a bedrock norm of international society, is no longer understood as undisputed control over territory but rather as comprising a set of conditional rights, dependent upon a state's respect for a minimum standard of human rights for its citizens.[93] Under this reconceptualization of sovereignty, while states are seen as the primary agents responsible for protecting their populations, outside actors can take on a remedial responsibility for protection without compromising sovereignty or the norm of non-intervention. Rather than viewing state sovereignty as limited by human rights, sovereignty and human rights thus become integrated in pursuit of the same (ultimate) objective.[94]

Another example of reconceptualization features centrally in Revisionist Just War theory. Unlike more conventional accounts of the ethics of war, which grant normative status to both states and individuals (thereby generating deep conceptual dilemmas), Revisionist theorists attribute clear normative primacy to individual human rights bearers. In short, they are both 'descriptive individualists' (claiming that only individuals—not collectives—act in war) and 'evaluative individualists' (arguing that only individuals morally matter in war).[95] This reconceptualization resolves a number of tensions raised by Traditional Just War theory, by building a coherent ethics of war from a human rights foundation. In doing so, however, it also raises new practical challenges relating to the difficulties and epistemic barriers in making micro-level judgements about the normative status of individuals in conflict situations.[96]

---

[93] For one key non-Western figure to address the conflict between sovereignty and human rights, see Francis Deng et al., *Sovereignty as Responsibility: Conflict Management in Africa* (Washington: Brookings Institution Press, 1996). For further discussion of the connection between sovereignty as responsibility and the 'responsibility to protect', see Jennifer M. Welsh, 'Implementing the Responsibility to Protect: Catalysing Debate and Building Capacity', in Alexander Betts and Phil Orchard (eds), *Implementation and World Politics: How Norms Change Practice* (Oxford: OUP, 2014), pp. 124–143; and Luke Glanville, *Sovereignty and the Responsibility to Protect: A New History* (Chicago: University of Chicago Press, 2013).

[94] In a similar formulation, Anne Peters develops the concept of 'humanized sovereignty', in which sovereignty exists to further the normative ends of humanity and implies responsibility for the protection of human rights. See 'Humanity as the A and Ω of Sovereignty', *European Journal of International Relations 20*, no. 3 (2009), pp. 513–544.

[95] Seth Lazar, 'Just War Theory: Revisionists Versus Traditionalists', *Annual Review of Political Science 20*, no. 1 (2017), pp. 37–54, at p. 40.

[96] See Dill, 'Towards a Moral Division of Labour' (2020); and Zehfuss, *War and the Politics of Ethics* (2018).

4.2 Reconciliation

A second approach along the spectrum, reconciliation, seeks not a general solution—prioritizing one norm over another—but rather the creation of context-specific relationships between competing norms and values. An illustration is the legal practice of 'interpretive complementarity', which is applied to situations where there are two legal regimes considered relevant and appropriate, with neither necessarily subordinate to the other. Both regimes thus apply, non-exclusively, to the same set of circumstances, often with one normative framework supplementing the other. Nehal Bhuta has explained how interpretive complementarity plays out in the case of armed conflict, where both international humanitarian law and international human rights law are said to have jurisdiction. Through interpretive complementarity, 'IHR rules and principles are used to inform and "humanize" IHL rules; or IHL rules are used to give content to IHR rules in certain exceptional states. In either case, one body of law supplements the other although the direction of this "supplementation" is not fixed.'[97] Similarly, in her analysis of the relationship between IHL and IHR rules, Helen Duffy observes courts and treaty bodies increasingly employing 'harmonious interpretation',[98] based on the common principles and values of both bodies of law, rather than denying the relevance of one or the other through the logic of *lex specialis*.

Another instance of reconciliation can be found in the legal framework regarding humanitarian relief operations in armed conflict. While the 1977 Additional Protocols to the Geneva Conventions provide that in cases where a civilian population is inadequately supplied with items indispensable for survival, humanitarian relief actions shall be undertaken, it also conditions such operations on the consent of the state to whose territory such action is to be conducted. In other words, there is both an obligation to conduct (and to accept) such humanitarian relief operations *and* a degree of discretion as to whether to accept them. The tension between these rules is resolved by accepting that while consent is required, such consent shall not be arbitrarily withheld and by a careful working out as to the circumstances in which it can be said that lack of consent is arbitrary. In this way, the requirements of both principles of law (which appear inconsistent) are met.[99]

4.3 Institutional Adaptation

A third way in which actors seek to resolve the tensions raised by individualization is through institutional adaptation: the design of policies or mechanisms to

---

[97] Nehal Bhuta, 'States of Exception: Regulating Targeted Killing in a "Global Civil War"', in P. Alston and E. Macdonald (eds), *Human Rights, Intervention, and the Use of Force* (Oxford: OUP, 2008), Ch. 7, at p. 252.

[98] Helen Duffy, 'Trials and Tribulations' (2020), at pp. 71–83.

[99] Dapo Akande and Emanuela-Chiara Gillard, 'Arbitrary Withholding of Consent to Humanitarian Relief Operations in Armed Conflict', *International Law Studies* 92 (2016), p. 483.

address dilemmas that arise between individual and collective values in certain contexts. One illustrative example is the Human Rights Due Diligence Policy of the United Nations, which responds to the potential for institutional complicity with armed actors engaged in violence against civilians. The policy stipulates that in the context of its peace operations, the UN cannot provide support to non-UN armed actors 'where there are substantial grounds for believing there is a real risk of the receiving entities committing grave violations of international humanitarian, human rights or refugee law'.[100] The UN's Human Rights Up Front initiative, launched in 2013, was an even more comprehensive form of institutional adaptation designed to address a central dilemma confronting the organization—namely, its need to retain the support of a government to help in delivering assistance to populations in need, while at the same responding to serious violations of international law that may require the UN to issue criticism of that same government. Human Rights Up Front represented a system-wide effort to prioritize the protection of populations from violence, through changes in the way that information is gathered and analysed, new training for all UN staff, and reform of the organization's decision-making structure.[101]

4.4 Ad Hoc Responses

Finally, the furthest end of the spectrum of strategies of resolution is marked by the *lack* of any systematic approach to addressing value conflicts. Where normative frameworks are seen as incompatible, analysts have identified at least three options for response: paralysis—i.e., no action; sequencing (whereby one value is pursued first and then the other); or principled inconsistency, through a case-by-case assessment of which value to privilege in any given situation.[102] While it would be tempting to see the second and third options as mere forms of 'organized hypocrisy', they can be underpinned by an actor's genuine commitment to both values and a reluctance to abandon either as part of its identity.

A well-known example is the 'peace first, justice later', or sequencing approach, to addressing the dilemmas that arise from efforts to pursue individual accountability for perpetrators of international crimes in situations of armed conflict.[103] Another illustration of a case-by-case assessment of which value to privilege in

---

[100] United Nations. Human rights due diligence policy on United Nations support to non-UN security forces. UN doc. A/67/775-S/2013/110, 5 March 2013.

[101] The initiative was prompted by the criticism of the UN's performance in the closing phase of the conflict in Sri Lanka in 2008-9. See Welsh, 'Humanitarian Actors and International Political Theory' (2018).

[102] Anchalee Ruland has conceptualized these response strategies—as well as others—in the context of analysing individual states' responses to situations of norm conflict. See *Norms in Conflict: Southeast Asia's Response to Human Rights Violations in Myanmar* (Lexington: The University Press of Kentucky, forthcoming 2022).

[103] For one influential argument that politics should 'lead, and justice 'follow', see Jack Snyder and Leslie Vinjamuri, 'Trials and Errors: Principle and Pragmatism in Strategies of International Justice', *International Security 28*, no. 3 (2004), pp. 5–44.

26 INTRODUCTION: UNDERSTANDING INDIVIDUALIZATION

a given situation is the provision in Article 53 of the ICC Statute, under which the Court may decline to prosecute international crimes where it would not be in the interests of justice. De Souza Dias and Akande provide an interpretive framework for this provision which would allow the Court to assess the circumstances in which temporarily setting aside criminal proceedings may lead to a form of justice that—in terms of quality and scope—is more desirable. This may be the case, they argue, in cases where negotiations are attentive to justice concerns and the interests of victims.[104]

5. The Contestation of Individualization

While we have theorized individualization as a 'from–to' process, involving the increased prominence of individuals, we do not assume a linear trajectory. Individualization has been and can be contested, in ways illuminated by the contributors to this volume. This leaves open the possibility that there may be moves backwards as well as forwards in the trajectory of individualization. Therefore, as a final feature of our conceptual framework, we adapt from the current literature on norm contestation within the field of international relations[105] to identify three kinds of contestation of the process of individualization:

- ***validity contestation:*** This form of contestation questions the very legitimacy of a move away from collectives towards individuals. It often takes the form of denying that individuals have any status or rights in armed conflict—as either agents or subjects—and arguing that collective and status-based categories best structure the practice of war and its normative assessment. One obvious example is the view of those states that question the extraterritorial application of international human rights law in situations in which these states are engaged in foreign armed conflicts, as Russia did before the European Court of Human Rights in the case regarding the 2008 Georgian–Russian war. The Court itself was ultimately divided on certain aspects of the case, including whether Russia could be held responsible for violation of the European Convention on Human Rights extraterritorially in an international armed conflict, and treated these aspects as matters of international humanitarian law.[106]

---

[104] Talita de Souza Dias and Dapo Akande, 'Peace Negotiations as "Interests of Justice"', in Richard H. Steinberg (ed), *The International Criminal Court: Contemporary Challenges and Reform Proposals* (Leiden: Brill Nijhoff, 2020), pp. 344–357.

[105] Nicole Deitelhoff and Lisbeth Zimmermann, 'Things We Lost in the Fire: How Different Types of Contestation Affect the Robustness of International Norms', *International Studies Review* 22, no. 1 (2020), pp. 51–76.

[106] In its long-awaited judgment, the Court did not establish that Russia had jurisdiction over territories in the war zone during the 'active period of hostilities' in August 2008, with the majority of judges

Other illustrations of validity contestation can be found in the scholarly literature, such as the counter-argument within the ethics of war to the practice of targeted killing, which denies the legitimacy of identifying 'high value' civilian targets,[107] or critiques of Revisionist Just War theory that either question whether the best rules to regulate war emanate from moral prescriptions related to human rights[108] or that defend a more collectivist approach.[109] Critical theorists, as we have noted, also express fundamental objections to individualization, by insisting that war is a particular 'institution, ideology and set of practices' that is not susceptible to forms of ethical reasoning that employ methodological individualism.[110]

- ***institutional contestation:*** A second form of contestation does not deny the legitimacy of placing increased emphasis on individuals as agents and subjects, but objects to the way in which individualization is currently institutionalized. An example can be found within the field of international criminal justice, where individual criminal responsibility per se is (usually) not contested, but rather the particular structure of the ICC or the way in which it has exercised its jurisdiction. This can be seen in efforts to set up a regional African criminal court as well as in the efforts to establish a hybrid tribunal for South Sudan. For its part, the African Union's contestation of the ICC is particularly focused the Court's application of its Statute to non-party states; most of its members do not challenge whether crimes committed by nationals or in the territory of states parties can generally fall within ICC jurisdiction. In the realm of peacekeeping, we can also see forms of institutional contestation concerning the Security Council's control of decision-making with respect to mission mandates and a perceived lack of consultation with troop-contributing countries.

- ***applicatory contestation:*** This type of contestation, like the one above, does not deny the legitimacy of individualization as such, but questions whether individualization should apply to a particular case of (or within) an armed conflict. Some legal scholars, for example, have argued that while there may

---

arguing that the 'very reality of armed confrontation and fighting between enemy military forces .... *In a context of chaos* means that there is no control over an area' (emphasis added). European Court of Justice, *Georgia v. Russia (II)*, 21 January 2021, para. 126. The Court did argue, however, that events after the active period of the war fell within Russia's jurisdiction and that Russia violated Articles 2, 3, and 8 of the European Convention.

[107] Jeremy Waldron, 'Death Squads and Death Lists: Targeted Killing and the Character of the State', *Constellations 23*, no. 2 (2016), pp. 292–307.

[108] Janina Dill and Henry Shue, 'Limiting Killing in War: Military Necessity and the St. Petersburg Assumption', *Ethics & International Affairs 26*, no. 3 (2013), pp. 311–333.

[109] See, for example, Lazar, 'Just War Theory'; and Saba Barzargan, 'Complicitous Liability in War', *Philosophical Studies 165*, no. 1 (2013), pp. 177–195.

[110] Hutchings, 'From Just War Theory to Ethico-Political Pacifism', p. 193. See also Zehfuss, *War and the Politics of Ethics*.

28 INTRODUCTION: UNDERSTANDING INDIVIDUALIZATION

be sound ethical reasons to apply international human rights law to considerations of both *jus ad bellum,* such a practice carries the risk of both depoliticizing war and securitizing human rights.[111] Within the domain of international criminal justice, applicatory contestation is manifest in the views of some scholars and diplomats that individual criminal accountability should not be pursued in the context of ongoing armed conflicts and, especially, during ongoing peace talks. Another example of this kind of contestation can be seen in relation to the principle of the 'responsibility to protect', where states debate whether the remedial responsibility of the international community has been activated, or whether states should be given greater time and scope to address threats to populations within their jurisdiction. Applicatory contestation is also apparent in debates among states as to whether the norm of 'protection of civilians' or the 'responsibility to protect' should apply to a given situation.[112]

6. Outline of the Volume

Building on the conceptualization presented above, our contributing authors address the different domains of the individualization of war and significantly advance our interdisciplinary understanding of its nature, effects, and controversies. The chapters that follow investigate individualization as both a normative claim—debated in the scholarship on the ethics of war—and an empirical phenomenon—manifest in 'real world' changes in the law and the practice of key actors engaged in armed conflict settings. Given that individualization has been explicitly and closely analysed in the philosophical literature, the book engages closely with the debate between so-called Revisionists and Traditionalists, featuring some of the leading scholars in this discussion who take the debate further forward in important new ways. But our examination of individualization extends beyond this particular philosophical exchange, to include legal and political analysis of how aspects of individualization affect the law of armed conflict, international institutions, and other related policy agendas.

The volume begins with essays that seek to extend the logic of individualization in the ethics and law of armed conflict. In Chapter 1, **Adil Haque** encourages us to rethink key aspects of the debate between Traditionalist and Revisionist just war scholars. Reductive individualists, such as Jeff McMahan, argue for the *application* of ordinary morality to the *factual* reality of war, while conventional collectivists, such as Michael Walzer, insist on the *adaptation* of ordinary morality to the *moral* reality of war. Haque contends that these distinctions rest on a fundamental mistake, insofar as the 'legal precept' of the Just War convention no longer exists in

---

[111] Lieblich, 'The Humanization of *Jus Ad Bellum*' (2021).
[112] Paddon Rhoads and Welsh, 'Close Cousins in Protection' (2019).

the wake of the Kellogg–Briand Pact's delegitimization of war as a legal institution. This prohibition of aggressive war, as he demonstrates, has transformed the law of armed conflict, its enforcement, and its relationship to other bodies of law. Nevertheless, these transformations are not complete within human rights law, which still imposes obligations on states (rather than on individuals), or within international criminal law (where there is no liability for ordinary soldiers for the crime of aggression). Haque concludes, however, by asserting that international law today more closely resembles the reductive individualism of Just War Revisionists. If this view prevails, and if the war convention adapts, he suggests that lawyers and philosophers alike will be better able to study the overall pattern of the law of armed conflict and ethically ground its rights and obligations.

In Chapter 2, **Anne Peters** analyses the individualization of international humanitarian law (IHL)—a process she argues has still not reached its limits. She begins by observing that when ascribing individual rights, there is a difference between legal rules which embody 'objective' standards of protection that impose obligations or duties on obligors, and rules which *additionally* confer 'subjective' rights on those persons whom the rules seek to protect. She then goes on to examine whether, and under what conditions, IHL generates such individual rights, and against whom. She argues that since case law has yet to settle which rules in IHL actually generate individual rights, this question must be determined in each case by interpreting the provisions or by clarifying the content of the underlying norm of customary law. In so doing, Peters suggests that the acknowledgement of IHL-based rights endorses the individual human being as the normative reference point of IHL. The principal modern purpose of IHL—to protect humans from the calamities of war—is best pursued, she concludes, by acknowledging direct IHL-based, special individual rights, rather than falling in the two extremes: either applying human rights across the board or denying individual rights altogether.

In Chapter 3, **Bradley Jay Strawser** focuses on how individualization affects those most engaged in waging war. Revisionist Just War theorists have argued that soldiers who serve in the military take on a risk that they will act in morally impermissible ways (if, for example, they are commanded to fight in a war that is objectively unjust) and that this provides a moral reason against participating in military service—especially in the absence of strong provisions for selective conscientious objection. Strawser strikingly turns this reasoning on its head, however, arguing instead that by voluntarily assuming a risk of moral wrongdoing, soldiers are actually performing a *noble* and morally supererogatory act. His 'Noble Risk Argument' starts from the premise that state militaries are at least in some cases both necessary and morally justified; we therefore require some individuals within our society to assume the risks of wrongdoing that military service entails. Those who serve in the military shoulder this moral burden on our behalf—knowing that they may thereby commit a severe moral wrong. Strawser then teases out the elements of this claim by showing how the assumption of moral risk closely tracks the praiseworthy way in which individuals may assume risk or harm in other contexts in order to help a society achieve important collective goals. He also examines how the idea of assuming risk connects with the way that soldiers frequently view their own activity and how the Noble Risk Argument provides support for a policy of conscription in order to fairly share the burden of moral risk.

The second section of the book invites us to rethink aspects of individualization, drawing on literature from moral philosophy and psychology. In Chapter 4, **Victor Tadros** provides a meta-analysis of the dispute between collectivists (such as Walzer) who conceive of war as a conflict between groups, and individualists (such as McMahan) who argue that the morality of war is straightforwardly reducible to the moral considerations that arise in the interpersonal conflict between individuals. Tadros's central task is to challenge the latter 'reductivist' account, by exploring three ways in which group membership can plausibly affect the morality of war. First, groups can have duties, and therefore can engage in wrongdoing, even if they are not moral agents in an ontological sense. Second, group membership can ground liability to harm in war, if we accept that attributing liability to harm on the basis of group membership may be the only way to fairly distribute the risks and harms entailed by fighting in a war within a community. Third, group membership can affect whether an individual is permitted, required, or prohibited from fighting in a just or unjust war due to the moral importance of the special relationships they share with other groups members. Although the role groups play in the morality of war leads Tadros to reject reductive individualism, it does not mean he supports the 'orthodox' interpretation of Just War theory. Rather, it suggests for him an even more radical form of Revisionism than that proposed by classic individualists like McMahan, because group membership on this view may support a more radical and far-reaching form of non-combatant liability to harm.

The defenders of traditional Just War theory—the collectivists—have in recent years forwarded both normative and practical objections to individualist Revisionists. In Chapter 5, **Benjamin Valentino** presents another crucial practical defence of the traditional view: 'situationism', which contends that human beings tend to *overestimate* the power of stable personal character traits while *underestimating* the effects external environment and context have in shaping behaviour. Valentino asserts that when applied to situations of war, situationism ought to have profound consequences for how we think about individual moral responsibility and justice, how we apportion blame and assign punishment, and how we regulate the conduct of war. In short, an appreciation of situationism ought to inform the ways we attempt to apply individualization to war in the real world. In taking situationism seriously, Valentino argues that we would do better to focus our efforts on restructuring the situations and institutions that encourage immoral behaviour in the first place—either by dividing authority to prevent one person from commanding total obedience, or by encouraging diversity among peer groups to prevent destructive conformity and peer pressure.

In the book's third section, our contributors elaborate on some of the key consequences of individualization, particularly for international law and international organizations. In Chapter 6, **Paola Gaeta and Abhimanyu George Jain** analyse the implications for IHL that stem from processes of criminalization. They begin by noting that while violations of IHL rules primarily implicate the responsibility of the parties to the conflict (usually states and non-state armed groups), it is widely acknowledged that wars are waged by people and that individuals may incur international criminal responsibility when charged with war crimes. In their view, this form of individualization—which prioritizes individual criminal accountability over state responsibility and other forms of collective international responsibility—has both desirable and undesirable consequences. In particular, they show that the individualization of IHL effectively places short-term gains over long-term rehabilitation of the flaws in the collective dimension of the international responsibility system, and consequently, potentially compromises the broader enforceability of IHL. The authors also identify a set of factors that are revealing the limitations of individual criminal responsibility, including a limited perspective of justice, false universalism, sexism, racism, and neocolonialism.

In Chapter 7, **Sarah Nouwen** engages with our conceptual framework by expanding on the tensions that the individualization of accountability can generate for different policy agendas related to armed conflict—including peacemaking; providing humanitarian relief IHL promotion; military action to address atrocity crimes; peacekeeping; economic cooperation; human rights promotion; rule-of-law promotion and democratization. Crucially, while international criminal law may itself create tensions, she focuses on the tensions created by the pursuit of individual criminal *accountability*—that is, attempts to transform liability into accountability through criminal proceedings. In so doing, Nouwen also evaluates the strengths and limitations of some of the strategies of resolution that we have set out in the Introduction. She concludes by suggesting that most of the tensions arising from individualization do not in fact exist at the normative level—the objectives themselves are not conflicting—but result from diverging logics: what is deemed necessary to pursue those objectives. She also notes that some of the tensions associated with individualization are not fully resolved but rather addressed through prioritization of one objective over another. Whether through law or ad hoc, these prioritizations are largely determined by political choice.

Chapter 8, by **Paul Williams**, returns to the first domain of individualization, protection, by analysing the evolution and consequences of 'protection of civilians' (PoC) mandates for UN peacekeepers. Since the end of the Cold War there has been a marked increase in UN peacekeeping operations seeking to stabilize war-torn countries, many of which are active sites of armed conflict where there is no peace to keep. Yet, until 1999, peacekeepers were not explicitly tasked to protect civilians in these conflict zones. Williams's review of practice in the first decades of the twenty-first century reveal that PoC mandates have been a useful addition

32 INTRODUCTION: UNDERSTANDING INDIVIDUALIZATION

despite raising local and international expectations about what UN peacekeepers can achieve in the field. Yet, while peacekeepers have been relatively success-ful in stopping, reducing, and mitigating many threats of physical violence to civilians, the underlying governance and political problems which generate these threats have largely been left unaddressed. In this sense, UN peacekeeping has witnessed both operational and tactical benefits for civilians but simultaneously a lack of strategic progress. Consequently, the UN's High-Level Independent Panel on Peace Operations (HIPPO) report, released in 2016, recommended that all UN peace operations ultimately be guided by *political* solutions to the conflict or crisis in question.

The final section of the book takes a different approach to analysing individual-ization, by acknowledging that while formal armed conflict is still a key feature of contemporary international relations, it is not the only or even the most important form of conflict and violence that takes place today. The Small Arms Survey Report of 2016 shows that out of the 560,000 violent deaths that occurred in that year, only 18 per cent were *direct conflict deaths*. Furthermore, of the five countries with the highest number of violent deaths in 2016, only two were experiencing active armed conflict.[113] The growing phenomenon of generalized violence accounts for the preponderant share of violent deaths around the world, and is concentrated in countries such as El Salvador, Guatemala, Brazil, Mexico, and Venezuela. In fact, the use of military force or militarized police operations against organized crime in Latin America has shown levels of destruction, death, and other forms of harm comparable to those situations of civil war. These 'situations other than war', as the ICRC refers to them, create particular challenges for actors seeking to pro-tect individuals from harm—in part because they create ambiguity in the status of particular individuals and raise questions about what legal obligations (if any) fall upon states and non-state actors.

Chapter 9, by **Pablo Kalmanovitz** and **Miriam Bradley**, shines a spotlight on these violent contexts which frequently do not meet the IHL thresholds for armed conflict and thus formally fall under a law enforcement or IHRL paradigm. Through a case of study of Mexico's war on organized crime, they illustrate how the qualification of a situation of organized violence as a non-international armed conflict (NIAC) or below the NIAC threshold has major implications for how pro-cesses of individualization operate. Starting from an IHRL baseline, Kalmanovitz and Bradley suggest that in contexts of criminal violence we are in fact encoun-tering a form of 'collectivization', in which collective designations become more prominent and normatively significant in the domains of protection and liability to harm. They further examine this process through a 'reverse analogy' with the

---

[113] Claire Mc Envoy and Gergely Hideg, 'Global Violent Deaths 2017: Time to Decide' *Small Arms Survey*, December 2017. Available at: https://www.smallarmssurvey.org/sites/default/files/resources/SAS-Report-GVD2017.pdf

process of individualization in armed conflict, and conclude that collectivization in these situations lacks an adequate underlying international legal framework, and therefore does not offer the same level of protection for individuals as exists in contexts of war. In forwarding this argument, they also illuminate the underlying structure of the process of individualization—its assumptions and conditions—and how it ultimately falls short of the move towards peacetime regulation of violence under IHRL.

References

Akande, D. (with C. Heyns, L. Hill-Cawthorne, and T. Chengeta). (2016) 'The International Law Framework Regulating the Use of Armed Drones', *International Comparative Law Quarterly*, 65, pp. 791.

Akande, D. and Gillard, E. (2016). 'Arbitrary Withholding of Consent to Humanitarian Relief Operations in Armed Conflict', *International Law Studies*, 92, p. 483.

Akande, D. and Shah, S. (2010) 'Immunities of States Officials, International Crimes, and Foreign Domestic Courts', *European Journal of International Law*, 21(4), pp. 815–852.

Akande, D. and Tzanakopoulous, A. (2018) 'The Crime of Aggression before the International Criminal Court: Introduction to the Symposium', *European Journal of International Law*, 29(30), pp. 829–833.

Akhavan, P. et al. (2014) *Open Letter to the UN on Humanitarian Aid*, 28 April 2014. Available at: https://www.ibanet.org/Article/NewDetail.aspx?ArticleUid=73b714fb-cb63-4ae7-bbaf-76947ab8cac6

Barry, C. and Christie, L. (2018) 'Moral Equality of Combatants', in S. Lazar and H. Frowe (eds), *The Oxford Handbook of Ethics of War*. Oxford: Oxford University Press, pp. 339–357.

Barzargan, S. (2013) 'Complicitous Liability in War', *Philosophical Studies*, 165(1), pp. 177–195.

Ben-Naftali, O. (ed.) (2011) *International Humanitarian Law and International Human Rights Law*. Oxford: Oxford University Press.

Bhuta, N. (2008) 'States of Exception: Regulating Targeted Killing in a "Global Civil War"', in P. Alston and E. Macdonald (eds), *Human Rights, Intervention, and the Use of Force*. Oxford: Oxford University Press, Ch. 7.

Blum, G. (2014) 'The Individualization of War: From War to Policing in the Regulations of Armed Conflicts', in A. Sarat, L. Douglas, and M. Umphrey (eds), *Law and War*. Redwood City, CA: Stanford University Press, pp. 48–83.

Bohrer, Z., Dill, J. and Duffy, H. (2020) *Law Applicable to Armed Conflict*. Cambridge: Cambridge University Press (Max Planck Trialogues).

Broomhall, B. (2004) *International Justice and the International Criminal Court: Between Sovereignty and the Rule of Law*. Oxford: Oxford University Press.

Buitelaar, T. and Hirschmann, G. (2021) 'Criminal Accountability at What Cost? Norm conflict, peace operations, and the International Criminal Court', *European Journal of International Relations*, 27(2), pp. 548–571

Coates, A.J. (1997) *The Ethics of War*. Manchester: Manchester University Press.

Crawford, J. (2013) *State Responsibility: The General Part*. Cambridge: Cambridge University Press.

34 INTRODUCTION: UNDERSTANDING INDIVIDUALIZATION

Dannenbaum, T. (2017) 'Why Have We Criminalized Aggressive War?', *Yale Law Journal*, 126(5), pp. 1242–1318.

Dannenbaum, T. (2018) *The Crime of Aggression, Humanity, and the Soldier*. Cambridge: Cambridge University Press.

De Souza Dias, T. and Akande, D. (2020) 'Peace Negotiations as "Interests of Justice"', in R. Steinberg (ed.), *The International Criminal Court: Contemporary Challenges and Reform Proposals*. Leiden: Brill Nijhoff, Chapter 31.

Deitelhoff, N. and Zimmerman, L. (2020) 'Things We Lost in the Fire: How Different Types of Contestation Affect the Robustness of International Norms', *International Studies Review*, 22(1), pp. 51–76.

Deng, F., Kimaro, S., Lyons, T., Rothchild, D., and Zartman, W. (1996) *Sovereignty as Responsibility: Conflict Management in Africa*. Washington, D.C.: Brookings Institution Press.

Dill, J. (2018) 'Just War Theory in Times of Individual Rights', in C. Brown and R. Eckersley (eds), *The Oxford Handbook of International Political Theory*. Oxford: Oxford University Press, Chapter 17.

Dill, J. (2019) 'Do Attackers Have a Legal Duty of Care? Limits to the "Individualization of War"', *International Theory*, 11(1), pp. 1–25.

Dill, J. and Shue, H. (2013) 'Limiting Killing in War: Military Necessity and the St. Petersburg Assumption', *Ethics & International Affairs*, 26(3), pp. 311–333.

Donini, A. (ed) (2012) *The Golden Fleece*. Boulder, CO: Kumarian Press.

Drezner, D. (2011) 'Sanctions Sometimes Smart: Targeted Sanctions in Theory and Practice', *International Studies Review*, 13(1), pp. 96–108.

Droege, C. (2007) 'The Interplay between International Humanitarian Law and International Human Rights Law in Situations of Armed Conflict', *Israel Law Review*, 40, pp. 310–355.

Drumbl, M. (2007) *Atrocity, Punishment, and International Law*. Cambridge: Cambridge University Press.

Erskine, T. (2001) 'Assigning Responsibility to Institutional Moral Agents: The Case of States and Quasi-States', *Ethics & International Affairs*, 15(2), pp. 67–85.

Erskine, T. (2010) 'Kicking Bodies and Damning Souls: The Danger of Harming "Innocent" Individuals while Punishing "Delinquent" States', *Ethics & International Affairs*, 24(3), pp. 261–285

European Court of Justice. (2021) *Georgia v. Russia (II)*, 21 January 2021.

Fabre, C. (2012) *Cosmopolitan War*. Oxford: Oxford University Press.

Fabre, C. and Lazar, S. (eds) (2014) *The Morality of Defensive War*. Oxford: Oxford University Press.

Fleming, S. (2020) *Leviathan on a Leash: A Theory of State Responsibility*. Princeton: Princeton University Press.

French, P. (1984) *Collective and Corporate Responsibility*. New York: Columbia University Press.

Frowe, H. (2014) *Defensive Killing*. Oxford: Oxford University Press.

Frowe, H. (2022) 'Intervening Agency and Civilian Liability', *Criminal Law and Philosophy*, 16(1), pp. 181–191. doi: 10.1007/s11572-020-09555-4.

Galand, A.S. (2020) 'Bemba and the Individualization of War: Reconciling Command Responsibility under Article 28 of Rome Statute with Individual Criminal Responsibility', *International Criminal Law Review*, 20(4), pp. 669–700.

Gordon J. (2010) *Invisible War: The United States and the Iraq Sanctions*. Cambridge, MA: Harvard University Press.

Gregory, D. (2011) 'The Everywhere War', *The Geographical Journal*, 177(3), pp. 238–250.

Gross, M. (2010) *Moral Dilemmas of Modern War*. Cambridge: Cambridge University Press.

Hakimi, M. (2012) 'A Functional Approach to Targeting and Detention, *Michigan Law Review*, 110, pp. 1365–1420.

Haque, A. (2017) *Law and Morality at War*. Oxford: Oxford University Press.

Hopgood, S. (2013) *The Endtimes of Human Rights*, Ithaca, NY: Cornell University Press.

Hutchings, K. (2019a) 'From Just War Theory to Ethico-Political Pacifism', *Critical Studies on Security*, 7(3), pp. 191–198.

Hutchings, K. (2019b) 'Cosmopolitan Just War and Coloniality', in D. Bell (ed.), *Empire, Race and Global Justice*. Cambridge: Cambridge University Press, pp. 211–227.

International Court of Justice. (2007) *Case Concerning the Application of the Convention on the Prevention and Punishment of the Crime of Genocide (Bosnia and Herzegovina v. Serbia and Montenegro)*. General List, no. 91, 26 February 2007.

Jorda, C. and de Hemptinne, J. (2002) 'The Status and Role of the Victim', in A. Cassesse, P. Gaeta, and J.R.W.D. Jones (eds), *The Rome Statute of the International Criminal Court: A Commentary*. Oxford: Oxford University Press, pp. 1378–1388.

Kendall, S. and Nouwen, S. (2014) 'Representational Practices at the International Criminal Court: The Gap between Juridified and Abstract Victimhood', *Law and Contemporary Problems*, 76, pp. 235–262.

Kendall, S. and Nouwen S. (2020) 'International Criminal Justice and Humanitarianism', in K.J. Heller, F. Mégret, S. Nouwen, J. Ohlin, and D. Robinson (eds), *The Oxford Handbook of International Criminal Law*. Oxford: Oxford University Press, Chapter 31.

Kersten, M. (2016) *Justice in Conflict: The Effects of the International Criminal Court's Interventions on Ending Wars and Building Peace*. Oxford: Oxford University Press.

Lang, Jr., A.F. (2011) 'Punishing Genocide: A Critical Reading of the International Court of Justice', in T. Isaacs and R. Vernon (eds), *Accountability for Collective Wrongdoings*. Cambridge: Cambridge University Press, pp. 92–118.

Lazar, S. (2017) 'Just War Theory: Revisionists Versus Traditionalists', *Annual Review of Political Science*, 20(1), pp. 37–54. doi: 10.1146/annurev-polisci-060314-112706.

Lazar, S. and Frowe, H. (eds) (2015) *The Oxford Handbook of Ethics of War*. New York: Oxford University Press.

Lieblich, E. (2021) 'The Humanization of *Jus Ad Bellum*: Prospects and Perils', *European Journal of International Law*, 32(2), pp. 579–612.

Lubell, N. (2007) 'Parallel Application of International Humanitarian Law and International Human Rights Law: An Examination of the Debate', *Israel Law Review*, 40, pp. 48–60.

Magone, C., Neumann, M., and Weissman, F. (eds). (2012) *Humanitarian Negotiations Revealed: The MSF Experience*. New York: Columbia University Press.

Mc Envoy, C. and Hideg, G. (2017) 'Global Violent Deaths 2017: Time to Decide' *Small Arms Survey*. Available at: https://www.smallarmssurvey.org/sites/default/files/resources/SAS-Report-GVD2017.pdf

McMahan, J. (2009) *Killing in War*. Oxford: Oxford University Press.

McMahan, J. (2010) 'Laws of War', in S. Besson and J. Tasioulas (eds), *The Philosophy of International Law*. New York: Oxford University Press, Chapter 24.

McMahan, J. (2016) 'The Limits of Self-Defense', in C. Coons and M. Weber (eds), *The Ethics of Self-Defense*. Oxford: Oxford University Press, Chapter 10.

Mégret, F. (2012) 'What Is the Specific Evil of Aggression?', Publisher unknown: http://dx.doi.org/10.2139/ssrn.2546732

Mégret, F. and Redaelli, C. (2022) 'The Crime of Aggression as a Violation of the Rights of One's Own Population', *Journal of the Use of Force in International Law*, 9(1), pp. 99–127.

Milanovic, M. (2010) 'Norm Conflict in International Law: Whither Human Rights?', *Duke Journal of Comparative & International Law*, 20(1), pp. 69–132.

Milanovic, M. (2016) 'The Lost Origins of *Lex Specialis*: Rethinking the Relationship between Human Rights and International Humanitarian Law', in J.D. Ohlin (ed.), *Theoretical Boundaries of Armed Conflict and Human Rights*. New York: Oxford University Press, pp. 78–117.

Murphy, S.D. (2015) 'The Crime of Aggression at the International Criminal Court', in M. Weller (ed.), *The Oxford Handbook of the Use of Force in International Law*. Oxford: Oxford University Press, Chapter 24.

Murray, D. et al. (consultant eds.). (2016) *Practitioners' Guide to Human Rights Law in Armed Conflict*. Oxford: Oxford University Press.

Nolkaemper, A. (2003) 'Concurrence between Individual Responsibility and State Responsibility in International Law', *International and Comparative Law* Quarterly, 52(3), pp. 615–640.

Nouwen, S. (2012) 'The International Criminal Court: A Peacebuilder in Africa?', in D. Curtis and G.A. Dzinesa (eds), *Peacebuilding, Power and Politics in Africa*. Athens: Ohio University Press, Chapter 9.

Orakhelashvili, A. (2008) 'The Interaction between Human Rights and Humanitarian Law', *European Journal of International Law*, 19, pp. 161–182.

Paddon Rhoads, E. (2016) *Taking Sides: Impartiality and the Future of the United Nations*. Oxford: Oxford University Press.

Paddon Rhoads, E. and Welsh, J.M. (2019) 'Close Cousins in Protection: The Evolution of Two Norms', *International Affairs*, 95(3), pp. 597–717.

Peters, A. (2009) 'Humanity as the A and Ω of Sovereignty', *European Journal of International Relations*, 20(3), pp. 513–544.

Peters, A. (2014) *Beyond Human Rights: The Legal Status of the Individual in International Law*. Cambridge: Cambridge University Press.

Peters, A. (2021) 'The Importance of Having Rights', *ZaöRV*, 81(1), pp. 7–22.

Reike, R. (2017) 'Book Review Essay: The International Criminal Court and Its Effects on Active Armed Conflict', *Journal of Intervention and Statebuilding*, 11(4), pp. 555–559.

Risse, T., Ropp, S.C., and Sikkink, K. (eds). (2013) *The Persistent Power of Human Rights*. Cambridge: Cambridge University Press.

Roberts, A. (2008) 'The Principle of Equal Application of the Laws of War', in D. Rodin and H. Shue (eds), *Just and Unjust Warriors: The Legal and Moral Status of Soldiers*. Oxford: Oxford University Press, Chapter 12.

Rodin, D. (2002) *War and Self-Defense*, Oxford: Oxford University Press.

Ruland, A. (2022) *Norms in Conflict: Southeast Asia's Response to Human Rights Violations in Myanmar*. Lexington: The University Press of Kentucky, forthcoming.

Schabas, W. (2002) 'Punishment of Non-State Actors in Non-International Armed Conflict', *Fordham International Law Journal*, 26(4), pp. 907–933.

Sikkink, K. (2011) *The Justice Cascade*. New York: W.W. Norton.

Simpson, G. (2009) 'Men and Abstract Entities: Individual Responsibility and Collective Guilt in International Criminal Law', in A. Nollkaemper and H. van der Wilt (eds), *System Criminality in International Law*. Cambridge: Cambridge University Press, Chapter 4.

Singer, P.W. (2009) *Wired for War*. New York: Penguin Books.

Snyder, J. and Vinjamuri, L. (2004) 'Trials and Errors: Principle and Pragmatism in Strategies of International Justice', *International Security*, 28(3), pp. 5–44.

Stilz, A. (2011) 'Collective Responsibility and the State', *Journal of Political Philosophy*, 19(2), pp. 190–208.

Strawser, B.J. (2010) 'Moral Predators: The Duty to Employ Uninhabited Aerial Vehicles', *Journal of Military Ethics*, 9(4), pp. 342–368.

Tadros, V. (2020) *To Do, To Die, To Reason Why: Individual Ethics in War*. Oxford: Oxford University Press.

Tomuschat, C. (2010) 'Human Rights and International Humanitarian Law', *European Journal of International Law*, 21, pp. 15–23.

Tostensen, A. and Bull, B. (2002) 'Are Smart Sanctions Feasible?', *World Politics*, 54(3), pp. 373–403.

United Nations. (2001) *Draft Articles on the Responsibility of States for Internationally Wrongful Acts*, Report of the International Law Commission on the Work of its Fifty-third Session, UN GAOR. UN doc. A/56/10.

United Nations. (2008) *United Nations Peacekeeping Operations: Principles and Guidelines*. New York: Department of Peacekeeping Operations.

United Nations (2013) *Human Rights Due Diligence Policy on United Nations Support to Non-un Security Forces*. UN doc. A/67/775-S/2013/110, 5 March 2013.

United Nations. (2018) *General Comment no. 36 on Article 6 of the International Covenant on Civil and Political Rights, on the Right to Life (GC 36)*. UN doc. CCPR/C/GC/36, 30 October 2018.

Van Schaack, B. (2011) 'The Crime of Aggression and Humanitarian Intervention on Behalf of Women', *International Criminal Law Review*, 11(3), pp. 477–493.

Verdirame, G. (2008) 'Human Rights in Wartime', *European Human Rights Law Review*, 6, pp. 689–705.

Waldron, J. (2015) 'Death Squads and Death Lists: Targeted Killing and the Character of the State', New York University Public Law and Legal Theory Working Papers. Paper 519. Available at: http://lsr.nellco.org/nyu_plltwp/519

Walzer, M. (2006) *Just and Unjust Wars*. New York: Basic Books.

Wegner, P.S. (2015) *The International Criminal Court in Ongoing Intrastate Conflicts: Navigating the Peace-Justice Divide*. Cambridge: Cambridge University Press.

Weinert, M. (2015) *Making Human: World Order and the Global Governance of Human Dignity*. Ann Arbor: University of Michigan Press.

Welsh, J.M. (2008) 'The Security Council and Humanitarian Intervention', in V. Lowe et al. (eds), *The United Nations Security Council and War: The Evolution of Thought and Practice since 1945*. Oxford: Oxford University Press, pp. 535–562.

Welsh, J.M. (2014) 'Implementing the Responsibility to Protect: Catalyzing Debate and Building Capacity', in A. Betts and P. Orchard (eds), *Implementation and World Politics: How Norms Change Practice*. Oxford: Oxford University Press, pp. 124–143.

Welsh, J.M. (2015) 'The Morality of 'Drone Warfare', in D. Cortright, R. Fairhurst, and K. Wall (eds), *Drones and the Future of Armed Conflict: Ethical, Legal and Strategic Implications*. Chicago: Chicago University Press, Ch. 2.

Welsh, J.M. (2016) 'The Responsibility to Protect after Libya and Syria', *Daedalus: Journal of the American Academy of Arts and Sciences*, 145(4), pp. 75–87.

Welsh, J.M. (2018) 'Humanitarian Actors and International Political Theory', in C. Brown and R. Eckersley (eds), *The Oxford Handbook of International Political Theory*. Oxford: Oxford University Press, Chapter 24.

Welsh, J.M. (2019a) 'Norm Robustness and the Responsibility to Protect', *Journal of Global Security Studies*, 4(1), pp. 53–57

Welsh, J.M. (2019b), 'The Individualization of War: Defining a Research Programme', *Annals of the Fondazione Luigi Einaudi*, 53 (1), pp. 9-28.

Zehfuss, M. (2018) *War and the Politics of Ethics*. Oxford: Oxford University Press.

PART I

EXTENDING INDIVIDUALIZATION IN THE ETHICS AND LAW OF ARMED CONFLICT

1

After War and Peace

Adil Ahmad Haque

1. Introduction

In his preface to *Killing in War*, Jeff McMahan writes that '[t]he prevailing view is that in a state of war, the practice of killing is governed by different moral principles from those that govern acts of killing in other contexts. This presupposes that it can make a moral difference to the moral permissibility of killing another person whether one's political leaders have declared a state of war with that person's country.'[1] Against this prevailing view, McMahan goes on to argue that '[a] state of war makes no difference other than to make the application of the relevant principles more complicated and difficult because of the number of people involved, the complexities of their relations with one another, and the virtual impossibility of having knowledge of all that is relevant to the justification of an act of killing.'[2]

The prevailing view that McMahan sets out to challenge is that of Michael Walzer, who famously proposes in *Just and Unjust Wars* that the morality of killing in armed conflict must be assessed by reference to what he calls the 'war convention', that is, 'the set of articulated norms, customs, professional codes, legal precepts, religious and philosophical principles, and reciprocal arrangements that shape our judgments of military conduct'.[3] Within the war convention, combatants and noncombatants enjoy war rights which differ from the moral rights they enjoy outside of war. Most notably, 'there is a license for soldiers, without regard to which side they are on; it is the first and most important of their war rights. They are entitled to kill.'[4] Indeed, soldiers are entitled to kill civilians as well as one another, at least within (different) limits. Civilians, in turn, are morally liable to collateral harm, again within limits, without regard to which side they are on; it is the first and most important abrogation of the moral rights they enjoy in peacetime.

Importantly, while McMahan calls for the application of ordinary morality to the factual reality of war, Walzer insists on the adaptation of ordinary morality to the moral reality of war. While McMahan and Walzer agree that ordinary morality provides for individual rights and responsibilities, Walzer describes war as

---

[1] Jeff McMahan, *Killing in War* (Oxford: Oxford University Press, 2009), p. vii.
[2] Ibid., p. 156
[3] Michael Walzer, *Just and Unjust Wars* (New York: Basic Books, 2nd ed., 1992), p. 44.
[4] Ibid., p. 36.

Adil Ahmad Haque, *After War and Peace*. In: *The Individualization of War*. Edited by: Jennifer Welsh, Dapo Akande, and David Rodin, Oxford University Press. © Adil Ahmad Haque (2023). DOI: 10.1093/oso/9780192872203.003.0002 'a coercively collectivizing enterprise; a tyrannical enterprise; it overrides individuality, and it makes the kind of attention that we would like to pay to each person's moral standing impossible; it is universally oppressive.'[5] For Walzer, the collectivizing reality of war explains why the war convention cannot be reduced to the individualized principles of ordinary morality, no matter how carefully applied. For McMahan, the argument runs the other way, from the moral imperatives of individualism to the rejection of the war convention.

The ethical debate between McMahan and Walzer—between reductive individualists and conventionalist collectivists—rests, in part, on a mistake. The 'legal precepts' that partly constitute Walzer's war convention, and that shape the 'prevailing view' that McMahan sets out to challenge, reflect an international law that no longer exists, if it ever did. For Walzer, 'the task of the moral theorist is to study the pattern as a whole, reaching for its deepest reasons.'[6] But Walzer misperceived the pattern and, as a result, its deepest reasons escaped his grasp. Perhaps, writing in 1977, he was standing too close. Or, perhaps, searching for a continuous social practice of moral argument and political criticism, he did not appreciate the radical discontinuity that occurred just a few decades earlier.

In the words of Hersch Lauterpacht, 'the place of war in the system of international law has undergone a fundamental change.'[7] However, the legal consequences of that fundamental change are not themselves embodied in express international agreements. Instead, these consequences must be determined 'by a reasonable application of the principle that newly enacted law, if it is of a general and fundamental character, alters rules inconsistent with it'. As Lauterpacht admits, this indirect method of ascertaining changes in the law 'introduces an element of uncertainty and conjecture', and 'appears to make the law flow not from the express will of states, but from deductions made by judges or writers .... However, there is a limit beyond which we should not ascribe to governments the desire to will things that are incompatible and contradictory. That limit in turn must curb any excessive rigidity of the positivist method.'

The fundamental change to which Lauterpacht referred was the outlawry of war and the general prohibition of interstate force. Its legal consequences transformed the law of neutrality, treaties, trade, and crime, as elegantly described by Oona Hathaway and Scott Shapiro.[8] Its legal consequences for the law of armed conflict, its enforcement, and its relationship with other bodies of international law are equally profound, though frequently unappreciated and often resisted.

---

[5] Michael Walzer. 'Response to McMahan's Paper', *Philosophia 34*, no.1 (2006), pp. 43–45.
[6] Walzer, *Just and Unjust Wars* (1992), p. 45.
[7] Hersch Lauterpacht, 'Rules of Warfare in an Unlawful War', in George A. Lipsky (ed.), *Law and Politics in the World Community: Essays on Hans Kelsen's Pure Theory and Related Problems in International Law* (1953), pp. 89–113.
[8] Oona Hathaway and Scott Shapiro, *The Internationalists* (New York: Simon & Schuster, 2017).

To see where we are, remember where we were. In 1863, at the height of the US Civil War, the United States government instructed its armies in the field to follow the so-called 'Leiber Code'. According to this 'Code', '[p]ublic war is a state of armed hostility between sovereign nations or governments' (art. 20).[9] The state of war is one that these collectives are free to enter, 'to obtain great ends of state, or ... in defense against wrong' (art. 30), within which only the law of war applies. On this view, '[t]he law of nations allows every sovereign government to make war upon another sovereign state, and, therefore, admits of no rules or laws different from those of regular warfare' (art. 67).[10]

The exclusive application of the law of war generates the 'license' of soldiers to fight within its limits. Accordingly, '[s]o soon as a man is armed by a sovereign government and takes the soldier's oath of fidelity, he is a belligerent; his killing, wounding, or other warlike acts are not individual crimes or offenses' (art. 57).[11] As for civilians, their liability to incidental harm stems from their membership in the collectivity: '[t]he citizen or native of a hostile country is thus an enemy, as one of the constituents of the hostile state or nation, and as such is subjected to the hardships of the war' (art 21). Nevertheless, 'as civilization has advanced ... [t]he principle has been more and more acknowledged that the unarmed citizen is to be spared in person, property, and honor as much as the exigencies of war will admit' (art. 22).

Of course, Walzer does not think that law or morality allows states to make war upon one another to obtain great ends of state, or even in defence against wrongs short of aggression and atrocity. Nevertheless, the war convention he describes seems mostly unaltered by the obliteration of its premise and context. Somehow, the nineteenth century *jus in bello* is supposed to survive the twentieth century *jus contra bellum*.

On one view, the state of war was a legal institution for the resolution of international disputes that states were free to enter at their discretion. States enjoyed a legal power, as well as a liberty or privilege, to alter their legal relationships with their adversaries (extinguishing claims to territorial integrity) and with other states (triggering duties of neutrality). While this view had competitors, its enduring influence is so tenacious, and its revival by Walzer so alluring (to some), that McMahan perceives it as 'the prevailing view' to this day.

---

[9] Article 20 continues: 'It is a law and requisite of civilized existence that men live in political, continuous societies, forming organized units, called states or nations, whose constituents bear, enjoy, suffer, advance and retrograde together, in peace and in war.'

[10] Similarly, '[t]here exists no law or body of authoritative rules of action between hostile armies, except that branch of the law of nature and nations which is called the law and usages of war on land' (art. 40).

[11] Similarly, '[a] prisoner of war is subject to no punishment for being a public enemy' (art. 56). Compare Walzer, *Just and Unjust Wars*, at p. 136 ('Soldiers fighting for an aggressor state are not themselves criminals').

44 AFTER WAR AND PEACE

In my view, when states 'condemn[ed] recourse to war for the solution of international controversies, and renounce[d] it, as an instrument of national policy in their relations with one another',[12] the state of war was thereby 'banished as a legal institution'.[13] The fact of armed conflict remains. The laws of war no longer form a special, self-contained legal regime. The law of armed conflict applies alongside the law of interstate force and international human rights law. Combatants are not entitled to kill, within limits, on behalf of their state. They are immune, within limits, from prosecution by opposing states, while subject to direct obligations and individual responsibility under international law. Civilians are not liable to harm within the limits of the law of war. They retain the human rights they enjoy in peacetime, though these rights must be applied (though not adapted) to the factual circumstances of armed conflict.

The pattern has changed, and its deepest reasons track McMahan's reductive individualism more closely than Walzer's conventionalist collectivism. Or so I shall argue. My aim in this paper is to trace some theoretical implications, for both law and philosophy, of the legal prohibition of aggressive war and armed force, with special emphasis on implications for the individualization of war. I will focus on the application of human rights law during armed conflict, individual rights and duties under the law of armed conflict, and individual criminal responsibility.

2. Human Rights in Armed Conflict

The view that human rights law applies only in peacetime, while the law of war exclusively governs the conduct of hostilities, has few adherents today. Most accept the statement of the International Court of Justice (ICJ) that the protection of human rights law 'does not cease in times of war' and that, 'in principle, the right not arbitrarily to be deprived of one's life applies also in hostilities'.[14] Controversy surrounds the succeeding statement, that '[t]he test of what is an arbitrary deprivation of life, however, then falls to be determined by the applicable lex specialis, namely, the law applicable in armed conflict which is designed to regulate the conduct of hostilities'.[15] Are we to apply human rights law to the factual circumstances of armed conflict (à la McMahan) or adjust human rights law to the legal reality of armed conflict (à la Walzer)?

No doubt, the application of human rights law to the context of hostilities should take into account relevant rules of the law of armed conflict.[16] If a deprivation of life violates the law of armed conflict, then it is (almost certainly) arbitrary under

---

[12] Kellogg–Briand Pact of 1928.
[13] Lauterpacht, 'Rules of Warfare in an Unlawful War', at p. 113.
[14] Legality of the Threat or Use of Nuclear Weapons, Advisory Opinion, 1996 ICJ Rep 226, para 25.
[15] Ibid.
[16] Vienna Convention on the Law of Treaties, art. 31(2)(c).

human rights law. However, the contrapositive—if a deprivation of life does not violate the law of armed conflict, then it is not arbitrary under human rights law—does not follow. In one respect, it cannot follow.

States that violate the general prohibition of interstate force may not benefit from their wrongdoing by avoiding or loosening their ordinary legal obligations. Nor may such states thereby deprive individuals of their human rights or diminish their legal protection. States have no legal power to alter their human rights obligations or the corresponding claims of individual right-holders. Nor should states have the de facto ability to trigger such alterations through their unlawful actions. This, too, would give states arbitrary control over the right to life of individuals. Accordingly, the general prohibition of interstate force excludes the Walzerian view that human rights must be adapted to—so as to be exhausted by—the legal conventions designed to regulate its conduct.

Unlawful armed force that does not violate the law of armed conflict nevertheless arbitrarily deprives those it kills of their lives under human rights law. The United Nations Human Rights Committee is therefore correct to state that 'acts of aggression ... resulting in deprivation of life, violate ipso facto' the human right to life.[17] As the Committee explains, 'a deprivation of life that lacks a legal basis or is otherwise inconsistent with life-protecting laws and procedures is, as a rule, arbitrary in nature'. Acts of aggression obviously fail on both counts.

This leaves open the possibility that deprivations of life in war violate human rights if and only if they violate either the law of interstate force or the law of armed conflict. But this view does not survive scrutiny. Consider that, for decades, the law of international armed conflict between states diverged from the law of non-international armed conflict between states and armed groups or between such groups.[18] Yet it is implausible that, in those decades, inflicting excessive harm on civilians, neglecting feasible precautions, and using civilians as human shields violated their human right to life in international armed conflict but not in non-international armed conflict. Similarly, it is implausible that such deprivations of life in non-international armed conflict were consistent with the right to life in the 1980s but are inconsistent with the right to life today. Finally, it is implausible that states could avoid or alter their human rights obligations by arbitrarily initiating a non-international armed conflict, even though the prohibition of interstate force may not apply.

No doubt, the contemporary law of armed conflict—international and non-international—does a far better job prohibiting arbitrary deprivation of life than its earlier incarnations. In part, this may reflect the increasing centrality of the

---

[17] Human Rights Committee, General Comment No. 36: General comment No. 36 (2018) on article 6 of the International Covenant on Civil and Political Rights, on the right to life, 124th Sess., UN Doc CCPR/C/GC/36 (30 October 2018).

[18] Compare Additional Protocols I and II to the 1949 Geneva Conventions, or articles 8(2)(a)–(b) and 8(2)(c)–(e) of the ICC Statute.

individual in this body of law. Early treaties, aimed at 'alleviating as much as possible the calamities of war',[19] seemed concerned with reducing aggregate suffering rather than respecting individual rights—what David Luban calls 'negative Benthamism'.[20] In contrast, more recent treaties (re)cast the 'humanitarian principles' of their predecessors in terms of 'respect for the human person'.[21] Recalling that then-recent human rights treaties 'offer a basic protection to the human person', they aim 'to ensure a better protection for the victims of ... armed conflicts'.[22]

Today, individual civilians enjoy general protection against the dangers arising from military operations, unless and for such time as they take a direct part in hostilities.[23] Violations of the opposing party do not release combatants from their legal obligations with respect to civilians, which are neither grounded in nor conditioned on reciprocity between the parties. This normative structure—categorical duties, protecting vital interests, controlled by the will of those protected—is that of individual rights.

There remain some arbitrary killings not prohibited by the law of armed conflict or the law of interstate force, which nevertheless violate the human right to life. The law of armed conflict only prohibits the killing of combatants under limited circumstances, such as capture, incapacitation, or surrender. It does not prohibit killing combatants whom it is feasible to capture, incapacitate, or offer an opportunity for surrender. This state of affairs is said to constitute 'status-based targeting', that is, targeting based on membership in a collective. Nevertheless, as the African Commission on Human and Peoples' Rights observes,

> Where military necessity does not require parties to an armed conflict to use lethal force in achieving a legitimate military objective against otherwise lawful targets, but allows the target for example to be captured rather than killed, the respect for the right to life can be best ensured by pursuing this option.[24]

The unnecessary killing of opposing combatants may not violate the law of armed conflict, yet violate human rights law. In this respect, civilians and combatants alike retain their individual human rights during armed conflict. States have no legal power to displace, diminish, or otherwise alter these rights by resorting to

---

[19] Declaration Renouncing the Use, in Time of War, of Explosive Projectiles Under 400 Grammes Weight. Saint Petersburg, 29 November/11 December 1868.

[20] David Luban, 'Human Rights Thinking and the Laws of War', in Jens David Ohlin (ed.), *Theoretical Boundaries of Human Rights and Armed Conflict* (Oxford: OUP, 2016), pp. 45–77, at p. 52.

[21] Additional Protocol II, preamble.

[22] Ibid.

[23] Protocol I, art. 51; Protocol II, art. 13.

[24] African Commission on Human and Peoples' Rights, General Comment No 3 on the African Charter on Human and Peoples' Rights: The Right to Life (Article 4) (PULP 2015), para 34.

unlawful force. While human rights law must be applied to the factual circumstances of armed conflict, its protections are not adjusted to the legal (non-)reality of war.

The same result follows from other human rights treaties. The European Convention on Human Rights prohibits intentional deprivations of life, with narrow exceptions. In time of war, states may take measures derogating from their obligations under the Convention, but only to the extent strictly required by the exigencies of the situation, and only if such measures are not inconsistent with their other obligations under international law.[25] Killing in furtherance of aggression is inconsistent with other obligations under international law. And killing opposing combatants who could be safely captured is not strictly required by the exigencies of the situation. No derogation from the right to life is permitted, except in respect of deaths resulting from lawful acts of war, that is, from acts governed but not prohibited by the law of armed conflict. It does not follow that any derogation from the right to life is permitted in respect of deaths resulting from lawful acts of war. Unlawful acts of war violate the human rights of those they kill. So do lawful acts of war that are not strictly necessary in the circumstances.[26]

The law of armed conflict still differs from human rights law in important respects. As we shall see, the law of armed conflict directly imposes legal obligations on individuals, while human rights law directly imposes legal obligations on states alone. While states necessarily act through their human agents, strictly speaking it is the state and not its human agents that bear legal duties to respect human rights. In this respect, contemporary international law retains some measure of collectivism despite its broader turn toward individualism.[27]

3. A Right to Fight?

Grant that civilians and combatants retain, in war, the individual human rights they enjoy in peace. Might combatants nevertheless acquire additional 'war rights' during armed conflict, most importantly the entitlement to kill on behalf of their political collective? No. So long as states claimed the right to resort to war, combatants could plausibly claim the right to fight in war. With the prohibition of aggressive war, combatants lost any true right to fight. As Hans Kelsen observed,

---

[25] Convention for the Protection of Human Rights and Fundamental Freedoms 1950, 213 UNTS 222, arts. 2 and 15.

[26] ECtHR, Georgia v. Russia (II), Appl. no. 38263/08, Judgment of 21 January 2021, paras 26–31 (concurring opinion of Judge Keller); Adil Ahmad Haque, 'Turkey, Aggression, and the Right to Life Under the ECHR' (EJIL: Talk!, 21 October 2019) < https://www.ejiltalk.org/turkey-aggression-and-the-right-to-life-under-the-echr/ > (accessed 12 April 2023).

[27] Thanks to Dapo Akande for pressing me on this point.

48 AFTER WAR AND PEACE

Normal acts of warfare performed by members of the armed forces involved in an unjust war forbidden by general international law or by a particular treaty, such as the Kellogg-Briand Pact, cannot be considered to be 'permitted', neither in a negative nor in a positive sense of the term, since the war as such is forbidden and, consequently, all the single acts which in their totality constitute the war must be considered as forbidden.[28]

International law does not permit acts of 'legitimate warfare', either in the negative sense that these acts are not forbidden, or in the positive sense that these acts are affirmatively authorized. The law of interstate force may forbid such acts, as component parts of an act of aggression, and only the law of interstate force may affirmatively authorize such acts, as component parts of an exercise of self-defence.

Today, 'the law relating to the conduct of hostilities is primarily a law of prohibition: it does not authorize, but prohibits certain things.'[29] The law of interstate force and the law of international armed conflict share a division of labour: one protecting states from aggression, the other protecting victims of armed conflict on all sides.[30]

Instead of a right to fight, members of state armed forces enjoy only a limited immunity from prosecution by adversary states for acts that conform to the law of armed conflict. Put the other way around, 'No prisoner of war may be tried or sentenced for an act which is not forbidden by the law of the Detaining Power or by international law.'[31] Acts forbidden by the law of the Detaining Power, but not by international law, may be punished if committed during detention or, in rare cases, if committed prior to capture but unrelated to the armed conflict.[32] Acts committed prior to capture, and related to the armed conflict, may be punished only if forbidden by international law.

If combatant immunity no longer rests on a legal entitlement to fight irrespective of one's cause (if it ever did), then what is its contemporary foundation? As Richard Baxter framed the issue,

---

[28] Hans Kelsen, 'Collective and Individual Responsibility in International Law with Particular Regard to the Punishment of War Criminals', *California Law Review 31*, no. 5 (1943), pp. 530–571, at p. 549.

[29] Protocol I Commentary para 2238. See also Richard R Baxter, 'The Law of War', *Naval War College Review 10*, no. 1 (1957), pp. 39–57, at p. 46 ('The law of war is essentially prohibitive law ... Accordingly, there is no "right" to injure the enemy, only a limitation on the way that violence can be employed.').

[30] See Protocol I, preamble ('recalling' the prohibition of armed force while 'believing it necessary nevertheless to reaffirm and develop the provisions protecting the victims of armed conflicts'). See also Draft Convention on Rights and Duties of States in Case of Aggression, *American Journal of International Law Supplement 33* (1939), pp. 827–830, art. 2 ('By becoming an aggressor, a State does not acquire rights or relieve itself of duties') and art. 14 (the forgoing does not 'excuse any State for a violation of the humanitarian rules concerning the conduct of hostilities').

[31] GC III art. 99.

[32] GC III Commentary, pp. 417–418.

the fundamental assumption that the soldier is exempt from enemy jurisdiction if he complies with international law ... should not be productive of any serious disagreement, although it is less clear on what theoretical basis it may be laid. It may be, as Professor Kelsen asserts, that the act of the soldier who conforms to the law of war and does not engage in private acts of warfare is an act of state depriving the enemy state of jurisdiction, or it may be that the humanitarian intervention of international law, which makes the soldier falling into the hands of the enemy not a criminal but a prisoner of war, subject only to prosecution for acts in violation of the law of war, produces that result in time of war.[33]

Put another way, it may be that the immunity of lawful combatants is a special application of the general rule of functional immunity enjoyed by state agents acting in their official capacity, or it may be that combatant immunity is a distinct rule of the law of armed conflict enjoyed only by combatants as such. While functional immunity protects the collective interests of the agent's state, combatant immunity protects the individual interests of each soldier. Accordingly, states may assert or waive the functional immunity of their agents, but not the combatant immunity of their soldiers.[34]

There is some basis for the view that, in the nineteenth century, the rule of functional immunity belonged to the law of peace, and was therefore abrogated upon the outbreak of war. Conversely, the rule of combatant immunity belonged to the law of war, and was therefore triggered upon its outbreak. While the rule of functional immunity facilitated the peaceful relations of states, the rule of combatant immunity protected the individual soldier when such peaceful relations were cast aside. The prosecution of foreign agents was and remains a hostile act, but in the state of war hostile acts were permitted (at least in the negative sense) unless specifically prohibited.

With the abolition of the state of war as a legal institution, and of the law of war as a self-contained legal regime, one might argue that the general rule of functional immunity continues to apply during international armed conflict, barring states from prosecuting the soldiers and other agents of their adversaries for their official acts. Functional immunity and combatant immunity would therefore apply in parallel, typically overlapping but occasionally diverging.[35]

---

[33] Richard Baxter, 'The Municipal and International Law Basis of Jurisdiction Over War Crimes', in Detley F. Vagts et al. (eds), *Humanizing the Laws of War* (Oxford: OUP, 2013), pp. 58–72.

[34] GC III art. 6. Note that combatants may not waive their own immunity either. Id. art. 7.

[35] If combatant immunity is *only* a special application of functional immunity, with no separate existence, then in principle states should retain the power waive the immunity of their soldiers even in respect of acts that conform to the law of armed conflict. On this view, GC III art. 6 would prohibit states from exercising that power. I will not pursue that possibility further.

50 AFTER WAR AND PEACE

This seems unlikely. Soldiers forfeit combatant immunity when they fail to properly distinguish themselves from civilians during military engagements.[36] If these soldiers nevertheless retained functional immunity, an important incentive to so distinguish themselves would be lost. There is no evidence that states would accept this result.

More dramatically, on this view, soldiers may enjoy functional immunity (but not combatant immunity) in respect of war crimes they commit on behalf of their states. This is because, according to many states, state agents enjoy functional immunity in respect of international crimes committed in their official capacity.[37] This implication would, of course, remove an important incentive for soldiers not to commit war crimes.

Of course, many states take the view that functional immunity does not apply in respect of international crimes, in or out of armed conflict.[38] The stakes of that debate would be raised even higher if functional immunity applies to the official acts of soldiers in armed conflict.

In any event, there is at least one reason of principle to doubt that functional immunity applies to the official acts of soldiers in armed conflict. On the prevailing view, the rule of functional immunity rests on the principle that states, as sovereign equals, may not sit in judgment of each other's acts. If one state alleges that another state has violated international law, the accused state may accept responsibility or consent to a legal procedure to determine responsibility. Importantly, in the nineteenth century, the state of war was viewed by many as just such a legal procedure, the outcome of which would settle any underlying legal dispute.

The prohibition of war abolished war as a legal procedure. In my view, it also undermined the principle that states may not judge each other's acts. This is because, under the new *jus contra bellum* regime, the resort to armed force in self-defence requires the legal judgment that an unlawful armed attack has occurred (or is underway, or will imminently occur). Conversely, states may not use force to resist lawful force—force that is itself justified as self-defence or authorized by the United Nations Security Council.

In this new context, it seems hard to object to a victim state applying its national criminal law to the acts of opposing combatants waging a war of aggression on the grounds that this prosecution would directly or indirectly judge the acts of an aggressor state. Presumably, the defending state has already found the aggressor

---

[36] See, e.g., Protocol I, art. 44(4). The fact that combatants may forfeit their immunity by failing to distinguish themselves from civilians seems to support the view that their immunity belongs to them as individuals and not to their state as a collective.

[37] These states include Australia, China, France, Germany, India, Iran, Ireland, Israel, Japan, Malaysia, Russia, Singapore, Spain, Sri Lanka, Switzerland, Thailand, the United Kingdom, and the United States. See Adil Ahmad Haque, *Immunity for International Crimes: Where Do States Really Stand?*, JUST SECURITY (17 April 2018), https://bit.ly/2qEQaYK.

[38] These states include Austria, Chile, Czech Republic, Denmark, El Salvador, Estonia, Finland, Greece, Hungary, Iceland, Italy, Mexico, Netherlands, New Zealand, Norway, Poland, Peru, Portugal, Romania, Slovakia, Slovenia, South Africa, Sweden, and Viet Nam. Id.

state collectively responsible for an unlawful act of aggression. Any special rule prohibiting the domestic prosecution of opposing combatants for ordinary crimes committed as part of a war of aggression must rest on a different legal and moral basis.[39]

The pragmatic case for the current scope of combatant immunity is straightforward. If states are free to punish opposing soldiers for carrying out acts of aggression against them then, in many conflicts, both sides will claim this right and punishment will fall on just and unjust combatants alike. Indeed, both sides may feel obliged to punish opposing soldiers, to demonstrate their conviction that they are in the right, or at least to keep up appearances. To take one example, in their 1967 conflict, Israel claimed to act in preemptive self-defence (against an imminent armed attack by Egypt), Egypt claimed to act in individual self-defence (against an actual armed attack by Israel), while Syria and Jordan claimed to act in collective self-defence (of Egypt). It is hard to see how freeing all sides to punish captured soldiers would have contributed to justice, let alone peace.[40] States may also use prisoners of war as bargaining chips in peace negotiations, giving states that care less about their soldiers' fate the upper hand.[41]

The case for exempting ordinary soldiers from criminal liability for the crime of aggression before international courts is less straightforward.[42] As currently defined, the crime of aggression can only be committed by individuals 'in a position effectively to exercise control over or to direct the political or military action of a State'.[43] Moreover, the ordinary rules that individuals may incur criminal liability by assisting the commission of an international crime, or by contributing to its commission by a group of persons acting with a common purpose, do not apply with respect to the crime of aggression.[44] These restrictions seem hard to justify as a matter of moral principle.

---

[39] It might be objected that the rule of functional immunity prohibits *the courts* of one state from judging the acts of another state, but does not prohibit the executive or legislative branches of one state from doing so. This view seems hard to sustain. Suppose that a state decides, as a matter of its own constitutional law, that executive or legislative decisions to resort to armed force against another state must be reviewed by a national court, to ensure conformity with international law. May that national court adjudicate whether that other state is responsible for an unlawful armed attack and therefore liable to lawful force in individual or collective self-defence? If international law permits the state to judge the acts of another state, then why should it prohibit the state from doing so through the judicial branch of its government, which may be best positioned to deliver an impartial, well-reasoned legal judgment?

[40] The February 2019 India–Pakistan conflict offers a recent example of a similar dynamic. India claimed to act in self-defence against a non-state actor based in Pakistan, while Pakistan claimed to defend its territory from an act of aggression by India. Pakistan captured an Indian pilot, held him as a prisoner of war, and repatriated him back to India, helping to de-escalate the conflict.

[41] See GC III, art. 119 (prisoners of war already convicted for an indictable offence may be detained until the completion of the punishment).

[42] For a revisionist view, see Alejandro Chehtman, 'Revisionist Just War Theory and the Concept of War Crimes', *Leiden Journal of International Law 31*, no. 1 (2018), pp. 171–194, at p. 171.

[43] ICC Statute, art. 8*bis*(1).

[44] ICC Statute, art. 25(3)*bis* ('In respect of the crime of aggression, [the various modes of criminal liability] shall apply only to persons in a position effectively to exercise control over or to direct the political or military action of a State').

52 AFTER WAR AND PEACE

Importantly, eliminating these restrictions need not result in unjust punishment of 'invincibly ignorant' soldiers who reasonably believed that they were fighting a just war of self-defence. The crime of aggression itself requires a 'manifest violation' of the United Nations Charter, imposing no criminal liability where international law is vague or unsettled.[45] Moreover, soldiers who commit crimes pursuant to superior orders may be relieved of criminal responsibility unless they know the orders are unlawful or the orders are manifestly unlawful.[46] These provisions should suffice to protect soldiers who are truly morally blameless. Even soldiers who carry out manifestly unlawful acts of aggression may have their sentence reduced in light of mitigating circumstances including youth, lack of education, or harsh penalties for disobedience.

It is often suggested that individual soldiers will be less willing to surrender to opposing forces, or to conform to the law of armed conflict, if they fear punishment for fighting at all. By pursuing justice, international courts may undermine peace. By punishing one international crime, international courts may create perverse incentives to commit others. Such claims are hard to evaluate. If the gravity of the threatened punishment and the likelihood of conviction are both sufficiently low, then it seems unlikely that soldiers will risk death on the battlefield to avoid a remote possibility of a few years in prison, or commit war crimes (increasing their potential sentence) to further reduce their (already low) chance of conviction. Given the track record of the International Criminal Court, these seem like plausible assumptions.[47] Marginal deterrence of war crimes could be achieved by keeping the punishment for fighting in a war of aggression low relative to the punishment for committing war crimes.

As a political matter, the prospects for effectively expanding liability for the crime of aggression to ordinary soldiers seem dim. Only forty-three of the International Criminal Court's 123 member states have accepted the Court's jurisdiction with respect to the crime of aggression as currently defined. Expanding the definition of the crime, or the relevant modes of liability, would require two-thirds of states parties to adopt an amendment and seven-eighths of states parties to ratify or accept it. Since the Court may not exercise jurisdiction over the crime of aggression unless both the aggressor state and the victim state consent, or the UN Security Council refers a situation of apparent aggression to the Prosecutor, there is little prospect of convicting ordinary soldiers for the crime of aggression anytime soon.

---

[45] ICC Statute, art. 8*bis*(1).

[46] ICC Statute, art. 33(1). I will set aside the possibility that some soldiers who execute acts of aggression may qualify for the duress defence. ICC Statute, art. 31(1)(d).

[47] To date, the Court has convicted three defendants of war crimes, sentencing them to nine, twelve, and fourteen years' imprisonment, respectively. Granted, it may be easier to prove that a defendant carried out, assisted, or contributed to an act of aggression than to prove that they committed, assisted, or contributed to a specific war crime. But the Court's jurisdiction over the crime of aggression is much more limited than its jurisdiction over war crimes. So the overall likelihood of conviction remains quite low.

The International Criminal Court does not recognize the personal or functional immunities of heads of state or other high government officials as a bar to the exercise of its jurisdiction or to the arrest and surrender of such officials by states parties as requested by the Court.[48] Notably, such immunities also do not apply between parties to an international armed conflict, who may detain each other's officials and prosecute them for international crimes according to the same rules protecting all prisoners of war.

As Quincy Wright explained, 'an enemy sovereign or chief of state cannot claim immunity from prosecution for breaches of the law of war.'

> The principle of the independence and equality of states ... is suspended in relations of opposing belligerents to each other by the very nature of war. Each is seeking to impose his will on the other and is free to use measures of coercion permitted by the law of war in order to bring about a complete submission of the enemy to his will. Thus the reasons which accord immunity to chiefs of state in the courts of another state in times of peace do not apply to actions against an enemy ruler for breaches of the law of war while the war is in progress nor would they apply to acts against an ex-ruler after the war is over.[49]

For his part, Kelsen thought an enemy head of state could be detained as a prisoner of war but not prosecuted for the crime of aggression or war crimes.[50] But Kelsen also thought that, '[i]n this respect there exists no difference between the Head of State and other State officials', including ordinary soldiers. A head of state's immunity from prosecution, like that of other state officials including soldiers, derived from not from a personal immunity but from 'the rule of international law that no State can claim jurisdiction, exercised by its courts, over acts of another State'. If the latter rule is suspended during armed conflict, as argued above and as Wright observed, then a detained head of state may be prosecuted for international crimes like any other prisoner of war.

4. Individual Obligations, Individual Responsibility

Well into the twentieth century, it was possible to maintain that the law of war imposed legal obligations on states but not on individual soldiers. Of course, the law of war obligated states to obligate their soldiers to conform to the law of war.

---

[48] Prosecutor v. Al-Bashir, Case No. ICC-02/05-01/09 OA2, Judgment in the Jordan Referral re Al-Bashir Appeal (May 6, 2019).

[49] Quincy Wright, 'War Criminals', *American Journal of International Law* 39, no. 2 (1945), pp. 257–285, at p. 278 ('A ruler recognized as such in the peace would doubtless from that fact acquire immunity from subsequent prosecution').

[50] Kelsen, 'Collective and Individual Responsibility', pp. 541–542.

54 AFTER WAR AND PEACE

But the legal obligations of individual soldiers arose under their national law, not under international law.[51]

Today, it is axiomatic that the law of armed conflict imposes legal obligations directly on individuals.[52] Moreover, individual criminal responsibility under international law arises directly from an individual's violation of her legal obligations, rather than derivatively or vicariously from her state's violation of its legal obligations. This development was not a direct legal consequence of the prohibition of war, but instead a solution to a related problem.

During the Second World War, Allied lawyers needed a theory of their anticipated case against Nazi leaders for planning and launching a war of aggression. While Germany was collectively responsible for violating the Peace Pact, the Pact did not explicitly impose individual legal obligations or individual criminal responsibility. For his part, Kelsen suggested that international law would permit the Allies to simply impose such individual responsibility retroactively, either with the consent of the German government as a condition of peace or in place of the German government after unconditional surrender or total defeat. This approach had a blunt candour to it, and Nazi leaders could hardly complain of unfairness.

As Hathaway and Shapiro describe, the Czech international lawyer Bohuslav Ečer suggested an alternative approach. According to Ečer, the Peace Pact did not impose legal obligations on individuals not to plan or initiate wars of aggression, but instead lifted the legal immunity protecting such individuals from criminal prosecution under the national law of their victim states. So long as states enjoyed a right to resort to war, individuals could not be punished for involvement in the exercise of that right. With that right abolished, and war prohibited, the accompanying immunity evaporated. Nazi leaders were therefore liable to prosecution for ordinary crimes of murder, kidnapping, arson, and the like under the national law of their victim states.[53]

Robert Jackson alluded to Ečer's approach in his opening argument before the Nuremberg Tribunal, stating that:

> War inevitably is a course of killings, assaults, deprivations of liberty, and destruction of property. ... The very minimum legal consequence of the treaties making aggressive wars illegal is to strip those who incite or wage them of every defense

---

[51] See, e.g., George Manner, 'The Legal Nature and Punishment of Criminal Acts of Violence Contrary to the Laws of War', *American Journal of International Law* 37, no. 3 (1943), pp. 407–435.

[52] See, e.g., Protocol I, art. 44(2)('all combatants are obliged to comply with the rules of international law applicable in armed conflict'); art. 57(2)(a)(requiring 'those who plan or decide upon an attack' to take specified precautions); art. 87(2)(commanders must 'ensure that members of the armed forces under their command are aware of *their* obligations under the Conventions and this Protocol').

[53] Hathaway and Shapiro, *The Internationalists*, p. 253.

the law ever gave, and to leave war-makers subject to judgment by the usually accepted principles of the law of crimes.[54]

Yet the Tribunal seemed to settle on the theory that the Peace Pact imposed legal obligations on individual Nazi leaders, their violations of which triggered their individual criminal responsibility. Why? What was so wrong with Ečer's approach that the Tribunal embraced a theory widely regarded, then and now, as legally dubious and even intellectually dishonest?

As Hathaway and Shapiro suggest, Ečer's approach may have proved too much. If the prohibition of aggressive war strips the immunities of war-makers, then it should also strip the immunities of war-fighters, leaving both leaders and soldiers exposed to prosecution by victim states under their national criminal law for the ordinary crimes they order or commit. Perhaps that was not a legal consequence that the Tribunal was prepared to accept.[55]

Now, we have already seen that a special rule of combatant immunity survives the prohibition of aggressive war. But, since combatant immunity extends to all members of state armed forces, it would seem to protect senior military leaders from prosecution by victim states under their national criminal law for acts that do not violate international law. Its invocation would protect military leaders as well as ordinary soldiers, which is also the wrong result.

It is possible, then, that the Tribunal felt that the best way to hold leaders individually criminally responsible for making aggressive war, without holding soldiers individually criminally responsible for waging aggressive war, was to create an international crime of aggression that only leaders can commit. So, while the prohibition of war did not itself entail individual legal obligations or individual criminal responsibility under international law, it created the context in which the latter seemed the best way to vindicate the former.

As we have seen, it is hard to identify a principled reason to exclude ordinary soldiers from criminal liability for executing, assisting, or contributing to the crime of aggression. At the same time, the idea of punishing leaders for the crime of

---

[54] R. H. Jackson, *The Nurnberg Case as Presented by Robert H. Jackson, Chief of Counsel for the United States, Together with Other Documents* (New York: Cooper Square Publishers, 1971), p. 84. See also United States: 'Report to the President from Justice Robert H. Jackson, Chief of Counsel for the United States in the Prosecution of Axis War Criminals', *American Journal of International Law 39*, no. S3 (1945), pp. 178–190, at p. 186 ('War necessarily is a calculated series of killings, of destructions of property, of oppressions. Such acts unquestionably would be criminal except that International Law throws a mantle of protection around acts which otherwise would be crimes, when committed in pursuit of legitimate warfare').

[55] For example, Hathaway and Shapiro suggest that Hartley Shawcross did not invoke Ečer's approach in his closing arguments because 'he may have understood the dangerous implications that such an account would have on the law of war', p. 283. They also discuss a similar criticism of a similar approach proposed by William Chandler, see Hathaway and Shaprio, p. 261.

aggression was already a major innovation. Punishing ordinary soldiers might have seemed like too much, too soon.

5. Conclusion

In this chapter, I have argued that the prohibition of aggressive war and interstate force transformed the law of armed conflict, its enforcement, and its relationship with other bodies of law. The transformation is not complete. Notably, human rights law still imposes obligations on states alone, not on individual state agents. International criminal law imposes no liability, primary or derivative, on ordinary soldiers for the crime of aggression. Nevertheless, international law today resembles the reductive individualism of just war revisionists more closely than the conventionalist collectivism of just war traditionalists. If this view prevails, and the war convention adapts, lawyers and philosophers alike can more fruitfully study the pattern as a whole and search for its deepest reasons.

References

Baxter, Richard R. (1957) 'The Law of War', *Naval War College Review*, 10(1), pp. 39–57.

Baxter, R. (2013) *Humanizing the Laws of War: Selected Writings of Richard Baxter, Humanizing the Laws of War.* Edited by D. F. Vagts et al. Oxford: Oxford University Press, pp. 58–72.

Chehtman, A. (2018) 'Revisionist Just War Theory and the Concept of War Crimes', *Leiden Journal of International Law*, 31(1), pp. 171–194. doi: 10.1017/S0922156517000498.

Hathaway, O.A. and Shapiro, S. (2017) *The Internationalists: How a Radical Plan to Outlaw War Remade the World.* New York: Simon & Schuster.

Jackson, R.H. (1945) 'Report to the President from Justice Robert H. Jackson, Chief of Counsel for the United States in the Prosecution of Axis War Criminals', *American Journal of International Law*, 39(S3), pp. 178–190. doi: 10.2307/2213922.

Jackson, R.H. and International Military Tribunal. (1971) *The Nurnberg case as presented by Robert H. Jackson, Chief of Counsel for the United States, Together with Other Documents.* New York: Cooper Square Publishers.

Kelsen, H. (1942) 'Collective and Individual Responsibility in International Law with Particular Regard to the Punishment of War Criminals', *California Law Review*, 31(5), pp. 530–571.

Lauterpacht, H. (1953) 'Rules of Warfare in an Unlawful War', in George A. Lipsky (ed.), *Law and Politics in the World Community: Essays on Hans Kelsen's Pure Theory and Related Problems in International Law.* Berkeley: University of California Press, pp. 89–113.

Luban, D. (2016) 'Human Rights Thinking and the Laws of War', in J.D. Ohlin (ed.), *Theoretical Boundaries of Armed Conflict and Human Rights.* Cambridge: Cambridge University Press (ASIL Studies in International Legal Theory), pp. 45–77. doi: 10.1017/CBO9781316481103.003.

Manner, G. (1943) 'The Legal Nature and Punishment of Criminal Acts of Violence Contrary to the Laws of War', *American Journal of International Law*, 37(3), pp. 407–435. doi: 10.2307/2192722.

McMahan, J. (2009) *Killing in War*. Oxford: Oxford University Press.

Walzer, M. (1992) *Just and Unjust Wars*. Second Edition. New York: Basic Books.

Walzer, M. (2006) 'Response to McMahan's Paper', *Philosophia* 34, pp. 43–45. doi: https://doi.org/10.1007/s11406-006-9008-x.

Wright, Q. (1945) 'War Criminals', *American Journal of International Law* 39(2), pp. 257–285. doi: https://doi.org/10.2307/2192345.

2

The Direct Rights of Individuals in the International Law of Armed Conflict

Anne Peters

1. Introduction and Statement of the Problem

Female inhabitants of occupied territories are protected against enforced prostitution. Do they also have a *right* not to be forced to prostitute (see Art. 27 Geneva Convention IV)? Ethnic minorities are protected against racial discrimination by the occupying power. Do they also enjoy—under IHL—the *right* not to be discriminated against? (Art. 27 Geneva Convention IV).

The legal background to these questions is that international law of armed conflict (now also called international humanitarian law, IHL) has in the nineteenth and twentieth centuries developed, firstly, as a law governing the relations between states.[1] Current IHL imposes obligations (duties) on parties to a conflict in several respects in relation to how they treat individuals (human persons). The traditional view is that these obligations are owed to the adverse party to the conflict. Given that many obligations are stipulated in treaties, the contractual perspective implies that these are obligations *inter partes*: they are owed by contracting parties to other contracting parties. However, this purely contractual perspective can not easily explain the direction of the relevant duties in non-international armed conflicts (with armed non-state groups on one or both sides) which form the majority of armed conflicts today.

The open question is—in all types of armed conflict—whether some obligations are owed to the individuals in question such that those individuals may be said to have a (direct) right under IHL. Asking this question about individual rights implies that there is a juridical conceptual difference between legal rules embodying so-called 'objective' standards of protection (imposing obligations/duties on the obligors) and rules which *additionally* confer 'subjective' rights[2] on those

---

[1] The rules on non-international armed conflict have been codified only in 1977 and arguably impose duties also on armed non-state groups, see below §6.2.

[2] I will occasionally use the terms 'claims' and 'entitlements' synonymously. The qualifier 'subjective' rights arises from German doctrine where rights are often called 'subjective' rights as opposed to 'objective' law. This chapter partly draws on and develops further ideas laid out in Anne Peters, *Beyond Human Rights* (Cambridge: CUP, 2016). Examples for the use of the mentioned terms by international and supranational bodies is given in ibid., pp. 526–527.

Anne Peters, *The Direct Rights of Individuals in the International Law of Armed Conflict*. In: *The Individualization of War*. Edited by: Jennifer Welsh, Dapo Akande, and David Rodin, Oxford University Press. © Anne Peters (2023).
DOI: 10.1093/oso/9780192872203.003.0003

persons whom the rules seek to protect. In other words, rules can address persons as mere *beneficiaries* or—and this is a different legal status—as actual *rights-holders* ('*titulaires*'). To illustrate the difference with an example: the painting of Mona Lisa benefits from the rule prohibiting anyone from scribbling on it. Everyone is *obliged* (has the duty) to desist from scribbling on the painting. However, Mona Lisa does not have a right not to be scribbled upon.

This chapter examines whether, under which conditions IHL indeed generates such individual rights, and against whom.[3] It also argues that where such individual rights do exist, they are so-called primary rights, and are distinct from secondary rights which may accrue from a relationship of responsibility between violator and victim in the event of a breach of a primary norm of IHL. The most relevant and controversial 'secondary' right is a right to reparation, notably in form of monetary compensation. Thirdly, another type of rights are individual procedural rights to a remedy in the sense of access to institutions (domestic or international) which decide on individual claims to reparation.[4]

The chapter recalls that various provisions of IHL speak of rights of individuals on the primary level (§2) and surveys the drafting history and the trend of 'humanization' of IHL (§3). Next, different views on the appropriate regulatory technique for achieving effective protection of humans in war are presented, notably the focus on duties (§4). I then explain and justify a reading of IHL which encompasses direct rights, and point out the symbolic and practical consequences, notably for remedies, reparation, and waiver (§5). It is then asked against whom the IHL-based rights are opposable, who are the duty-bearers (§6). The chapter concludes that the recognition of IHL-based rights is helpful for steering IHL between the two evils of overextended human rights thinking and a static and paternalist fixation on states (§7).

2. The Treaty Language

The starting point for the analysis of potential direct rights under IHL are the texts of the four Geneva Conventions, and their two Additional Protocols. Their wording is mixed. Several provisions require not only the protection of individuals

---

[3] This question is rarely discussed explicitly. See in passing Marco Sassòli, 'State Responsibility for Violations of International Humanitarian Law', *IRRC 84*, no. 846 (2002), pp. 401–434, at p. 419; in more detail see Oliver Dörr, 'Völkerrechtliche Deliktsansprüche Privater—auf der Grundlage und in den Grenzen einer völkerrechtlichen Schutznormlehre', in Martin Breuer, Astrid Epiney, Andreas Haratsch, Stefanie Schmahl, and Norman Weiß (eds), *Der Staat im Recht: Festschrift Eckart Klein zum 70. Geburtstag* (Berlin: Duncker & Humblot, 2013), pp. 765–782, esp. at p. 779.

[4] It is difficult to place this right to remedy in one of the doctrinal categories of traditional international law, whether it is a 'primary' or 'secondary' right. It has a human rights–like quality and is at least partly covered by the human rights conventions' guarantees such as Art. 13 ECHR.

60 RIGHTS IN THE INTERNATIONAL LAW OF ARMED CONFLICT

but expressly refer to the 'rights', 'claims', 'entitlements', 'liberty', or 'guarantees' in regard to the individual.

Rights and entitlements are mentioned in the Hague Regulations respecting the Laws and Customs of War on Land,[5] the Third Geneva Convention relative to the Treatment of Prisoners of War (GC III),[6] the Fourth Geneva Convention relative to the Protection of Civilian Persons in Time of War (GC IV),[7] the Protocol Additional to the Geneva Conventions relating to the Protection of Victims of International Armed Conflicts (AP I of 1977),[8] and the Protocol Additional to the Geneva Conventions relating to the Protection of Victims of Non-International Armed Conflicts (AP II of 1977).[9]

In contrast, most of the provisions in the Geneva Conventions and the Additional Protocols expressly stipulate state obligations and do *not* clothe them in the language of rights. The provisions are generally formulated as prohibitions addressed to the state or as state duties of protection without a reference to the 'rights' of protected persons. Customary international law as included in the ICRC database also appears prima facie to define prohibitions and precepts or standards of treatment but not individual rights. An example of a norm formulated as objective law is Common Article 3 of the Geneva Conventions. Even the important list of fundamental guarantees set out in Article 75 of AP I is phrased as protection requirements and prohibitions, not as rights.

In the end, it is not clear from the wording whether the mentioned provisions really generate individual rights or are a misnomer. Concomitantly, it is an open question whether all other provisions which do not use the language of rights could never generate individual rights. The German case law has simply assumed that numerous provisions of the Geneva Conventions and their Additional Protocols stipulate individual rights. For instance, the Federal Constitutional Court of Germany (*Bundesverfassungsgericht*) speaks of the 'primary legal right of the affected person to compliance with the prohibitions of international humanitarian law'.[10]

---

[5] Article 3, Article 12, Article 13, Article 18, Article 23(1)(h), Article 32, and Article 46(1) of the Annex to Hague Convention (IV) respecting the Laws and Customs of War on Land of 1907 (205 CTS 277). The Annex consists of the regulations respecting the laws and customs of war on land.

[6] Article 6(1), Article 7, Article 14(1), Article 50(2), Article 54(2), Article 78(1) and (2), Article 84(2), Article 96(4), Article 105(1), Article 106, Article 113(1), Article 129(4), and Article 130 of GC III.

[7] Article 5(3), Article 7(1), Article 8, Article 27(1), Article 35(1) and (2), Article 38, Article 40(4), Article 43(1), Article 48, Article 52(1), Article 72(1), Article 73, Article 75(1), Article 76(3), (6), and (7), Article 78(2), Article 80, Article 101(1) and (2), Article 146(4), and Article 147 of GC IV.

[8] Article 11(5) ('right' to refuse surgical operation), Article 32 ('right' of families), Article 44(2), (5), and (6) ('rights' of combatants and prisoners of war), Article 45 ('claim' to the status of prisoner of war), Article 56(3) ('entitlement' of the civilian population to protection), Article 79(2) ('right' of journalists), and Article 85(4)(e) ('rights' of fair and regular trial) of AP I.

[9] Article 4(1), Article 5(1)(e), Article 6(2)(a) and (e), and Article 6(3) of AP II.

[10] *Entscheidungen des Bundesverfassungsgerichts* (BVerfGE) 112, 1 et seq., (2 BvR 1379/01) ECLI: DE:BVerfG:2004:rk20040628.2bvr137901, decision of 28 June 2004, paragraph 38 (translation mine)—*italienische Militärinternierte*. The German Federal Court in Civil Matters (*Bundesgerichtshof in Zivilsachen*) left the question open in BGHZ 169, 348 (III ZR 190/05), judgment of 2 November 2006—*Varvarin*, paragraph 15.

This was no unconscious move, because those same courts took care to split off secondary rights to reparation (as will be discussed below).

That case law has not yet settled which rules in the law of armed conflict actually generate individual rights. This must be determined in each case by interpreting the provisions (or clarifying the content of the underlying norm of customary law). Further study must identify how to recognize an individual IHL-based right and which types of rights exist. For example, the 'right' to participate directly in hostilities (Art. 43(2) AP I), does not seem to be a 'claim right' in the Hohfeldian sense but rather (as the traditional term of the law of war, 'combat immunity', expresses) an immunity right,[11] granting immunity from criminal prosecution.

In order to identify and circumscribe better the 'rights' content of the law, we must clarify the concept.

3. The Concept of Rights under IHL

The language of rights was deliberately chosen in the law of armed conflict only after the Second World War, and the relationship between IHL and human rights became a major issue only in the new millennium.[12]

3.1 Negotiating History and Codification of IHL Post–Second World War

The drafting of the Geneva Conventions of 1949 stood under the impression of the extreme violations of the rights and dignity of humans. The drafters therefore used the language of rights deliberately. The negotiating history of the Geneva Conventions suggests that their provisions should not be thought of solely as objective norms of protection. Rather, this history indicates that certain provisions should be interpreted so as to generate individual rights. At the Diplomatic Conference in 1949, the early proposal in regard to the non-renunciation clause—'the rights which it stipulates on their behalf'—was abandoned in favour of the formulation 'the rights which it confers upon them'.[13] This change can be read as an indication of the intention to provide individual ownership of the claim. The Conference was of the view that the phrase 'on their behalf' would have implied only 'an

---

[11] Adil A. Haque, *Law and Morality at War* (New York: Oxford University Press, 2017), p. 28.

[12] Before the Second World War, the word 'right' was anodyne, and most likely no special meaning was attached to it: Hague Regulations Respecting the Laws and Customs of War on Land (Annex to the Hague Convention) of 18 October 1907 stipulates 'rights' of prisoners, parlementaires, and commanders (Art. 3; 12; 32–34). The Geneva Convention Relative to the Treatment of Prisoners of War of 27 July 1929 (entered into force 19 June 1931), (118 LNTS 343) mentions 'rights' of prisoners of war in Art. 42, 62, 64.

[13] Final Record of the Diplomatic Conference of Geneva of 1949 (New York: William S. Hein & Co., 2004), Vol. II, Sec. B, 76 (Special Committee, Joint Committee, 23rd meeting).

62 RIGHTS IN THE INTERNATIONAL LAW OF ARMED CONFLICT

"indirect" benefit resulting from the attitude prescribed to the States'. For this reason, the Diplomatic Conference preferred the formulation previously proposed by the ICRC ('confers upon them'), according to the authoritative Pictet commentary on the Geneva Conventions.[14]

At the same time, the Pictet commentary shows that this 'individualization' of the law of armed conflict, i.e., the charging of precepts and prohibitions with individual claims, represented a novelty in the law of armed conflict after the Second World War. In regard to Convention (III) Relative to the Treatment of Prisoners of War, the Pictet commentary notes: 'At the outset, however, the treatment which belligerents were required to accord to persons referred to in the Convention was not presented, nor indeed clearly conceived as constituting a body of "rights" to which they were automatically entitled ...: It was not ... until the Convention of 1949 (in particular in Articles 6 and 7[15]) that the existence of "rights" conferred on prisoners of war was affirmed.'[16] The Pictet commentary attributes the conscious and deliberate focus on individual rights to the influence of the recognition of international human rights.[17] The result was the codification of rights that are related to, but distinct from human rights.

3.2 'Humanization', 'Righting', and Human Rights–Based Approaches

The idea of applying *human* rights in armed conflict arose only later. In a seminal book of 2006, Theodor Meron analysed the 'radiation'[18] of human rights into IHL. What Meron described as 'humanization' of IHL is part of the broader phenomenon that human rights have become relevant in all areas of international law, both in the special issue areas and in its general parts. This phenomenon has been accompanied by so-called 'human rights–based approaches' (for example the human rights–based approach to development) and to 'X and human rights' debates (for example 'investment and human rights').[19] The loading of various

---

[14] René-Jean Wilhelm, 'Art. 7' in: Jean Pictet (ed.). *Commentary of the Geneva Conventions of 12 August 1949, Vol. I*: Geneva Convention I for the Amelioration of the Condition of the Wounded and Sick in Armed Forces in the Field. Geneva: ICRC, 1952, pp. 82–83.

[15] The non-renunciation clause and the prohibition of special agreements.

[16] René-Jean Wilhelm, 'Art. 7' in: Jean Pictet (ed.). *Commentary on the Geneva Conventions of 12 August 1949, Vol. III*:, Geneva Convention III Relative to the Treatment of Prisoners of War. Geneva: ICRC, 1960, p. 91(footnote added).

[17] René-Jean Wilhelm, 'Art. 7' in: Pictet, *Commentary on the Geneva Conventions, Vol. I*, at p. 83, stating the formulation was influenced by 'the concomitant trends of doctrine, which also led to the universal proclamation of Human Rights'.

[18] Theodor Meron, *The Humanization of International Law* (Leiden: Martinus Nijhoff, 2006), p. xv.

[19] Depending on the issue area and on the concrete problems at hand, human rights function as a reinforcement of the regimes' overall objectives (for example in the law of migration) or rather as a counterpoint (for example in trade law), and sometimes as both.

international legal regimes with human rights has also been called their 'righting',[20] or their 'rightsification'.[21]

The overall imbuement of global governance activities, including responses to armed conflict, with human rights was initially deemed to lend a higher legitimacy to those agendas, and also had the effect to legalize the fields more (because they became oriented at human rights as *legal* standards). The seeping of human rights into IHL has also promoted novel interpretations of traditional concepts. However, this 'humanization' has come under fire.[22] The imbuement of IHL with human rights considerations has been criticized as an inappropriate or even strategical deflection from the actual objectives of IHL. We must therefore turn to these objectives.

4. Rights or Duties?

Today, probably most commentators agree that the purpose of international humanitarian law is to go 'beyond the interstate levels' and to reach for 'the level of the real (or ultimate) beneficiaries of humanitarian protection, i.e., individuals and groups of individuals'.[23] However, some controversy persists over the adequate legal techniques to realize this ultimately broad objective, and over distinct specific finalities on a more concrete plane.

4.1 Different Logics?

Some authors underline the different logics of human rights law on the one side, and IHL on the other side. David Luban has argued that '[t]here is no intrinsic connection between the humanitarian project and the human rights project.'[24] According to that view, IHL and human rights law do not share the same essence. Historically, IHL was not designed to protect human dignity but to reduce human suffering.[25] This is—according to Luban—a more utilitarian (Benthamite) rationale than a Kantian one.[26]

---

[20] The term 'righting' was coined by Karen Knop and applied in a critical spirit to the law of occupation by Aeyal Gross. See Aeyal Gross, The Writing on the Wall: Rethinking the International Law of Occupation (Cambridge: CUP, 2017), ch. 5.

[21] John Gershman and Jonathan Morduch, 'Credit Is Not a Right', in Tom Sorell and Luis Cabrera (eds), *Microfinance, Rights and Global Justice* (Cambridge: CUP, 2015), pp. 14–26, at p. 21.

[22] Cf. Lawrence Hill-Cawthorne, 'Rights under International Humanitarian Law', *EJIL 28*, no. 4 (2017), pp. 1187–1215, at pp. 1212–1213.

[23] Georges Abi-Saab, 'The Specificities of Humanitarian Law', in Christophe Swinarski (ed.), *Studies and Essays of International Humanitarian Law and Red Cross Principles in Honour of Jean Pictet* (Geneva: ICRC, 1984), pp. 265–281, at p. 269.

[24] David Luban, 'Human Rights Thinking and the Laws of War', in Jens David Ohlin (ed.), *Theoretical Boundaries of Armed Conflict and Human Rights* (Cambridge: CUP, 2016), pp. 45–77, at p. 49.

[25] Ibid., p. 45.

[26] Ibid., p. 50.

Françoise Hampson has very usefully explained the differences as follows:

> Philosophically, human rights law and humanitarian law start from very differ-
> ent premises. The rules are designed to fulfil different functions, human rights
> law being applicable to varying degrees in all situations and humanitarian law
> only in time of armed conflict. The rules also concern different actors. By way of
> illustration, it is helpful to think of a pebble hitting a pond. In the case of human
> rights law, the pebble is the individual whose rights are to be protected. The rip-
> ples encompass many different State agents, depending on the situation. In the
> case of humanitarian law, the pebble is the member of the armed forces, rather
> than a potential victim. The ripples are the different categories of people with
> whom he/she has to deal. In the first case, it is the State agents (the ripples) who
> are limited in the actions they can take. In the latter, it is the member of the armed
> forces (the pebble) who is restricted.[27]

This image illustrates that not only the starting point of the legal analysis is ostensibly a different one but also, most importantly, that the focus is on different
duty-bearers. Human rights are opposable to states (acting through their agents).
In contrast, IHL-based rights are opposable to those actors which commit violent act in war. The question of duty-bearers will be discussed in detail in §6.
At this point it suffices to conclude, with Hampson, that '[w]hilst the form of the
rules is therefore very different, nevertheless the effect of the two bodies of rules is
strikingly similar.'[28]

4.2 Duty-Based IHL?

The traditional view was that individuals are the *objects* of protection but not *subjects (legal persons)*, at best 'beneficiaries', but not holders of rights under IHL. The
treaty provisions were interpreted as giving rise to obligations *between states*, the
fulfilment of which was owed only to the other contracting states.

Recent scholarship reiterates this view. According to Françoise Hampson, the
rules of IHL:

> are not based on any notion of the 'right' of the individual civilian not to be
> attacked, the 'right' of the prisoner of war to good treatment or the 'right' of
> the injured to medical care. The Conventions are based rather on the recipro-
> cal *obligations* of States. This is given effect by imposing obligations on members
> of armed forces, for the breach of which international law requires that they be
> punished. The State itself is also responsible for the conduct of its armed forces.[29]

[27] Françoise Hampson, 'Human Rights Law and Humanitarian Law: Two Coins or Two Sides of the Same Coin?' *Bulletin of Human Rights 1* (1991), pp. 46–54, at p. 49).
[28] Ibid.
[29] Ibid., at p. 49.

According to René Provost, '[p]rotection given to individuals [...] would not be in the nature of rights, either for the state or the individual, but more in the nature of standards of treatment.'[30] And Ziv Bohrer finds 'a core difference between IHL and IHRL [international human rights law]: the former being obligations-based and the latter rights-based.'[31] Bohrer enumerates several benefits of a duty-based system. First, it can easily be applied extraterritorially because 'obligations are attached to the obligation-bearers and, as such, tend to follow them.'[32] Secondly, the focus on obligation-bearers should make it more likely that the acting commanders actually implement the legally prescribed measures.[33] Rights-based systems, by contrast, refer to the rights of third persons, and are therefore more prone to disregard. Thirdly, Bohrer finds obligation-based systems more adequate for protecting the disempowered, those who are incapable to 'demand the protection of their rights.'[34] Fourthly, Bohrer points out that the traditional chivalry narrative, reflected in the status orientation of IHL, has been the 'basis for imposing certain demanding ethical-legal soldierly duties.'[35] By contrast, the rights orientation effaces that aspect. The focus on rights finally might, as Bohrer warns, even incite soldiers to place their own individual rights first, as reflected in the debates on 'force protection', a trend that should not be welcomed.[36]

4.3 Further Objections against IHL-Based Rights

The idea of IHL-based rights also alerts champions of an international legal order that is and must in their view remain a primarily interstate order. Those voices insist that 'in principle, the individual *remains an object of protection. ...* [T]he overstretched concept of the individualisation of international law has reached its useful limits.'[37]

Along this line, three further arguments have been made against the rights-based view and in favour of an understanding of the law of armed conflict based

---

[30] René Provost, *International Human Rights and Humanitarian Law* (Cambridge: CUP, 2002), pp. 27–34, esp. at p. 33; see also ibid., p. 116. See in this sense also Kate Parlett, *The Individual in the International Legal System* (Cambridge: CUP, 2011), pp. 176–228, esp. at p. 224.

[31] Ziv Bohrer, 'Divisions over Distinctions in Wartime International Law', in Helen Duffy, Janina Dill, and Ziv Bohrer, *Law Applicable to Armed Conflict*, Max Planck Trialogues on the Law of Peace and War vol. 2 (Anne Peters and Christian Marxsen series eds, Cambridge: CUP, 2019), pp. 106–196, at p. 175, see ibid., pp. 182–186.

[32] Bohrer, 'Divisions over Distinctions in Wartime International Law', p. 180.

[33] Cf. ibid., p. 186.

[34] Ibid.

[35] Ibid., p. 189.

[36] I summarize Bohrer's position relying on Christian Marxsen and Anne Peters, 'Conclusions: Productive Divisions', in Duffy et al., *Law Applicable to Armed Conflict*, Max Planck Trialogues on the Law of Peace and War vol. 2 (Anne Peters and Christian Marxsen series eds, Cambridge: CUP, 2019), pp. 266–279, at p. 275.

[37] Klaus Ferdinand Gärditz, 'Bridge of Varvarin', *AJIL 108*, no. 1 (2014), pp. 86–93, at p. 91(italics mine).

66 RIGHTS IN THE INTERNATIONAL LAW OF ARMED CONFLICT

purely on duties and on 'objective' law (as opposed to 'subjective' rights). Firstly—according to Kate Parlett—the 'objective' interpretation is easier to reconcile with the non-renunciation clauses and the prohibition of special agreements because these types of clauses prohibit both individuals and states from deviating from the standards.[38] Secondly, the 'objective' interpretation is compatible with a legal framework in which the individuals do not have any legal or even any factual possibility to enforce their rights.[39] And finally, according to Parlett, the purely objective legal construction is not necessarily less effective for the protection of the individual.[40] All three considerations are comprehensible but not compelling. As discussed below, the non-renunciation clauses are intended to move the guarantees into the vicinity of human rights, i.e., the individual rights par excellence (section 5.5). The prohibitions of deviations by way of agreements between states are ambivalent: on the one hand, they imply that certain guarantees are subject to state disposition; but they also withdraw other guarantees from the power of the states. If the states are not the obligees (receivers) of the owed duties of protection, then individuals must be the obligees.

4.4 The Priority of Rights over Duties

The reported body of scholarship provokes the question of the relationship between rights and duties (obligations). Do rights trigger the other side's obligation or is it the other way round? In the early *ius naturae et gentium*, obligations were seen as the primary concept.[41] The 'classic' view was that obligations (against God, against oneself, and against others) gave rise to correlative rights.[42]

Most likely, it was the rise of the sovereign state which triggered the prioritization of rights. According to Richard Tuck, Hugo Grotius' *De iure belli ac pacis*[43] is 'in fact the first reconstruction of an actual legal system in terms of rights rather than laws. Consequently it is the true ancestor of all the modern codes which have

---

[38] See for a detailed analysis of these two types of clauses below §5.2.

[39] Parlett, *The Individual in the International Legal System*, p. 187; Bohrer, p. 186.

[40] See Parlett, pp. 224, 225, and 228.

[41] Gerald Hartung, *Die Naturrechtsdebatte: Geschichte der obligatio vom 17. bis 20. Jahrhundert* (2d ed Freiburg: Alber, 1999); Stephan Stübinger, 'Hegel und das moderne Verständnis der Person im Recht', in Kurt Seelmann and Benno Zabel (eds), *Autonomie und Normativität: Zu Hegels Rechtsphilosophie* (Tübingen: Mohr Siebeck, 2014), p. 69.

[42] Samuel Pufendorf, *De officio hominis et civis juxta legem naturalem libri duo* (1678 edn): chapter IV (De officio hominis erga deum, seu de religione naturali), pp. 52–67; chapter V (De officio hominis erga seipsum), pp. 67–91.

[43] According to Grotius's definition, '[I]us est qualitas moralis personae competens ad aliquid iuste habendum vel agendum' ('Ius is the moral quality of a person enabling that person to have something or do something rightfully'); Hugo Grotius, *De iure belli ac pacis libri tres* (1625), liber primus, caput 1, n IV, ed. B. J. A. de Kanter-van Hettinga Tromp (Leiden: E. J. Brill, 1939; online 2009 dbnl). See Peter Haggenmacher, 'Droits subjectifs et système juridique chez Grotius', in Luc Foisneau (ed.), *Politique, droit et théologie chez Bodin, Grotius et Hobbes* (Paris: Éditions Kimé, 1997), pp. 73–130.

rights of various kinds at their centre.'[44] But not until John Locke, and especially Immanuel Kant, was the 'central position of the subjective right in modern legal thinking' established.[45]

Near the end of eighteenth century, the reversal of the order between rights and obligations was completed. The concept of right (moral or legal, sometimes conflated) had superseded the concept of obligation.[46] The 'right' became to symbolize liberty and free will.[47] Since then, secular Western legal systems tend to conceive of rights as the primary concept which then prompt the other side's duties. It can be said that 'rights' are the 'paradigmatically modern answer' to the basic problem of every society, namely the separation between individual reason and a social order no longer experienced as necessary but rather as malleable.[48] And exactly these 'modern' issues of moral responsibility, liberty, sociability, and objectives of human action have also become relevant for the international legal order, as highlighted by Emmanuel Roucounas.[49]

4.5 Assessment

The contemporary critique against the 'righting' of IHL seems to suggest going back in history and giving a priority to duties.[50] However, the renewed focus on duties does not solve the puzzle. On a very abstract level, the problem of any legal analysis taking rights (as opposed to the duties) as the starting point seems to be that the obligors (duty-bearers) are not entirely determined from the outset. As Joseph Raz writes, 'one may know of the existence of a right ... *without knowing who is bound by duties* based on it or what precisely are those duties.'[51]

However, independently from what comes 'first', the exact addressees of duties and of rights need to be identified. Who are the rights-bearers and who are the duty-bearers? The renewed focus on duties cannot absolve from these questions, and the answers seem independent of the question of priority. The traditional

---

[44] Richard Tuck, *Natural Rights Theories: Their Origin and Development* (Cambridge: CUP, 1979), p. 66.

[45] Marietta Auer, Der privatrechtliche Diskurs der Moderne (Tübingen: Mohr Siebeck, 2013), pp. 24–29, at p. 27.

[46] Friedrich von Gentz, Ueber den Ursprung und die obersten Prinzipien des Rechts, Berlinische Monatsschrift 18, pp. 370–396, at p. 379.

[47] Cf. Stephan Stübinger, 'Hegel und das moderne Verständnis der Person im Recht', in K. Seelmann and B. Zabel, (eds), *Autonomie und Normativität: Zu Hegels Rechtsphilosophie* (Tübingen: Mohr Siebeck, 2014), p. 84.

[48] Marietta Auer, 'Subjektive Rechte bei Pufendorf und Kant', *Archiv der civilistischen Praxis 208*, no. 5 (2008), pp. 584–634, at p. 633 (my translation).

[49] Emmanuel Roucounas, 'Facteurs privés et droit international public', *Recueil des Cours: Collected Courses of The Hague Academy of International Law 299* (2002), pp. 9–419, at p. 47 (para. 43).

[50] Actually the priority of duties has persisted in some legal systems, for example in Jewish law see Robert M. Cover, 'Obligation: A Jewish Jurisprudence of the Social Order', *Journal of Law and Religion* 5(1) (1987), pp. 65–74.

[51] Joseph Raz, *The Morality of Freedom* (Oxford: OUP, 1988), p. 184.

paradigm was that IHL-based duties were incumbent on states, the parties to the relevant treaties, owed to the other state parties. These 'recipients' of the obligations were understood to be bearers of the concomitant rights to compliance. However, even where states have been seen as the rights-holders, individuals have been seen as the '*beneficiaries*'. The states' duties gave rise to a beneficial reflection for human beings. The idea of IHL-based rights is simply to conceptualize human beings as the recipients of the extant duties, to shift the direction of the duties which are otherwise left untouched. The duty-bearers will be analysed in § 6.

5. The Utility of IHL-Based Rights

Against the sceptical voices, this section explains the utility of IHL-based rights.

5.1 Emancipation

Rights empower people, if not judicially then at least politically.[52] As Cass Sunstein put it: 'It is surely plausible that the recognition of rights often converts people from victims into citizens. Certainly a major point of rights guarantee is to do precisely this.'[53]

In IHL, the particular aspect of empowerment is that IHL-based rights may be asserted by the individual person, *irrespective of the view the individual's home state takes on this point*. Precisely that point had been addressed by the ICRC at the Preliminary Conference convened in 1946 to prepare a revision of the Geneva Conventions: '[T]he Commission unanimously recommended that the rights conferred by the Convention on prisoners of war should have a personal and intangible character, allowing the latter to claim them irrespective of the attitude adopted by their home country.'[54] The (non-litigative) empowerment of individuals can be regarded as an expression of the overall paradigm shift of IHL, away from a law that mainly serves to empower states to broaden their discretion in conducting military operations.[55]

It is my view that this emancipation is best suited to the moral status of the individual within the international legal order.[56] Treating the human being as an

---

[52] See, e.g., Michael Ignatieff, 'Human Rights as Idolatry', in Amy Gutman (ed.), *Human Rights as Politics and Idolatry* (Princeton: Princeton University Press, 2001), pp. 53–100, at p. 57: Rights language is a language of empowerment.

[53] Cass Sunstein, 'Rights and Their Critics', *Notre Dame Law Review 70*, no. 4 (1999), pp. 727–768, at p. 754.

[54] International Committee of the Red Cross, 'Report on the Work of the Preliminary Conference of National Red Cross Societies for the Study of the Conventions and of Various Problems Relative to the Red Cross' (Geneva, 26 July–3 August 1946) (Geneva, 1947), at p. 71. The 'Commission' was one of the three Conference committees; in this context, it gave its opinion on the planned revised agreement on prisoners of war.

[55] Cf. Amanda Alexander, 'A Short History of International Humanitarian Law', *EJIL 26*, no. 1 (2015), pp. 110–138, at p. 110.

[56] Anne Peters, 'Humanity as the A and Ω of Sovereignty', *EJIL 20*, no. 3 (2009), pp. 513–544.

object in the law of armed conflict—a relic of the nineteenth century—would be out of sync with the presumption of international legal personhood of the individual. If we want to preserve the paradigm shift from sovereigntism to humanism, the recognition of IHL-based rights is warranted.

5.2 Increased Protection against Infringement

The second non-enforcement related advantage of having rights as opposed to being merely beneficiaries of standards of conduct is an increased and stronger protection. The recognition of rights carries with it a powerful message of prima facie inviolability (which the metaphors of 'trump',[57] 'stop-sign', 'shield', or 'armour',[58] and the like express). The protection is not perfect, but it is stronger than without rights. Rights are not absolutes, because they can be interfered with, curtailed or restricted up to a certain point. The heightened protection offered by a right lies in the fact that curtailments and restrictions of rights must *be specifically justified*. Acknowledging a right places a burden of explanation and justification on the actor who wants to restrict the right. Only if the justification fails, the right is deemed to be violated.[59]

Exactly this burden of justification implies that cloaking the question of our social and political interactions, and of the ensuing conflicts between antagonist interests in the language of rights *channels the discourse*.

> Introducing the notion of something having a 'right' (simply speaking that way), brings into the legal system a flexibility and open-endedness that no series of specifically stated legal rules like R1, R2, R3, ... R. can capture. Part of the reason is that 'right' (and other so-called 'legal terms' ...) have meaning—vague but forceful—in the ordinary language, and the force of these meanings, inevitably infused with our thought, becomes part of the context against which the 'legal language' of our contemporary 'legal rules' is interpreted.[60]

This modification of the discourse is in turn apt to impact on behaviour, as social constructivists have argued. The rights discourse and the burden of justification going with it 'socializes' the relevant actors. This has been empirically shown with

---

[57] Ronald Dworkin, 'Rights as Trumps', in Jeremy Waldron (ed.), *Theories of Rights* (Oxford: OUP, 1984), pp. 153–167.

[58] Frederick Schauer, 'A Comment on the Structure of Rights', *Georgia Law Review 27*, no. 2 (1993), pp. 415–434, at p. 429.

[59] I here follow the terminology of the European Court of Human Rights with regard to human rights: interference/restriction—justification—violation.

[60] Christopher D. Stone, 'Should Trees have Standing? Toward Legal Rights for Natural Objects', *Southern California Law Review 45*, no. 2 (1972), pp. 450–501, at p. 488.

regard to human rights, as an effect of endorsing and ratifying international human rights conventions.[61]

Third, the rights-related balancing differs from the utilitarian calculus. Although the identification of the point where an interference with a right amounts to an inadmissible violation of that right involves balancing, too, the right confers a legal position which changes the equation.[62] For example, balancing the *protection* of civilians against military advantages (as in the IHL standard of 'military necessity') is structurally biased against civilians. In contrast, individual *rights* flowing from IHL would allow a fair balancing in which the proper value of fundamental human interests could be integrated.

The fourth function of rights—short of their enforceability—lies in their dynamic and overshooting content. This means that the protection created through rights may become stronger (or weaker) with the circumstances. For example, the provision of Art. 5(1) e) of AP II grants interned or detained persons 'the benefit of working conditions and safeguards similar to those enjoyed by the local civilian population'. If this provision is construed as a right, it is particularly open and dynamic. Art. 5(2) c) of AP II states that 'places of internment and detention shall not be located close to the combat zone'. Again, reading this as a right will allow law-appliers to adapt its exact content to the technical development of combat.

5.3 Remedies

A very practical advantage of rights is to facilitate proceedings in court. Indeed, some legal systems have traditionally defined rights by their judicial enforceability: 'no rights without remedy'. IHL-based specific remedies (in the sense of access for individuals to international monitoring bodies or courts) do not exist. It has therefore been asserted that it is pointless to speak of IHL-based rights as long as an IHL-based international enforcement mechanism, accessible to individuals, is lacking.[63] Such assertions reflect the classic, Anglo-Saxon-coloured link between the *substantive* legal status of the individual under international law and his/her

---

[61] Beth A. Simmons, *Mobilizing for Human Rights: International Law in Domestic Politics* (Cambridge: CUP, 2009); Ryan Goodman and Derek Jinks, *Socializing States: Promoting Human Rights through International Law* (Oxford: OUP, 2013); Thomas Risse and Stephen C. Ropp, 'Introduction and Overview', in Thomas Risse, Stephen C. Ropp, and Kathryn Sikkink (eds), *The Persistent Power of Human Rights: From Commitment to Compliance* (Cambridge: CUP, 2013), pp. 3–25 on the 'spiral model of human rights change' which social constructivist authors had developed since 1998.

[62] Jeremy Waldron, 'Rights in Conflict', in his *Liberal Rights: Collected Papers 1981–1991* (Cambridge: CUP, 1993), pp. 203–224, esp. at pp. 210–211.

[63] Lars C. Berster, '"Duty to Act" and Commission by Omission in International Criminal Law', *International Criminal Law Review 10*, no. 5 (2010), pp. 619–646, at p. 627.

procedural legal status.[64] I call this view the 'coupling thesis' (coupling substance and procedure).

However, this link between substance and (judicial) procedure is doubtful: the availability of a judicial remedy (justiciability in the sense of being enforceable through a court) is no universal feature of all kinds of rights. Probably all legal systems of states now distinguish between substantive and procedural rights. Contemporary domestic law is based on an ideal-typical distinction between rights and legal protection.

Recent international judgments as well distinguish between substantive rights and actionability. Already the Permanent Court of International Justice held: 'It is scarcely necessary to point out that the capacity to *possess* civil rights does not necessarily imply the capacity to *exercise* those rights oneself.'[65] Also in the *LaGrand* case, the ICJ stated without further ado that the VCCR 'creates individual rights' that can (only) be asserted by the home state before the court.[66]

The 'procedural' conception of international rights of the individual ignores that the enforcement of rights can occur at different levels, i.e., at both the domestic and international levels. Actually, the decentralized enforcement of individual rights through *domestic* institutions on the basis of a recognition of the direct effect of international legal norms protecting the individual is probably the main type of enforcement.[67] The coupling thesis which links international rights to the availability of international remedies underestimates the important role of domestic institutions in the decentralized enforcement of international law, generally speaking. This type of decentralized enforcement in domestic institutions, notably courts, is not only an emergency measure where a fully elaborated, international, court-like system for the protection of individual rights is lacking, but it also is desirable on normative grounds because it respects the general legal principle of subsidiarity.

For all these reasons, the proceedings available to the individual before international enforcement bodies are no defining characteristic of international rights of the individual. To conclude, the question of possessing a right (as a part of substantive law) and the question of how and in which forums to enforce it (procedural law), are two separate issues. Nevertheless, the weakness of international

---

[64] Rosalyn Higgins, *Problems and Process: International Law and How We Use It* (Oxford: OUP, 1995), pp. 52–53. She tended towards decoupling substance and process: '[W]e are not unaccustomed to separating our definition of a right from our appraisal of a remedy.' 'My own view is that the individual does have certain rights owed to him under international law (and not just to his state).'

[65] PCIJ, *Peter Pàzmàny University Case*, Ser. A/B, No. 61 (1935), p. 231 (italics mine). See also IACtHR, *Judicial Condition and Human Rights of the Child*, Advisory Opinion No. 17, 28 August 2002, holding 1 of the opinion (p. 79) and concurring opinion of Antônio A. Cançado Trindade, paragraphs 6 and 8: The child is a holder of (human) rights, irrespective of the child's capacity to act, i.e., the capacity to exercise those rights.

[66] ICJ, *LaGrand Case (Germany v. United States of America)*, ICJ Reports 2001, 466, paragraph 77.

[67] Peters, *Beyond Human Rights*, ch. 16.

72 RIGHTS IN THE INTERNATIONAL LAW OF ARMED CONFLICT

enforcement options raises the question of the practical utility of substantive international rights that are difficult to enforce procedurally.

5.4 Reparation

The finding of a primary right under IHL bolsters individual claims for reparation and compensation (secondary rights). Such claims are controversial.[68] Reparation to individuals for war-related harms are being increasingly recognized by international, transnational, and hybrid bodies such as special war crimes tribunals and truth commissions. They are stipulated in special agreements in post-conflict situations, and they are foreseen, e.g., in Art. 75 ICC-Statute. The 2005 General Assembly's Basic Principles and Guidelines on the Right to a Remedy and Reparation for Victims of Gross Violations of International Human Rights Law and Serious Violations of International Humanitarian Law[69] postulate that individual rights to reparation can be found in various international instruments but do not in itself create these rights as a matter of hard law. National courts are normally reluctant to award IHL-based reparation. Three lines of argument are worth discussing in this context.

A first idea is that the controversial individual right to reparation in the field of armed conflict is distinct from the rules of state responsibility and might be seen as a *sui generis*, independent of the familiar two-level scheme in general international law.[70] However, such a novel conceptualization creates complexity and lacks foreseeability.[71] Stepping out of the established structure of international law would in any case require a thorough doctrinal and normative explanation.

A second idea is to separate the two levels of international law. Notably, the German case law on reparations operates on the idea that the ownership of the international rights (claims) on the primary level and on the secondary level of state responsibility is split: while the owner of the claim in substance may be the individual, the ownership of the secondary claim to reparation is assigned to the state. In a ruling of 2004, the Federal Constitutional Court held:

> This right to damages under secondary law, however, exists only in the public-international-law relationship between the states involved and is subject to their

---

[68] See out of the abundant literature Cristián Correa, Shuichi Furuya, and Clara Sandoval, *Reparation for Victims of Armed Conflict*, Max Planck Trialogues on the Law of Peace and War vol. 3 (Anne Peters and Christian Marxsen series eds, Cambridge: CUP, 2021).

[69] Basic Principles and Guidelines on the Right to a Remedy and Reparation for Victims of Gross Violations of International Human Rights Law and Serious Violations of International Humanitarian Law of 16 December 2005 (UN Doc. A/RES/60/147).

[70] Hill-Cawthorne, 'Rights under International Humanitarian Law', p. 1208.

[71] See on state responsibility towards individuals Anne Peters, *Beyond Human Rights*, ch. 6, pp. 167–193.

disposition. In this respect, the claim to damages differs from the involved persons' entitlement under primary law that the prohibitions of humanitarian public international law be observed; this [primary] claim exists in the public-international-law relationship between the state occupying a territory and the population living in this territory.[72]

This 'separation approach' distributes the ownership of the claim at the levels of primary and secondary law between two different persons (subjects): the victim on the one hand, and the victim's home state on the other.

The case law of the Federal Court of Justice stated that not every 'rule *relating* to human rights' in treaties actually *assigned* individual rights. The Court thus created an opposition between an 'individual right' of the affected natural person on the one hand and the mere 'factual privilege' of that person or a 'legal reflex' to that individual's benefit.[73] 'In particular, the rule continues to apply that— independently of any primary legal claim by the affected persons for compliance with international law—claims for damages under secondary law arising from acts of State in violation of international law against citizens of foreign States continue to be due only to the home State as a matter of principle.'[74]

In its ensuing inadmissibility decision, the German Federal Constitutional Court endorsed this reasoning. It held:

Despite the—continuously progressing—developments in the area of human rights which has led to a recognition of a partial legal personality of the individual and to the establishment of treaty-based complaint mechanisms, a similar development on the level of secondary claims cannot be ascertained. *Rights to reparation for breaches of international law by a State towards aliens still belong, as a matter of principle, only the individual's State of nationality.*[75]

The same stance was taken both by the Federal Court of Justice in Civil Matters and the Constitutional Court in the case of *Distomo*.[76] In *Kunduz*, the German

---

[72] BVerfG – *Militärinternierte* (n. 10) paragraph 38 (translation mine).

[73] BGHZ 169, 348 et seq.—*Varvarin* (n. 10), paragraph 11 (translation and italics mine).

[74] (Ibid. According to the Court, the holder of the secondary claim for damages arising from Article 3 of the Hague Convention (IV) and Article 91 of AP I continues to be the home state. (Ibid., paragraphs 12–21). The wording, history, and case-law especially of Article 91 of AP I does not give rise in practice to any individual (secondary) claim for reparation. (Ibid., paragraphs 15–20 with references from the treaty materials in paragraph 12).

[75] *Bundesverfassungsgericht* (BVerfG), (2 BvR 2660/06 and 2 BVR 487/07), ECLI: DE:BVerfG:2013:rk20130813.2bvr266006, inadmissibility decision of 13 August 2013—*Varvarin*, esp. paragraphs 43–47, quotation paragraph 46, translation and italics mine.

[76] BVerfG (2 BvR 1476/03), ECLI:DE:BVerfG:2006:rk20060215.2bvr147603, inadmissibility decision of the 1st Chamber of 15 February 2006, paragraph 20—*Distomo*. The Constitutional Court continued in this case: 'Irrespective of developments at the level of the protection of human rights, which have led to recognition of a partial international legal subjectivity of the individual and to the

74 RIGHTS IN THE INTERNATIONAL LAW OF ARMED CONFLICT

Federal Court of Justice in Civil Matters stated in 2016: 'For treaties under public international law, the [secondary] obligation of responsibility is limited to the international legal relationship between states. It exists only between the state parties and is distinct from the primary entitlement of the affected person to have the norms of IHL complied with.'[77]

This split between rights *of the individual person* on the level of the primary law (i.e., in the field of IHL) on the one side and exclusive rights *of the state* on the level of secondary law (pertaining to the field of international state responsibility) is overly complicated. It seems more straightforward to either acknowledge both primary and secondary rights of individual persons, or to deny rights on both levels of law.

The by far most plausible and much less convoluted legal solution is to look, as in the established structures of state responsibility, for violations of primary rights. Where a direct individual right can be identified, individuals are entitled to compliance with the primary norm of IHL. We then see a 'primary' legal relationship between the obligor and the entitled individual (the obligee). On the premise that individual rights to reparation are a kind of prolongation of primary rights, they arise upon violation of such primary rights in the first place. If, from the outset on, IHL does not *entitle* individuals to protection, it seems much more difficult to allow for an individual right to reparation.

5.5 Waivers

The ownership of IHL-based rights has legal consequences for the possibility of waiving them. Waiver of the primary rights of protected persons is expressly ruled out by two types of non-disposal clauses.

1. Non-renunciation clauses

First, each of the four Geneva Conventions contains a non-renunciation clause.[78] Convention (III) relative to the Treatment of Prisoners of War states, for example: 'Prisoners of war may in no circumstances renounce ... *the rights secured to them*

---

establishment of individual complaints procedures set out in treaties, secondary claims for damages arising from acts of a State in violation of international law against foreign nationals continue to be assigned only to the home State in principle.' (ibid., paragraph 21 (translation mine). Along similar lines, the lower court decision of the Federal Court of Justice in Civil Matters (*Bundesgerichtshof in Zivilsachen*) (III ZR 245/98), BGHZ 155, 279; judgment of 26 June 2003, section IV.1. —*Distomo*.

[77] BGH (III ZR 140/15), BGHZ 212, 173; ECLI:DE:BGH:2016:061016UIIIZR140.15.0; judgment of 6 October 2016—*Kunduz*, paragraph 16 (translation mine). Along the same line the lower court: *Landgericht* (LG) Bonn, (1 O 460/11), ECLI:DE:LGBN:2013:1211.1O460.11.00, judgment of 11 December 2013, paragraphs 41–43. BverfG (2 BvR 477/17), order of 2nd chamber of 18 November 2020 did not see any violation of HL and thus did not discuss the question of direct rights.

[78] On the parallel question in international investment protection law whether an investor's waiver of ICSID proceedings is permissible, see Anne Peters, *Beyond Human Rights*, ch. 10.

by the present Convention ....'[79] According to Article 11 of AP I, no scientific experiments may be conducted or organs removed or similar acts performed, even with the consent of the person concerned. The wording of these non-renunciation clauses indicates that rights are granted to or conferred on the individual directly by the conventions themselves, not only once domestic law has been enacted by the contracting parties.

The purpose of granting protected persons their own rights was not to let the affected persons decide themselves whether the provisions should be applied or not. Rather, the purpose was to remove those persons from the interference and sovereignty of their home states.[80] Typically, the affected persons—such as prisoners of war—are put under pressure by the custodial states to renounce their rights. The non-disposal rule was intended precisely to prevent this type of extortion and to take any incentive away from the states to exercise coercion. In light of the typical plight of protected persons (as injured persons or prisoners in the hands of the enemy), in which free decision-making is unlikely, the recognition of the affected persons' power of disposal over their rights would create only a 'pseudo-liberté'.[81] The Pictet commentary says of the non-renunciation clause in Convention (IV) relative to the Protection of Civilian Persons that it is 'of the greatest assistance to all protected persons. It allows them to claim the protection of the Convention, not as a privilege, but as a right ....'[82]

Moreover, the non-renunciation clauses signal that these rights are of the utmost importance. The legal idea of non-renunciation is familiar from the field of human rights. In that context, the notion of 'inalienable' human rights underscores precisely this importance and by no means implies that human rights do not belong to individuals as the holders of those rights. The non-disposability of the protective norms can thus be read as an indication of the high rank of the protected rights. This reading is best suited to the intention of the treaty-makers to 'safeguard the dignity of the human person'.[83]

2. Savings clauses

The second indicator of individual rights is found in the prohibitions of all special agreements (saving clauses) that are contained in each of the conventions. Article 6 of Convention (I) for the Amelioration of the Condition of the Wounded and Sick

---

[79] Article 7 of GC III (italics mine). According to Article 8 of Convention (IV) relative to the Protection of Civilian Persons in Time of War, 'Protected persons may in no circumstances renounce in part or in entirety the *rights secured to them* by the present Convention, and by the special agreements referred to in the foregoing Article, if such there be.' (italics mine). Similarly, see Article 7 of GC I, Article 7 of GC II.

[80] See René-Jean Wilhelm, 'Le caractère des droits accordés à l'individu dans les Conventions de Genève', *Revue internationale de la Croix-Rouge 32* (1950), pp. 561–590, at p. 587.

[81] Ibid.

[82] N.a., 'Art. 8' in: Jean Pictet (ed.). *Commentary on the Geneva Conventions of 12 August 1949, Vol. IV*: Geneva Convention IV Relative to the Protection of Civilian Persons. Geneva: ICRC, 1958, p. 79. Similarly, see René-Jean Wilhelm, 'Art. 7' in: Pictet, *Commentary Geneva Conventions, Vol. I*, p. 84 on GC I on wounded and sick persons.

[83] René-Jean Wilhelm, 'Art. 7' in: Pictet, *Commentary on the Geneva Conventions, Vol. I*, p. 82.

in Armed Forces in the Field states: 'No special agreement shall adversely affect the situation of the wounded and sick, of members of the medical personnel or of chaplains, as defined by the present Convention, nor restrict the rights which it confers upon them.'[84] According to Article 6 of Convention (III) relative to the Treatment of Prisoners of War, 'No special agreement [by the High Contracting Parties] shall adversely affect the situation of prisoners of war ... nor restrict the rights which it confers upon them.' Similarly, the provision in Article 7 of Convention (IV) relative to the Protection of Civilian Persons in Time of War states: 'No special agreement shall adversely affect the situation of protected persons, as defined by the present Convention, nor restrict the rights which it confers upon them.'[85] The wording of this saving clause again indicates that rights are conferred on individuals, and again directly by the international agreement itself.

These explicit prohibitions to depriving individuals of rights conferred on them in the Geneva Conventions by way of any special agreements between states are a novelty of the 1949 Geneva Conventions. With these prohibitions, the authors of the Geneva Conventions responded to the practice of special agreements to the detriment of prisoners of war during the Second World War. The Pictet commentary refers to this novelty as being 'of paramount importance' for the purpose of ensuring the comprehensive application of the conventions without exception as the standard regime under all circumstances.[86]

3. Waiver of secondary rights

The acknowledgement of direct individual rights under IHL also determines the lawfulness of waivers and interstate lump sum agreements about reparation and compensation.[87] Reparation and compensation are *secondary rights*. In peace treaties, states have often reciprocally waived claims to reparations.[88] For instance, the Allied states in the Second World War waived all reparation claims, other state claims, and all claims of their citizens that might have arisen from the conduct of Japan or of Japanese citizens during the war.[89]

---

[84] Article 6, sentence 2 of GC I. Similarly, see Article 6 of GC II.

[85] Italics mine.

[86] René-Jean Wilhelm, 'Art. 6' in: Pictet (ed.), *Commentary on the Geneva Conventions, Vol. I*, pp. 71–72.

[87] See in recent scholarship on this problem, e.g., Alessandro Bufalini, 'On the Power of a State to Waive Reparation Claims Arising from War Crimes and Crimes against Humanity', *Zeitschrift für ausländisches öffentliches Recht und Völkerrecht 77*, no. 2 (2017), pp. 447–470; Shuichi Furuya, 'Right to Reparation for Victims of Armed Conflict: The Intertwining Development of Substantive and Procedural Aspects', in C. Correa, S. Furuya, and C. Sandoval, *Reparation for Victims of Armed Conflict*, Max Planck Trialogues on the Law of Peace and War vol. 3 (Anne Peters and Christian Marxsen series eds) (Cambridge: CUP, 2021), pp. 27–36.

[88] See the numerous references to such waiver clauses in peace treaties in BVerfGE 94, 315 (2 BvL 33/93), decision of 13 May 1996, paragraphs 55 et seq. (1996)—*jüdische Zwangsarbeiter*.

[89] Article 14(b) of the Treaty of Peace between the Allied Powers and Japan of 8 May 1951 (Treaty of San Francisco).

The Geneva Conventions and the Additional Protocols do not contain specific rules on these types of waiver. But the Conventions prohibit disclaimers of responsibility for grave breaches (Article 51 GC I; Article 52 GC II; Article 131 GC III, Article 148 GC IV).[90] According to the historical view, these provisions referred only to the punishment of war criminals, from which the contracting parties were not allowed to absolve themselves. These clauses might, however, be interpreted dynamically as a prohibition of the waiver of reparations by states *for grave breaches*.

Secondly, compliance with peremptory international norms, from which no derogation is possible, can as a matter of logic not be waived. This prohibition arguably also extends to the ensuing claims for reparation for such violations, because such waivers indirectly confirm the breach of the norms themselves. Therefore states cannot waive reparation claims for the violation of *ius cogens*.[91]

Beyond these two parameters, the question of the lawfulness of waivers of claims to reparation for breaches of the laws of armed conflict is open. The ICJ did not resolve it in its pronouncement in the case of *Jurisdictional Immunities of the State*. Here the Court merely said that there is no 'rule *requiring* the payment of full compensation to each and every individual victim' as a rule 'from which no derogation is permitted'.[92] This statement was expressly limited to the question of a peremptory norm (*ius cogens*). It did not say anything on other norms of international law which might govern reparations to individuals. Moreover, the Court only said that international law (*ius cogens*) does not require a full compensation to each and individual victim. The Court remained silent on the exactly opposite question whether international law may in certain cases *prohibit* states to completely renounce on payments potentially due to them for the benefit of their nationals, or due directly to the victims themselves.

In two judgments in 2007, the Supreme Court of Japan found the waiver clauses in the Treaty of San Francisco to be valid and accordingly dismissed a group of compensation claims relating to forced labour and sexual slavery lodged by Chinese citizens.[93] The claimants had argued that the individual rights of citizens attributable to them in a personal capacity could not be limited by an agreement

---

[90] See, e.g., Article 51 GC I: 'No High Contracting Party shall be allowed to absolve itself or any other High Contracting Party of any liability incurred by itself or by another High Contracting Party in respect of breaches referred to in the preceding Article.'

[91] See Marco Sassòli, 'Reparation', in Vincent Chétail (ed.), *Post-Conflict Peacebuilding: A Lexicon* (Oxford: OUP, 2009), pp. 279–290, esp. at pp. 284–285.

[92] ICJ, *Jurisdictional Immunities of the State* (Germany v. Italy: Greece Intervening), Judgment of 3 February 2012, ICJ Reports 2012, para. 94 (italics mine).

[93] See *Nishimatsu Construction Co v. Song Jixiao*, 61 Minshu 1188, 1969 Hanrei Jiho 31, 2004 (Ju) No. 1658 (Supreme Court of Japan, 2nd Petty Bench), Judgment of 27 April 2007 (judgment concerning paragraph 5 of the Joint Communiqué of the Government of Japan and the Government of the People's Republic of China). *Kō Hanakao et al. v. Japan*, 1969 Hanrei Jiho 38, Supreme Court of Japan (1st Petty Bench), Judgment of 27 April 2007. Annotations of both judgments by Mark A. Levin in 'Nishimatsu Constructions Co. v. Song Jixiao et al; Kō Hanako et al. v. Japan', *AJIL 102*, no. 1 (2008), pp. 148–154.

between states. The Japanese Supreme Court rejected this legal allegation with the argument that, in virtue of its sovereignty, the state is able to dispose of the international claims of its citizens.[94] The Court drew attention to the legitimate goals of reciprocal waivers conferred by treaties. But it interpreted treaty waivers as a procedural clause, not in a substantive sense: the treaty arrangement was able solely to defeat the power to bring claims. Because this did not affect the substantive claims, the obligors were at liberty to satisfy the claims on a voluntary basis.

This pragmatic argumentation should be considered critically. On the one side, it appears to be a requirement of legal logic to deny the possibility of state waiver when individuals are seen as the owners of the right: as soon as it is recognized that compensation claims belong to the individuals themselves (possibly alongside state claims for compensation), a waiver by the home state of these individual claims does not appear possible, because the state does not own the claim.

A radical argument would be that states do not have any power at all to dispose over these third-party rights. The better approach is to accept some state power in this matter, by qualifying the state waiver as a *conceivable limitation of the individual rights to reparation*. From this perspective, a mere reference to state sovereignty would not suffice as a legal basis for a waiver. Rather, the waiver must satisfy the normal requirements for lawfully restricting or limiting an individual right. Such a limitation of an individual rights to reparation must notably pursue legitimate public interests and it must be proportionate. The first prong is easily satisfied: waivers relating to compensation claims after armed conflicts can in principle be motivated by legitimate public interests: they serve to bring about lasting peace in society, they create legal certainty, and they prevent the involved states from being overwhelmed by numerous unforeseeable claims. But are the waiver clauses also proportionate? An argument against proportionality appears to be that the waiver does not merely limit the right to reparation, but defeats it entirely—which seems disproportionate. The core and essence of that right to reparation can only be safeguarded if some kind of redress is offered, which would not inevitably have to be in the form of a monetary compensation.

In the final analysis, assigning the ownership of primary rights under IHL to the individual victims (followed by a secondary right to reparation) allows us to give a meaningful answer to the currently unresolved question of the legality of waivers for war-related compensation claims: there is no unconditional and limitless power of disposal by the state over these claims, but proportionate restrictions of any individual right to reparation may be admissible.

---

[94] 2004 (Ju) No. 1658, Section II, 2. (3): 'However, upon entering into a peace treaty to end a war, each nation has the power to dispose all relevant claims including claims held by individuals based on its sovereignty over citizens.'

6. Rights against Whom?

A key question for the utility of rights is against whom they are opposable. Jean Pictet writes,

> Rights entail obligations. With reference to the individual, ... the rules of the Conventions, or certain of them, can also be considered as obligations directly incumbent on the persons protected. It is an indisputable fact that certain *obligations*, such as the respect due to the wounded and sick under Article 16, are also laid upon *persons* who can claim protection under the Convention.[95]

This assertion requires some deeper analysis. Who are the bearers of the concomitant obligation to respect the IHL-based rights?

6.1 Opposability against States

For human rights which have been invented against the state, the duty-bearer is clear. IHL-based rights are somewhat different. They protect against military violence and are therefore prima facie addressed against the opposing party to the conflict.

When the opposing party to the conflict is a state, no specific difficulty arises. In international armed conflict, the primary actors are members of the state armed forces, whose conduct is attributed to the involved state parties to the conflict. For this reason, the question of a direct imposition of obligations specifically on these persons (combatants for purposes of international humanitarian law) has hardly been asked, as the relevant obligations are in the end state obligations. But also in international armed conflict, it would be helpful to impose IHL-based obligations directly on individuals. Indeed, the criminal responsibility of individual perpetrators for war crimes presupposes that it is *also* their personal duty not to commit crimes. Individual obligations even beyond the remit of crimes would strengthen the protection of the especially important legal goods (such as life and physical integrity) that are almost always at stake in war.

6.2 Opposability against Armed Groups

The legal situation is different in non international armed conflicts. Here, the military operations of non-state actors cannot sensibly be attributed to the state they are fighting. The question then is whether IHL-based rights are opposable to other

---

[95] Pictet, *Commentary on the Geneva Conventions, Vol. IV*, p. 79 (italics mine).

80 RIGHTS IN THE INTERNATIONAL LAW OF ARMED CONFLICT

individuals or groups as holders of the concomitant primary obligations under international humanitarian law.

In regard to those IHL-based obligations whose violation is criminalized, international law reaches beyond the smokescreen of the state. Article 25(4) of the Rome Statute makes clear that parallel international responsibility of states and individuals exists: 'No provision in this Statute relating to individual criminal responsibility shall affect the responsibility of States under international law.'

Outside the realm of criminal law, IHL-based obligations of individuals (natural persons) are conceivable, too. The subjection of armed opposition groups in non-international armed conflict to the relevant provisions of international humanitarian law (i.e., to Common Article 3 of the Geneva Conventions, AP II, and customary international law) is largely recognized in practice.[96] Still, it is sometimes unclear who exactly is being addressed: the armed group as an autonomous entity or its individual members. Moreover, it is not easy to explain the binding nature of the IHL-based obligations in regard to these groups of individuals.[97]

Traditionally, recognized insurgents are granted limited international legal personality in the domain of international humanitarian law. This means the individuals who have come together as an opposition group *can* in principle be holders of international obligations under international humanitarian law.[98] But this does not yet indicate which obligations actually apply to a group in a specific case and how these obligations arise. Besides obligations flowing from 'special agreements' under common Article 3(2) of the Geneva Conventions, and from unilateral declarations made by numerous armed opposition groups (in which they declare that they will respect the relevant rules of international humanitarian law), it is disputed whether and how common Art. 3 of the Geneva Conventions and AP II legally bind opposition groups *qua treaty*. Bindingness has been denied by several states at the Diplomatic Conference that prepared the AP II. According to that view, the AP II, especially, only creates legal obligations among the contracting parties.[99] These obligations are owed only to the other contracting parties (not to the opposition groups). The states parties have an obligation to enact national laws in which they require opposition groups to observe the provisions of AP II. According to this view, the mediation of opposition groups is complete. Their rights and duties arise only from the national law that the states parties must enact to implement their obligations set out in AP II.

---

[96] For evidence from practice and case law to this effect, see Liesbeth Zegveld, *Accountability of Armed Opposition Groups in International Law* (Cambridge: CUP, 2002), pp. 10–12.

[97] Seminally, Antonio Cassese, 'The Status of Rebels under the 1977 Geneva Protocol in Non-International Armed Conflict', *ICLQ 30*, no. 2 (1981), pp. 416–439; Sandesh Sivakumaran, 'Binding Armed Opposition Groups', *ICLQ 55*, no. 2 (2006), pp. 369–394.

[98] Sivakumaran, 'Binding Armed Opposition Groups', p. 374.

[99] For references to the positions held by the states, see Cassese, 'Status of Rebels', pp. 420–422.

According to a second view, rebels are 'third parties' under treaty law, to whom the binding nature of a treaty may be extended only by way of an exception to the *pacta tertiis* principle (by analogy to Articles 34–36 VCLT).[100] For this purpose, the contracting parties would have to intend to impose legal obligations on third parties, and the third parties would have to consent to being bound in that way. Finally, they would become contracting parties only by way of their consent. This conception builds on a misleading analogy with private law. It is, however, not normatively appropriate to conceive of IHL as a purely contractual framework, in which natural persons would be 'third parties' within the meaning of the *pacta tertiis* rule. Rather, IHL can and should be seen as a public-purpose based international legal order of war. The ultimate telos of this international regulatory framework is the protection of natural persons from the calamities of war.

In this paradigm, it can be argued that direct international obligations of armed groups can flow from Common Article 3, irrespective of the group's consent and irrespective of the enactment of state implementing norms. In the early literature on the Geneva Conventions, this way of binding the groups was affirmed, assuming that 'the obligations imposed by the article [common Article 3] devolve upon the whole of the population of the State concerned, at any time ... This would, if correct, be an instance of *obligations, international in nature, inhering directly in individuals*.'[101]

A possible explanation is the 'principle of legislative competence'. When a state ratifies a treaty, it does this for all individuals (or for all actors that are deemed to have international legal capacity in principle) in its territory; it represents them in an international legal sense.[102]

However, in the context of non-international armed conflict, any mandate of the government to act on behalf of, or with a legal effect for, the rebels is implausible. Such conflicts are defined by the fact that the rebels deny the legitimacy of the government and its very entitlement to represent them. On the contrary—they fight the government by military means. It would be a contradiction of values to bind the armed opposition groups by norms that their enemy had consented to 'for them'. Potential direct international obligations of armed opposition groups arising directly from Common Article 3 can therefore not easily be explained with reference to the principle of legislative competence.

Another explanation is the idea of a rule of customary international law that presumably extends the consequences of ratification carried out by a state to every new subject of international law coming into being in its territory.[103] The

---

[100] See ibid., pp. 423–429.

[101] Gerald Irving Anthony Dare Draper, 'The Geneva Conventions of 1949', *Recueil des Cours 114* (1965/I), pp. 59–165, at p. 96 (italics mine).

[102] See, especially, Sivakumaran, 'Binding Armed Opposition Groups', pp. 381–382.

[103] See Michael Bothe, 'Conflits armés et droit international humanitaire', *RGDIP 82*, no. 1 (1978), pp. 82–102, at p. 92. On the practice underlying this view, see Zegveld, *Accountability*, pp. 14–18.

obligations of the members of the armed group are then not themselves based on customary law, but rather they are obligations arising from Article 3, whose circle of addressees is expanded in virtue of customary law.

This view might be bolstered by the principle of effectiveness: there is a specific risk in non-international armed conflict of under-regulation by national law. Individual obligations *should* arise from Article 3 because that provision protects important legal goods, and because without imposing obligations directly on individuals, a regulatory deficit would emerge. The obligations set out here must apply *erga omnes* in order to be effective. The extension of the direction of the obligations to include individuals is easily reconcilable with the open wording of Article 3. The deduction of individual obligations from Article 3 is also foreseeable, given the long legal and political debate on the topic for sixty years now. This means these direct international obligations are also covered by the principle of legality. An additional question is whether and how parallel customary rules bind armed groups, and whether such rules emerge not only from the *opinio juris* and practice of states but also from the legal opinion and practice of those groups themselves.

But *who exactly* are the addressees of the obligations postulated here? In practice and in the legal discussion, no clear conceptual distinction has crystallized so far between armed groups and their members.[104] This aspect will be examined in more detail in the following discussion.

6.3 Opposability against Individuals

Obligations of individuals under IHL are controversial. As a general matter, direct international law-based obligations should not be imposed lightly on natural persons because such obligations constrain the latters' liberty and thus restrict the latter's *own rights*. Such limitations must satisfy conditions of legality and legitimacy. Direct IHL-based obligations should therefore be recognized only if they are necessary for the effective protection of global legal goods (if there is a risk of regulatory deficit) and if they rest on a legal basis that defines the obligations so unambiguously that they are foreseeable for natural persons as obligors.[105]

Another reason for the call 'for some limiting principle' is that otherwise that body of law would displace all other (including national) criminal norms applicable in an armed conflict.[106] Such a limiting principle could, for instance, rely on the motives or nature of the violation or on a nexus to the conflict.[107]

One group of authors postulates that '[i]nternational humanitarian law creates obligations for all individuals in times of armed conflicts. The relationship

---

[104] Parlett, *The Individual in the International Legal System*, p. 227, see also p. 197.
[105] Peters, *Beyond Human Rights*, ch. 4.
[106] Provost, *International Human Rights*, p. 98.
[107] Ibid., pp. 98–99.

between an individual and his or her state is irrelevant to that fact.'[108] '[I]ndividuals clearly have an active role to play as bearers of individual rights and obligations under international humanitarian law.'[109]

Other authors are sceptical:

> The Geneva Conventions and their Additional Protocols are international treaties and as such, in principle, are binding on states only. Even if it were accepted that some of their provisions might be self-executing and would therefore apply to individuals qua treaty, none of those provisions, not even their grave breaches sections, were ever meant to be regarded per se as an international criminal code the breach of which could entail international criminal responsibility directly under the treaty regime.[110]

This statement mingles three aspects: the question of substantive individual obligations, the question of direct effect (self-execution), and the question of criminality. We are here interested in the question of IHL-based primary obligations only. The starting point of the analysis should be the wording of the codified law of armed conflict. Only in very scattered provisions do the Geneva Conventions explicitly mention obligations of individuals, and then only in relation to less fundamental aspects (see, e.g., Article 17 and Article 39(2) of Geneva Convention (III)).

Beyond such textual mentioning of duties, individual obligations may arise also from other rules that do not explicitly address individuals. For example, an important rule is the individual's obligation to tolerate internment, which at the same time constitutes deprivation of liberty relevant to fundamental rights. Internment in international armed conflicts has its legal basis in the Geneva Conventions and customary international law for prisoners of war and civilian persons. The source of the individual person's obligation to tolerate this treatment in international armed conflict is international law itself.[111] In contrast, there is no international legal basis for internment in non-international armed conflict.

The explanation for direct IHL-based duties of individuals can be found in the regulatory (not contractual) quality of IHL, in the highest ranking of the legal goods in question (right to life, etc.), and the experience that imposing obligations only on states in all types of armed conflict typically does not suffice to protect these legal goods in an effective way. For this reason, every individual combatant and every civilian should be acknowledged as a direct addressee of those norms

---

[108] Ibid., p. 98.

[109] Dieter Fleck, 'The Role of Individuals in International Humanitarian Law and Challenges for States in Its Development', in Michael Schmitt and Leslie Green (eds), *The Law of Armed Conflict: Into the Next Millennium* (Newport: Naval War College, 1998), pp. 119–139, at p. 136.

[110] Guénaël Mettraux, *International Crimes and the Ad hoc Tribunals* (Oxford: OUP, 2005), p. 8.

[111] Article 21 of GC III (prisoners of war); Article 118 of GC III; Article 42(1) of GC IV. See also Article 42 of GC IV on voluntary internment and Article 78 of GC IV.

of international humanitarian law *relevant to his or her situation*, where permitted by the wording of the norms (condition of specificity) and if the imposition of obligations is sufficiently predictable for the person concerned (condition of foreseeability). These are requirements set by the principle of legality which also applies in international law. Numerous prohibitions of international humanitarian law are sufficiently specific and unconditional to satisfy that principle of legality. This is why—as it is submitted here—international humanitarian law prohibits every single combatant from employing methods of warfare that cause unnecessary suffering (Article 35(2) of AP I), carrying out indiscriminate attacks (Article 48 of AP I), or attacking civilian objects (Article 52 of AP I). International humanitarian law also prohibits every civilian from taking part directly in hostilities, sanctioning breaches with the loss of civilian immunity (Article 51(3) of AP I). According to the view put forward here, these obligations are addressed directly to individuals, not only to their home states or supreme commanders of the troops in question. Provided the condition of specificity and foreseeability is met, individuals are likewise bound by the obligations under customary international law that almost always exist in parallel with the treaty norms.

In regard to the norms of international humanitarian law enforced by criminal sanctions, the status of the individual as a duty-bearer can be deduced from the fact that the violation of these norms entails individual criminal responsibility. The legal status as an addressee of obligations and the status as a subject in the second level relationship of responsibility are two different things. Nevertheless, the imposition of a punishment on the person allows one to draw the conclusion that that person was obligated from the outset not to commit certain acts.[112]

Examination and analysis of future practice must clarify these threshold requirements or triggering conditions for individual obligations based on concrete norms of the law of armed conflict.

7. Conclusion

The acknowledgement of IHL-based rights endorses the individual human being as the normative reference point of IHL. Against critical voices, this chapter has argued that the individualization of IHL has *not* reached its limits. The principal modern purpose of IHL—which I see in effectively protecting humans from the calamities of war—can be best pursued by acknowledging direct IHL-based, special individual rights, rather than falling in the two extremes: either applying human rights across the board or denying individual rights altogether.

The negotiating history of the current provisions of the law of armed conflict points in this direction. Moreover, the frequent use of the term 'rights' presumably

---

[112] Provost, International Human Rights, p. 75.

means what it says, namely 'rights'. On this basis, (some) provisions of the law of armed conflict can be reasonably read as setting out obligations owed not (only) to other states, but (also) *directly to individuals*. Correspondingly, these provisions embody individual rights to fulfilment. The differences between having a right and being the object of a protective standard are symbolic, political, and practical. Because rights trigger an obligation to justify their curtailment, because of the weight afforded to them in a balancing exercise, because of their overshooting tendency and the indeterminacy of the obligations flowing from rights, legal rights offer a stronger protection than the concrete and selective obligations to accord humans a specific treatment under international law. 'Ainsi, tout se passe comme si les "personnes protégées" étaient elles-mêmes "sujets" du droit international';[113] 'les Conventions de 1949, une fois de plus, renforcent la position et les droits des "personnes protégées", bref, de l'individu.'[114] The state claim for compliance with international humanitarian law can, theoretically, persist alongside the individual right. The follow-up question then is how the putative individual rights relate to the presumably persisting state's rights and which consequences this parallelism entails for claims to reparation.

To conclude, the acknowledgement of IHL-based rights which are distinct from human rights (although they partly serve similar values) is apt to square the clear wording of the relevant provisions of IHL—which speak of 'rights'—with the justified scepticism against applying human rights in this context. The conceptualization of IHL-based rights distinct from international human rights strikes a doctrinally sound and in legal policy terms beneficial compromise between the two poles of exaggeration: 'human rightism'[115] on the one hand and nineteenth-century statism on the other.

References

Abi-Saab, G. (1984) 'The Specificities of Humanitarian Law', in C. Swinarski (ed.), *Studies and Essays of International Humanitarian Law and Red Cross Principles in Honour of Jean Pictet*. Geneva: International Committee of the Red Cross; Martinus Nijhoff, pp. 265–281.

Alexander, A. (2015) 'A Short History of International Humanitarian Law', *European Journal of International Law*, 26(1), pp. 109–138. doi: 10.1093/ejil/chv002.

Auer, M. (2008) 'Subjektive Rechte bei Pufendorf und Kant. Eine Analyse im Lichte der Rechtskritik Hohfelds', *Archiv für die civilistische Praxis (AcP)*, 208(5), pp. 584–634. doi: 10.1628/000389908785978711.

Auer, M. (2014) *Der privatrechtliche Diskurs der Moderne*. Tübingen: Mohr Siebeck.

---

[113] Wilhelm, 'Le caractère des droits accordés', p. 562.
[114] Ibid., p. 585.
[115] Alain Pellet, '"Human Rightism" and International Law', *Italian Yearbook of International Law*, 10(1) (2003), pp. 3–16.

Berster, L. C. (2010b) '"Duty to Act" and "Commission by Omission" in International Criminal Law', *International Criminal Law Review*, 10(5), pp. 619–646. doi: 10.1163/157181210X527046.

Bohrer, Z. (2020) 'Divisions over Distinctions in Wartime International Law', in H. Duffy, J. Dill, and Z. Bohrer, *Law Applicable to Armed Conflict*. Cambridge: Cambridge University Press (Max Planck Trialogues on the Law of Peace and War), (Anne Peters and Christian Marxsen series eds), pp. 106–196. doi: 10.1017/9781108674416.003.

Bothe, M. (1978) 'Conflits armés et droit international humanitaire', *Revue générale du droit international public*, 82(1), pp. 82–102.

Bufalini, A. (2017) 'On the Power of a State to Waive Reparation Claims Arising from War Crimes and Crimes against Humanity', *Zeitschrift für ausländisches öffentliches Recht und Völkerrecht*, 77(2), pp. 447–470.

Cassese, A. (1981) 'The Status of Rebels under the 1977 Geneva Protocol on Non-International Armed Conflicts', *The International and Comparative Law Quarterly*, 30(2), pp. 416–439.

Correa, C., Furuya, S., and Sandoval, C. (2020) *Reparation for Victims of Armed Conflict*. Cambridge: Cambridge University Press (Max Planck Trialogues on the Law of Peace and War), (Anne Peters and Christian Marxsen series eds). doi: 10.1017/9781108628877.

Cover, R.M. (1987) 'Obligation: A Jewish Jurisprudence of the Social Order', *Journal of Law and Religion*, 5(1), pp. 65–74. doi: 10.2307/1051017.

Dörr, O. (2013) 'Völkerrechtliche Deliktsansprüche Privater—auf der Grundlage und in den Grenzen einer völkerrechtlichen Schutznormlehre', in M. Breuer et al. (eds), *Der Staat im Recht: Festschrift Eckart Klein zum 70. Geburtstag*. Berlin: Duncker & Humblot, pp. 765–782.

Draper, G.I.A.D. (1965) 'The Geneva Conventions of 1949', *Recueil des Cours: Collected Courses of The Hague Academy of International Law*, 114, pp. 59–165.

Dworkin, R. (1984) 'Rights as Trumps', in J. Waldron (ed.), *Theories of Rights*, Oxford: Oxford University Press, pp. 153–167.

Final Record of the Diplomatic Conference of Geneva of 1949 (New York: William S. Hein & Co., 2004), Vol. II, Sec. B, 76 (Special Committee, Joint Committee, 23rd meeting).

Fleck, D. (1998) 'The Role of Individuals in International Humanitarian Law and Challenges for States in Its Development', in M. Schmitt and L. Green (eds), *The Law of Armed Conflict: Into the Next Millennium*. Newport: Naval War College, pp. 119–139.

Gärditz, K.F. (2014) 'Bridge of Varvarin', *American Journal of International Law*, 108(1), pp. 86–93. doi: 10.5305/amerjintelaw.108.1.0086.

Gentz, F.V. (1791) 'Ueber den Ursprung und die obersten Prinzipien des Rechts,' *Berlinische Monatsschrift*, 18, pp. 370–396.

Gershman, J. and Morduch, J. (2015) 'Credit Is Not a Right', in T. Sorell and L. Cabrera (eds), *Microfinance, Rights and Global Justice*. Cambridge: Cambridge University Press, pp. 14–26. doi: 10.1017/CBO9781316275634.002.

Goodman, R. and Jinks, D. (2013) *Socializing States: Promoting Human Rights through International Law*. Oxford: Oxford University Press.

Gross, A. (2017) *The Writing on the Wall: Rethinking the International Law of Occupation*. Cambridge: Cambridge University Press. doi: 10.1017/9781316536308.

Grotius, H. (1625) *De iure belli ac pacis libri tres*, liber primus, caput 1, n IV, ed. B. J. A. de Kanter-van Hettinga Tromp. Leiden: E. J. Brill 1939; online 2009 dbnl.

Haggenmacher, P. (1997) 'Droits subjectifs et système juridique chez Grotius', in L. Foisneau (ed.), *Politique, droit et théologie chez Bodin, Grotius et Hobbes*. Paris: Éditions Kimé, pp. 73–130.

Hampson, F. (1991) 'Human Rights Law and Humanitarian Law: Two Coins or Two Sides of the Same Coin', *Bulletin of Human Rights*, 1, pp. 46–54.

Hartung, G. (1999). *Die Naturrechtsdebatte: Geschichte der obligatio vom 17. bis 20. Jahrhundert*. Freiburg: Alber 2nd ed.

Higgins, R. (1995) *Problems and Process: International Law and How We Use It, Problems and Process*. Oxford: Oxford University Press.

Hill-Cawthorne, L. (2017) 'Rights under International Humanitarian Law', *European Journal of International Law*, 28(4), pp. 1187–1215. doi: 10.1093/ejil/chx073.

Ignatieff, M. (2001) 'Human Rights as Idolatry', in A. Gutmann (ed.), *Human Rights as Politics and Idolatry*. Princeton: Princeton University Press, 53–100.

International Committee of the Red Cross. (1946–47) 'Report on the Work of the Preliminary Conference of National Red Cross Societies for the Study of the Conventions and of Various Problems Relative to the Red Cross'. Geneva: International Committee of the Red Cross.

Luban, D. (2016) 'Human Rights Thinking and the Laws of War', in J.D. Ohlin (ed.), *Theoretical Boundaries of Armed Conflict and Human Rights*. Cambridge: Cambridge University Press (ASIL Studies in International Legal Theory), pp. 45–77. doi: 10.1017/CBO9781316481103.003.

Marxsen, C. and Peters, A. (2020) 'Conclusions: Productive Divisions', in H. Duffy, J. Dill, and Z. Bohrer, *Law Applicable to Armed Conflict*. Cambridge: Cambridge University Press (Max Planck Trialogues on the Law of Peace and War) (Anne Peters and Christian Marxcsen series eds), pp. 266–279. doi: 10.1017/9781108674416.005.

Meron, T. (2006) *The Humanization of International Law*. Leiden: Martinus Nijhoff.

Mettraux, G. (2005) *International Crimes and the Ad Hoc Tribunals*. Oxford: Oxford University Press.

Parlett, K. (2011) The Individual in the International Legal System: Continuity and Change in International Law. Cambridge: Cambridge University Press. doi: 10.1017/CBO9780511921858.

Pellet, A. (2003) '"Human Rightism" and International Law', *The Italian Yearbook of International Law*, 10(1), pp. 3–16. doi: 10.1163/221161300X00013.

Peters, A. (2009) 'Humanity as the A and Ω of Sovereignty', *European Journal of International Law*, 20(3), pp. 513–544. doi: 10.1093/ejil/chp026.

Peters, A. (2016) *Beyond Human Rights: The Legal Status of the Individual in International Law*. Cambridge: Cambridge University Press. doi: 10.1017/CBO9781316687123.

Pictet, J. (ed.). (1952) *Commentary of the Geneva Conventions of 12 August 1949, Vol. I:, Geneva Convention I for the Amelioration of the Condition of the Wounded and Sick in Armed Forces in the Field*. Geneva: ICRC.

Pictet, J. (ed.). (1958) *Commentary of the Geneva Conventions of 12 August 1949, Vol. IV: Geneva Convention IV Relative to the Protection of Civilian Persons*. Geneva: ICRC.

Pictet, J. (ed.). (1960) *Commentary of the Geneva Conventions of 12 August 1949, Vol. III: Geneva Convention III Relative to the Treatment of Prisoners of War*. Geneva: ICRC.

88 RIGHTS IN THE INTERNATIONAL LAW OF ARMED CONFLICT

Provost, R. (2002) *International Human Rights and Humanitarian Law*. Cambridge: Cambridge University Press.

Pufendorf, S. (1715) *S. Puffendorfii De officio hominis et civis juxta legem naturalem libri duo*. Cantabrigi: Typis academicis. Impensis Jacobi Knapton Londini.

Raz, J. (1988) *The Morality of Freedom*. Oxford: Oxford University Press.

Risse, T. and Ropp, S.C. (2013) 'Introduction and Overview', in K. Sikkink, S.C. Ropp, and T. Risse (eds), *The Persistent Power of Human Rights: From Commitment to Compliance*. Cambridge: Cambridge University Press (Cambridge Studies in International Relations), pp. 3–25. doi: 10.1017/CBO9781139237161.003.

Roucounas, E. (2002) 'Facteurs privés et droit international public', *Recueil des Cours: Collected Courses of The Hague Academy of International Law*, 299, pp. 9–419.

Sassòli, M. (2002) 'State Responsibility for Violations of International Humanitarian Law', *International Review of the Red Cross*, 84(846), pp. 401–434. doi: 10.1017/S1560775500097753.

Sassòli, M. (2009) 'Reparation', in V. Chétail (ed.), *Post-Conflict Peacebuilding: A Lexicon*. Oxford: Oxford University Press, pp. 279–290.

Schauer, F. (1993) 'A Comment on the Structure of Rights', *Georgia Law Review*, 27(2), pp. 415–434.

Simmons, B.A. (2009) *Mobilizing for Human Rights: International Law in Domestic Politics*. Cambridge: Cambridge University Press.

Sivakumaran, S. (2006) 'Binding Armed Opposition Groups', *International & Comparative Law Quarterly*, 55(2), pp. 369–394. doi: 10.1093/iclq/lei085.

Stone, C.D. (1972) 'Should Trees Have Standing?—Toward Legal Rights for Natural Objects', *Southern California Law Review*, 45(2), pp. 450–501.

Stübinger, S. (2014) 'Hegel und das moderne Verständnis der Person im Recht', in K. Seelmann and B. Zabel (eds), *Autonomie und Normativität: Zu Hegels Rechtsphilosophie*. Tübingen: Mohr Siebeck, pp. 69–96.

Sunstein, C.R. (1999) 'Rights and Their Critics', *Notre Dame Law Review*, 70(4), pp. 727–768.

Tuck, R. (1979) *Natural Rights Theories: Their Origin and Development*. Cambridge: Cambridge University Press.

Waldron, J. (1993) *Liberal Rights: Collected Papers 1981–1991*. Cambridge: Cambridge University Press.

Wilhelm, R.-J. (1950) 'Le caractère des droits accordés à l'individu dans les Conventions de Genève', *Revue internationale de la Croix-Rouge*, 32 (380), pp. 561–590.

Zegveld, L. (2002) *Accountability of Armed Opposition Groups in International Law*. Cambridge: Cambridge University Press.

3
The Supererogatory Moral Risks of Military Service

Bradley Jay Strawser

1. Introduction: The Noble Risk Argument

Individuals who voluntarily choose to serve in a modern state's military take on an array of extraordinary risks. These risks include the possibility of being ordered by their state to wage war and therein face the physical risks of severe injury or death as well as the risks of tremendous psychological harm, such as post-traumatic stress.[1] However, there is another kind of risk that individuals incur when they serve. Namely, they take on *moral* risks, which are both numerous and weighty. These moral risks include the likes of failing to serve honourably in the grim tasks of waging war itself—perhaps failing to make a correct split-second decision over life-or-death stakes under extreme epistemic uncertainty and duress. But it also includes the moral risk that individuals could be morally misused more generally, as instruments of the state they serve by being commanded to fight in an unjust war. Individuals choose to become soldiers for a wide range of motivations, be it a genuine desire to selflessly serve one's country or perhaps for the financial incentives military service can garner, or a multitude of other, perfectly legitimate reasons. Yet, as Jeff McMahan has written, 'Whatever their motivation, they are committing themselves to become weapons controlled by others whose purposes cannot be reliably predicted.'[2]

Taking this moral risk as a starting point, some have asked if it is morally permissible (much less prudential or wise) for individuals to knowingly take on the potentially extreme moral risk of military service. In this paper, I explore one possible line of response to this question which argues not only that it is permissible, but that it can be, in fact, a noble or supererogatory act for an individual

---

[1] I use the term post-traumatic stress as opposed to post-traumatic stress disorder (PTS vs. PTSD) intentionally. There has been a small movement of late within the US military to shift away from using the term disorder. The idea is that responding negatively to the kinds of traumatic events that occur in war is not in some way disordered or abnormal, but actually quite a reasonable and understandable response.
[2] Jeff McMahan, 'The Moral Responsibility of Volunteer Soldiers: Should they say no to fighting in an unjust war?', November 2013, forum in *Boston Review*. Available at: https://www.bostonreview.net/forum/moral-wounds-ethics-volunteer-military-service/

Bradley Jay Strawser, *The Supererogatory Moral Risks of Military Service*. In: *The Individualization of War*. Edited by: Jennifer Welsh, Dapo Akande, and David Rodin, Oxford University Press. © Bradley Jay Strawser (2023). DOI: 10.1093/oso/9780192872203.003.0004

90   THE SUPEREROGATORY MORAL RISKS OF MILITARY SERVICE

to knowingly assume the moral risks of military service.[3] A supererogatory act is one in which an agent goes 'above and beyond' there basic moral duties or obligations. For many it will seem nearly obvious that one should *not* willingly take on the kinds of risks just discussed if they can possibly help it. But what if we, collectively, actually *need* someone to take on those risks? Including the particular moral risk that we, collectively, may morally fail in sending that person to wage an unjust war? In that case, one might plausibly conclude that the wilful assumption of such moral risk is, in fact, a morally praiseworthy act—one that goes above and beyond the call of duty.

The rough-and-ready argument for this kind of view runs as follows. First, begin with the premise that in the contemporary world a state military is a necessary—and thereby morally justified—institution for at least some modern liberal democracies. Second, given that it is necessary and justified, it follows that it will be necessary and justified for some subset of individuals within such a society to serve in the military. But this entails that it will be necessary for some individuals to take on the moral risks of military service—including the particular moral risk I focus on here, that they may end up doing wrong by actively participating in an unjust war that their nation wages. As such, given that society needs some subset of its number to assume this risk, it can be a supererogatory act for an individual to voluntarily do so and willingly bear the burden of this moral risk on behalf of the many.[4] These individuals carry out a noble, selfless act in their willingness to volunteer and shoulder such moral risk so that the rest of us do not have to; and for that their voluntary service should be rightfully morally praised as going 'above and beyond'.[5] Call this the Noble Risk Argument for voluntary military service. There are several important caveats and qualifications that will be explored below, but this gives us a baseline articulation of the argument to work from. Right

---

[3] Note on usage of terms: I will use 'noble' on occasion, and in naming the argument itself, as a stand-in for supererogatory. The terms are not perfect matches; but noble and other terms around exemplary moral actions are the kinds of terms one might hear used by soldiers themselves in articulating this kind of argument.

[4] This line of reasoning is making an important assumption on these incurred risks. Namely, that the moral risk here incurred is that they may fight in an unjust war. However, in a functioning democracy, one could argue that the rest of the population similarly bears the risk of being responsible for ordering those soldiers to fight in an unjust war. I'm here assuming that there is a relevant difference on the extent to which these moral risks should be weighed, and that the greater moral risk is actually fighting in an unjust war, bringing with it the risk of oneself being the person who kills non-liable people. (Thanks to Helen Frowe for this point.)

[5] Similar to the previous note, here again I must clarify. (Thanks again to Helen Frowe.) One might worry this formulation assumes a rather narrow view of the moral responsibility we all hold for our respective countries going to war; but that is mistaken. On my view, we all (combatants and non-combatants alike) risk *causing* unjust killings in war (be it by voting for a government that choses to wage war, or by paying taxes to support that war effort, or some other contribution, and so on); whereas some subset of the population (combatants) risk actually being the ones inflicting those wrongful killings. It's an important point and I cannot resolve it here. But the Noble Risk Argument presumes that there is a non-trivial relevant difference in the moral weight of these risks (i.e., that it's morally worse to be the person who actually does the killing, rather than one of millions of people sharing in a distributed decision.)

away, we see that this argument has some counter-intuitive features. One looming puzzle, for example, is that if this reasoning is correct, then those individuals do *right*, in part, by agreeing to take on the risk of doing *wrong*.

Some here may think this argument doesn't even get out of the gate, however, because of objections to the notion of 'taking on' of moral risks (or moral responsibility, and so on) *on behalf of* others. This is complex; but to give some intuitive appeal to the basic concept, consider a dilemma the characters come across in Margaret Atwood's *The Handmaid's Tale*. The characters are attempting a life-and-death stakes escape attempt and realize, tragically, that their cat creates a problem.[6]

> The cat, is what he said.
> Cat? I said, against the wool of his sweater.
> We can't just leave her here.
> I hadn't thought about the cat. Neither of us had. Our decision had been sudden, and then there had been the planning to do. I must have thought she was coming with us. But she couldn't, you don't take a cat on a day trip across the border. Why not outside? I said. We could just leave her.
> She'd hang around and mew at the door. Someone would notice we were gone. We could give her away, I said. One of the neighbors.
> Even as I said this, I saw how foolish that would be.
> I'll take care of it, Luke said. And because he said it instead of her, I knew he meant kill. That is what you have to do before you kill, I thought. You have to create an it, where none was before ...
> Luke found the cat, who was hiding under our bed. They always know. He went into the garage with her. I don't know what he did, and I never asked him. I sat in the living room, hands folded in my lap. I should have gone out with him, taken that small responsibility. I should at least have asked him about it afterwards, so he didn't have to carry it alone; because that little sacrifice, that snuffing out of love, was done for my sake as well.[7]

Presume that killing the cat was a justified, perhaps even necessary act, all things considered for the characters in that scenario. It is this notion of Luke taking on 'that small responsibility' on her behalf that is operative here. If we want to make the parallels to the Noble Risk Argument even stronger, we could presume that there's a moral risk they are getting the decision wrong. In which case Nick taking on that risk, in a different way than she is by being the one to actually carry out

---

[6] I am indebted to Casey Johnson for this example.

[7] *The Handmaid's Tale*, Deluxe Edition (New York: Ecco, 2019), pp. 192–193. 'This quotation from *Handmaid's Tale* is used under Section 107 of the Copyright Act of 1976 wherein allowance is made for "fair use" for purposes such as "criticism, comment, news reporting, teaching, scholarship, and research." Fair use is a use permitted by copyright statute that might otherwise be infringing. Non-profit, educational, or personal use tips the balance in favor of use.'

the deed himself, is in some sense a noble shielding of her (at least partially) from the acts of that moral risk. The analogy is imperfect on several fronts because, as will be discussed below in §2.1, the act does not include the kind of 'big picture' moral risk required for the Noble Risk Argument. Further, one might think this is simply a kind of taking on of a dirty hands problem on behalf of another, but that misses the mark as well, as will be discussed in §2.2. However, what the story does show, is this simple first step of the idea of some moral act being done 'for my sake as well', by the other. Someone had to take on this necessary, grim task; it was noble that Nick did it so she could be spared, not only from the trauma itself, but in some sense (at least partially) from the moral trauma as well.

It is worth stressing at the outset that something like this kind of moral reasoning is regularly voiced by military members serving today, which is precisely why I find it worthy of careful philosophical exploration. Perhaps it will come as a surprise to some readers, but many individual soldiers are keenly aware of not only the physical but also the *moral* risks their military service entails. For anecdotal evidence of this, I offer my own personal experience educating hundreds, if not thousands, of military members over the past decade, including members across all ranks and services, as well as from dozens of different countries. I have heard various versions of this Noble Risk Argument presented explicitly while teaching ethics at the Naval Postgraduate School. Of note is that, anecdotally, the prevalence of this kind of argument has seemed to grow in recent years. Many then view their own service as a kind of self-sacrificial assumption of those risks for the good of the rest of society. It is a classic supererogation claim of 'going above and beyond'—to 'pay out more than is due', to quote the Latin literally—but it rests on the confounding notion that the morally praiseworthy act in question is being willing to risk the potential of doing great wrong. I aim to take this view seriously and see what can be made of it. Can a coherent philosophical position be constructed out of this Noble Risk Argument? I believe it can, though it will take some modification.

It must also be admitted at the outset that this supposedly righteous act of volunteering for the moral risk of military service wears thin when we view it in light of those cases where the risk goes wrong. Just how 'noble' do we regard the act of moral risk undertaken by a soldier choosing to serve his country that then goes on to wage an unjust war? Choose whichever historical example of an unjust war you like, and the intuitions for this argument are challenged significantly. For example, was it a morally supererogatory act for a German soldier to assume the risk of military service on behalf of the many in the 1930s? This consideration alone seems to throw cold water on the argument's prospects. I'll return to this below. Still, despite these kinds of cases, this notion of supererogatory good runs deep in the self-understanding of many individual soldiers who serve today and it deserves careful treatment. In this paper, I take this view seriously, aim to unpack and develop it, and see if a philosophically defensible version of the argument can be found.

In what follows, I will first clarify the argument in §2, showing what is being claimed and what is not. This requires some discussion of the military as a necessary institution for modern states and whether the argument is merely an elaborate dirty hands problem. (I conclude that it is not.) Next, in §3, I delve into the concept of moral risk and what is entailed for individuals when they voluntarily assume such risk. In §4, I discuss the concept of supererogation and whether the intentional assumption of moral risk can fit the bill for going above and beyond the call of duty. Finally, in §5, I survey a modified version of the argument that treats moral risk as a kind of harm and that justice demands that harm be fairly distributed. I conclude that, with some important caveats, the wilful individual assumption of necessary moral risk on behalf of the many can, indeed, be a supererogatory act. Moreover, in some cases, this will be true of voluntary military service, and can thereby serve as a partial basis to not only justify but give positive moral weight to the decision to serve in the military. It does, however, point us strongly in the direction of a moral preference for conscription, among other considerations.

2. What the Argument Is and Is Not

2.1 *Jus ad Bellum* 'Big Picture' Risk

The Noble Risk Argument, as I've initially described it, centres on the moral risk to the individual who volunteers to serve in a military which then engages in a wrongful war. There are countless other moral risks an individual bears, of course, in serving in the military, but I set those aside in this formulation for the purpose of focusing on the risk of being misused by the state on behalf of an unjust cause. Recognizing and wrestling with this particular moral risk of military service has only recently returned to critical attention by just war theorists.[8] This is in large part because orthodox just war theory, as articulated paradigmatically by Michael Walzer, holds to a separation of *jus ad bellum* and *jus in bello* concerns.[9] It thus contends that the individual soldier need not concern herself with the overall justice of a cause and thereby assumes no moral risk in military service itself, broadly

---

[8] Though the concern has a fascinating historical pedigree. For one example, see the work of Francisco de Vitoria, the Spanish theologian and philosopher famous for his defence of the rights of Native Americans to fight against colonial aggressors, among other work. Francisco de Vitoria, 'De Indis Relectio Posterior, Sive de Jure Belle [On the Law of War]', in Jeremy Lawrence and Anthony Pagden (eds), 2.2 *Vitoria: Political Writings* (Cambridge: Cambridge University Press, 1991), §§22, 25. On the point at hand, here is David Rodin explaining Vitoria's view, 'Francisco de Vitoria argued that ordinary soldiers are not obligated to investigate the justness of the wars in which they fight, but that they should not fight if they happen to discover that their war is not just.' David Rodin, 'The Liability of Ordinary Soldiers for Crimes of Aggression', *Washington University Global Studies Law Review* 6, no. 3 (2007), pp. 591–607, at p. 595. If that's the case, then it's clear they take a moral risk in signing up to fight, given that they may come to discover a cause is unjust.

[9] Michael Walzer, *Just and Unjust Wars* (New York: Basic Books, 1977).

94 THE SUPEREROGATORY MORAL RISKS OF MILITARY SERVICE

speaking. For if the state the soldiers serve enters into an unjust war, the injustice of the war itself does not rest upon their shoulders.[10] Rather, on this view, the individual soldier's moral risks are entirely confined to specific acts within war. That is, the risks that they may morally fail to follow the strictures of *jus in bello*, such as harming a non-combatant or acting disproportionately, due to any number of reasons. But they are not at moral risk for serving on behalf of a *jus ad bellum* unjust war, on this account.

Shakespeare's famous lines from the play *Henry V* are appropriate in this discussion, specifically the notion that the injustice of a cause undertaken by a state does not fall on the soldiers themselves. In the scene in question, soldiers are discussing their individual responsibility for the justice (or injustice) of the battle they are about to partake in the next morning, as well as the epistemic limitations they face in actually knowing the justice of the cause.

> 'Methinks I could not die anywhere so contented as in the king's company, his cause being just and his quarrel honourable.'
> 'That's more than we know.'
> 'Ay, or more than we should seek after, for we know enough if we know we are the king's subjects. If his cause be wrong, our obedience to the king wipes the crime of it out of us.'[11]

However, the individualization of war and the concurrent development of revisionist just war theory brings this 'big picture' moral risk of military service to the fore. Revisionists challenge that the justice of the cause is indeed relevant to the individual soldier's service and that participation on behalf an unjust war is itself morally impermissible.[12] On this view, there is no strict separation between *jus ad bellum* and *jus in bello*; serving in an unjust war, indeed, is something for which the individual is morally responsible and should not do. Therefore, on this revisionist account, military service is fraught with moral risk that one may act wrongly in fighting on behalf of an unjust cause.[13]

---

[10] Shakespeare's famous lines from *Henry V* are appropriate in this discussion. The soldiers in the scene are discussing their individual responsibility for the justice (or injustice) of the battle they are about to partake in, as well as the epistemic limitations they face in actually knowing the justice of the cause. 'Methinks I could not die anywhere so contented as in the king's company, his cause being just and his quarrel honorable.' 'That's more than we know.' 'Ay, or more than we should seek after, for we know enough if we know we are the king's subjects. If his cause be wrong, our obedience to the king wipes the crime of it out of us.' Act 4, Scene 1. *Henry V.*

[11] Act 4, Scene 1. *Henry V.*

[12] See the work of Jeff McMahan, Cecile Fabre, and Helen Frowe, among many other prominent theorists, on this point.

[13] It is interesting here to consider a recent argument made by Massimo Renzo for a middle way between the two approaches to an individual soldier's moral responsibility to not fight in an unjust war. See Renzo, 'Political Authority and Unjust Wars', *Philosophy and Phenomenological Research 99*, no. 2 (2018), pp. 336–357. Renzo acknowledges the relevance of the justice of a cause for permissibility to fight, while also asking us to consider implications of combatants as members of political bodies. While I cannot develop it here, I tentatively think that the Noble Risk Argument could work on either a revisionist account, or Renzo's modified approach.

The Noble Risk Argument is born out of this latter, revisionist view of the moral responsibility of individual soldiers. As such, a revisionist handling of the puzzle the argument raises, specifically as it pertains to the moral risk to individuals for serving in a military whatsoever, is in wont of exploration and explanation. Note, of course, there could be alternative versions of the argument that rest the supererogatory act claim on the assumption of *other* moral risks that soldiers assume by volunteering to serve in the military—such as *jus in bello* moral mistakes made in warfare. But such versions will all be importantly different. This is because such versions of the argument will inevitably not be significantly different from other, far more standard cases of moral risk that individuals in different roles in society take on daily.

To see this, consider a simple example. Society needs medical surgeons to engage in acts whereby they have significant moral risk of getting certain high stakes decisions wrong in the operating room. The fact that they volunteer to bear this kind of moral risk willingly is likely something to be praised morally. But notice that the entire enterprise of, say, *being* a surgeon *qua* surgeon does not carry with it the kind of 'big picture' risk under examination. That is, we don't think that volunteering to become a surgeon puts one at moral risk that they may then be misused by the society they serve for some larger unjust aim. We think this, even though we are aware—and those who volunteer to be surgeons are aware—that the job itself may regularly include morally risky decisions. But we do not think that the overall efforts of performing surgeries and the like—the overall mission of being a surgeon, to use military parlance—is itself morally risky in its cause. It is this particular, significant 'big picture' moral risk of serving on behalf of an unjust war that forms the basis for the Noble Risk Argument. I will return to this below in a more detailed discussion of moral risk.

It's worth thinking through which other professions carry with them this kind of 'big picture' moral risk of misuse of the individual by the larger society, *and* also are necessary. I am not here arguing for a special pleading for military service; I do not presume it is unique in this regard. Here's a short list of potential vocations that come to mind of having this dual nature (moral risk of broad misuse of the individual's efforts by the larger society and yet also necessary to society). Police officers and law enforcement individuals in general; civil servants in various capacities; judges or other actors in jurisprudence. More controversially, potentially scientific researchers, or even university professors and teachers, could even potentially fit the bill. To be clear, for these cases to have the kind of big picture risk under discussion, there would have to exist a genuine risk that the society or state would use the given occupation (police departments, say) for unjust ends as part of a larger overall unjust cause for which they are instrumental; not simply that these occupations themselves may fall into abuse and injustice. That seems plausible in some cases; more outlandish (though not impossible) in some of the others.

96 THE SUPEREROGATORY MORAL RISKS OF MILITARY SERVICE

2.2 Dirty Hands

Before moving on, it's important to be clear on just how potentially odd this moral reasoning may sound, at first blush. As noted, the argument insists that it can be morally *good* to knowingly take on a moral risk that one might end up doing grave *wrong*. This is puzzling. In fact, on the surface one might think that it forms a peculiar version of the classic dirty hands problem. Walzer himself, of course, is well known for his work on the dirty hands problem.[14] However, Walzer primarily viewed the dirty hands problem for military ethics as a question for political leaders and for intentional *jus in bello* violations in cases of so-called 'supreme emergency'.[15] Or one might be reminded of Bernard Williams 'Jim and the Indians' case.[16] In that case, Jim must kill an innocent villager to save nineteen others. In all of these kinds of cases, one must commit a pro tanto wrong in order to achieve a greater, justified good.

But here we are asking a different question for individual soldiers who volunteered to serve. The Noble Risk Argument is not grounded on what would otherwise normally be considered wrongful acts that a soldier may be compelled to knowingly undertake in war, because the war or the need for the military and so forth is somehow deriving a sufficient greater good. Rather, it rests on voluntarily taking on the moral risk of serving on behalf of others, and the specific moral risk they take on is that they may end up fighting on behalf of an unjust cause in the first place. The act of assuming the moral risk itself is, the argument contends, not a wrongful act, but a morally good, supererogatory act. To be clear, then, the Noble Risk Argument is not a version of a dirty hands problem. The issue is not whether someone should do something that violates usual moral norms for some greater good, as the dirty hands problem is often formulated. But rather, the question is whether someone should take on the moral risk that they *might* do grave wrong, when there exists a compelling, morally necessary reason that someone take on such risk. The Noble Risk Argument contends that not only should someone take on that risk, but that individuals actually go above and beyond in doing so.

It's good to note here that for many this discussion will immediately lead one to consider ways we could avoid this kind of individualized risk and instead share this burden in a fair manner. Perhaps we could draw lots, for example, for this necessary duty. In other words: conscription, or some version of it. I will return to this below in §6, and I take this instinctive response to the Noble Risk Argument as counting in its favour.

---

[14] Michael Walzer, 'Political Action: The Problem of Dirty Hands', *Philosophy and Public Affairs 2*, no. 2 (1973), pp. 160–180.

[15] Ibid.

[16] Bernard Williams, 'A Critique of Utilitarianism' in Bernard Williams and J.C. Smart, *Utilitarianism: For and Against* (Cambridge: Cambridge University Press, 1973), pp. 75–150.

2.3 Commensurate Risk Calculation

However, one might think that once the decision to serve is formulated in this way, there is no puzzle here at all. For perhaps the moral risk of military service is simply *commensurate* with the moral need that taking on that risk is fulfilling. That is, the real worry might simply be whether or not the moral need is actually worth the corresponding moral risk; and the soldier volunteering to serve either gets that risk calculation right or wrong. Of course, on such a reading, whether or not the individual gets *that* conclusion right itself then becomes its own moral risk to weigh. An individual must determine whether a given society's military really is a justified and necessary institution, for example.[17] And that determination will carry its own risk of getting that call wrong. And so on, down for all the epistemic pieces of this puzzle. We'll return to the depth of the moral risk more below, but, in other words, one might think that this is simply one 'big picture' moral risk calculation all the way down.

Yet I'm dubious of this conclusion as well and that the assumption of the moral risks of military service is *merely* a brute risk calculation, full stop. There is something plausible in the notion of a kind of nobility in shouldering that necessary moral risk on behalf of others. Remember, the Noble Risk Argument is not merely contending that volunteering is permissible—like a permissible, rational risk calculus to take, given various contingent circumstances and competing goods—but rather that it is a supererogatory act to take on that risk on behalf of others. If it is merely a risk calculation the individual can get right or wrong, it will be impossible to derive a supererogatory conclusion from it.[18] We will return to this view of the moral phenomenon of volunteering for military service as simply a brute risk calculation below.

2.4 Lazar and Moral Courage

As already mentioned, I conceived of an embryonic version of this argument many years ago. Subsequently I heard this kind of claim for the supererogatory nature of voluntary military service—specifically derived from its inherent moral risk that one could be misused by one's state, articulated by soldiers themselves. However, I was pleased to discover—to my surprise—that something along these lines had indeed recently been formulated by a philosopher who works on the

---

[17] Some baseline level of that determination seems like it must be the case on *any* version of this argument. For example, do we really think any version of the Noble Risk Argument could possibly hold for someone choosing to volunteer to serve in a cartoonishly evil military enterprise, such as volunteering to serve for ISIS?

[18] One is not self-sacrificially going above and beyond when they make the correct, rational moral risk calculation.

ethics of war. Seth Lazar offered a quick articulation of moral praise for volunteer soldiers specifically for their taking on moral risks in a discussion piece hosted by the *Boston Review*.[19] Looking carefully at Lazar's argument will help bring the above points in §2 together nicely.

As we'll see, Lazar's claim has a clear family resemblance to the Noble Risk Argument. In the piece, he is responding to McMahan on the moral risks of voluntary military service.[20] To answer the question of whether taking on such risks is morally permissible, Lazar focuses on whether a given military is a justified institution or not. Once we answer that, he argues, it follows whether service within it (and its concomitant moral risks) would thereby be permissible or impermissible. He bases this on whether the expected value for a given institution one would serve is predicted to be overall morally better or worse for the world. Lazar writes, 'Whether it is permissible to volunteer depends on whether your expectation of doing good is greater than your expectation of doing ill.'[21] In the resulting discussion, Lazar comes to the case of what he calls a minimally justified military. These are cases where, simply, it is 'morally permissible to have these armed forces, compared with having none at all', and the expectation of good is greater than wrong.[22]

In cases of minimally justified militaries, Lazar recognizes that military service in those cases, while permissible, could still carry significant moral risk to the individual. His way of stating the case is as follows:

> ... perhaps minimally justified armed forces include roles that are necessary for their functioning but are impermissible for those who take them up because their expectation of wrong is greater than their expectation of good. To have these justified institutions, some people must take moral risks that one *ought* not take. If minimally justified institutions require that some operatives *get dirty hands*, then all of those able should have an equal prospect of bearing those moral risks: we should endorse conscription. But suppose that some among us volunteer to take on that burden. How should we evaluate their decision? Barring wrongful motivations, and if the decision is genuinely voluntary, we should celebrate it as a remarkable display of not only physical but also moral courage. They are putting both their lives and their souls at risk so others don't have to, to sustain a morally justified institution from which we all benefit.[23]

On a first pass, the above may sound quite similar to the rough-and-ready version of the Noble Risk Argument outlined in §1. However, many of the similarities are only superficial, and Lazar's view here is crucially different in a foundational way. And that is that Lazar couches the decision to volunteer and assume the moral risk of military service as something that, *prima facie*, one should not do. That

---

[19] Seth Lazar, 'Response to Moral Wounds', November 2013, forum in *Boston Review*.
[20] McMahan, 'The Moral Responsibility of Volunteer Soldiers'.
[21] Lazar, 'Response to Moral Wounds'.
[22] Ibid.
[23] Ibid. Emphasis mine throughout.

is, he takes the act as to be a kind of dirty hands problem. On his reading, we need some number of people to take on acts for which they actually have a higher expectation of wrongdoing *individually*, but that will thereby allow for institutions which creates an all-things-considered greater good for all. In order to have these military institutions that, on par, do more good than wrong in the world, Lazar holds that it's likely some must take on these kinds of moral risks. These are risks the individuals themselves have good reason to believe have a morally *negative* expected value and thereby are risks they ought *not* take. However, for the rest of us and the world, it is good and well that they do take them.

To understand how this contrasts with the Noble Risk Argument, focus on Lazar's claim that for these military volunteers their expectation of doing wrong via their military service could well be greater than their expectation of doing good. To understand why he would think that they should still serve in spite of that expectation—or have the 'moral courage' to serve—we must return to his under-standing of a minimally justified military. Recall that by it he simply means it is better for them to exist than not, and that the overall expectation of good is greater than wrong for the institution as a whole.[24] Given that, I take it that Lazar intends his claim about the individual's expectation of greater wrong than good to reference specific acts that they may have to undertake in war. Perhaps he here means things like so-called 'collateral damage' or some other moral issue surrounding a specific *jus in bello* practice or act that would be a pro tanto wrong, even though the overall existence of the military makes such wrongs justifiable costs. In any case, why he would then take this as a Dirty Hands case emerges clearly enough, given that understanding.

Hence, we see why Lazar's praise for these individuals' moral courage is so far afield from the Noble Risk Argument. If it really is the case that these are moral risks that the individuals ought *not* take by volunteering, as Lazar contends, then it's unclear how they could possibly be praiseworthy, much less supererogatory actions to so take them. At best, it seems they would be making a correct, ratio-nal risk calculation, like that discussed above, and we should be thankful that the individuals got that calculation right. We should be thankful because it's better than not that the institution should exist; but this doesn't leave much room for the volunteering itself to be a particularly noble act.[25]

There are really two things going on in the contrast here with Lazar. First, the Noble Risk Argument is focused on the moral risk specifically that a soldier may

---

[24] Frowe points out that this is an exceedingly low bar and that it is dubious whether such a bar could make something morally justified. I agree. But recall that Lazar's point with that standard here is to simply get the military institution to what he calls 'minimally justified', which simply means that it is permissible to have the military as opposed to having none at all. Thanks to Helen Frowe for discussion on this point.

[25] Lazar's formulation *does* have a kind of self-sacrificial nature to it; but it is misleading. The self-sacrificial nature of their volunteering on his reading is that they may be willing to commit pro tanto wrongs, for the greater good of all. He sees volunteer soldiers shouldering *that* burden. But what the Noble Risk Argument claims is that the act of volunteering and shouldering the moral risk is itself a morally good act; indeed, it is supererogatory.

fight in an unjust war; the *jus ad bellum* risks, not the *jus in bello* risks, as shown above. Lazar's reasoning here suggests he's focused on the moral risks of *jus in bello* wrongdoing for the individual. As discussed in §2.1, the moral risks of failing in some *jus in bello* aspect of war do not seem particularly different in kind than the moral risks other roles in society face in the goings about of their professions, such as a surgeon. Whereas soldiers have this 'big picture' moral risk that the entire enterprise of soldiering might be wrong, if they are sent to wage an unjust war. The Noble Risk Argument is focused on this later moral risk, which gives the grounds for supererogatory action.

But, even setting that aside, second, the bigger disparity is that the Noble Risk Argument runs the logic Lazar employs from a different direction, which delivers a subtle, but importantly different conclusion. To wit: the Noble Risk Argument starts from the justification and necessity of a military, and the corollary that we therefore need some subset of individuals to serve within it. Granting that there are 'big picture' *jus ad bellum* moral risks associated with such service, we need some individuals to bear that burden. Those who are willing to do so, are going above and beyond in willingly shouldering that burden on behalf of others. That shouldering of the *risk* of doing wrong in the first instance is the basis for the moral praiseworthiness of their volunteer act itself; not a willingness to *do* wrong that they 'bravely' take on, as Lazar concludes.

2.5 The Duty to Not Fight in an Unjust War

The discussion in §2 thus far helps clarify just what, and what not, the Noble Risk Argument is claiming. One final clarifying note is needed to shore up the argument further, before moving onto to a closer look at the nature of moral risk and supererogation.

In my view, if an individual enlists in a military and she comes to conclude that the military is engaging in an unjust war, she should not fight. That is, she should find a means by which to get out of the commitment to the military so as to not fight in an unjust war if possible.[26] The Noble Risk Argument does not require, in other words, that the moral risk works out. It could go wrong—that's the point— and even though the taking on of the moral risk in the first place may have been morally supererogatory, if she goes on to knowingly participate in an unjust war, that participation itself is still wrong. Put another way: the goodness of the act of volunteering for the risk of wrongdoing doesn't somehow shield the individual from the wrongness of thereafter participating in an unjust war. The argument allows, however, for the fact that many soldiers will simply not have the epistemic vantage to know with any degree of certainty whether a given war is just or unjust.

---

[26] This will be revisited below in §5.2 in a discussion on selective conscientious objection.

But that, of course, is yet another piece of the moral risk inherent in the initial decision to volunteer, if not in fact the *primary* driver of the moral risk, as will be discussed next in §3.

3. Moral Risk

3.1 Uncertainty about Empirical Realities

Moral risk occurs when an agent does something that has a non-zero probability of being morally wrong. When one knowingly commits an act under moral risk, they are aware that they are doing something that has a non-zero probably of being wrong. Many of us take on some level of moral risk every day, even if it is usually quite small. For each moral risk we take, it is an open question whether it is morally permissible to assume that risk. Often, it is impermissible to take a moral risk, even if the given risk works out for the good and the potential wrong never occurs; simply taking the moral risk itself may be impermissible. Whether one is justified in taking a given moral risk hinges on the costs of avoidance and the stakes of the risk. On most accounts and in most scenarios, we think moral risk is something one should try to avoid, if possible, depending on the costs of that avoidance and the good to be attained. As a general rule, if one can avoid moral risk at no or minimal cost, or if there is a means to attain the good sought by a non- or less-morally-risky means, then we think one should do so. Intentionally taking on moral risk seems like a bad idea not only because the risk may go bad (the potential wrong comes about), but we also think that even the act of knowingly taking a moral risk can itself be wrongful. This can be especially true when the moral stakes are high.

Moral Risk can mean many different things. To get some clarity on it, we do well to start with the concept of uncertainty and acting under varying degrees of uncertainty. Exploring what is morally right, rational action under conditions of uncertainty has received a great deal of attention of late.[27] When one is acting under uncertainty, there are different ways he can be unsure of things. Most commonly, one can simply be unsure about the empirical facts surrounding a case, or his predictive certainty about how an act will play out or impact others. That is, uncertainties about the probabilities of forecasts regarding the empirical facts to come. But, in the first instance, those empirical facts, and the uncertainties about them, can include certain normative features of the world. Moreover, moral risk can also mean acting under varying degrees of uncertainty about the normative

---

[27] See Michael Zimmerman, *Living with Uncertainty: The Moral Significance of Ignorance* (Leiden: Cambridge University Press, 2010). See also Seth Lazar's recent work across a variety of articles on this general topic, such as 'In Dubious Battle: Uncertainty and the Ethics of Killing', *Philosophical Studies* 17, no. 4 (2018), pp. 859–883.

facts themselves. So, there are (at least) two ways one can be uncertain in these cases: about the empirical realities or the normative realities. But often, those two will coincide and interrelate. The moral risk is that one may be mistaken on any one of these metrics and end up doing wrong. Again, in other words, we take moral risk when we do something that has a non-zero probability of being morally wrong.

Some simple cases will help elaborate. Here is a case of empirical uncertainty whereby the agent will do something that has a non-zero probability of being morally wrong.

Uncertain Hunter

Jim is on a hunting trip with his friend Tom. They are dressed in camouflage, but they also wear orange-coloured hats so as to not be confused with an animal. They have split up in their hunt and Jim is not sure exactly where Tom is. Meanwhile, Jim sees what he thinks is an elk coming up a ridgeline near him, soon to be emerging from some brush. Jim thinks he'll only have one very brief chance to take a shot at the elk. Right before he does so, he second guesses himself, and questions whether or not he saw the colour orange or not emerging from the brush. He is fairly certain he did not, but he has some doubt, and he knows there's a real chance he could be mistaken on this and he might accidentally be shooting at Tom.

If Jim decides to shoot, he is assuming significant moral risk. The moral risk is that his shooting, while it may turn out to be permissible if indeed it is an elk, could also turn out to be morally wrong if it turns out to be a person, like his friend Tom. Presumably here, the stakes are low. If he waits and does not shoot, he may miss this chance to get the elk, but most will conclude that's not worth the risk of shooting his friend. In fact, given the stakes, we think on just about *any* reasonable amount of uncertainty about what he's shooting at, he should err on the side of caution, and not take that risk. This would be an impermissible moral risk for Jim to presume. Notice we think it would be wrong for Jim to take this moral risk, even if it turned out he was correct and it wasn't Tom but an elk. We would think his assumption of moral risk was reckless and impermissible even though it turned out the risk didn't go bad in this case.

But notice how the stakes involved can change these conclusions very quickly. Consider a different hunter example, but this time the hunter is hunting to provide for a starving village.

Starving Village Hunter

A remote village is about to enter into a long winter. Due to some disaster, they are in the midst of a famine and facing starvation. In desperation, they send Jim and Tom out on one last hunting trip before winter sets in. This will be the last chance to get food for the village for several months. The village will be cut off, their supplies will run low, and if Jim and Tom are unsuccessful in coming back with some game, many will surely die.

From here, the case proceeds identically to *Uncertain Hunter*. In this case, we think taking the moral risk of shooting is justified. Notice that the relevant empirical uncertainty is identical, and it is certainly still true that Jim is doing something with a non-zero probability of being wrong. But the stakes are so high in this case—if he doesn't get an elk, many in the village will starve—that we think it is a permissible moral risk to take. In fact, depending on the relative confidence Jim has that this may be his one and only chance to get the elk and thereby save many villagers from starvation, one might even think it's *obligatory* to take on the moral risk of shooting.[28]

3.2 Uncertainty about Moral Realities

But there is another kind of uncertainty under which we act with a non-zero probability of acting wrongly. Namely, moral uncertainty about what the right thing to do is itself. That is, there are cases where the agent is not only uncertain about relevant empirical realities, but unsure about the moral realities as well. Imagine if an agent is unsure which moral theory, for example, is the right one, and two competing moral theories prescribe different actions for him to take. In that case, the agent is again doing something that has a non-zero probability of being wrong. But the risk comes from an uncertainty about normativity itself.

Here's a generalized example. Imagine any given applied ethics topic for which there is sustained disagreement among experts as to what the right action is. Simplify this to two broad camps; one argues that A is the morally correct action and the other that ~A is morally preferred. Each side has a series of arguments they employ to make their cases. An individual is wrestling over a decision to do A or ~A. She is mostly convinced by the arguments in favour of A. But she admits that she is not completely sure; she could be wrong, and the moral arguments for ~A could well turn out to be correct and the arguments for A could be mistaken.[29]

In such a case, when she does act A, she acts under moral risk. One can insert nearly any applied ethics topic for A here and we see this kind of moral risk is pervasive. Of course, one need not be wrestling over some broad topic for this kind of moral risk to occur. It could be a simple, one-off event in an agent's life where she is simply uncertain what the right moral course of action is, due to uncertainties within her own moral reasoning and deliberation on the matter.

---

[28] Cases of obligatory moral risk-taking are controversial. I will not engage that debate here.

[29] See Dan Moller, 'Abortion and Moral Risk', *Philosophy 86*, no. 3 (2011), pp. 425–443, for a superb paper working through precisely this kind of reasoning for a major applied ethics topic.

There is a view that argues an agent should 'hedge' her moral bets in these kinds of cases of moral risk. As Christian Tarsney explains, 'Advocates of moral hedging claim that an agent should weigh the reasons put forward by each moral theory in which she has positive credence, considering both the likelihood that that theory is true and the strength of the reasons it posits.'[30] Agents should count their uncertainty and the chance that the moral arguments or moral theory they think is false could actually turn out to be correct, as part of their overall decision on what to do. As such, the chance that they could be getting it wrong (morally) can serve as its own deterrent and reason to 'err on the side of caution' just as it does in the cases of morally relevant empirical uncertainty. The thought is that if uncertainties about the empirical state of the world matter for moral risk as discussed above, then so do uncertainties about the basic principles of morality as well.[31] Or, going further, so too for uncertainties about the strength of a given moral argument for an act; or so too for uncertainties about one's own moral decision-making deliberation and ability. And so on.[32]

The result is that moral risk comes about in a great many of the decisions and actions we undertake. The majority of the time, thankfully, the risk of wrongdoing is rather low. And, as such, even though there is a non-zero probability that we are acting wrongly, the probability is low enough that it should not prohibit action. Eventually, however, in some cases that moral risk probability gets high enough that we should not act.

The above discussion on moral risk is controversial. There is no clear consensus among those working on moral risk, for example, on whether this kind of normative uncertainty should give rise to hedging one's actions.[33] Some even argue that we have no reason to avoid moral risk, full stop. Although I find such a view of moral risk utterly bizarre, Elizabeth Harmon and Brian Weatherson each argue, for example, that we have no reason to avoid moral risk, even in the simplest of cases.[34] On this view, what one ought to do is simply the output of their beliefs about the world plus the true moral theory. Of course, Tarsney and others respond

---

[30] Christian Tarsney, 'Rationality and Moral Risk: A Moderate Defense of Hedging', PhD dissertation, Digital Repository at the University of Maryland (2017).

[31] Ibid.

[32] The so on here is that the rabbit hole simply doesn't seem to ever stop. Deliberating about what the good is, for example, is itself a moral action, and hence could be something we are wrong about. That is, sometimes the good thing in the world could be to *not* deliberate. These second-order moral risk problems seem nearly endless. Notice, simply saying, 'I'm not going to put myself in a morally risky position', assumes that *that* inaction is itself less morally risky. Perhaps sitting on the fence is worse in some cases. On these 'metanormative' problems, see William MacAskill's excellent work, 'Normative Uncertainty', PhD dissertation, University of Oxford (2014).

[33] To say that the lack of consensus among experts on this issue forms a beautiful meta-irony for the debate itself is perhaps obvious. I found it to be one of those hilarious yet profound hiccups of contemporary moral analytic philosophy.

[34] See Elizabeth Harmon, 'The Irrelevance of Moral Uncertainty', in R. Shafer-Landau (ed.), *Oxford Studies in Metaethics*, Vol. 10 (Oxford: Oxford University Press, 2015), Chapter 3; and Brian Weatherson, 'Running Risks Morally', *Philosophical Studies 167*, no 1 (2014), pp. 141–163.

with the quite reasonable question: but what if one doesn't know the true moral theory?[35] I cannot address that debate here. For the purposes of this paper, I help myself to the hedging view and the stance that moral risk is real and pervasive across a wide swath of our moral decisions. This will be critical for the Noble Risk Argument. If it turns out there is no need to avoid moral risk, then it will be hard to see how the modification to the argument based on harm would work below in §4.

3.3 Moral Risk of Military Service

Now return to the case at hand: the moral risk of voluntary military service. Here we have a wide combination of uncertainties. There is the uncertainty about whether a given military is morally justified and a necessary institution to begin with. Depending on the case, this can be a kind of empirical uncertainty or a normative uncertainty, or both. Moreover, there is also uncertainty about how a given state will act in the future. This future, predictive uncertainty can be, again, empirical, or normative, or both—and this uncertainty forms the basis for the primary moral risk that drives the Noble Risk Argument. Again, we are here assuming the revisionist stance that an individual is morally responsible for fighting on behalf of an unjust war. We are also assuming the corollary that if a soldier does come to the conclusion that a given war is unjust, she should not fight. But the epistemic uncertainties of determining if a war is unjust or not, especially for an individual soldier already serving, will often be daunting, to say the least.

So we have strong reason to conclude that volunteering for military service involves taking on significant moral risk. Just how great that moral risk is will depend on a combination of the empirical facts and the epistemic predictive ability of an individual, as well as his own moral deliberation abilities. Imagine an individual, Bill, considering enlisting. First, a premise of the Noble Risk Argument is that, in some cases, a state military is necessary and justified. Bill could get this determination wrong for the given state he serves, in any number of ways. I mentioned above in a note the extreme case of someone considering fighting for ISIS.[36] But set aside such relatively 'easy' cases. For most modern states, their continued existence is likely often justified, but their military may not be. (In such cases, it may be that the existence of *a* military of some kind is justified, but *this* particular military is not.)[37] This will depend on a complicated calculus. Depending on how the world is arranged, there could be any number of ways a given state's military

---

[35] Tarsney, 'Rationality and Moral Risk'.

[36] I assume that we agree that the existence of ISIS's military is *not* justified and necessary. This is because the continued existence of ISIS itself is not justified; to say nothing of the ongoing unjust ends the ISIS military pursues.

[37] Thanks to Helen Frowe for this point.

is unnecessary and unjustified. Other countries can, and do, glean a kind of collective security from the military might of other, allied nations, for example.[38] So perhaps for some states, it is not necessary that they themselves have a military, so long as their allies do.[39] Bill could get this determination wrong.

Next, once Bill decides to volunteer to serve in a given military, there is now the worry that they may engage in an unjust war. Here is where the primary driver of moral risk for the Noble Risk Argument enters. The state presumably will argue that the war they are waging is just. So, Bill must worry whether the leaders above him who made the decision to go to war got it right. But they could be wrong. Even if he trusts that they are acting in good faith—that trust creating its own massive source of moral risk—the leaders of his state could have simply gotten it wrong. Moreover, his own deliberation on the justness of the cause could be mistaken. Perhaps he concludes on the evidence and arguments he's been given that a war is just; he could be mistaken on the conclusion. And so on. By volunteering to serve, Bill takes on the massive moral risk that he may end up fighting on behalf of an unjust war.

4. Supererogation

4.1 Optional but Praiseworthy

Now that we've discussed a bit of how complex moral risk can be, let us return to the concept of supererogation. This is central to the Noble Risk argument, for it claims that not only is it morally permissible for an individual to take on the moral risk of military service—it is not merely a rational risk to take in some cases—but, in at least some cases, the act of assuming that risk is actually morally exemplary or an act of 'going above and beyond' what one is morally required to do.

---

[38] We see this prominently with the United States military and NATO more broadly.

[39] Though, in those cases, there are likely important moral questions about free-riding that need to be addressed. But there are many other possible arrangements of how the world could be and how international security could play out. Of course, there are logically possible worlds where there is no need for a military whatsoever, for any state. But one can also imagine some closer possible worlds where instead of states having militaries, perhaps there is a collective 'world' military, run by an international organization like an advanced United Nations, or something similar. In any of these cases other than those worlds where we simply no longer need militaries—may such a world come with haste—there will still remain the necessity for some subset of the population to serve in the military, whatever form or shape that takes. All that will be different is the distribution of the necessity, and the distribution of what subset must thereby serve. Each of these possibilities would present ways Bill could get his moral reasoning wrong on this first step of his decision. Importantly, some of the above alternative arrangements to militaries as institutions could significantly increase (or decrease) the given moral risk at play when one voluntarily serves. That is, if a better arrangement for collective defence resulted in a much lower likelihood of a given military engaging in an unjust war, that would, in turn, reduce the severity of the moral risk the individual takes on. Of course, the irony then, according to the Noble Risk Argument is that it would be *less* supererogatory in such cases—for the risk the individual was bearing on behalf of the many would be that much less.

Cases of supererogatory actions are those which lie at the intersection of something that is both morally praiseworthy to do yet non-obligatory at the same time.[40] Supererogatory actions often have the feature of requiring some real cost to the agent—some kind of sacrifice—which is considered giving more than one is morally required to give. Hence, the literal Latin of 'paying out more than is due'.[41] Many supererogatory acts have not only the element of 'oversubscription' in this regard, but also a component of real risk to the agent.[42] However, even though it is a common element of supererogatory action, David Heyd explains that it cannot 'be the source of the value of supererogation, since ... it is neither a necessary nor a sufficient condition of supererogatory action'.[43] Heyd goes on to argue that the source of supererogatory value includes two further features: 'the good intended *consequences* on the one hand, and the *optional* nature of the act on the other'.[44] The optional element is central, because, again, for an act to be supererogatory it cannot be morally obligatory—it must be going above and beyond duty. But for that to be the case, it must in some sense be optional for the individual agent. Importantly, on the intended good consequences element, the value of the supererogation does not rest on the *success* of those good intended consequences coming to pass. Again, Heyd, 'The good promoted is typically of an altruistic nature and thus an act may be supererogatory even if the overall good is not promoted'.[45] Lastly, although somewhat controversial, many also argue that the good intentions of a supererogatory act must be others-focused.[46]

The above gives us something like the following list of elements for a supererogatory action: a morally praiseworthy act that is nevertheless non-obligatory, and optional in nature, voluntarily undertaken by an agent who often does so at risk, cost, or sacrifice to herself, with beneficent or altruistic intent of good consequences towards others. Heyd gives a nice example of volunteering for a risky medical experiment, that can't be simply assigned to someone, which hits all of the above points:

> When a job or a task must be done by a group of people, the group might select the individual who will do the job on the basis of some principle of justice or desert or, in the absence of such principle, by lot. In extreme cases, such as taking part in a highly risky medical experiment, it may be the case that no selection process, including lottery, should be deployed. If an individual volunteers to take upon herself the task rather than leaving it to the selected person, and particularly

---

[40] David Heyd, 'Supererogation', *Stanford Encyclopedia of Philosophy* (2015 entry revised in 2019 by Edward N. Zalta).

[41] Ibid., *super-erogare*.

[42] Joel Feinberg, 'Collective responsibility', *Journal of Philosophy* 65, no. 21 (1968), pp. 674–688.

[43] Heyd, 'Supererogation'.

[44] Ibid.

[45] Ibid.

[46] This is a divergence from the original Christian tradition, though non-Christian Kantian versions of supererogation with strong self-regarding duties also exist. See Heyd, 'Supererogation'.

when it is wrong to select *anyone*, then clearly her act is supererogatory. Volunteering highlights the optional nature of supererogatory action in its purest form (the agent can hardly hide behind the morally modest expression 'I only did my duty').[47]

However, in this paper we are considering a situation for which it is, in fact, required for some members of a larger group to take on a certain cost. So does that mean that the optional nature of supererogation is missing for military service? No. Because the key is that no specific individual person needs to take on the given burden; even though it may be required that *some* subset does.[48] Imagine a simple case of a community of 1000 people. They come to the conclusion that they will need some small subset number of their group to take on the physical risks associated with being firefighters. They need some individuals to bear this burden; it is required in that sense. But it is not required for all to bear this burden. Further, presume that for some reason—perhaps the requirements of extensive training, or some other pragmatic reason—that this is a burden which cannot be divided and shared across the 1000 in some fair distribution. In that case, if some individuals volunteer to bear this burden on behalf of the rest, precisely so that others need not bear the physical risk, this would be a paradigmatic example of supererogatory action.

4.2 Moral Risk of Military Service as Supererogatory

In returning to the Noble Risk Argument, remember again how if one runs the argument's logic in a different direction, one can come to very different results on whether or not one ought to take on the moral risk of military service; much less this notion that it can be supererogatory. We saw this above in Lazar's formulation. Here's McMahan heading down a similar road:

> There seems to be a moral presumption against enlistment, based on the serious risk that enlisting will lead one to attack and kill people in the service of unjust aims. Such killings are unjust. Yet most political communities require a military to protect their security and ensure their survival. The best response to this dilemma is to adopt provisions for selective conscientious objection by active-duty soldiers.[49]

[47] Ibid.
[48] Of course, if no one volunteers, then some kind of forced conscription mechanism will be required. This could be an overall moral gain, even as it would rule out the supererogatory piece. I will return to this below.
[49] McMahan, 'The Moral Responsibility of Volunteer Soldiers'.

The move to some form of selective conscientious objection (SCO) for soldiers is a good one, no doubt. Anyone who agrees with the revisionist view that individual soldiers have moral responsibility for fighting in unjust wars should likely agree that SCO would be a significant moral improvement for those individuals barring the moral risks of military service. I certainly share that view and endorse the move.[50]

Notice, however, that even something like SCO would not 'solve' for the moral risks for military service. Even then, they would still abound, as the uncertainties, both empirical and normative, still abound. Indeed, some have argued that SCO would actually increase a different kind of moral risk—getting the SCO decision wrong.

But before we even get to SCO, notice that McMahan takes the *risk* of doing wrong as itself an automatic presumption against enlistment, even though he agrees that 'most political communities require a military to protect their security and ensure their survival.' This is a mistake. Rather, the logic should work in the other direction, or so contends the Noble Risk Argument. That is, *if* political communities require a military, and it is thereby morally justified to have one, *and* if enlisting in that military entails significant moral risk that one may end up wrongly waging an unjust war, *then* we need some to take on that moral risk. Taking on the moral risk is not itself the wrongful act, even if that risk coming to pass would, indeed, result in a wrongful act.

The question then is whether the act of taking on the moral risk itself can constitute an act of supererogation. I think it quite clearly can, depending on the kind of risk. Voluntarily taking on a physical risk, like with the firefighter case, hits the mark. But does taking on the *moral* risk that one might do wrong? If it does, then the case appears to work. Namely: the kind of voluntary military enlistment whereby one takes on the moral risk that they may be used wrongly by their state to prosecute an unjust war, in cases where it is necessary for that state to have a military and thus necessary for some to bear that moral risk, seems to hit all the marks of supererogation laid out above. In it, we have an agent who is committing a morally praiseworthy act that is non-obligatory to herself specifically, which is optional in nature, voluntarily undertaken by her at serious risk to herself, with

---

[50] There's a surprising result of instituting an SCO that emerges quite starkly here in the face of the moral risk of military service. Namely, if there is a relatively easy 'escape route' via SCO for an individual to get out of military service if they are convinced a given war is unjust, then this may actually *increase* the moral risk they assume in military service. (And, resultantly and oddly, increase the supererogatory nature of the act.) This is because, presumably, soldiers who do not have an SCO route, will have some partial blameworthiness mitigated for serving in an unjust war because extraditing themselves is particularly difficult or costly. But those who have SCO available would likely have an increased moral responsibility to not serve in an unjust war. To be clear, on my view, soldiers both with an SCO option and those without should not serve in an unjust war. But those without an SCO do have a greater mitigating excuse. For some interesting thoughts on this, see David Whetham's publications from 2017 and Andrea Ellner, Paul Robinson, and David Whetham (eds), *When Soldiers Say No: Selective Conscientious Objection and the Modern Military* (New York: Routledge, 2016).

the beneficent, altruistic intent of good consequences towards others. Namely, in this case, the good consequences intended towards others is precisely that the rest of the group need not bear this moral risk.[51] Moreover, of course, the *intent* of the soldier is here presumed to be that she will actually then only serve on behalf of just wars, even though she is aware of the moral risk that her enlistment may lead her to serve in unjust wars.

Note, importantly, that it is the very fact that she may do wrong which makes this act of enlistment it morally risky in the first place and, thereby, supererogatory on this account. It's the taking on of risk, after all, which is the going above and beyond here. If the act of military service *didn't* involve any of this moral risk—if somehow individuals could have certainty that they would not be used on behalf of an unjust cause—then it wouldn't be supererogatory to volunteer to take it on. In that case, it could still be—and likely would be—supererogatory for *other* reasons; such as the assumption of the physical and psychological risks of military service and such.[52] However, here we are aiming only to see if we can make sense of the assumption of the 'big picture' moral risk itself as supererogatory, to test the Noble Risk Argument. And, to return to that point, it is the risk of doing wrong itself, that is the cost to the individual which succeeds in making it a possible act of supererogation.

5. Moral Risk as Harm and Distribution

So far, so good for the Noble Risk Argument. It appears to have some plausible philosophical footing, despite its initial counter-intuitive and puzzling nature. However, one further refinement is worth considering. Namely, some view imposing moral risk on others as a kind of harm that is done to them. This is Claire Finkelstein's view. She argues that from a victim's perspective, exposure to 'risk harm' results in a loss of welfare and is as real as 'outcome harm'.[53] In her view, harm from moral risk persists even if a risk does not 'actually materialize'.[54] I find Finkelstein's argument here compelling. This is significant for our investigation because it opens another potential line of reasoning for

---

[51] Many here object that this is surely not plausibly why *most* soldiers enlist. (Thanks to discussions with Judith Lichtenburg, Jeff McMahan, Forrest Crowell, Helen Frowe, Rob Birch, and many of my students on this point.) I do not deny the objection. And I am not making the case that this is a common intent behind enlistment—though a surprising number of my military officer students, anecdotally, do report that this kind of thinking underlies their service at some deep level. Rather, for those who do serve for such reasons, the argument seems to hold. It will surely be a subset of soldiers for whom this applies.

[52] In that regard, the supererogatory nature of many instances of voluntary military enlistment may well likely be overdetermined.

[53] Claire Finkelstein, 'Is Risk a Harm?', *University of Pennsylvania Law Review 151*, no. 3 (2003), pp. 963–1001, at p. 966.

[54] Ibid., p. 993.

the 'noble risk' view. Indeed, I believe that this understanding of moral risk can significantly strengthen the Noble Risk Argument for voluntary military service and help explain its supererogatory nature via a just distribution of harm argument.

First grant the assumption that bearing moral risk can be a kind of harm. Yet imagine we find in a given society that a particular harm is unavoidable, yet not fully divisible so as to be fairly distributed among all members of the society. That is, it is a harm that must be borne by some smaller subset of the population. Moreover, the society finds that this harm is unavoidable and necessary for the continued existence of the society and the greater good of all members. In such a case, this given society has a just distribution of harm problem. If a member of the society steps up in that circumstance and willingly volunteers to be the one to bear this harm, so that others need not, then it seems we have a straightforward case of supererogatory good.[55] Simply in virtue of being the one to volunteer to willingly bear the necessary harm that must befall someone in the group, such an individual would be committing a praiseworthy but non-obligatory instance of supererogation. Thus, if the moral risk of military service is a kind of necessary harm that must be distributed to some subset of people, and some willingly volunteer to 'take the hit for the team' as to this harm, then the Noble Risk Argument for supererogation goes through easily.

Further still, on Finkelstein's view, this harm persists even when a risk does not 'actually materialize'.[56] This is helpful to resolve the difficult issue of how the noble act can persist even when the moral risk of service never materializes and so, one might think, there really never was a harm that the agent bore. Finkelstein's point is that the harm persists, regardless. Think of a simple case of non-moral risk imposition to see this. If I drive recklessly, swerving my car wildly onto the sidewalk where you are walking as a pedestrian, this view holds that I have harmed you, even if I don't end up actually hitting you. That is, again to use Finkelstein's terms, I have exposed you to 'risk harm', which results in a loss of welfare that is just as real as any 'outcome harm' that can also befall you. The same would be true for the harm the soldier takes on in the assumption of moral risk of wrongdoing, even if that risk never materializes.

However, this approach to the Noble Risk Argument, while in many ways improving the position, has an uncomfortable result. And that is that from the perspective of many soldiers who hold this view of the supererogatory nature of their service, most do not think of their assumption of moral risk, itself, as a kind of harm that has befallen them. This is because many grow weary of the notion of the veteran as a kind of victim. Michael Robillard makes this point well.

---

[55] Again, intent matters here. If someone is stepping into that risk for other reasons, it may not thereby qualify as a supererogatory act.

[56] Ibid.

112 THE SUPEREROGATORY MORAL RISKS OF MILITARY SERVICE

Indeed, when it comes to the issue of what society owes military veterans, we find too often within mainstream discourse an assumed debt to veterans coupled with the prevalence of two dominant, unquestioned narratives of 'veteran as hero' or 'veteran as victim'. Such knee-jerk lionization or pitying of veterans can frequently stymy more nuanced discussions concerning the normative foundations of our presupposed debts to veterans as well as the ethics of particular wars with which the concept of veteran gets too frequently conflated.[57]

Hence, many will view the moral risk as harm version of the Noble Risk Argument sceptically because of the apparent 'victim' narrative that comes from it. The worry is that the soldier is seen as a victim who simply bears this harm. However, this moral risk as harm version of the Noble Act Argument actually delivers us something else, because the soldier bears the harm for others. Consequently, it delivers the 'veteran as hero' claim *precisely* because of a simultaneous 'veteran as victim' claim contained in the soldier being the bearer of this harm. Looked at carefully, on this account we see that the veteran is not *either* a victim or a hero—forced to make a choice between these narratives—but rather is *both* hero and victim at the same time. Surprisingly enough, the basis for them being understood as a hero is due to them willingly being a victim—in this case, by volunteering to be the victim of this risk harm that must be borne by someone in society.

While I think the logic here works, this is an unhappy conclusion. I share Robillard's desire to move away from such simplistic narratives of victim or hero—or both, as this result gives us. But such a conclusion for the ethical status of volunteer soldiers might be unavoidable. If the Noble Risk Argument is true (which in at least some cases it appears plausible), and if the bearing of moral risk is properly understood in some cases as a kind of risk harm to the individual (which also seems at least plausible), then the volunteer soldier as both hero and victim seems to follow.

6. Conclusion

A few remaining comments and issues are worth addressing. Recall the worry at the outset that the Noble Risk Argument may sound plausible in some cases but will cut against many intuitions when a soldier does indeed go on to serve in an unjust war. As I wrote above, 'For example, was it a morally supererogatory act for a German soldier to assume the risk of military service on behalf of the many

---

[57] Michael Robillard, 'A Case for Gratitude: A Response to Stephen Kershnar's Gratitude toward Veterans', *Reason Papers 39*, no. 1 (2017), pp. 65–74. Robillard is here writing in response to Stephen Kershnar, who argues at length that veterans are not proper recipients of gratitude for their service. See, Stephen Kershnar, *Gratitude toward Veterans: Why Americans Should Not Be Very Grateful to Veterans* (Lanham, MD: Lexington Books, 2014). This is a view which, for obvious reasons, would conflict rather diametrically with that set forth in this paper; though perhaps the Noble Risk Argument might be a good rebuttal to some of Kershnar's arguments in that book.

in the 1930s?' To that I respond that we must be very careful just what the claim is that the Noble Risk Argument is making. The proper claim is that the German soldier's act to volunteer to serve, and to take on the moral risk that he may end up being used for unjust ends, could be a supererogatory act worthy of praise, if, indeed, it was necessary for him to do so on behalf of others.[58] If that's true, keep clear that it was the volunteering act of willingly bearing the moral risk of military service that is supererogatory and good. The soldier's subsequent act of then actually serving on behalf of an unjust war was certainly not a good or praiseworthy act. Indeed, serving on behalf of an unjust war is morally condemnable. Those two moral acts—the supererogatory volunteering and the blameworthy fighting in an unjust war—can come apart conceptually.

Another closing point is that the Noble Risk Argument, if true, points us strongly in the direction of conscription. This is not because, as Lazar argues, these necessary institutions require that 'some operatives get dirty hands' but because, instead, some operatives take on the burden—and harm—of moral risk in supererogatorily volunteering to serve. Given that this necessary risk harm exists, the argument goes, if we can find a way to more fairly distribute that harm more justly across society through a mechanism of conscription, then we should. Conscription could theoretically provide a means for all members of a society to share in shouldering the harm of the moral risk of military service. Israel is a nice example of a present-day modern liberal democracy that requires military service of all its citizens. In such an arrangement, the *need* for some to supererogatorily take on the 'extra' necessary duty of moral risk is now evenly distributed to all, rather than a small slice of the population. If, however, the second-order costs to conscription are too high or for some other reason it is morally ruled out, then, similar to those volunteers in David Heyd's risky experiment example, we should be grateful that some are willing to volunteer to bear this harm on behalf of the rest of us.

I, for one, am grateful.[59]

---

[58] Of course, at some point in the 1930s, especially by the late 1930s, this would no longer be true, once it was apparent that the regime itself was not minimally justified, in the Lazarian sense discussed above. Hence, it was not necessary to serve in a military promoting its ends. Indeed, at some point in the evolution of the Nazi state—perhaps quite early—it would be actively wrong to serve, because of the abundant evidence that the risk of being used wrongly was exceedingly high, *and* that the regime itself should no longer justify having a military in the minimal sense. In the example I'm describing above, imagine a soldier who joins the German military at some point historically before such conclusions would have had epistemic warrant, whenever that would have been.

[59] This paper has been a long time in the making. I first considered this kind of argument over a lunch conversation with Jeff McMahan in early 2010. I was then surprised to hear it again, years later, while teaching US Military Special Forces Officers at the Naval Postgraduate School. These men (they were all men) understood the concepts of moral risk discussed here at length and believed sincerely they were undertaking a noble act by voluntarily assuming that risk. This has been repeated across several iterations of students. I am indebted to all of my active duty military students over the years who I have discussed this with, including and especially: John Huntsman, Bart Fray, Espen Ulvebne, Curtis Tucker Knie, Andy Anderson, Forest Crowell, Scott Orr, and Rob Birch. Moreover, I received tremendous help thinking through the central idea of this paper in generous conversations with Christian Tarsney, Jeff McMahan, Victor Tadros, David Heyd, David Rodin, Helen Frowe, Judith Lichtenburg, David Luban,

References

Ellner, A., Robinson, P., and Whetham, D. (2016) *When Soldiers say No: Selective Conscientious Objection in the Modern Military.* New York: Routledge.

Feinberg, J. (1968) 'Collective Responsibility', *Journal of Philosophy*, 65(21), pp. 674–688. doi: 10.2307/2024543.

Finkelstein, C. (2003) 'Is Risk a Harm?', *University of Pennsylvania Law Review*, 151(3), pp. 963–1001.

Harman, E. (2015) 'The Irrelevance of Moral Uncertainty', in Shafer-Landau, R. (ed.) *Oxford Studies in Metaethics*, Volume 10. Oxford: Oxford University Press, Chapter 3.

Heyd, D. (2019) 'Supererogation', in Zalta, E.N. (ed.) *The Stanford Encyclopedia of Philosophy.* Winter 2019. Metaphysics Research Lab, Stanford University. Available at https://plato.stanford.edu/archives/win2019/entries/supererogation/ (Accessed: 5 April 2021).

Kershnar, S. (2014) *Gratitude toward Veterans: Why Americans Should Not Be Very Grateful to Veterans.* Lanham, MD: Lexington Books.

Lazar, S. (2013) 'Response to Moral Wounds', *Boston Review.* Available at: https://www.bostonreview.net/forum_response/seth-lazar/ (Accessed: 5 April 2023).

McMahan, J. (2013) *The Moral Responsibility of Volunteer Soldiers, Boston Review.* Available at: http://bostonreview.net/forum/jeff-mcmahan-moral-responsibility-volunteer-soldiers (Accessed: 5 April 2021).

Moller, D. (2011) 'Abortion and Moral Risk', *Philosophy*, 86(3), pp. 425–443. doi: 10.1017/S0031819111000222.

Renzo, M. (2019) 'Political Authority and Unjust Wars', *Philosophy and Phenomenological Research*, 99(2), pp. 336–357. doi: https://doi.org/10.1111/phpr.12487.

Robillard, M. (2017) 'A Case for Gratitude: A Response to Stephen Kershnar's Gratitude toward Veterans', *Reason Papers*, 39(1), pp. 65–74.

Rodin, D. (2007) 'The Liability of Ordinary Soldiers for Crimes of Aggression', *Washington University Global Studies Law Review*, 6(3), pp. 591–607.

Tarsney, C. (2017) 'Rationality and Moral Risk: A Moderate Defense of Hedging'. doi: 10.13016/M2K931684.

Vitoria, F. de (1991) *Vitoria: Political Writings.* Edited by A. Pagden and J. Lawrance. Cambridge: Cambridge University Press (Cambridge texts in the history of political thought).

Walzer, M. (1973) 'Political Action: The Problem of Dirty Hands', *Philosophy & Public Affairs*, 2(2), pp. 160–180.

Walzer, M. (1977) *Just and Unjust Wars: A Moral Argument with Historical Illustrations.* New York: Basic Books.

Weatherson, B. (2014), 'Running Risks Morally', *Philosophical Studies*, 167 (1), pp. 141–163

Williams, B. (1973) 'A Critique of Utilitarianism' in B. Williams, and J.C. Smart (eds), *Utilitarianism: For and Against.* Cambridge: Cambridge University Press.

Zimmerman, M.J. (2008) *Living with Uncertainty: The Moral Significance of Ignorance.* Leiden: Cambridge University Press (Cambridge Studies in Philosophy).

Adil Haque, Dan Moller, Donald J. Joy, Eric Jensen, and John Arquilla. Thanks to all participants at the 2018 Individualization of War Conference and the attendees and participants at the 2018 Grover Lecture at the University of Connecticut—with particular thanks to Casey Johnson for her excellent comments.

PART II

RETHINKING INDIVIDUALIZATION

PHILOSOPHICAL AND PSYCHOLOGICAL PERSPECTIVES

4
Collective Values in Just and Unjust Wars

Victor Tadros

1. Introduction

In the ongoing conflict in the academic community working on the morality and legality of war, the battle lines tend to be drawn between self-styled collectivists and self-styled individualists. Michael Walzer is commander in chief of the first view, and Jeff McMahan of the second.

Walzer defended the view that war is primarily a conflict between states or groups, and only secondarily a conflict between individuals, and that individuals do not bear responsibility for fighting unjust wars because the fact that the war is unjust is the responsibility of the group rather than the individual. This led to a doctrine that is called 'the moral equality of combatants', where the moral status of a combatant is independent of the justice or injustice of the war.[1]

McMahan, in contrast, defended an individualist view, where war is primarily a conflict between individuals, albeit on a mass scale, where the moral questions that pertain to war are primarily questions about the moral principles that govern the ethics of individual self-defence. As a person's liability to be harmed in self-defence depends on the reasons why they are being attacked, and particularly whether they themselves have launched unjust attacks on others, the moral equality of combatants is false. Furthermore, contrary to conventional wisdom, as individuals can make themselves liable to be harmed in self-defence by causing others to pose unjust threats, some non-combatants are liable to be harmed or killed in self-defence.[2]

This tendency to divide the ethics of war into collectivists and individualists is unhelpful. This is partly because questions about the relationship between individuals and groups have been bound up with orthogonal questions about the extent to which war is a distinctive enterprise.[3] Those who believe that it is not distinctive are sometimes also called 'reductivists'.[4] Assessing whether war is special is difficult because it depends on difficult empirical and conceptual questions about what

---

[1] See, especially, Michael Walzer, *Just and Unjust Wars* (New York: Basic Books, 1977)
[2] See, especially, Jeff McMahan, *Killing in War* (Oxford: Oxford University Press, 2009).
[3] For a similar concern, see Seth Lazar 'Method in the Morality of War,' in Seth Lazar and Helen Frowe, *The Oxford Handbook of Ethics of War* (Oxford: OUP, 2018).
[4] See, for example, Lazar, 'Method in the Morality of War.

Victor Tadros, *Collective Values in Just and Unjust Wars*. In: *The Individualization of War*.
Edited by: Jennifer Welsh, Dapo Akande, and David Rodin, Oxford University Press.
© Victor Tadros (2023). DOI: 10.1093/oso/9780192872203.003.0005

118 COLLECTIVE VALUES IN JUST AND UNJUST WARS

facts are exclusively facts about war, and difficult moral questions about whether any of those facts are morally salient.[5]

It is partly because it has often been assumed that the central question about the relationship between individuals and groups is about the existence, and importance, of group agents or group responsibility. But this is only one kind of group relationship. Here I assess a broad range of ideas that might be thought of as being concerned with the significance of groups. One kind of group is made up of individuals who just bear certain similarities, where these similarities are in no way relational. For example, the group of redheads includes all redheads. But there is nothing relational about being a redhead. Other group-making facts are relational. For example, a family is a relational group—one becomes a member of that group by certain biological or social relations with other members of the group.

Even more importantly, the standard division is unhelpful because group membership might matter in some ways rather than others, and crudely drawn battle lines have contributed to a failure adequately to distinguish the ways in which groups or relationships between people might matter. And it has often been assumed that groups or relationships matter morally in a way that will help to support more conventional views about the ethics of war. I am especially keen to challenge this last assumption.

Here are three of the most important questions. First, do groups have duties, and can groups be blamed? Second, can membership of a group make a person liable to be harmed or killed in war? And third, does a person's membership of a group affect that person's permissions or duties to kill in war? I aim to sketch out a view about all three issues, indicating where groups matter morally. Although it is only a sketch, it is enough to indicate some directions of travel in our thinking about the importance of groups in the ethics of war.

If groups matter morally in any of these ways, a view that is sometimes called 'reductive individualism' is false, at least if that view is understood in the following way, a way that is natural given the label. Reductive individualism, as I will understand it, is the view that the morality of war is reducible to the moral considerations that arise in interpersonal conflict between individuals. This view is false if the moral considerations that determine what it is permissible or wrong to do in war are grounded in facts about groups. As there are many different ways in which facts about groups might ground the permissibility or wrongness of killing in war, showing that reductive individualism is true is a hard task—it requires ruling out many possible ways in which groups might matter.

I think that there are many reasons why reductive individualism is false: there are many ways in which group membership is relevant to the ethics of war. At least in a sense, groups can have permissions and duties in war. Group membership can

---

[5] Lazar summarizes different possibilities nicely in 'Method in the Morality of War', at pp. 28–33.

ground liability to be harmed or killed in war. And people can have permissions or duties in war that are grounded in their membership of certain groups.

This may seem to align my views with Walzer over McMahan. But it does not. Although group membership can be morally salient in several ways, its salience does little to vindicate orthodox views in just war theory. The main way in which orthodox scholars believe that group membership is important is that it grounds a permission to fight in an unjust war, and to explain why individuals who do so are not responsible for the wrongful deaths that are inflicted on the just side of a war. This view strikes me as patently absurd—the idea that no fault is attached to those who fought for the most evil causes in history is hard to believe. And there is no merit in the view that any responsibility that a state or a government has for a war deprives individuals of responsibility for their choices to respond to decisions of the state or government.

In fact, the significance of group membership, I will argue, should lead us to an even more radical rejection of conventional views about war than the individualist programme suggests. There is at least some prospect for individualists to restrict the scope of liability to be harmed or killed in war to those who participate in wars. Once we see that group membership can ground liability, though, this restriction must go, and that leads to revisionist conclusions about the moral status of non-combatants.

2. Can Groups Have Duties?

One question about the morality of killing in war is who is required or permitted to kill or not to kill in war (or to cause or not to cause deaths). It is uncontroversial that individuals have such permissions or duties. Mostly, individuals are permitted or required to fight in just wars, and they are permitted or required not to fight unjust wars, as individualists such as McMahan have ably shown.[6] More controversially, some are permitted or required to fight in unjust wars; and some are permitted or required not to fight in just wars.[7]

Of course, some claim that the permission that individuals have to fight a war derives from the fact that their state is fighting a war. A standard orthodox view is that a person is permitted to fight in an unjust war if and because her state has authorized her to do so. But this is not to deny that individuals have duties and permissions in war; it is a controversial claim about the source of duties and permissions.

---

[6] See, especially, McMahan, *Killing in War*.

[7] For defence of the latter view, see, for example, Saba Bazargan, 'The Permissibility of Aiding and Abetting Unjust Wars', *Journal of Moral Philosophy* 8, no. 4 (2011), pp. 513–529; Victor Tadros 'Unjust Wars Worth Fighting For', *Journal of Practical Ethics* 4, no. 1 (2016), pp. 52–78.

The related question concerning groups is whether groups, and especially states, have permissions or duties to kill or not to kill. David Luban once seemed to deny that there is any distinctive question about the morality of war that applies to states. He suggested that 'wars are not fought by states, but by men and women,'[8] arguing that we can bypass questions about what states do, or have rights to, and focus just on individuals.

There is a common-sense question, though, about whether a particular state is permitted or required to fight a particular war, and any theory of the morality of war that made this question unintelligible would be hard to accept. The question is not whether it is intelligible, but how it is to be understood, and how it relates to questions about individual duty and permission. Luban's view might then be understood as the view that the question about whether a state is permitted or required to fight a particular war is reducible to the question whether particular individuals are permitted or required to fight in that war, or perhaps whether particular individuals are permitted or required to authorize others to do so.

But even understood thus, this view does not seem to capture all of our judgements about war. Suppose that it was wrong for the UK to fight the war that it began to fight in Iraq in 2003. This judgement seems to be one about the collection of acts that together constitute that war. But there is no individual who performed that collection of acts. Furthermore, the wrongness or permissibility of the collection of acts does not seem reducible to the aggregate wrongness of each act of the individuals who together performed that set of acts.[9]

This question about group duties and permissions is related to the more familiar question whether groups can be responsible or blameworthy. It is often suggested that certain groups are the appropriate targets of warranted blame for wrongdoing, and that this is so because they can be responsible for wrongdoing. For example, people blame corporations or states for wrongdoing, and some claim that this practice is warranted because corporations and states can be responsible for wrongdoing, independently of the responsibility of the individual members. This view is sometimes supported by attempts to show that corporations and states can be agents where their agency is not reducible to the agency of their members.[10]

It is highly plausible that only entities that have duties can be blamed because the standard thing that we blame people for is wrongdoing, and wrongdoing just is the violation of a duty. Only those who have duties can violate them, so only those

---

[8] David Luban, 'Just War and Human Rights', *Philosophy and Public Affairs 9*, no. 2 (1980), pp. 160–181, at p. 166.

[9] For a very sophisticated demonstration of this idea, and its unsettling implications, see Patrick Tomlin, 'Proportionality in War: Revising Revisionism', *Ethics 131*, no. 1 (2020), p. 34.

[10] Probably the most sophisticated and best known of the recent defences of this view is Christian List and Philip Pettit, *Group Agency: The Possibility, Design, and Status of Corporate Agents* (Oxford: OUP, 2011). For discussion in the context of war, but with scepticism about the implications for liability, see François Tanguay-Renaud, 'Can States Be Corporately Liable to Attack in War?', in Saba Bazargan and Samuel C. Rickless (eds), *The Ethics of War: Essays* (Oxford: OUP, 2017).

who have duties can be blamed. Some might also find it plausible that only agents can have duties, and thus the blameworthiness of groups depends on the existence of group agents. This view is plausible because the primary role of duties is in the context of practical reasoning. When an entity has an all-things-considered duty not to *v*, *v*ing is 'ruled out' in practical reasoning. And it is because wrongdoers act in a way that is ruled out that they may be blamed. Thus, wrongdoing is to be understood as a feature of a set of options that an entity selects between. But, at least at first blush, it is hard to understand the idea of an entity selecting between options, where some are ruled out and others are not, without invoking agency.

Altogether, this set of views seems to put pressure on us to acknowledge the existence of group agents—it seems that the UK may have acted wrongly in Iraq in some sense irreducible to the wrongness of the individual acts that constitute the war; that this is so only if the UK had a duty not to prosecute that war; and that this is true only if the UK is an agent. But if the UK is an agent, it is a collective agent.

We should resist this argument. A preliminary reason why is that the common-sense judgement that the UK acted wrongly in prosecuting the war in Iraq does not seem to rely on group agency. To see this, note that scepticism that the conditions of group agency are met does not seem to imply scepticism about the wrongness of the war. Suppose, for example, that certain procedural conditions must be met for a group to be able to form intentions independent of its members, and that such intentions are necessary for group agency. Now suppose that the UK fails to meet those procedural conditions. This does not seem, on its surface, to affect the judgement that the war was wrong.

So which part of the argument should we reject? We have already seen a reason why only agents have obligations, and I think that there is a strict sense in which this is true. But there is also a sense, albeit an attenuated sense, in which an entity can have an obligation without its being an agent. Grasping this distinction between senses in which we can have obligations helps us to clarify both the idea that the UK acted wrongly in prosecuting the war in Iraq, and also the air of mystery in the idea that a group can have obligations.

Let me clarify. There is a strict sense of an obligation where only an agent can have an obligation for the reason given earlier—that duties, and thus wrongdoing, are distinguished by their role, their role is in practical reasoning, and only agents engage in practical reasoning. It may be that more than mere agency is necessary for an entity to have a duty in this sense. I think that more is required, for I think that the significance of the contrast between duties and permissions is best understood by considering the attitudes that the entity should have both to the values that are external to her, and the value of personal autonomy. She thus needs a valuable life of her own, as well as the ability to self-reflect.[11]

---

[11] I sketch out an account like this in Victor Tadros, *Wrongs and Crimes* (Oxford: OUP, 2016), ch. 3.

122 COLLECTIVE VALUES IN JUST AND UNJUST WARS

However, there is a looser sense of an obligation where groups can have obligations—a sense where obligations do not depend on agency. For this reason, group obligations do not depend on group agency. To see that this is a common-sense idea, consider an example where there is a group obligation to do something that no individual has an obligation to do, or even to contribute to. Suppose that you and I can together rescue a person from death; neither of us could do this individually; neither of us is at all motivated to act; and neither of us can be persuaded or forced to participate. Now assume that 'ought implies can', so that if a person cannot perform some action or bring about some outcome, she cannot be required to perform that action or bring about that outcome.

It follows that you are not required to rescue the person, for you can't rescue the person without my help and you can't get me to help. And I am not required to rescue the person, for I can't rescue the person without your help and I can't get you to help. As neither of us can persuade the other to act, there is nothing for either of us to do, taken individually, which will result in the person being rescued. Are *we*, then, required to rescue the person? Strictly, we are not. *We* are not an integrated conscious agent that is capable of reasoning about its own life. Indeed, *we* are not an agent at all—we are neither an individual nor a group agent, on any plausible account of agency.

But we are required to rescue the person in a loose sense. Let me describe that sense. There is a set of things that we can bring about if each of us act, but that neither of us can bring about given what the other will do. I cannot influence you to act, and you cannot influence me, so neither of us is in a position to bring about the good outcome; not even by attempting to coordinate with the other. Now consider those things that we can bring about, and consider which of them is ruled out by the disvalue of those options. In considering this we can take account of the significance of each of us having autonomous control over what we do. The disvalue of refraining from rescuing the person makes the option of rescuing her best. And this option is not one that is permitted because of the importance of either of us controlling our lives.

As we are not an agent with a life of its own, we lack some of the features that are central to the significance of having obligations. But in a more attenuated sense, we have an obligation to rescue the person from death, in that the disvalue of failing to rescue the person from death makes that option 'morally best' both in the sense that it is the most valuable, and in the sense that the value of that option would decisively ground an obligation were further agential conditions of obligations met, such as the condition that ought implies can.

This idea relies on noticing two distinct sets of properties that ground obligations: properties concerned with the values that ground them on the one hand and their agential conditions on the other. The attenuated sense of obligation arises in cases where the values would be sufficient to ground an obligation were the agential conditions fulfilled, but some such condition is unfulfilled. This attenuated sense of obligation, then, is applicable to entities that lack agency. This kind of obligation is also one that the UK has. And that explains why it seems natural to conclude that the UK was required not to go to war in Iraq without invoking any special metaphysical claims about group agents.

We might then ask whether there is any special role for group agents to play in the philosophy of war. I cannot decisively show that there is not here, but I have my doubts. Group agency is insufficient for an entity to have obligations in the strict sense, because a group agent lacks features that give the contrast between obligations and permissions its importance. And it is unnecessary for it to have obligations in the loose sense, because those obligations turn simply on the value of certain options, including the value of individuals in the group being able to shape their own lives. It does not depend on whether groups have the power to make decisions independently of their members. Discussion of collective agency in the morality of war, I therefore suspect, is just a distraction, at least when we are considering the obligations and permissions to go to war, or to kill in war.

3. Groups and the Grounds of Liability

A second set of questions concerns the grounds of liability. The central question here is whether relationships between members of groups can make a person liable to be harmed in war. Reductive individualists about this issue claim that the only facts that make a person liable as such are facts about the individual, such as whether she poses a threat, or the culpable or responsible choices that she makes. Even these facts are relational—individualists typically believe that people are liable to be harmed because they are culpable or responsible for posing threats *to others*. What they deny is that one person can be liable simply because of their relationship with other of a group where other members of that group, or the group itself, are culpable or responsible for posing threats to others.

Again, the question of group agency has tended to occlude the relevant considerations. Some defend the view that at least compensatory harm can be justified on the basis of group agency. On this view, members of a group agent are liable to bear compensatory costs because a group agent is culpable or responsible for wrongly causing harm to others.[12] And some might be tempted to extend this view of liability to defensive harm.

Just as I am sceptical about group agency in the context of duties and permissions, I am sceptical about the role of group agency in grounding liability, even if there are group agents. This is not for the standard reason that group membership cannot ground liability because that would make liability a matter of luck rather

---

[12] See, for example, Anna Stilz, 'Collective Responsibility and the State', *Journal of Political Philosophy 19*, no. 2 (2011), pp. 190–208.

than choice. Rather, even if we accept that it is sometimes fair to distribute liability amongst a group, and not only to those members who are responsible or culpable for causing or posing threats, it is not clear why the fairness of doing this depends on, or is grounded in, group agency. When determining whether some group has a shared fate, why should it matter whether their group is an independent agent—whether, for example, it can take decisions or form intentions independently of the decisions or intentions of the group?

The remaining question is whether considerations of fairness do indeed sometimes ground shared liability amongst a group due to relationships between members of the group, where some are responsible for posing or causing unjust threats and others are not. Elsewhere, I have defended the view that they do: that a person can be liable because of her relationship with others who make wrongful choices. I argued for this on the grounds that a fair distribution of risk and harm in a society sometimes requires some innocent people to bear the costs that will otherwise be inflicted on those who choose wrongly.[13]

The basic reason why is that people who join the military are put in a position where they are charged with making decisions that, if they decide wrongly, ground liability. Those decisions are difficult, and in the course of a career those who join the military are likely to act wrongly some of the time. In taking on such roles, they relieve other people in the society of having to take those decisions. If liability is concentrated on the military, the increased risk of being harmed or killed that they anyway bear by being willing to fight is increased further, whereas the risks that non-combatants face is further reduced. In those circumstances, perhaps subject to further considerations, it is often fair that any costs that arise through wrongdoing are shared amongst the group.

To see the case for this in the abstract, consider a society that needs protection from outside threats. The military role is created, and must be filled, in order to meet these threats. Suppose, first, that there is a conditional obligation on members of that society to take up that role—each member is required to take up that role if others do not do so in order to ensure adequate protection for all. It is plausible that people in many societies have such obligations, because everyone receives greater protection from external threats if some take up that role, including those who join the military and their families. The society gives people adequate incentives to join the military under a fair scheme of equality of opportunity. If insufficient numbers join up under these conditions, the society conscripts. It is justified in doing so because of the conditional obligation that people have that I have just described.

---

[13] See Victor Tadros, 'Orwell's Battle with Brittain: Vicarious Liability for Unjust Aggression', *Philosophy and Public Affairs 42*, no. 1 (2014), pp. 42–77, and see, further, Victor Tadros, *To Do, To Die, To Reason Why* (Oxford: OUP, 2020), ch. 11.

Those in the military face difficult questions of judgement about matters of life and death: they are under social pressure to follow orders, they must assess whether to go to war or not, and during war they face difficult decisions how to act. In the course of a military career, it is likely that most people will sometimes decide wrongly, at least in a world where external threats occur reasonably often. If they make the wrong choice, they will sometimes be responsible for posing or causing unjust lethal threats to others, and are liable to be killed on this basis, most people agree. Thus, in the course of a person's military career, that person is likely at some point to be liable to be killed.

The risks of that person being killed when she is liable, though, may be diminished if she shares liability with other members of the society: where each member is jointly and severally liable. Joint and several liability is a kind of vicarious liability—liability that some members of a group have as a result of the liability-incurring choices of other members of the group. Where joint and several liability of this kind occurs, a person who will otherwise be the victim of a wrongful attack may defend herself in a way that inflicts harm on a member, or some members, of the group of people who is jointly and severally liable. In selecting between members to be harmed, the victim may select either the person who wrongly poses or causes the threat, or some other member of the group. The fact that she may select in this way, if it is subject to appropriate constraints, offers greater protection to victims by providing further opportunities for defensive force. More importantly for our purposes, though, it both reduces the risk that each person in the group faces of being killed, and reduces the death toll on the unjust side. This latter set of facts helps to make it fair to distribute liability on the group.

To see both the reduction in risk, and why this might be a fair way of reducing risk, let us consider just one of many kinds of case. Suppose that X is a member of the armed forces who joins an unjust war, and wrongly creates a threat to V. V can avert the threat in one of two ways—the first way will certainly harm X, whereas the second poses a 40 per cent chance of killing X, a 40 per cent chance of killing an innocent person, Y, who is a member of X's political community, and a 20 per cent chance of harming no one.

If only X is liable, it seems that if V decides to avert the threat, she must do so in the first way. Posing a 40 per cent chance of killing an innocent person to avert a threat, rather than killing the only person who is liable to be killed to avert that threat, seems hard to justify. But if X and Y are jointly and severally liable, V is required to pick the second route rather than the first. Doing so has the potential to reduce the death toll, as it may result in no one being killed, and it distributes the risks fairly between those who are liable to avert the threat posed to Y. Thus, the risks to X are reduced. If such decisions are iterated throughout a war, risk is distributed more evenly amongst the group, and the overall magnitude of death and harm that war causes to the unjust side is reduced.

If Y benefits from X being in the military, because this relieves her of joining the military herself, and Y would have wrongly caused threats had she joined up, it seems fair that liability is shared between X and Y other things equal. Some might put constraints on the application of this principle—for example the constraint that the overall expected death toll does not increase, or decreases, compared with X alone being liable. But limits of this kind are consistent with liability to be harmed on the basis of group membership.

Furthermore, this view can take account of different modes of harming. For example, suppose that it is especially hard to justify winning a war by killing some people to terrorize a population. This might constrain the way in which harm is inflicted. It may be easier to justify killing more combatants to eliminate threats they pose than to kill fewer non-combatants to terrorize the population. And then there are difficult questions about the permissibility of using terror by killing combatants.[14] But these are just complications about the application and scope of the view under consideration and not about its merits.

This narrow case for extending liability on the basis of groups can plausibly be extended. For example, we have so far considered the case where X takes on a military role that would otherwise be occupied by Y, and other things are equal. Now suppose that Y lacked the capabilities to join the military. A fairness-based argument might extend joint and several liability to Y even in this case, because Y would otherwise benefit from X having protective capacities that Y lacks, and were Y not liable, X would bear greater risks because of his capacities to protect Y.

And we have considered only just societies, where those who join the military against a background of fair occupational choice. The case for joint and several liability is even stronger in societies where people who join the military do so with an unfairly restricted set of occupational opportunities. And almost all societies are like this. In such societies, if the only people who are liable are members of the military, those who are beneficiaries of unfair opportunities when compared with those who join the military benefit from their unjust opportunity both by being protected from the risks of fighting, and from the liabilities that arise from the decisions of victims of injustice, who join the military and act wrongly as a result.

Obviously, there is much more to say to develop the case for vicarious liability, and I do not have space for a full account here. But whatever the scope of the right fairness-based view of joint and several liability, we have seen enough to conclude that at least some case for liability to be harmed can be mounted on grounds of the fair distribution of risk and harm in a society. And this suggests that simple relational facts ground liability in some cases.

---

[14] I discuss these issues further in Tadros, *To Do, To Die, To Reason Why,* ch.11.

Perhaps self-described individualists will be happy with this conclusion, for perhaps they do not intend to rule out simple relational sources of liability. But it is then unclear what individualism amounts to. A natural way of drawing the contrast between reductive individualist views about the sources of liability and their opponents is that reductive individualists think that liability arises due to facts that are only about the individual. These include, for example, what the individual has done, or caused. Those who deny this think that purely relational facts, such as the relationship between two people, X and Y, can ground X's liability, even where X has done nothing, or caused nothing, that has moral significance. At least if that is how we draw the contrast between reductive individualists and their opponents, I reject reductive individualism.

This rejection of reductive individualism does not have implications that conventionalists will find attractive, though. It does not permit fighting unjust wars. Nor does it suggest that individuals who do so lack responsibility for the threats they wrongly pose. On the contrary, responsible choice is the very basis for vicarious liability. The whole point of vicarious liability is that some people can be liable to bear costs in order to avert threats that others are responsible for posing.

We can clarify this by distinguishing different kinds of responsibility. Attribution responsibility is responsibility for certain actions or their consequences. Prospective responsibility is the responsibility that people have for performing certain tasks. Often, attribution responsibility gives rise to prospective responsibility—a person who is attribution responsible for negligently harming another, for example, is prospectively responsible for compensating that person. In the case of vicarious liability, though, attribution responsibility and prospective responsibility come apart. All members of the group have prospective responsibility to address harms and threats of harm that some members are attribution responsible for creating.

Traditionalists deny that combatants are attribution responsible for posing unjust threats. In contrast, I claim that all members of the group are prospectively responsible for responding to threats that individual members are attribution responsible for posing or causing, and that as a result liability is shared amongst the group between those who are attribution responsible and those who are not.

4. Groups and the Grounds of Obligations

A third set of questions is whether group membership can ground individual permissions and obligations to kill in war. On the view that it can, the fact that a person is a member of a certain group makes it true that this person is permitted or required to kill, or not to kill, in war.

4.1 Special Relationships and the Grounds of Duty

The idea that certain relationships ground permissions and duties is familiar. The most powerful case is that of family members—I am required to care for close family, even where I could do more good by caring for strangers, and it of course follows that I am permitted to do so, at least if the differences between family members and strangers is not too stark.

It is plausible that such permissions and obligations extend to other relations, such as those of friendship. And it is plausible that my relationship with other members of a democratic state can ground at least some obligations, such as the obligation to foster and protect the democratic institutions that we share. Perhaps I have a stronger obligation to foster and support those institutions that govern my group than those institutions that govern strangers.

Assuming that this general idea is right, what role can it play in the ethics of war? To make progress, we should distinguish different ways in which relationships might give rise to obligations. Relationships might be permission or duty grounding because members of those relationships have special reasons to care about the fate of those who they are related to. This seems true, for example, of family members and friends and comrades in arms. But it seems less plausible, or at least much less powerful, in the case of members of a political community, who will typically not know each other personally. This is confirmed by the intuition that there seems no stronger reason to rescue a member of my own political community from harm than a member of some other community: if a Brit and a Swede fall off a boat and I can rescue only one, I have no more reason to rescue the Brit than the Swede, and I ought to flip a coin to determine whom to rescue.

However, members of a political community might have obligations to each other on a different basis, and that may also give rise to special permissions and duties. They may have special reasons to act in accordance with the judgements or decisions that are taken by that community or its representatives out of respect for them as mutual participants in a democratic society, where members aim to shape their fate together through collective reflection and choice. Consider the distinctive value of a community that shapes the institutions, laws and policies that govern its members by encouraging active participation of those members. Such a community has a special kind of value, for its members show respect for each other as autonomous agents who have reason to care about shaping their own fate, rather than having their fate determined by decisions of others without their involvement.

Duties might also arise as a result of a person occupying a certain role in a society based on a fair division of labour. This is plausible in the case of the military. The military role includes a permission to fight where others might be required not to do so, and an obligation to protect the group from being killed. Resources are provided to those who occupy that role based on the importance of the role, and the permissions and obligations that go with it. And that funding is provided by other activities that members of the group engage in to develop the resources available to that society. In other words, the particular role that members of the military have in a cooperative scheme is constituted in part by permissions and obligations that are justifiably attached to that role, and these permissions and obligations are justified in virtue of the benefits to all members of a division of roles and responsibilities.

4.2 The Deontic Implications of Groups

Just as we should distinguish different relationships whose value might give rise to permissions and duties, we should distinguish different deontic implications of such relationships. Consider some war. A person may be required to fight that war, permitted but not required to fight that war, or required not to fight that war. The view that groups ground duties and permissions in war is the view that group membership can make a difference between which of things this is true of a person.

There are many possibilities. First, take a person who would be permitted but not required to fight a war were she not a member of a group. Group membership may make her required to fight that war, or required not to fight it. Second, take a person who would be required to fight a war were she not a member of a group. Group membership may make her permitted but not required not to fight that war, or required not to fight it. Third, take a person who would be required not to fight a war were she not a member of a group. Group membership may make her permitted but not required to fight that war, or required to fight it.

4.3 Decisions to Fight Internally Just Wars

Typically, those who think that groups are important aim to show that the last of these things is true, but I think that whilst group membership can make a person permitted or required to fight a war that she would otherwise be required not to fight, this is only true in restricted circumstances. It cannot normally permit or require a person to fight in a war that is unjust because of the lack of a just cause, or because the war is insufficiently important to justify the harm that will be inflicted.

First consider a person who would be permitted not to fight a certain war, even though that war would be just were the person to fight it—it has a just cause, and is necessary and proportionate. Can group membership ground a requirement to fight? I have already indicated a reason why it can—members of the military might have such an obligation because the political community together decides to fight that war, and this can ground an obligation of members of the military to participate. And by taking up a military role, with the funding that goes with it, the person acquires an obligation to fight. A stranger may be permitted to join the war, because it has a just cause and is proportionate—normally, assisting a person to defend a group that she is permitted to defend is also permissible. But members of the military may have an obligation to do what others are merely permitted to do because of their role in a political community. Of course, difficult questions arise about the political conditions that are sufficient for such obligations to arise; it obviously does not normally arise in deeply unjust states, for example. But at least such obligations arise under reasonably fair political conditions.

Furthermore, group membership can require a person to fight a war that it would otherwise be wrong to fight. Suppose that there is a civil war going on in two countries, X and Y, where each war is fought between a clearly just side and a clearly unjust side. All is equal between these wars. Combatants in X could either fight on the just side in X, or the just side in Y. Special relationships between combatants in X and those who will be protected if they fight in X may require those combatants to fight the civil war in X rather than the civil war in Y, where they would be permitted to fight in Y were they not members of the group of people who are threatened by unjust forces in X.

A similar thing may be true of the military in a democratic society, where a democratic decision is taken to fight a war. Suppose once again that there is a civil war going on in two countries, X and Y, where each has a clearly just and a clearly unjust side. Combatants in a humanitarian peacekeeping force of a third country, Z, could join either of these civil wars on the just side. If Z decides to commit troops to support the just side in X, it is wrong for Z to join the just side in Y, and vice versa. And combatants should wait until the democratic decision is taken to decide which war to join.

The democratic decision, in this case, triggers a requirement to fight an internally just war. Here is why. The decision-maker has two options, where it is permitted to choose either option. When it picks one of these options, combatants who follow this decision do not, therefore, follow a command to kill others that the decision-maker was wrong to issue. Thus, their decision to follow orders is consistent with both substantive and procedural justice—a society governed in this way does what is just, and does so by involving its members in an appropriate way in doing what is just.

But this conclusion depends on the specific features of this case—that each of the wars is internally just, and that there is nothing to choose between them. These facts are insufficient to require or even permit a person to fight such wars. It is insufficient to require the person to fight the war, because the person may have personal prerogatives not to fight. It is insufficient to permit the person to fight because the person may have conflicting personal duties that she will violate if she fights. Group membership can alter whether the person has such prerogatives or duties, and so group membership can ground a requirement to fight a war that the person would otherwise be permitted or required not to fight.

4.4 Decisions to Fight Internally Unjust Wars

Can group membership permit or require a person to fight internally unjust wars that either lack a just cause, or fail to satisfy proportionality or necessity constraints?

To address this question, we should first get a tighter grip on it in two ways. First, we should acknowledge that it is not always wrong to participate in unjust wars quite independently of group membership. A combatant might contribute to just phases of unjust wars. Or she might ameliorate rather than exacerbate the injustice of an unjust war, and that is sometimes sufficient to permit fighting that war.[15] So we should be clear that we are focused on internally unjust wars where it would be wrong to join those wars except for the democratic decision to authorize participation.

Second, decisions of members of one's group may make a difference to the permissibility of fighting a war for contingent reasons. These are not the reasons that we are exploring here. For example, democratic decision-making might be epistemically reliable—wars that a democratic body decides to fight after the appropriate kind of deliberation might be more likely to be just wars than wars that it decides not to fight. Thus, democratic decision-making can contribute to the evidential case that a war is just, and that might result in a combatant being evidence-relative permitted or required to fight a war that she would otherwise be required not to fight.

Similarly, the democratic decision of a state to fight a war might result in other combatants fighting that war—both those governed by the state and outsiders. This may alter its prospects of success, or whether it meets the proportionality or necessity constraint. Obviously enough, these features of democracy have nothing to do with group membership as such—they affect the justice of fighting for both group members and for non-members. They only show that democratic decision-making can 'trigger' some fact that makes fighting a war just or unjust, but they do not show that it makes a difference to the justice of fighting wars as such, simply because the person is a member of the relevant democratic community.[16] I thus set these features of democracy aside.

I now outline the central objection to the view that group membership can make it just to fight an internally unjust war. Where a war is internally unjust, this is because of the importance of the lives of some people who will be killed in war. The deaths that war causes need to be justified by some goal—the just cause of the war—and that goal must be sufficiently important to outweigh deaths caused to

[15] See Bazargan, 'The Permissibility of Aiding and Abetting Unjust Wars'; Tadros, 'Unjust Wars Worth Fighting For', p. 52.
[16] For the contrast between triggering and more fundamental ways in which duties and permissions arise, see David Enoch, 'Authority and Reason-Giving', *Philosophy and Phenomenological Research 89*, no. 2 (2014), pp. 296–332; Tadros, *To Do, To Die, To Reason Why*, ch. 4.

combatants and non-combatants. An internally unjust war is a war where any just cause is insufficient to outweigh these deaths. The view that group membership makes a difference to the permissibility of fighting a just war, then, is the view that membership can tip the balance. The just cause is insufficiently important to justify deaths caused, but group membership helps to justify causing these deaths.

We can now consider two proposals that group membership can make this kind of difference. The first is that certain agent-relative prerogatives permit fighting an internally unjust war. The second is that democratic decision-making authorizes fighting such a war by giving people duties even where the decision-maker was wrong to authorize the war. Neither of these proposals succeeds.

To see how the first proposal works, consider an internally unjust war that some country decides to fight. The idea under consideration is that once that war starts, people are permitted to kill in war in order to protect those who they have special relationships with, even though protecting those people by killing in war would be wrong were it not for these relationships.

This proposal thus relies on the idea that agent-relative prerogatives affect proportionality. Though I cannot offer a full argument for it here, this view seems false. Whilst we have agent-relative permissions and prerogatives to refrain from saving others, we do not normally have such prerogatives to cause harm to others.

The best explanation for agent-relative prerogatives is twofold: there is value in our freedom to use our personal resources to pursue ends that we set for ourselves; and there is disvalue in others involving our resources in their projects against our will. This pair of ideas helps to explain the powerful intuition that a person is permitted not to rescue others at grave personal cost, as well as the intuition that she is permitted to withdraw her resources from being used for the sake of some important goal where she needs those resources to serve her own ends.

Neither idea is engaged where a person is harmed against her will, and this explains the equally powerful intuition that it is normally wrong to harm a person in order to protect oneself, even where it would be permissible to refrain from saving a person in order to protect oneself. For example, it seems wrong to divert a threat from oneself to another innocent person, who will then be harmed as a side effect, even though one would be permitted not to save another person from being harmed where the cost to oneself is much less.

The second proposal is that democratic decision-making can give people duties to follow a decision even where that decision was wrongly made. Whilst this idea has some plausibility in some contexts, it lacks all plausibility in the case of killing in war. To see why, suppose that some democratic body is deciding whether to engage in a war, where members are unsure about the justice of the war. They consider the lives that will be lost, as well as the goal that might be secured, and wrongly conclude that the war is just.

Now consider the idea that respect for democratic decision-making requires combatants to follow orders. This idea seems false, simply because respect for democratic decision-making requires one to respond appropriately to the attitudes of the decision-makers themselves. The decision-makers, if they are deliberating appropriately, have no reason to value the fact that their decisions are followed in cases where they decide to authorize wrongful killing. To think otherwise is to treat them as though the fact of their decision has some importance to them where life and death is at stake. And those who reason appropriately in matters of life and death do not think this.

To put it crudely, those who take decisions in matters of life and death ought to give lexical priority to substantive justice over any procedural values. The most important thing is to ensure that one does not authorize unjust killing; how one comes to that conclusion is a secondary matter. If the decision-maker gets things wrong, they have every reason to hope that their decisions are not followed, for if they are followed they will be the authors of unjust killings. Thus, those who follow unjust decisions about matters of life and death out of a misguided sense of respect for decision-makers show decision-makers a grave disrespect—they treat them as though they care about their decisions where, if they have appropriate attitudes about the value of the substantive issues and of deliberation itself, they do not care about this at all.[17]

5. Conclusion

We have seen three ways in which groups matter in the ethics of war. First, in a sense at least, if only an attenuated sense, groups have duties. Second, group membership can ground liability to be harmed or killed in war. Third, group membership can ground permissions and duties to kill in war, albeit only in limited circumstances.

But the implications of these ways that groups matter are largely in line with the revisionist conclusions that reductive individualists draw. My arguments do little to support standard conventionalist views, such as the moral equality of combatants, or the wrongness of killing non-combatants. Group membership does not ground a permission to fight in internally unjust wars. Any state responsibility for such wars does nothing to eliminate individual responsibility for the part they play.

Furthermore, the idea that group membership grounds liability is significantly more revisionist than standard reductive individualist views. Familiar individualist views claim that non-combatants can be liable on the basis of their moral or causal responsibility for unjust threats posed in war, or on the basis of complicity.[18] The group-based view that I have defended extends liability of non-combatants to

[17] See, further, Tadros, *To Do, To Die, To Reason Why*, ch. 3.
[18] See, for example, Helen Frowe, *Defensive Killing* (Oxford: OUP, 2014), ch. 6 on non-combatant liability; and Saba Bazargan, 'Complicitious Liability in War', *Philosophical Studies 165*, no. 1 (2012), pp. 177–195 on complicity.

those who are not responsible in any way for unjust threats, either as perpetrators or accomplices. If anything, then, the individualist programme has led us significantly to underestimate just how badly misguided the conventionalist view is.

References

Bazargan, S. (2011) 'The Permissibility of Aiding and Abetting Unjust Wars', *Journal of Moral Philosophy*, 8(4), pp. 513–529. doi: 10.1163/174552411X592185.

Bazargan, S. (2012) 'Complicitous Liability in War', *Philosophical Studies*, 165(1), pp. 177–195. doi: 10.1007/s11098-012-9927-2.

Bazargan-Forward, S. (2018) 'Non-Combatant Immunity and War-Profiteering', in H. Frowe and S. Lazar (eds), *The Oxford Handbook of Ethics of War*. New York: Oxford University Press, pp. 358–82.

Enoch, D. (2014) 'Authority and Reason-Giving', *Philosophy and Phenomenological Research*, 89(2), pp. 296–332. doi: https://doi.org/10.1111/j.1933-1592.2012.00610.x.

Frowe, H. (2014) *Defensive Killing*. Oxford: Oxford University Press.

List, C. and Pettit, P. (2011) *Group Agency: The Possibility, Design, and Status of Corporate Agents*. Oxford: Oxford University Press.

Luban, D. (1980) 'Just War and Human Rights', *Philosophy & Public Affairs*, 9(2), pp. 160–181.

McMahan, J. (2009) *Killing in War*. Oxford: Oxford University Press.

Stilz A. (2011) 'Collective Responsibility and the State', *Journal of Political Philosophy*, 19(2), pp. 190–208. doi: 10.1111/j.1467-9760.2010.00360.x.

Tadros, V. (2014) 'Orwell's Battle with Brittain: Vicarious Liability for Unjust Aggression', *Philosophy & Public Affairs*, 42(1), pp. 42–77. doi: 10.1111/papa.12025.

Tadros, V. (2016) 'Unjust Wars Worth Fighting For', *Journal of Practical Ethics*, 4(1), pp. 52–78.

Tadros, V. (2016) *Wrongs and Crimes*. Oxford: Oxford University Press (Criminalization series).

Tadros, V. (2020) *To Do, To Die, To Reason Why: Individual Ethics in War*. Oxford, New York: Oxford University Press.

Tanguay-Renaud, F. (2017) 'Can States Be Corporately Liable to Attack in War?', in S. Bazargan and S.C. Rickless (eds), *The Ethics of War: Essays*. Oxford: Oxford University Press, pp.116–138.

Tomlin, P. (2020), 'Proportionality in War', *Ethics*, 131(1), pp. 34–61.

Walzer, M. (1977) *Just and Unjust Wars*. New York: Basic Books.

5

Situationism and the Individualization of Responsibility in War

Benjamin Valentino

1. Introduction

In recent years, a growing number of philosophers of war and scholars of international law have endeavoured to conceive of ethical principles and legal institutions that privilege the rights and responsibilities of individuals during times of war. This effort has been motivated in large part by the desire to develop ethics and laws of war that are more consistent with the ethics and laws governing violence in other contexts. Outside of war, we almost always conceive of rights and duties as inhering in individuals. Indeed, efforts to expunge the vestiges of collective responsibly from our legal and ethical doctrines can be credited with an important part in the evolution of law and morality in Western societies over the last several centuries.[1]

In contemporary debates about the laws and ethics of war, proponents of individualization are often associated with the 'revisionist' camp of just war scholarship, while collectivists are associated with 'traditionalism'.[2] Defenders of traditionalist just war theory have forwarded both normative and practical objections to individualist revisionists. Normatively, some traditionalists contend that collective entities such as states or cultures have special significance and intrinsic value that cannot be reduced entirely to the interests of their individual members.[3] Arguing from a practical standpoint, traditionalists have objected that meaningful individualization of the laws of armed conflict would be nearly impossible to realize and, given the lack of an objective arbiter in international politics capable of adjudicating rival claims and enforcing verdicts, could actually lead to less moral conduct in war.[4]

---

[1] Joel Feinberg, 'Collective Responsibility', *The Journal of Philosophy* 65, no. 21 (1968), pp. 674–688.
[2] As Seth Lazar notes, however, that correspondence is not perfect. Seth Lazar, 'Just War Theory: Revisionists Versus Traditionalists', *Annual Review of Political Science* 20, no. 1 (2007), pp. 37–54.
[3] Michael Walzer, 'Terrorism and Just War', *Philosophia* 34, no. 1 (2006), pp. 3–12.
[4] Henry Shue, 'Do We Need a "Morality of War"?', in David Rodin and Henry Shue (eds), *Just and Unjust Warriors* (Oxford: Oxford University Press, 2008), pp. 87–111; and Dan Zupan, 'A Presumption of the Moral Equality of Combatants: A Citizen-Soldier's perspective', in David Rodin and Henry Shue (eds), *Just and Unjust Warriors* (Oxford: OUP, 2008), pp. 214–225. Some revisionists also acknowledge these practical issues and admit that they may limit how deeply international law may be individualized, at least in current circumstances. See Jeff McMahan, *Killing in War* (Oxford: OUP, 2009), p. 108; and

Benjamin Valentino, *Situationism and the Individualization of Responsibility in War.* In: *The Individualization of War.*
Edited by: Jennifer Welsh, Dapo Akande, and David Rodin, Oxford University Press. © Benjamin Valentino (2023).
DOI: 10.1093/oso/9780192872203.003.0006

136   SITUATIONISM AND INDIVIDUALIZATION OF RESPONSIBILITY IN WAR

A related, but potentially larger concern with the practical application of the individualization of war, however, has not received as much attention from scholars. This concern arises from empirical research on the causes of unethical behaviour in situations like war. Beginning in the 1960s, a robust body of psychological research has accumulated establishing that human beings tend to overestimate the power of stable personal character traits and other differences between individuals and underestimate the effects of our external environment and context ('situations') in shaping our own and others' behaviours. This perspective on human behaviour has come to be known as situationism.

Situations have been demonstrated to exert potent effects on individual behaviour—including motivating participation in acts of extreme violence and other harms. A wide range of historians, sociologists, and political scientists who study war, genocide, and military organizations have found this scholarship valuable in understanding the behaviour of soldiers and perpetrators of mass atrocities. The situation of war, in other words, appears to exert a powerful collectivizing effect on individual behaviour in ways that do not always have clear analogues in the domestic criminal contexts in which individual responsibility for harm is usually adjudicated. If the situationist interpretation is correct, therefore, this ought to have profound consequences for how we think about individual moral responsibility and justice in times of war. Situationism should have the most profound effects on individualization in post-war efforts to apportion blame and assign punishments for immoral acts. But it also has some implications for what kind of laws and rules we ought to prefer for regulating the conduct of war.

In this chapter, I argue that an appreciation of situationism ought to inform the ways we attempt to apply individualization to war in the real world. To be clear, I do not argue that situationism and individualism are incompatible. Most versions of situationism leave ample room for notions of individual responsibility, liability, and accountability. If soldiers who participate in unjust wars or even perpetrate war crimes, however, are doing what almost any other individual in the same situation would have done, it calls into question how morally responsible they are for the unjustified threats they pose to soldiers and civilians on the other side. If nearly all citizens tend to enlist when called upon to enlist and nearly all soldiers shoot when called upon to shoot (regardless of the target), then whether one fights for a just or an unjust cause could be little more than luck. This would be an unsound basis for punishing those on the unlucky side. Rather, situationism suggests that the political and military elites who have the power to shape the collective environments that define war bear much of the responsibility for the actions of the individual soldiers and civilians who are the agents and underwriters of war's violence. This conclusion, in turn, suggests that even traditional just

David Rodin, 'The Moral Inequality of Soldiers', in David Rodin and Henry Shue (eds), *Just and Unjust Warriors* (Oxford: OUP, 2008), pp. 58–59.

war theory's emphasis on the responsibility of individual soldiers for violating the rules of *jus in bello* might need to be tempered by insights from situationism and related psychological research.

2. Situationism in Psychology

Although it is possible to trace the origins of situationism to the 1920s, this line of research garnered relatively little attention until the late 1960s when experiments in social psychology began to accumulate increasing evidence that personality traits were not nearly as stable as most people—including most professional psychologists and psychiatrists at the time—believed.[5] Many credit the publication of Walter Mischel's book, *Personality and Assessment*, in 1968 as the foundational text of contemporary situationism.[6] In *Personality and Assessment*, Mischel reviewed evidence from his own original research and a wide range of previous studies on individual behaviour, including moral behaviours like student cheating in academic settings. He discovered a surprisingly low level of correlation in the behaviour of individuals across disparate situations. Mischel concluded that the then dominant view in psychology that individual behaviour was governed by measurable personality traits that remained largely stable across time and context was 'untenable'. Instead, Mischel was surprised to find that 'the behaviors which are often construed as stable personality trait indicators actually are highly specific and depend on the details of the evoking situations.'[7]

Other researchers soon built upon Mischel's work with a series of what would become some of the most famous experiments in psychology. Arguably, the most prominent among these are the series of 'obedience experiments' conducted by the Yale psychologist Stanley Milgram. Although the original experiments were conducted between 1961 and 1962, it was not until the publication of his book, *Obedience to Authority*, in 1974, that Milgram explored the broader implications of this research and connected it to the ongoing debates about personality and situation. Milgram's experiments showed that more than two-thirds of subjects would deliver what they believed were dangerous electrical shocks to an innocent stranger when directed to do so by a scientist. Although Milgram believed that there must be personality traits or other individual-level characteristics that explained why some subjects obeyed authority and others did not, he was ultimately unable to identify any robust determinants of variation in obedience. He acknowledged that his 'overall reaction was to wonder at how few correlates there were of obedience and disobedience and how weakly they are related to the

---

[5] For an early 'situationist' perspective see Hugh Hartshorn and Mark A. May, *Studies in the Nature of Character I: Studies in Deceit* (New York: Macmillan, 1928).

[6] Walter Mischel, *Personality and Assessment* (New York: John Wiley and Sons, 1968).

[7] Ibid., p. 146.

138   SITUATIONISM AND INDIVIDUALIZATION OF RESPONSIBILITY IN WAR

observed behavior.'[8] Rather, changes in the structure of the experimental situation (e.g., the physical proximity of the victim or the presence of 'peers' who disobeyed the experimenter's instructions) had a much more profound effect on behaviour than any of the individual traits Milgram had measured.

The Milgram experiments are often discussed in the context of the dangers of excessive obedience to authority. Today, however, many psychologists see their chief significance as providing the evidentiary foundation of the broader situationist perspective.[9] As the influential social psychologist, Lee Ross, concluded,

> the importance of [Milgram's] research clearly does not lie in the demonstration that subjects obey authority figures or that conformity pressures excited by peers have an impact. That would be dull, obvious, and scientifically unproductive. Rather, they demonstrate that these variables are important relative to other personal and situational influences that most of us had previously thought to be far more important determinants of behavior.[10]

The situationist perspective was bolstered further by another famous experiment conducted at Stanford University in 1971 by Philip Zimbardo. Zimbardo randomly selected psychologically normal, college-age men to play the roles of prisoners and guards in a mock prison that Zimbardo had constructed in the basement of the psychology department building to study the psychological effects of imprisonment. Although Zimbardo did not tell the guards how to behave, and physical violence was forbidden, the guards quickly began to abuse the prisoners— humiliating them verbally, stripping them naked, forcing them to do strenuous exercises and exiling them to solitary confinement. The guards' behaviour became so alarming that Zimbardo was ultimately forced to end the experiment after only six of a planned fourteen days. Zimbardo concluded that the simulation had demonstrated:

> the relative ease with which sadistic behavior could be elicited from normal non-sadistic people .... [T]he pathology observed in this study cannot be attributed to any pre-existing personality differences of the subjects. Rather, their abnormal social and personal relations were a product of their transaction with an environment whose norms and contingencies supported the production of behavior which would be pathological in other settings, but were 'appropriate' in this prison.[11]

---

[8] Stanley Milgram, *Obedience to Authority* (New York: Harper and Row, 1974), p. 208.

[9] See Lee D. Ross, 'Situationist Perspectives on the Obedience Experiments', *Contemporary Psychology* 33, no. 2 (1988), pp. 101–104; Lee Ross and Richard Nisbet, *The Person and the Situation: Perspectives of Social Psychology* (Philadelphia: Temple University Press, 1991), especially pp. 52–58; and Philip Zimbardo, 'The Psychology of Evil: A Situationist Perspective on Recruiting Good People to Engage in Anti-Social Acts', *Research in Social Psychology* 11, no. 2 (1995), pp. 125–133.

[10] Lee Ross, 'The Intuitive Psychologist and His Shortcomings: Distortions in the Attribution Process', *Advances in Experimental Social Psychology* 10, (1977), pp. 173–220, at p. 213.

[11] Philip Zimbardo et al., 'The Psychology of Imprisonment: Privation, Power and Pathology', in David L. Rosenhan and Perry London (eds), *Theory and Research in Abnormal Psychology* (New York: Holt, Rinehart and Winston, 1975), pp. 270–287.

A third situationist experiment, conducted by John Darley and Daniel Batson in 1971 at Princeton Theological Seminary, explored the effects of situational pressures on bystanders rather than perpetrators of violent or immoral behaviour.[12] On the pretext of studying religious education and vocations, Darley and Batson asked seminary students to walk to a building across campus to record a short lecture. One third of the students was told that they were running very late and that they would need to hurry to make it to the recording studio. One third was told that they were right on time. The final third was told that they were ahead of schedule, but that they should leave immediately anyway and that they could wait a few minutes once they arrived at their destination. Along the way, Darley and Batson arranged for the students to pass an actor-confederate slumped over in a hallway in obvious respiratory distress. Of the students who were early for their appointment, 63 per cent stopped to help the man. Only 45 per cent of those who were on time stopped, however, and just 10 per cent of those who were told they were late stopped. Many students in the 'late' condition literally stepped over the victim in order to pass by. None of the individual measures of personality or religiosity that Darley and Batson collected from the students proved significant determinates of helping. Indeed, even subjects who had been asked to read the parable of the Good Samaritan to prepare for their lecture were no more likely to provide help than those who had read a dull passage on the kinds of jobs that seminary students might enjoy.

Although each of the three famous experiments described above has attracted significant criticism,[13] they have been replicated repeatedly in countries around the world (the Milgram experiment was most recently replicated in 2015 in Poland).[14] Dozens of related experiments reaching comparable conclusions about power of situational pressures have been conducted in subsequent years. Perhaps even more compellingly, disconcertingly similar patterns of behaviour have been documented outside of the laboratory. In one particularly distressing example,

[12] John Darley and C. Daniel Batson, 'From Jerusalem to Jericho: A Study of Situational and Dispositional Variables in Helping Behavior', *Journal of Personality and Social Psychology 27*, no. 1 (1973), pp. 100–118.

[13] Daniel C. Batson et al., 'Failure to Help When in a Hurry: Callousness or Conflict?', *Personality and Social Psychology Bulletin 4*, no. 1 (1978), pp. 97–101; Gregg Topo, 'Time to Dismiss the Stanford Prison Experiment?' *Inside Higher Ed*, 20 June 2018. Available at: https://www.insidehighered.com/news/2018/06/20/new-stanford-prison-experiment-revelations-question-findings; Richard Griggs and George Whitehead, 'Coverage of recent criticisms of Milgram's obedience experiments in introductory social psychology textbooks', *Theory and Psychology 25*, no. 5 (2015), pp. 564–580.

[14] See Dariusz Doliński et al., 'Would You Deliver an Electric Shock in 2015? Obedience in the Experimental Paradigm Developed by Stanley Milgram in the 50 Years Following the Original Studies', *Social Psychology and Personality Science 8*, no. 8 (2017), pp. 927–933; Jerry M. Burger, 'Replicating Milgram: Would People Still Obey Today?' *American Psychologist 64*, no. 1 (2009), pp. 1–11; Arthur G. Miller, *The Obedience Experiments: A Case Study of Controversy in Social Science* (New York: Praeger, 1986), esp. pp. 67–87; Alan Elms, 'Obedience in Retrospect', *Journal of Social Issues 51*, no. 3 (1995), pp. 21–31; W.H.J. Meeus and Q.A.W. Raaijmakers, 'Obedience in Modern Society: The Utrecht Studies', *Journal of Social Issues 52*, no. 3 (1995), pp. 155–175; Kenneth Ring, Kenneth A. Wallston, and Michael Cory, 'Mode of Debriefing as a Factor Affecting Subjective Reactions to a Milgram-Type Experiment: An Ethical Inquiry', *Representative Research in Social Psychology 1* (1970), pp. 67–85; and S.H. Lovibond, M. Adams, and W.G. Adams, 'The Effects of Three Experimental Prison Environments on the Behavior of Nonconflict Volunteer Subjects', *Australian Psychologist 14*, no. 3 (1979), pp. 273–287.

between 1995 and 2004, police determined that a man made over seventy phone calls to fast food restaurants around the United States, impersonating a police officer and asking managers to strip search and sometimes sexually assault employees on the pretext that the employee was suspected of having stolen money or goods.[15] Dozens of managers complied with the voice on the phone. Interviewed about the crimes later, Philip Zimbardo declared that the perpetrator 'was very skilled in human psychology—he may have even read about Milgram'.[16]

Today, the dominant school of thought in this area of psychology is known as 'interactionism', which, sensibly, sees behaviour as a product of the interaction between individual traits and the external environment. Few psychologists, however, deny the fundamental insights of these early situationist experiments, which demonstrated that situations are often stronger predictors of behaviour than personality traits. Despite the mounting evidence of the power of situations to determine behaviour, psychologists find that most people continue to believe in consistent personality traits like honesty, trustworthiness, and kindness—and remain unaware of the powerful effects that situations exert on their own and others' actions and attitudes.[17] Even when presented with indisputable evidence of the power of situational forces, people seem to cling to dispositional explanations. In a series of famous experiments, for example, Edward Jones found that readers tended to infer that essay writers genuinely believed in the arguments they forwarded in their essays—even when readers were told explicitly that the writer's position had been assigned randomly by the experimenter.[18] In some cases, subjects were just as likely to assume that the writers believed what they had written when subjects were told the argument has been randomly assigned as when subjects were explicitly told the writers had been free to choose their positions.

Most people, in other words, are unswerving 'dispositionists'. Indeed, the propensity to privilege dispositional explanations for behaviour is so powerful that psychologists have termed this tendency the 'fundamental attribution error'.[19] As a result, people regularly misattribute responsibility for their own and others' actions and they make poor predictions about how they and others are likely to behave—especially in stressful and unfamiliar situations infused with strong social expectations. War is clearly one such situation.

---

[15] Andrew Wolfson, 'A Hoax Most Cruel', *Louisville Courier-Journal*, 9 October 2005.
[16] Ibid.
[17] Richard Nisbett and Timothy Wilson, 'Telling More than We Can Know: Verbal Reports on Mental Processes', *Psychological Review 84*, no. 3 (1977), pp. 231–259.
[18] Edward Jones, 'The Rocky Road from Acts to Dispositions', *American Psychologist 34*, no. 2 (1979), pp. 107–117.
[19] Ross, 'The Intuitive Psychologist and His Shortcomings'.

3. Situationism in the Study of War and Wartime Atrocities

Can situationism help us understand the behaviour of soldiers during war and the perpetrators of wartime atrocities? Unsurprisingly, the situations facing individuals in times of war are much more complex and ambiguous than those facing subjects in experiments like Milgram's, Zimbardo's, or Darley and Batson's. Some aspects of wartime situations almost certainly make compliance with authority or bystanding less likely. Unlike the subjects of Milgram and Zimbardo's experiments, for example, soldiers in war sometimes must engage in, or at least witness, extreme levels of violence, sometimes at very close range, with all the blood and terror those kinds of situations entail. Bystanders in war are not merely asked to pass by a stranger suffering in a hallway, but to look on as friends and neighbours are killed or dragged away for forced relocation.

Yet, it is easy to overstate the influence of these countervailing forces. Even in times of war, most soldiers will never fire their weapon at another human being.[20] Increasingly, those who do engage in combat employ long-range weapons such as artillery, aircraft, and missiles that separate shooters from their targets, ensuring that many will never witness the full effects of their weapons. Civilians, the ultimate underwriters of war, are even more insulated. Most will never directly witness the violence carried out in their name.

Conversely, war generates a number of powerful situational pressures not present in the psychological experiments described above. These pressures seem likely to supersede individual traits that might dispose some people to refuse to participate in war or atrocities, let alone to take active measures to resist war and protect its innocent victims.

First, unlike both soldiers and civilians in times of war, none of the subjects in the situationists' experiments had any reason to believe they might be entering a situation that could involve harming another person (or helping a person avoid harm). As participants in what they believed to be routine academic studies, they were surprised and wholly unprepared for what they encountered. Soldiers, by contrast, are expressly trained to kill and inured to violence by military organizations that draw on techniques that have been perfected over thousands of years to ensure compliance with orders.[21]

Second, although both Milgram and Zimbardo explored the effects of peer pressure, the 'peers' in their studies were, in fact, complete strangers to the experiments' subjects (sometimes confederates of the experiment) who just happened to find themselves in the same situation as the subjects did. These peers are manifestly weak facsimiles of the close friends and family members that young men and

---

[20] David Grossman, *On Killing: The Psychological Cost of Learning to Kill in War and Society* (London: Back Bay Books, 1995).

[21] Gwynne Dyer, *War* (New York: Crown Publishers, 1985), pp. 102–129.

women must confront when deciding whether or not to fight in war and how to conduct themselves if they do.

Third, subjects in the situationists' experiments understood that the disturbing and stressful situations into which they had been thrown also were created by strangers whose only authority stemmed from their positions in respected academic institutions. In war, on the other hand, individuals know that the decision to fight is decided upon by national leaders who frequently enjoy widespread respect and legitimacy by virtue of their positions. Likewise, orders on the battlefield are usually conveyed by commanders who are known personally to soldiers, with whom they have lived and trained for extended periods, and upon whom they depend for their survival in combat, often in foreign lands.

Fourth, whereas the subjects of the situationists' experiments received little or no justification for their participation beyond the requirements of the experimental exercise, civilians and soldiers in times of war usually have been subject to years or even generations of implicit or explicit propaganda and indoctrination designed to reinforce the justness of their own cause, the superiority and value of their nation, the honour of military service, and the depravity of their adversaries.[22]

Finally, the strongest sanctions for non-compliance with which Milgram could threaten his subjects were a series of simple verbal commands that 'the experiment requires that you continue' or 'you have no choice, you must go on.'[23] Neither Zimbardo nor Darley and Batson gave their subjects any orders to harm or not to help others. In times of war, of course, orders to engage in violence are ubiquitous. Citizens who refuse to serve are threatened with prison (or worse) and soldiers who refuse to follow orders on the battlefield are routinely shot.

Given the potent mix of situational forces that defines war, it is not surprising that many scholars of war and mass atrocities have found that situationist research provides important insights into the behaviour of the soldiers who fight wars and the civilians who finance and support them.

Stanley Milgram's research took place as America's involvement in the Vietnam War was just beginning. While over 60 per cent supported the war in 1965, by 1971, 61 per cent were opposed.[24] In his 1974 book, Milgram could not help but wonder why so many young men had been willing to kill and be killed in such a war. His research, he concluded, implied that motivating participation in war was easier than many believed. 'A few changes in newspaper headlines, a call from the draft board, orders from a man with epaulets, and men are led to kill with little

---

[22] Alan Page Fiske and Tage Shakti Rai, *Virtuous Violence* (Cambridge: Cambridge University Press, 2015).

[23] Arthur G. Miller, *The Obedience Experiments: A Case Study of Controversy in Social Science* (New York: Praeger, 1986), p. 8.

[24] Jeffrey M. Jones, 'Latest Poll Shows High Point in Opposition to Iraq War', 11 July 2007, *Gallup Polls*. Available at: http://news.gallup.com/poll/28099/latest-poll-shows-high-point-opposition-iraq-war.aspx

difficulty.'[25] The history of warfare suggests that Milgram was largely correct. War resistance is exceedingly rare, even in relatively unpopular wars and even when the penalties for evading service are mild. During the Vietnam War, for example, only 4 per cent of the 27 million draft age males in the United States are estimated to have been deserters, draft violators or resistors.[26] This was the highest rate of resistance in the history of any US war. Fewer than 9000 men were ultimately convicted of draft evasion, and only 3250 served any time in prison.[27] Prison sentences for those who did serve time ranged from an average of 37 months in 1968 to 17.5 months in 1973.[28] Even deserters typically received just six months in prison and a dishonourable discharge.[29] If fear of legal punishment was the only factor driving young men to participate in the war, we should have expected much higher rates of resistance.

In Israel, a movement called 'Courage to Refuse' has been collecting the signatures of Israeli soldiers who are willing to serve in the Israel Defense Forces (IDF), but refuse to fight in the occupied territories in a conflict that they believe has 'nothing to do with the security of our country' and serves 'the sole purpose of perpetuating our control over the Palestinian people.'[30] Although recent polls show that approximately a third of Israeli Jews believe that settlements in the occupied territories actually *hurt* Israel's security, only 623 soldiers signed the letter between 2002 and 2018—a fraction of 1 per cent of IDF membership over that time.[31] Again, the penalties for refusing to serve are surprisingly light, even in Israel. Only 280 of the signatories have served any time in prison—with a maximum sentence of only thirty-five days.[32]

Most scholars who have studied combat motivation generally agree that, once individuals have been integrated into military organizations, they are driven more powerfully by small-group dynamics, primarily the desires to protect fellow soldiers, conform to group expectations, and avoid the appearance of cowardliness,

---

[25] Stanley Milgram, *Obedience to Authority* (New York: Harper and Row, 1974), p. 6.

[26] Lawrence Baskir and William Strauss, *Chance and Circumstance: The Draft, the War, and the Vietnam Generation*, (New York: Vintage Books, 1978), p. 5, 114.

[27] David Harris, 'I Picked Prison over Fighting in Vietnam', *The New York Times*, 23 June 2017. Available at: https://www.nytimes.com/2017/06/23/opinion/vietnam-war-draft-protests.html

[28] Ford Foundation, *Amnesty—Ford Foundation Study of Effects of Vietnam on Veterans, Deserters and Evaders* (Ann Arbor: Gerald R. Ford Library), p. ii–10. Available at: https://www.fordlibrarymuseum.gov/library/document/0067/1562799.pdf

[29] Ibid., pp. ii–13.

[30] Randy Friedman, 'The Challenge of Selective Conscientious Objection in Israel', *Theoria: A Journal of Social and Political Theory*, no. 109 (April 2006), p. 84.

[31] In 2013, 35 per cent of Israeli Jews said the settlements hurt Israel's security, while 31 per cent said it helped; in 2015, 42 per cent said it helped and 30 per cent said it hurt, see Pew Research Center, 'Israel's Religiously Divided Society', 8 March 2016, at p. 185. Available at: http://assets.pewresearch.org/wp-content/uploads/sites/11/2016/03/Israel-Survey-Full-Report.pdf; http://assets.pewresearch.org/wp-content/uploads/sites/11/2016/03/Israel-Survey-Full-Report.pdf; http://www.seruv.org.il/english/movement.asp

[32] http://www.seruv.org.il/english/movement.asp

144 SITUATIONISM AND INDIVIDUALIZATION OF RESPONSIBILITY IN WAR

than by a carefully considered commitment to the justice of the war or its conduct.[33] In their book exploring human motivations for violence, Alan Fiske and Tage Rai argue that, 'on the battlefield soldiers are killing to protect each other—they feel intensely morally committed to do so, even if they die looking out for each other.'[34] Similarly, Gwynne Dyer's study of men in combat concludes that although many soldiers

> do feel the need for some patriotic or ideological justification for what they do ... which nation, which ideology, does not matter: men will fight as well and die as bravely for the Khmer Rouge as for 'God, King, and Country'. Soldiers are the instruments of politicians and priests, ideologues and strategists, who may have high moral purposes in mind, but the men down in the trenches fight for more basic motives.[35]

Unfortunately, many of the same situational pressures that seem to motivate soldiers in combat also appear to impel their participation in war crimes and mass atrocities. Indeed, historians and political scientists who have studied war crimes frequently refer explicitly to the situationist literature to help make sense of the behaviour of the perpetrators of these atrocities.[36] In Arthur Miller's review of studies on the perpetrators of the Holocaust, for example, he observes 'a remarkable degree of consensus regarding the generalizability of the obedience experiments. Clearly they are viewed by many commentators from a diversity of disciplines and orientations as convincing and meaningful to an understanding of the Holocaust, and of other instances of what is often referred to as "social evil".'[37] Likewise, the historian Donald Bloxham concludes that 'the very existence of mass participation in most genocides shows that the context is generally more important than the disposition and beliefs of the individual perpetrator, since in the "right" situation so many people of demonstrably different characters and values participate ....'[38] Although most people find it difficult to accept (precisely as the fundamental attribution error expects them to), the excuse so often proffered by those of accused of

---

[33] See Richard Holmes, *Acts of War: The Behavior of Men in Battle* (New York: Free Press, 1986), pp. 270–359; Anthony Kellett, *Combat Motivation: The Behavior of Soldiers in Battle* (Boston: Kluwer, 1982), pp. 167–213; Walter Laqueur, *The Guerrilla Reader: A Historical Anthology* (Philadelphia: Temple University Press, 1977), pp. 272–273; E.A. Shils and Morris Janowitz, 'Cohesion and Disintegration in the Wehrmacht in World War II', *Public Opinion Quarterly 12*, no. 2 (1948), pp. 280–315; and S.L.A. Marshall, *Men against Fire* (New York: William Morrow, 1947).

[34] Fiske and Rai, *Virtuous Violence*, p. 102.

[35] Dyer, *War*, p. 104.

[36] For a review of studies of perpetrators of mass atrocities see Benjamin Valentino, *Final Solutions: Mass Killing and Genocide in the Twentieth Century* (Ithaca: Cornell University Press, 2004), pp. 30–65.

[37] Arthur G. Miller, *The Obedience Experiments: A Case Study of Controversy in Social Science* (New York: Praeger, 1986), p. 203.

[38] Donald Bloxham, 'The Organisation of Genocide: Perpetration in Comparative Perspective', in O. Jensen and C.C.W. Szejnmann (eds), *Ordinary People as Mass Murderers: Perpetrators in Comparative Perspectives* (London: Palgrave Macmillan, 2008), p. 187.

war crimes—'I was just following orders'—may, in fact, be a valid construal of the motivations of many perpetrators of mass atrocities.

One of the most compelling applications of situationism to the study of war can be found in the historian Christopher Browning's celebrated history of the German 'Order Police', the military police units tasked with carrying out the extermination of Polish Jews in the early months of the Holocaust, before the death camps had been constructed. Browning concludes that 'Zimbardo's spectrum of guard behaviors bears an uncanny resemblance' to the units he studied and that 'many of Milgram's insights find graphic confirmation in the behavior and testimony of the men' who participated in the killings.[39] Although soldiers in the units he studied were offered the option of not participating in the executions, Browning found that:

> 80 to 90 percent of the men proceeded to kill, though almost all of them—at least initially—were horrified and disgusted by what they were doing. To break ranks and step out, to adopt overtly nonconformist behavior, was simply beyond most of the men. It was easier for them to shoot. Why? First of all, by breaking ranks, non-shooters were leaving the 'dirty work' to their comrades. Since the battalion had to shoot even if individuals did not, refusing to shoot constituted refusing one's share of an unpleasant collective obligation. It was in effect an asocial act vis-à-vis one's comrades. Those who did not shoot risked isolation, rejection, and ostracism—a very uncomfortable prospect within the framework of a tight-knit unit stationed abroad among a hostile population, so that the individual had nowhere else to turn for support and social contact.[40]

Scholars studying the perpetrators of mass atrocities in other cases have reached similar conclusions. To cite just one example, David Chandler's history of the Toul Sleng (also known as S-21) prison where nearly 14,000 Cambodians were tortured and killed under the Khmer Rouge, also references Milgram and Zimbardo to understand the behaviour of the prison guards and interrogators.[41] According to Chandler, 'what we know about the workers at S-21 points in most cases ... to their ordinariness and banality. Bonded with people like themselves and abjectly respectful of those in charge, the workers at S-21, like the prisoners, were trapped inside a merciless place and a pitiless scenario.'[42] 'Explanations that place the blame for evil entirely on "evil people"', Chandler concludes,

[39] Christopher R. Browning, *Ordinary Men: Reserve Police Battalion 101 and the Final Solution in Poland* (New York: HarperCollins, 1992), p. 174.

[40] Ibid., pp. 184–186. For a further argument stressing the power of situational factors over anti-Semitism, see Jürgen Matthäus, 'What about the "Ordinary Men"? The German Order Police and the Holocaust in the Occupied Soviet Union', *Holocaust and Genocide Studies 10*, no. 2 (1996), pp. 134–150.

[41] David P. Chandler, *Voices from S-21: Terror and History in Pol Pot's Secret Prison* (Berkeley: University of California Press, 1999), pp. 147–149.

[42] Ibid., p. 147.

fail to consider that what all of us share with perpetrators of evil is not a culture, a doctrine, or an innate tendency to kill but our similarity as human beings and, in particular, our tendencies toward acculturation and obedience ... The implication is that what is permitted, or commanded, however awful, is usually what occurs; resistance is rarer than compliance and immorality ... is often socially conditioned.[43]

4. Implications of Situationism for the Individualization of War in Ethics and Law

It was not until the early 1990s that philosophers began to grapple explicitly with the implications of situationism for ethics.[44] The most important early contributions to this conversation were registered by Gilbert Harman and John Doris.[45] Both Harman and Doris argued that insights from situationist social psychology severely undermined the conception of moral character or moral virtues, which traces its roots back at least to Aristotle. As Doris put it, 'If we took situationism to heart in our ethical practice, we would revise certain habits of moral-psychological assessment—we would hesitate to evaluate persons by reference to robust traits or evaluatively consistent personality structures, on the grounds that these are unreasonable standards to expect actual persons to approximate'.[46]

In his 2004 book, Doris speculated on how this conclusion might affect our judgements of individual behaviour in times of war. 'Despite familiar convictions to the effect that the moral quality of our lives is somehow "up to us"', he argued, 'people's moral status may to a disquieting degree be hostage to the vagaries of fortune ... Had I lived in Nazi Germany or Rwanda ... I might have led a life that was morally reprehensible, despite the fact that the life I lead now is perhaps no worse than morally mediocre. There, but for the grace of God, do I.'[47] Doris rejects the idea that situationism renders moral evaluation impossible. However, he argues that situationism does imply that 'high intensity situations' may constitute 'excusing conditions' for otherwise seemingly immoral behaviour

---

[43] Ibid., p. 155.
[44] For a review of philosophical debates about the implications of situationism see Candace L. Upton, 'Virtue Ethics and Moral Psychology: The Situationism Debate', *The Journal of Ethics 13*, no. 2–3 (2009), pp. 103–115.
[45] Gilbert Harman, 'Moral Philosophy Meets Social Psychology: Virtue Ethics and the Fundamental Attribution Error', *Proceedings of the Aristotelian Society 99*, no. 1 (1999), pp. 315–331; John M. Doris, 'Persons, Situations, and Virtue Ethics', *Noûs 32*, no. 4 (1998), pp. 504–530. See also Peter Vranas, 'The Indeterminacy Paradox: Character Evaluations and Human Psychology', *Noûs 39*, no. 1 (2005), pp. 1–42. For rebuttals to the situationist critique of virtue ethics see Rachana Kamtekar, 'Situationism and Virtue Ethics on the Content of Our Character', *Ethics 11*, no. 3 (2004), pp. 458–491; and John Sabini and Maury Silver, 'Lack of Character? Situationism Critiqued', *Ethics 115*, no. 3 (2005), pp. 535–562.
[46] Doris, 'Persons, Situations, and Virtue Ethics', pp. 513–514.
[47] John Doris, *Lack of Character: Personality and Moral Behavior* (Cambridge: CUP, 2002), p. 117.

and that we ought to pay special attention to situations in which the vast majority of people behave similarly—since this may reflect the influence of powerful, if sometimes subtle, situational forces.[48] As I have tried to demonstrate above, war would seem to be one such situation. Indeed, in a subsequent article on the perpetrators of wartime atrocities (written with Dominic Murphy), Doris advanced what he acknowledged was an 'unsettling' conclusion. 'Perpetrators of atrocity' Doris and Murphy claimed, 'typically occupy excusing conditions and are therefore not morally responsible for their conduct. While nothing justifies atrocity, many perpetrators manifest cognitive impairments [most notably, "cognitively degrading circumstances"] that profoundly degrade their capacity for moral judgment, and such impairments ... preclude the attribution of moral responsibility.'[49]

Coincidentally, it was not long after moral philosophers like Doris and Harman began to explore the implications of situationism for ethics that a different group of philosophers reignited an ancient debate about the ethics and laws of war. These scholars would come to be known as the just war theory revisionists. Revisionists levelled many critiques against traditional interpretations of just war theory, but much of the debate has centred on the traditional principle of the moral equality of combatants. Traditional interpretations of just war theory hold that judgements about the justice of a war's cause should remain separate from the conduct of those who fight it. Thus, the theory maintains that it is possible to wage an unjust war justly and to wage a just war unjustly. Even soldiers who knowingly volunteer for an unjust war are entitled to the presumption of moral equality as long as they uphold the *jus in bello* rules of war. As Michael Walzer, the most prominent contemporary proponent of the traditionalist interpretation of just war theory puts it, 'The rules of war apply with equal force to aggressors and their adversaries ... Soldiers fighting for an aggressor state are not themselves criminals: hence their rights are the same as those of their opponents. Soldiers fighting against an aggressor state have no license to become criminals: hence they are subject to the same restraints as their opponents.'[50]

Revisionists object that this approach to the ethics of war contradicts the ways we think about violence in contexts outside of war, without a convincing justification for drawing a distinction. As revisionist scholar Jeff McMahon writes, traditionalism's moral equality of combatants 'has no plausibility outside the context of war. In contexts other than war, the morality of conflict is almost invariably asymmetric. Those who are in the right may be permitted to use force and violence but those who are in the wrong are not.'[51] An armed robber, for example, is

---

[48] Ibid., pp. 137–138.

[49] John Doris and Dominic Murphy, 'From My Lai to Abu Ghraib: The Moral Psychology of Atrocity', *Midwest Studies in Philosophy 31*, no. 1 (2007), pp. 25–55, at p. 26.

[50] Michael Walzer, *Just and Unjust Wars* (New York: Basic Books, 1977), p. 136.

[51] McMahan, *Killing in War*, p. 3.

not permitted the right of self-defence against a shopkeeper who tries to protect himself and his business when the robber breaks into his store.

More importantly, in contexts other than war, judgements about moral liability to harm are almost always rendered at the level of the individual, whereas traditional just war theory and much of the international laws of war seem to define the liability of both soldiers and civilians collectively. In Walzer's view, war is a 'coercively collectivizing enterprise ... it overrides individuality, and it makes the kind of attention that we would like to pay to each person's moral standing impossible'.[52] For Walzer, therefore, a soldier—even one fighting for an unjust cause—'is not a member of a robber band, a willful wrongdoer, but a loyal and obedient subject and citizen, acting sometimes at great personal risk in a way he thinks is right'.[53] Thus, in traditional just war theory and in the laws of armed conflict, all soldiers on both sides of the war are deemed liable to attack, regardless of their personal motives or their individual contributions to the war. Conversely, civilians on both sides are held immune from attack, regardless of whether they play a role inciting their nation to initiate the war or whether they organize a protest against it. According to McMahon,

> individual morality has principles that govern the conduct of individuals in their roles as members of collectives and it is a person's guilt or innocence relative to these principles that is largely determinative of his or her liability for actions taken by the collective. If this is right, then it cannot simply be irrelevant to how an unjust combatant may be treated whether he is morally innocent or guilty for his individual action, even if he acts as an agent of the collective. Similarly, civilian noncombatants may also contribute to the war-related acts of the collective and may not be absolved of all liability for those acts simply by virtue of their noncombatant status.

The insights of situationism clearly reinforce Walzer's claim that war is a 'collectivizing enterprise'. As we have seen, the pressures of war appear to force most individuals to behave similarly regardless of their character, their beliefs and intentions, or most other morally relevant individual-level attributes. This does not mean, however, that situationism is fundamentally incompatible with the individualization of war. In principle, it ought to be possible to centre the moral responsibility of individual soldiers and civilians while still giving due consideration to the specific situational forces each person experienced before and during the war. It should also be possible to evaluate whether certain individuals were morally culpable for voluntarily entering into situations they should have known would generate irresistible pressures to behave unjustly. In practice, making these kind of evaluations undoubtedly would be difficult, and sometimes impossible,

---

[52] Michael Walzer, 'Response to McMahan's Paper', *Philosophia 34*, no. 1 (2006), pp. 43–45.
[53] Walzer, *Just and Unjust Wars*, p. 39.

because the effects of situations so often depend on subtle and unforeseen features of the environment. The situationists' experiments are so compelling in large part because of their ability to control away the complexity of the real-world and reveal the dramatic effects that seemingly small variations in the structure of situations exert on human behaviour. It is difficult to imagine how these kinds of considerations could be adequately weighed in a courtroom, let alone in the heat of battle when many of the most fateful moral decisions in war must be made.

What might an individualist approach to the ethics of war that took situationism seriously look like? The implications of situationism for the way we judge and sanction individuals *after* war are probably more significant for individualism than they are for the rights and duties of soldiers during war. During war, soldiers fighting for a just cause would still seem to have a much greater claim to use force than soldiers fighting for the unjust side, even if situationism tells us that those on the unjust side are not morally 'responsible' for the threats they pose. As McMahan argues, to conclude otherwise is to conflate ex post 'excuses' for unjust killing with the ex ante 'permission' to kill justly.[54] Indeed, even in the cases where soldiers are clearly coerced to fight for an unjust cause, this would not seem to give them 'permission' to kill just soldiers on the other side any more than a man dying of heart failure would have permission to kill his neighbour to obtain a life-saving transplant.

Situationism, however, does suggest that most soldiers are unlikely to perceive themselves as fighting for an unjust cause and, therefore, unlikely to change their behaviour in war, even if all were to agree on new rules of war derived from individualism. As Yuval Feldman argues, while classical approaches to law and morality assume that people 'consider the situation, recognize the moral conflict, and then decide what to do', the results of contemporary psychological research shows that most people 'decide what seems to be the right thing to do based on their highly motivated perception of the situation. Their behaviour may be immoral, but they still view themselves as moral people because they frame the situation in such a way that it "allows" immoral behavior.'[55] One of the most powerful effects of the situations that surround war is to convince people that the violence they commit is, in fact, moral, or at least that they are not responsible for any moral wrongs that result from it. As noted above, in most societies, nationalism generates powerful incentives for citizens to think that their countries have inherent value—and often that their country is morally superior to others. In addition, most societies intentionally or spontaneously promote the belief among citizens that their national leaders are legitimate and their decisions are just. In practice,

---

[54] McMahan, *Killing in War*, p. 115.
[55] Yuval Feldman, *The Law of Good People: Challenging States' Ability to Regulate Human Behavior* (Cambridge: CUP, 2018), p. 17.

therefore, few soldiers seem to question the justice of their cause. As Fiske and Rai conclude, 'people in most cultures and subcultures deem it a moral duty to kill the enemy—and in many cases soldiers feel that they *should* kill, enslave, torture, rape, or starve enemy captives or civilians. Philosophers and religious leaders often exhort men ... to fight, extolling the noble virtues of warfare ....'[56] Soldiers, in other words, are likely to act as if they are morally equal, even if, objectively, they are not.

Many revisionists concede that history gives us no reason to expect that people or states would be able to judge the justice of their own causes objectively. As McMahan admits, in the real world, 'most combatants believe that the war they are fighting in is just and lawful' and would 'claim the legal prerogatives accorded to just combatants.'[57] Rodin concurs, observing that 'the majority of wars have been claimed to be just on both sides.'[58] But McMahan also suggests that it is reasonable to hold soldiers responsible for failing to appreciate the possibility that their war might be unjust and that 'soldiers have a stringent moral responsibility to seek to overcome the epistemic constraints that typically characterize their situation.'[59] Situationism helps us understand why meeting this responsibility may be so much harder than it seems.

Even in those relatively rare instances in which soldiers do become convinced that their war is unjust, other powerful situational pressures apply that encourage compliance. In the Milgram experiments, for instance, most subjects appear to have understood that they were participating in an unjust act. As Milgram observed, 'Many of the people studied in the experiment were in some sense against what they did to the learner, and many protested even while they obeyed. ... Some were totally convinced of the wrongness of what they were doing but could not bring themselves to make an open break with authority.'[60] Even though subjects could easily have refused to participate, Milgram believed that most subjects convinced themselves that any wrongs they committed were really the responsibility of the experimenter who ordered them to deliver the shocks.

The same mentality is often apparent in soldiers and perpetrators of mass atrocities.[61] Fisk and Rai contend that 'the foundational morality of organized armies throughout history and across cultures is simply, "Kill whoever you are ordered to kill whenever you are ordered to kill them, even if you must die trying". ... Soldiers must not make their own private moral decisions ... the duty to obey superiors *is* military morality.'[62]

---

[56] Fiske and Rai, *Virtuous Violence*, p. 93 (emphasis original).
[57] McMahan, *Killing in War*, p. 108.
[58] David Rodin, 'The Moral Inequality of Soldiers', pp. 58–59.
[59] McMahan, *Killing in War*, p. 185.
[60] Milgram, *Obedience to Authority*, p. 10; Ross, 'Situationist Perspectives on the Obedience Experiments', p. 103.
[61] Valentino, *Final Solutions*.
[62] Fiske and Rai, *Virtuous Violence*, pp. 101–102 (emphasis original).

Similarly, one Jewish Holocaust survivor, who worked and lived with German soldiers while serving as an interpreter (under a disguised identity) for German forces during the invasion of the Soviet Union recalled: 'I think that the whole business of anti-Jewish moves, the business of Jewish extermination, they considered unclean. The operations against the partisans were not in the same category. For them a confrontation with the partisans was a battle, a military move. But a move against the Jews was something they might have experienced as "dirty".'[63] These soldiers, in other words, seemed to understand that their actions against Jews were, at least in some sense, wrong, but they complied with their orders to kill nonetheless.

Counteracting the situational pressures to kill when called upon, therefore, would almost certainly require much more than simply discrediting the idea that a soldier does no wrong by agreeing to fight in an unjust war (although that might still be worthwhile). Rather, it would require dismantling the deep social scaffolding that supports not only compliance with political and military leaders in times of war, but many other social structures and institutions that depend on at least some level of moral 'outsourcing' and obedience to authority.

The implications of situationism for the real-world application of individualization are even more profound when we turn to judging the behaviour of combatants ex post, since it is then that considerations of excuse usually matter more. If some of the most important reasons why some people fight in wars and others do not, or why some soldiers perpetrate war crimes and others do not, come down to powerful situational factors outside of the control of individual soldiers, there would seem to be little basis for using these behaviours to decide who deserves to be punished and who should be excused or commended. McMahan seems to recognize this, acknowledging that for 'most people it may be more a matter of luck than anything else that they have not fought in an unjust war. Had they been ordered to by their government, most would have readily followed their country into an unjust war, as others have done throughout history ....'[64] But McMahon concludes that 'part of the explanation for this lies in an idea that we share ... with most people in most cultures at all times in history. This is the idea that one does no wrong, or acts impermissibly, merely by fighting in a war that turns out to be unjust.'[65]

The situationist perspective, however, suggests that the problem runs deeper than McMahon suggests. If situationism is correct, simply persuading people of the abstract principle that it is wrong to fight in a war they believe to be unjust would do relatively little to change behaviour, since situationism explains just how difficult it is for most people to recognize that they are serving on the unjust side.

---

[63] Quoted in Matthäus, 'What about the "Ordinary Men"?', p. 144.
[64] McMahan, *Killing in War*, p. 3.
[65] Ibid.

Indeed, for the same reason, it seems unlikely that the principle of moral equality plays much role in motivating soldiers to fight today—if they are even aware of it.

Although one aim of the individualization of war is to make the ethics and laws of war more consistent with the ways that we think about the use of force in contexts outside of war, it is apparent that the implications of situationism have not been fully incorporated even in those other contexts. As David Rodin writes, although many have argued that soldiers in unjust wars

> are excused by reason of duress or of non-culpable ignorance ... these claims do not cohere with our normal standards of liability in criminal law or interpersonal ethics. Although soldiers at war do face tremendous coercive pressures of various kinds, in many cases this pressure falls short of the threat of execution for those who refuse to fight. Even in cases in which a soldier faces death if he or she does not fight, this may not furnish an excuse of wrongful killing because duress has not traditionally been recognized as an excuse for wrongful homicide in most jurisdictions.[66]

As we have seen, Rodin is correct that most soldiers comply with orders to fight and kill, even when the punishments for refusing are much less severe than execution. While Rodin takes this to mean that there is something wrong with the way we currently judge soldiers in times of wars, situationism suggests that we may have once again underestimated the power of situations and, therefore, that something may instead be wrong with the way we judge individuals—even in domestic contexts. For this reason, a growing number of psychologists, neuroscientists, and legal scholars have begun to argue that most societies may need to fundamentally reorganize their criminal justice systems to account for what we now know about the sources of human behaviour.[67]

The question of exactly how situationism should influence the ways we judge and punish individuals who engage in unjust wars or atrocities is a difficult one. At one extreme, situationism might seem to bleed into a form of radical free will scepticism. This, in turn, could lead to the conclusion that no one—whether in war or in any other context—ought to be held liable or punished for any of their actions, no matter how abhorrent, since whether or not any particular person engaged in those activities is only a matter of unlucky circumstances or genetic factors outside of his or her control.[68] As noted above, however, most psychologists

---

[66] Rodin, 'The Moral Inequality of Soldiers', p. 51.

[67] J Lee Ross and Donna Shestowsky, 'Contemporary Psychology's Challenges to Legal Theory and Practice', *Northwestern University Law Review 97*, no. 3 (2002–2003), pp. 1081–1114; Anders Kaye, 'Does Situationist Psychology Have Radical Implications for Criminal Responsibility', *Alabama Law Review 59*, no. 3 (2008), pp. 611–678; and Joshua Greene and Jonathan Cohen, 'For the Law, Neuroscience Changes Nothing and Everything', *Philosophical Transactions of the Royal Society 359*, no. 1451 (2004), pp. 1775–1785. Also see the Law and Neuroscience Project web page (http://www.lawneuro.org/publications.php) for an extensive bibliography of recent publications on these subjects.

[68] Although criminals might still need to be quarantined or rehabilitated. Luis Chiesa, 'Punishing without Free Will', *Utah Law Review*, no. 4 (2011), pp. 1403–1460.

today do not contend that individuals have no power over their behaviour at all. Even among soldiers in the same units, we often observe a spectrum of behaviour, with some soldiers carrying out their orders reluctantly and shirking whenever possible, while others seem to seek out opportunities to engage in violence and invent new cruelties for their victims.[69] Milgram and Zimbardo observed the same spectrum of behaviours in their experiments. A more moderate interpretation of situationism, therefore, would simply caution us to take the power of situations seriously when evaluating individual moral responsibility and avoid the involuntary but potent tendency to commit the fundamental attribution error when assigning blame and meting out punishment.

In overwhelmingly intense situations like war, this might mean that all but the most extreme perpetrators—those whose behaviour stands out from their peers in the same situations—would ultimately be judged relatively lightly. How to determine the appropriate punishment for such individuals is complicated because, as Doris and Murphy argue,

> Although they are closely connected, the questions of moral responsibility and criminal liability are detachable, and we believe it is in this context [of wartime atrocities] sometimes necessary to detach them, to allow judicial punishment of the most serious offenders, even where they occupy excusing conditions. Unfortunately, this conclusion might be thought no more appealing than exculpation, for imposing criminal liability on those who lack moral responsibility apparently invokes a doctrine of strict liability, and this doctrine has been widely criticized, and reasonably so, by legal theorists. If our conclusion regarding responsibility for atrocity is established, then, an ugly dilemma emerges: we are driven to embrace either exculpation or strict liability.[70]

There is, on the other hand, at least one area in which reckoning with situationism ought to make moral and legal judgements simpler. While the civilians and rank-and-file soldiers who find themselves trapped in the situation of war may be entitled to at least some excuse for their actions, the military and political leaders who knowingly create those situations have much less recourse to a situationist defence. Leaders are hardly immune to situational pressures, but some of the most powerful social and cognitive forces identified by psychologists—such as obedience to authority, peer pressure, diffusion of responsibility, and coercion ought to be significantly attenuated among elites. Nor can leaders evade moral responsibility based on the lack of access to information, since elite decision makers have much greater access to the available information about the justice or injustice of a war than do rank and file combatants.

---

[69] Valentino, *Final Solutions*.

[70] Doris and Murphy, 'From My Lai to Abu Ghraib', p. 28. See also Judith Lichtenberg, 'How to Judge Soldiers Whose Cause Is Unjust', in David Rodin and Henry Shue (eds), *Just and Unjust Warriors* (Oxford: OUP, 2008), pp. 112–130.

It might even be justified to hold wartime leaders at least partly responsible for the actions of all those who were foreseeably influenced by the situations leaders created. This conclusion might hold even in cases in which leaders did not explicitly order their troops to commit atrocities or to violate other *jus in bello* principles—just as Zimbardo did not order his guards to abuse the prisoners in his mock prison. By now, it should be reasonably foreseeable that the situation of war will provoke these kinds of behaviours unless leaders implement extensive measures (probably more extensive than almost any military organization applies today) to prevent them. Indeed, when Zimbardo was called upon in 2004 to testify on behalf of an American soldier accused in the Abu Ghraib prison torture case, he told the court that the entire 'military is on trial, particularly all the officers ... who should have known what was going on, should have prevented it, should have stopped it, and should have challenged it'.[71] If the low-ranking soldier who actually carried out the mistreatment of prisoners was to be punished, Zimbardo argued, 'whatever his sentence is, has to be ... mitigated by the responsibility of the whole chain of command'.[72] If this view is correct, then both traditional just war theory and revisionism may actually *underestimate* the moral culpability of war leaders, both in instigating war and in waging it.

5. Conclusions

The individualization of war agenda has been spurred to a significant degree by its proponents' desires to rectify the perceived injustice of the current ethical and legal principles that govern war. Under current laws and moral theories, soldiers who fight simply to defend themselves and their homelands from aggression are just as liable to attack as soldiers who enthusiastically join the war of aggression on the other side. Meanwhile, civilians who incite others into fighting or even goad them to commit atrocities, receive the same protections from attack as civilians who take to the streets to protest an unjust war. Situationism, however, cautions that adopting laws and principles of individualization that do not take the power of situational factors adequately into account could risk trading one kind of injustice for another.

As Harman writes, ordinary moral intuitions, which privilege dispositions over situations, often have 'deplorable results, leading to massive misunderstanding of other people, promoting unnecessary hostility between individuals and groups, distorting discussions of law and public policy'.[73] Indeed, evidence from public opinion polls suggests that the public is likely to fall victim to the fundamental

---

[71] Philip Zimbardo, *The Lucifer Effect: Understanding How Good People Turn Evil* (New York: Random House, 2007), p. 381.
[72] Ibid.
[73] Harman, 'Moral Philosophy Meets Social Psychology', p. 330.

attribution error when evaluating the wartime behaviour of soldiers. In a survey experiment conducted with Scott Sagan, for example, I found that Americans were just as likely to judge the behaviour of soldiers in a hypothetical unjust war as unethical when the soldiers were described as enthusiastic volunteers as when they were described as reluctant conscripts—even though soldiers on both sides adhered to *jus in bello* rules.[74] More than 56 per cent of subjects supported prison terms for the soldiers who had volunteered for the unjust war, as did 48 per cent for the conscripts. Perhaps more disturbingly, 40 per cent of subjects approved of executing the volunteer soldiers for their participation in the unjust war, as did 22 per cent even when the soldiers were described as unenthusiastic conscripts. Revisionists like McMahan explicitly reject these kinds of punishments, but these findings suggest that we may not be able to trust real-world justice to match the prescriptions of revisionist theory.[75]

Incorporating the insights of situationism into the law and ethics of war is complicated both in theory and in practice. Theoretically, it will be difficult to allow situationism to revise our views of moral responsibility without doing away with responsibility altogether. Practically, situationists have offered few clear solutions for countering the power of situations to induce or facilitate immoral behaviour. Moral education might seem to provide one attractive way out, but the evidence that education can produce meaningful changes in moral behaviour is mixed at best. One meta-analysis of twenty-five business ethics programmes, for example, concluded that that 'business ethics instructional programs have a minimal impact on increasing outcomes related to ethical perceptions, behavior, or awareness.'[76] In fact, despite mandatory ethics training in most business schools, business students appear to cheat significantly more than their non-business school peers.[77] Even moral philosophers do not seem to behave more ethically than their peers in other subfields of philosophy or in unrelated departments, and they are no more likely to avoid common cognitive traps in moral reasoning.[78]

---

[74] Scott Sagan and Benjamin Valentino, 'Just War and Unjust Soldiers: American Public Opinion on the Moral Equality of Combatants', *Ethics and International Affairs 33*, no. 4 (2019), pp. 411–444.

[75] Jeff McMahan, 'Rethinking the "Just War," Part 2', *The New York Times*, 12 November 2012. Available at: http://opinionator.blogs.nytimes.com/2012/11/12/rethinking-the-just-war-part-2/ (Accessed: 30 August 2016).

[76] Ethan P. Waples et al., 'Meta-Analytic Investigation of Business Ethics Instruction', *Journal of Business Ethics 87*, no. 1 (2009), pp. 133–151. See also Ronald D. Jewe, 'Do Business Ethics Courses Work? The Effectiveness of Business Ethics Education: An Empirical Study', *The Journal of Global Business Issues*, no. 1 (2008), pp. 1–6; and James Konow, 'Does Studying Ethics Affect Moral Views? An Application to Economic Justice', *Journal of Economic Methodology 24*, no. 2, (2017), pp. 190–203.

[77] Donald L. McCabe, Kenneth D. Butterfield, and Linda Klebe Trevino, 'Academic Dishonesty in Graduate Business Programs: Prevalence, Causes, and Proposed Action', *Academy of Management Learning and Education 5*, no. 3 (2006), pp. 294–305.

[78] Eric Schwitzgebel and Joshua Rust, 'The Moral Behavior of Ethics Professors: Relationships among Self-Reported Behavior, Expressed Normative Attitude, and Directly Observed Behavior', *Philosophical Psychology 27*, no. 3 (2014), pp. 293–327; and Eric Schwitzgebel and Fiery Cushman, 'Expertise in Moral Reasoning? Order Effects on Moral Judgment in Professional Philosophers and Non-Philosophers', *Mind & Language 27*, no. 2 (2012), pp. 135–153.

156 SITUATIONISM AND INDIVIDUALIZATION OF RESPONSIBILITY IN WAR

If situations frequently have the power to override individual moral judgement, as situationists claim, perhaps it should not be surprising that interventions at the individual level have not proved widely effective. Rather, situationism suggests that we would do better to focus our efforts on restructuring the situations and institutions that encourage immoral behaviour in the first place. Phillip Zimbardo calls this approach fixing the 'bad barrel', rather than attempting to remove the 'bad apples'.[79] In practice, this might mean restructuring military organizations to ensure divisions of authority at all levels to prevent any one person from commanding total obedience. More generally, it might mean encouraging greater diversity among peer groups to prevent destructive conformity and peer pressure.

The risk of embracing a policy of individualism untempered by situationism is not merely that society might judge and punish some soldiers too harshly, but also that soldiers might judge themselves by the same excessive standards. In her interviews with American soldiers on the ethics of war, Nancy Sherman found that soldiers do 'feel morally accountable not just for how they fight but what they fight for. They feel accountable for their participation in the collective end that defines a particular war .... Soldiers actually do struggle hard with their individual accountability for participating in a war of others' making.'[80] Relating the story of one American veteran of the Vietnam War, Sherman writes, 'because of the war he fought, he feels contaminated. His assessment of himself, and how he views others assessing him, are wrapped up with moral luck and a coerced choice.'[81] Situationism suggests that this soldier's pain and self-doubt are likely symptoms of the fundamental attribution error—an error both he and society have made. Worse, his efforts and those of the rest of society to individualize his responsibility for participating in the war may detract from the effort to hold responsible those military and political leaders who created the situation whose effects we are still grappling with today.

References

Baskir, L. and Strauss, W. (1978) *Chance and Circumstance: The Draft, the War, and the Vietnam Generation.* New York: Vintage Books.
Batson, C.D. et al. (1978) 'Failure to Help When in a Hurry: Callousness or Conflict?', *Personality and Social Psychology Bulletin*, 4(1), pp. 97–101. doi: 10.1177/014616727800400120.

---

[79] Zimbardo, *The Lucifer Effect.*
[80] Nancy Sherman, *The Untold War: Inside the Hearts, Minds, and Souls of Our Soldiers* (New York: WW Norton, 2010), pp. 41–45. See also Brett T. Litz et al., 'Moral Injury and Moral Repair in War Veterans: A Preliminary Model and Intervention Strategy', *Clinical Psychology Review 29*, no. 8 (2009), pp. 695–706.
[81] Sherman, *The Untold War*, p. 53.

Bloxham, D. (2008) 'The Organisation of Genocide: Perpetration in Comparative Perspective', in O. Jensen and C.C.W. Szejnmann (eds), *Ordinary People as Mass Murderers: Perpetrators in Comparative Perspectives*. London: Palgrave Macmillan (The Holocaust and Its Contexts), pp. 185–200. doi: 10.1057/9780230583566_9.

Browning, C.R. (1992) *Ordinary Men: Reserve Police Battalion 101 and the Final Solution in Poland*. New York: HarperCollins.

Burger, J.M. (2009) 'Replicating Milgram: Would People Still Obey Today?', *The American Psychologist*, 64(1), pp. 1–11. doi: 10.1037/a0010932.

Chandler, D.P. (1999) *Voices from S-21: Terror and History in Pol Pot's Secret Prison*. Berkeley: University of California Press.

Chiesa, L.E. (2011) 'Punishing Without Free Will', *Utah Law Review*, 4, pp. 1403–1460.

Darley, J.M. and Batson, C.D. (1973) '"From Jerusalem to Jericho": A Study of Situational and Dispositional Variables in Helping Behavior', *Journal of Personality and Social Psychology*, 27(1), pp. 100–108. doi: 10.1037/h0034449.

Doliński, D. et al. (2017) 'Would You Deliver an Electric Shock in 2015? Obedience in the Experimental Paradigm Developed by Stanley Milgram in the 50 Years Following the Original Studies', *Social Psychological and Personality Science*, 8(8), pp. 927–933. doi: 10.1177/1948550617693060.

Doris, J.M. (1998) 'Persons, Situations, and Virtue Ethics', *Noûs*, 32(4), pp. 504–530. doi: https://doi.org/10.1111/0029-4624.00136.

Doris, J.M. (2005) *Lack of Character: Personality and Moral Behavior*. Cambridge: Cambridge University Press.

Doris, J.M. and Murphy, D. (2007) 'From My Lai to Abu Ghraib: The Moral Psychology of Atrocity', *Midwest Studies in Philosophy*, 31(1), pp. 25–55. doi: 10.1111/j.1475-4975.2007.00149.x.

Dyer, G. (1985) *War*. New York: Crown Publishers.

Elms, A.C. (1995) 'Obedience in Retrospect', *Journal of Social Issues*, 51(3), pp. 21–31. doi: 10.1111/j.1540-4560.1995.tb01332.x.

Feinberg, J. (1968) 'Collective Responsibility', *The Journal of Philosophy*, 65(21), pp. 674–688. doi: 10.2307/2024543.

Feldman, Y. (2018) *The Law of Good People: Challenging States' Ability to Regulate Human Behavior* (1 online resource vol). Cambridge: Cambridge University Press.

Fiske, A.P. and Rai, T.S. (2014) *Virtuous Violence: Hurting and Killing to Create, Sustain, End, and Honor Social Relationships*. Cambridge: Cambridge University Press. doi: 10.1017/CBO9781316104668.

Ford Foundation (1974) *Amnesty—Ford Foundation Study of Effects of Vietnam on Veterans, Deserters and Evaders*. Ann Arbor: Gerald R. Ford Library.

Friedman, R. (2006) '"The Challenge of Selective Conscientious Objection in Israel", *Theoria: A Journal of Social and Political Theory*, no. 109, pp. 79–99.

Griggs, R. and Whitehead, G. (2015) 'Coverage of Recent Criticisms of Milgram's Obedience Experiments in Introductory Social Psychology Textbooks', *Theory and Psychology*, 25(5), pp. 564–580.

Grossman, D. (1995) *On Killing: The Psychological Cost of Learning to Kill in War and Society*. London: Black Bay Books.

Harman, G. (1999) 'Moral Philosophy Meets Social Psychology: Virtue Ethics and the Fundamental Attribution Error', *Proceedings of the Aristotelian Society*, 99, pp. 315–331.

Harris, D. (2017) 'I Picked Prison over Fighting in Vietnam', *The New York Times*, 23 June. Available at: https://www.nytimes.com/2017/06/23/opinion/vietnam-war-draft-protests.html (Accessed: 13 March 2021).

Hartshorn, H. and May, M.A. (1928) *Studies in the Nature of Character I: Studies in Deceit*. New York: Macmillan.

Holmes, R. (1986) *Acts of War: The Behavior of Men in Battle*. New York: Free Press.

Jewe, R.D. (2008) 'Do Business Ethics Courses Work? The Effectiveness of Business Ethics Education: An Empirical Study', *Journal of Global Business Issues*, 2 (1), pp. 1–6.

Jones, E. (1979) 'The Rocky Road from Acts to Dispositions', *The American Psychologist*, 34(2), pp. 107–117.

Jones, J.M. (2007) 'Latest Poll Shows High Point in Opposition to Iraq War', *Gallup*. Available at: https://news.gallup.com/poll/28099/Latest-Poll-Shows-High-Point-Opposition-Iraq-War.aspx (Accessed: 13 March 2021).

Kamtekar, R. (2004) 'Situationism and Virtue Ethics on the Content of Our Character', *Ethics*, 114(3), pp. 458–491.

Kaye, A. (2007) 'Does Situationist Psychology Have Radical Implications for Criminal Responsibility?', *Alabama Law Review*, 59(3), pp. 611–678.

Kellett, A. (1982) *Combat Motivation: The Behavior of Soldiers in Battle*. Boston: Kluwer-Nijhoff Pub (International series in management science/operations research).

Konow, J. (2017) 'Does Studying Ethics Affect Moral Views? An Application to Economic Justice', *Journal of Economic Methodology*, 24(2), pp. 190–203. doi: 10.1080/1350178X.2017.1309812.

Laqueur, W. (1977) *The Guerrilla Reader: A Historical Anthology*. Philadelphia: Temple University Press.

Lazar, S. (2017) 'Just War Theory: Revisionists Versus Traditionalists', *Annual Review of Political Science*, 20(1), pp. 37–54. doi: 10.1146/annurev-polisci-060314-112706.

Litz, B.T. et al. (2009) 'Moral Injury and Moral Repair in War Veterans: A Preliminary Model and Intervention Strategy', *Clinical Psychology Review*, 29(8), pp. 695–706. doi: 10.1016/j.cpr.2009.07.003.

Lovibond, S.H., Mithiran and Adams, W.G. (1979) 'The Effects of Three Experimental Prison Environments on the Behaviour of Non-Convict Volunteer Subjects', *Australian Psychologist*, 14(3), pp. 273–287. doi: https://doi.org/10.1080/00050067908254355.

Marshall, S.L.A. (1947) *Men against Fire*. New York: William Morrow.

Matthäus, J. (1996) 'What About the "Ordinary Men"?: The German Order Police and the Holocaust in the Occupied Soviet Union', *Holocaust and Genocide Studies*, 10(2), pp. 134–150. doi: 10.1093/hgs/10.2.134.

McCabe, D.L., Butterfield, K.D. and Treviño, L.K. (2006) 'Academic Dishonesty in Graduate Business Programs: Prevalence, Causes, and Proposed Action', *Academy of Management Learning & Education*, 5(3), pp. 294–305.

McMahan, J. (2009) *Killing in War*. Oxford: Oxford University Press.

Meeus, W.H.J. and Raaijmakers, Q.A.W. (1995) 'Obedience in Modern Society: The Utrecht Studies', *Journal of Social Issues*, 51(3), pp. 155–175. doi: 10.1111/j.1540-4560.1995.tb01339.x.

Milgram, S. (1974) *Obedience to Authority: An Experimental View*. New York: Harper & Row.

Miller, A.G. (1986) *The Obedience Experiments: A Case Study of Controversy in Social Science.* New York: Praeger (Praeger special studies).

Mischel, W. (1968) *Personality and Assessment.* New York: Wiley (Series in psychology).

Nisbett, R.E. and Wilson, T.D. (1977) 'Telling More than We Can Know: Verbal Reports on Mental Processes', *Psychological Review*, 84(3), pp. 231–259. doi: 10.1037//0033-295X.84.3.231.

Ring, K., Wallston, K.A., and Cory, M. (1970) 'Mode of Debriefing as a Factor Affecting Subjective Reactions to a Milgram-Type Experiment: An Ethical Inquiry', *Representative Research in Social Psychology*, 1 (1), pp. 67–88.

Rodin, D. and Shue, H. (2008) *Just and Unjust Warriors: The Moral and Legal Status of Soldiers.* Oxford: Oxford University Press.

Ross, L. (1977) 'The Intuitive Psychologist and His Shortcomings: Distortions in the Attribution Process', *Advances in Experimental Social Psychology*, 10, pp. 173–220. doi: 10.1016/S0065-2601(08)60357-3.

Ross, L.D. (1988) 'Situationist Perspectives on the Obedience Experiments', *Contemporary Psychology: A Journal of Reviews*, 33(2), pp. 101–104. doi: 10.1037/025376.

Ross, L. and Shestowsky, D. (2002) 'Contemporary Psychology's Challenges to Legal Theory and Practice Empirical Legal Realism: A New Social Scientific Assessment of Law and Human Behavior', *Northwestern University Law Review*, 97(3), pp. 1081–1114.

Ross, Lee. and Nisbett, R. E. (1991) *The Person and the Situation: Perspectives of Social Psychology.* Philadelphia: Temple University Press.

Sabini, J. and Silver, M. (2005) 'Lack of Character? Situationism Critiqued', *Ethics*, 115(3), pp. 535–562. doi: 10.1086/428459.

Sagan, S.D. and Valentino, B.A. (2019) 'Just War and Unjust Soldiers: American Public Opinion on the Moral Equality of Combatants', *Ethics & International Affairs*, 33(4), pp. 411–444. doi: 10.1017/S0892679419000431.

Schwitzgebel, E. and Cushman, F. (2012) 'Expertise in Moral Reasoning? Order Effects on Moral Judgment in Professional Philosophers and Non-Philosophers', *Mind & Language*, 27(2), pp. 135–153. doi: 10.1111/j.1468-0017.2012.01438.x.

Schwitzgebel, E. and Rust, J. (2014) 'The Moral Behavior of Ethics Professors: Relationships among Self-Reported Behavior, Expressed Normative Attitude, and Directly Observed Behavior', *Philosophical Psychology*, 27(3), pp. 293–327. doi: 10.1080/09515089.2012.727135.

Sherman, N. (2010) *The Untold War: Inside the Hearts, Minds, and Souls of Our Soldiers.* New York: WW Norton.

Shils, E.A. and Janowitz, M. (1948) 'Cohesion and Disintegration in the Wehrmacht in World War II', *The Public Opinion Quarterly*, 12(2), pp. 280–315.

Upton, C.L. (2009) 'Virtue Ethics and Moral Psychology: The Situationism Debate', *The Journal of Ethics*, 13(2–3), pp. 103–115.

Valentino, B.A. (2004) *Final Solutions: Mass Killing and Genocide in the Twentieth Century.* Ithaca, NY: Cornell University Press (Cornell studies in security affairs).

Vranas, P.B.M. (2005) 'The Indeterminacy Paradox: Character Evaluations and Human Psychology', *Noûs*, 39(1), pp. 1–42.

Walzer, M. (1977) *Just and Unjust Wars.* New York: Basic Books.

Walzer, M. (2006) 'Response to McMahan's Paper', *Philosophia*, 34(1), pp. 43–45.

Walzer, M. (2006) 'Terrorism and Just War', *Philosophia*, 34(1), pp. 3–12. doi: 10.1007/s11406-006-9004-1.

Waples, E.P. et al. (2009) 'A Meta-Analytic Investigation of Business Ethics Instruction', *Journal of Business Ethics*, 87(1), pp. 133–151.

Zimbardo, P. et al. (1975) 'The Psychology of Imprisonment: Privation, Power and Pathology", in David L. Rosenhan and Perry London (eds), *Theory and Research in Abnormal Psychology*. New York: Holt, Rinehart and Winston, pp. 270–287.

Zimbardo, P. (1995) 'The Psychology of Evil: A Situationist Perspective on Recruiting Good People to Engage in Anti-Social Acts', *Research in Social Psychology,* 11(2), pp. 125–133.

Zimbardo, P. (2007) The Lucifer Effect: Understanding How Good People Turn Evil. New York: Random House.

PART III
THE CONSEQUENCES OF INDIVIDUALIZATION

6

The Individualization of IHL Rules through Criminalization for War Crimes

Some (Un)Intended Consequences

Paola Gaeta and Abhimanyu George Jain

1. Introduction

Violations of rules of international humanitarian law (IHL) primarily implicate the responsibility of the parties to the conflict,[1] usually states and non-state armed groups.[2] However, paraphrasing the well-known dictum of the International Military Tribunal at Nuremberg, wars are waged, and the rules of IHL are implemented, by '[people], not by abstract entities'.[3] Transgressions of some rules of IHL, therefore, may also give rise to the international criminal responsibility of individuals under war crimes charges. Consequently, certain unlawful conduct in warfare could trigger two different forms of international responsibility: the responsibility of the relevant party to the conflict, if the conduct in question violates a rule of IHL and the violation is attributable to that party to the conflict, and the international criminal responsibility of the individual, to the extent that this conduct also constitutes the material element (*actus reus*) of a war crime and is carried out with the required mental element (*mens rea*).

Notwithstanding the fact that these two forms of responsibility arguably perform different functions (the former—restorative, the latter—retributive) and are

---

[1] In its decision on the defence's jurisdictional appeal, the Appeals Chamber of the International Criminal tribunal for the Former Yugoslavia (ICTY) defined an armed conflict in the following terms: 'an armed conflict exists whenever there is a resort to armed force between States or protracted armed violence between governmental authorities and organized armed groups or between such groups within a State.' See, *Prosecutor v Duško Tadić, IT-94-1-A (Decision on the Defence Motion for Interlocutory Appeal on Jurisdiction)* (International Criminal Tribunal for the Former Yugoslavia) [70].

[2] In the field of the international responsibility of the parties to an armed conflict, a key outstanding issue includes enhancing the enforcement of the regime of state responsibility in light of the weakness of existing institutional mechanisms and the progressive ban on decentralized means in the form of belligerent reprisals. Given the increased participation of contemporary non-state armed actors in so-called asymmetric warfare, the discussion is also open as to the identification of the applicable regime for their international responsibility when they commit violations of the relevant rules of IHL in the course of a non-international armed conflict.

[3] *The Trial of German Major War Criminals* (1946) 22 Proceedings of the International Military Tribunal Sitting at Nuremberg, p. 447.

Paola Gaeta and Abhimanyu George Jain, *The Individualization of IHL Rules through Criminalization for War Crimes*. In: *The Individualization of War*. Edited by: Jennifer Welsh, Dapo Akande, and David Rodin, Oxford University Press. © Paola Gaeta and Abhimanyu George Jain (2023). DOI: 10.1093/oso/9780192872203.003.0007

164 INDIVIDUALIZATION OF IHL RULES THROUGH CRIMINALIZATION

subject to different sets of rules and standards of evidence before a competent court or tribunal, they coexist and apply in parallel to the same conduct. Their relationship has sparked vivid scholarly debate in the context of the general discussion on the relationship between state and individual responsibility under international law. At the same time, at least under the scheme of key IHL treaties such as the 1949 Geneva Conventions (individually GC I, GC II, GC III, and GC IV, and collectively GCs)[4] and the 1977 Additional Protocol I (AP I),[5] the criminal responsibility of individuals for war crimes is expressly provided for only with respect to a specific set of unlawful behaviours, the so-called 'grave breaches'. The High Contracting Parties are subject to specific obligations relating to the repression through criminal sanction of persons allegedly responsible for a grave breach, while in relation to other breaches of the GCs and AP I they are allowed discretion to 'take measures necessary for ... [their] ... suppression'.[6] By contrast, the international responsibility of the relevant state party to the conflict may arise for the violation of *any* rule contained therein. This is made explicit in a common provision of the GCs, whereby the High Contracting Parties are not allowed to absolve themselves of any liability incurred in respect of violations of these Conventions.[7] The same principle is also enunciated in Article 3 of the Hague Convention (IV) of 1907 (HC IV) and in Article 91 of AP I, according to which a High Contracting Party is responsible for the violations of the rules of the Conventions and the Protocol that are attributable to it. This responsibility persists regardless of whether the unlawful conduct may give rise to criminal responsibility for war crimes and individual authors have been punished. In other words, under relevant IHL treaties, state responsibility provides the primary consequence in case of transgressions, while the individual criminal responsibility for war crimes supplements the former and is only mandatory for the so-called grave breaches.

In recent decades, however, the establishment of modern international and 'mixed' criminal courts and tribunals and the emergence of the so-called 'fight

---

[4] Geneva Convention for the Amelioration of the Condition of the Wounded and Sick in Armed Forces in the Field 1949 (75 UNTS 31) (GC I); Geneva Convention for the Amelioration of the Condition of Wounded, Sick and Shipwrecked Members of Armed Forces at Sea 1949 (75 UNTS 85) (GC II); Geneva Convention Relative to the Treatment of Prisoners of War 1949 (75 UNTS 135) (GC III); Geneva Convention Relative to the Protection of Civilian Persons in Time of War 1949 (75 UNTS 287) (GC IV).

[5] Protocol Additional to the Geneva Conventions of 12 August 1949, and Relating to the Protection of Victims of International Armed Conflicts 1977 (1125 UNTS 3) (AP I).

[6] GCs, Common Article 49/50/129/146; AP I, Article 85. In relation to grave breaches, states parties are required to criminalize the underlying conduct and prosecute or extradite the perpetrators of such conduct. See also, Theodor Méron, 'International Criminalisation of Internal Atrocities', *The American Journal of International Law 89*, no. 3 (1995), pp. 554–577, at p. 564. The International Committee of the Red Cross has noted that although states have discretion as to the means of suppression of other breaches, an increasing number of states apply criminal sanction to a number of other breaches: Knut Dörmann and others (eds), *Commentary on the Second Geneva Convention: Convention (II) for the Amelioration of the Condition of Wounded, Sick, and Shipwrecked Members of Armed Forces at Sea* (Cambridge: CUP, 2017), paras 3006–3007.

[7] GCs, Common Article 49(3)/50(3)/129(3)/146(3).

against impunity' paradigm, have contributed to emphasizing the importance of criminal repression of violations of IHL. Individualization of guilt for wartime atrocities and other atrocity crimes has been suggested as being more suitable than collective forms of responsibility such as state responsibility by reference to a variety of reasons.[8] At the same time, there are scholars who underline that focusing on individual criminal responsibility as the primary means of enforcement of IHL fails to capture the systemic dimension of war crimes and other atrocity crimes.[9] These scholars therefore warn that state responsibility and other forms of collective responsibility should not be left behind, since they reflect the structural nature of wartime atrocities and other atrocity crimes better than individualization of guilt through criminal law.

This chapter intends to contribute to this debate from a different perspective. After sketching the origins of the process of individualization of IHL rules through individual responsibility for war crimes (§2), it will explain the acceleration of the process in recent decades (§3). It will then explain which requirements have been identified to ground individualization of IHL rules through the notion of war crimes (§4). The chapter will finally draw out some of the tensions produced by this process, focusing upon some of its consequences for the relevant IHL norms (§5).

The argument presented in this chapter is not against the individualization of IHL norms through individual criminal responsibility for war crimes. It is an argument against reckless enthusiasm for the process of individualization and an argument for consideration of what is lost in this process. In this endeavour, this chapter sits within the broader theme of the tensions of individualization outlined in the Introduction to this volume.

---

[8] These include facilitating reconciliation and longer-lasting peace among groups or nations once at war. Shifting the focus onto the individuals may have a cathartic or healing effect: it helps the victims of atrocities committed in wartime to understand that 'the enemy' as an abstract and collective entity did not commit them. The additional seed of hatred against the enemy group or nation that the notion of 'collective' guilt may plant may thus have no reason to grow. In addition, holding criminally accountable those who violate the rules of IHL in wartime is propounded as a more 'just' means of enforcement than resorting to collective responsibility, in the form of reparation or reprisals. Only the alleged culprit will suffer the negative consequences of illegal behaviour. The individualization of guilt through criminal punishment for violations of the rules of IHL is therefore presented as more consonant with the notion of responsibility developed in modern legal systems, which is a notion of personal rather than collective responsibility. In this sense, individual criminal responsibility is seen as contributing to the increasing sophistication of the international legal systems in line with developments in national legal orders. See, e.g., Marco Sassòli, 'Humanitarian Law and International Criminal Law', in Antonio Cassese (ed.), *The Oxford Companion to International Criminal Justice* (Oxford: OUP, 2009), p. 113.

[9] See, e.g., Frédéric Mégret, 'International Criminal Justice: A Critical Research Agenda', in Christine E.J. Schwöbel (ed.), *Critical Approaches to International Criminal Law: An Introduction* (New York: Routledge, 2014), pp. 28–30.

2. The Origins of Individualization through Criminalization

Individualization of IHL rules through individualization of responsibility for their violations is at the core of the concept of war crimes. Until the Second World War, the traditional position had always been that the prosecution of individuals responsible for violations of IHL through war crimes charges was restricted to municipal law and had to be based in criminalization of the impugned conduct under IHL in the relevant domestic system.[10] The notion that rules of international law could directly provide the basis for criminal punishment of individuals allegedly responsible for their transgression was alien to international law. Though the Versailles peace treaty concluded at the end of the First World War contemplated the criminal trial of the German Kaiser for the crime of aggression under *international law*,[11] there was still significant discomfort with the idea of the criminalization of the waging of war in international law.[12] Indeed, the Australian Prime Minister argued that persons could not be tried for 'making war', and equated the criminalization of war with 'treason against mankind'.[13] Eventually, the contemplated trial of the Kaiser did not take place as planned, owing to the refusal of the Netherlands, where he had sought refuge, to extradite him.[14]

The International Military Tribunal at Nuremberg and the International Military Tribunal for the Far East represented a significant but exceptional instance of the trial of individuals for war crimes under international law. These tribunals drew on international law prohibitions which applied to states and extended them to individuals charged with war crimes by referring to the necessity of states acting through individuals.[15] This conversion of prohibitions on state conduct

---

[10] This characterization of the history of war crimes law is advisedly referred to the 'traditional' understanding. While Nuremberg and Tokyo may reasonably be seen as the starting points of modern war crimes law, having been reified as such by convention and usage, there are broader and more critical histories of the idea and practice of 'internationalized' war crimes trials. See, e.g., Kevin Jon Heller and Gerry J. Simpson (eds), *The Hidden Histories of War Crimes Trials* (Oxford: OUP, 2013); Immi Tallgren and Thomas Skouteris (eds), *The New Histories of International Criminal Law: Retrials* (Oxford: OUP, 2019).

[11] Article 227 of the Versailles peace treaty provides: 'The Allied and Associated Powers publicly arraign William II of Hohenzollern, formerly German Emperor, for a supreme offence against international morality and the sanctity of treaties.' Article 227 contemplated the establishment of a special tribunal comprising five members, one each from the United States, Great Britain, France, Italy, and Japan, to try the Kaiser. In contrast, criminal jurisdiction over other 'acts in violation of the laws and customs of war' was vested in the military tribunals of the Allied and Associated Powers. See, Treaty of Peace Between the British Empire, France, Italy, Japan and the United States (the Principal Allied and Associated Powers), and Belgium, Bolivia, Brazil, China, Cuba, Czechoslovakia, Ecuador, Greece, Guatemala, Haiti, the Hedjaz, Honduras, Liberia, Nicaragua, Panama, Peru, Poland, Portugal, Roumania, the Serb-Croat-Slovene State, Siam, and Uruguay, and Germany, Signed at Versailles 1919 (225 CTS 188).

[12] Gerry J. Simpson, *Law, War and Crime: War Crimes Trials and the Reinvention of International Law* (Cambridge: Polity, 2007), pp. 124–125.

[13] Gerry J. Simpson, 'NM 68226 84912; TQ 30052 80597', in Jessie Hohmann and Daniel Joyce (eds), *International Law's Objects* (Oxford: OUP, 2018), p. 301.

[14] William Schabas, *The Trial of the Kaiser* (Oxford: OUP, 2018), pp. 4, 266–291.

[15] *Supra* note 3 and accompanying text.

into individual crimes—the individualization of IHL norms—was one of the key analytical contributions of these tribunals.

The developments at Nuremberg and Tokyo were then taken further in the national trials conducted after the Second World War. In some countries of civil law tradition, these trials encountered the significant obstacle that the relevant national laws did not criminalize the impugned conduct at the time of their commission, leading to the passage of ad hoc criminal legislation. The idea of prohibition/criminalization in international law applied at the Nuremberg and Tokyo Tribunals was therefore crucial to circumventing the challenge of retroactive application of criminal law and violation of the principle of legality in criminal matters.[16] The inclusion of provisions for the criminal repression of the so-called grave breaches in the newly adopted 1949 GCs also served the purpose of legitimizing those national trials, 'recognizing' that these trials were in conformity with international law.[17] At the same time, the permissibility of international law as a basis for criminalization was confirmed by Article 7(1) of the European Convention on Human Rights, entered into in 1950, a mere few years after the end of the Second World War and the first modern war crimes trials.[18]

The grave breaches provisions incorporated in the GCs, however, did not go so far as to envisage the direct criminalization of those breaches. Under the GCs, criminal repression of grave breaches rests in the hand of national jurisdictions, based on their domestic criminal legislation. Even the choice to refer to the punishable unlawful conducts as 'grave breaches' instead of 'war crimes' signals that the drafters of the GCs did not seek to enact criminal law provisions. Some delegations also expressly noted that the GCs' provisions on grave breaches were insufficiently detailed to work on their own as a criminal code on which to ground directly criminal charges against allegedly responsible individuals. In 1977, AP I, in expanding the list of grave breaches, expressly declared that those breaches had to be considered as 'war crimes' but did not alter the scheme of the GCs on the topic. The international provisions on grave breaches still needed to be implemented and complemented by national criminal rules and were not intended to form the direct basis of criminal charges.

It was the establishment of the two UN ad hoc Tribunals for the former Yugoslavia (ICTY) and Rwanda (ICTR) that continued and developed the legacy of the Nuremberg and Tokyo trials. The UN Security Council created these two Tribunals to punish those allegedly responsible for, inter alia, serious violations

---

[16] See amplius, Paola Gaeta, 'Grave Breaches of the Geneva Conventions', in Andrew Clapham, Paola Gaeta, and Marco Sassòli (eds), *The 1949 Geneva Conventions: A Commentary* (Oxford: OUP, 2015), pp. 617–620.

[17] Ibid.

[18] A similar reliance was placed on Article 15(2) of the International Covenant on Civil and Political Rights by the Mucić trial chamber in response to a legality challenge by the defence: *Prosecutor v Zdravko Mucić et al. (Trial Chamber)* [1998] International Criminal Tribunal for the Former Yugoslavia IT-96-21-T [313].

of IHL. The jurisdiction of the ICTY therefore included both grave breaches of the GCs (Article 2 of the ICTY Statute)[19] and violations of the laws and customs of war (Article 3). By contrast, in light of the non-international nature of the armed conflict in Rwanda, the jurisdiction of the ICTR comprised serious violations of Article 3 common to the GCs and of Additional Protocol II (AP II)[20] (Article 4 of the ICTR Statute).[21] Since these developments, followed by the adoption of the Rome Statute for the International Criminal Court (ICC) and a host of other international and 'mixed' criminal courts and tribunals, it is widely recognized that international rules alone can constitute the basis for criminal punishment including for violations of the rules of IHL through the concept of war crimes.

3. The Progressive Criminalization of Violations of IHL Rules

The ICTY, and subsequent international criminal courts and tribunals building upon its jurisprudence, have been particularly prolific in the ascription of individual criminal responsibility for violations of IHL rules. Increasingly, these courts and tribunals have construed 'serious' violations of IHL rules[22] as war crimes implicating the international criminal responsibility of individuals.

The most emblematic instance of this is the construal of Common Article 3 of the GCs as giving rise to individual criminal responsibility by the ICTY. Common Article 3 of the GCs provides a baseline of minimum guarantees which operate in non-international armed conflicts, and was, until AP II, the only source of IHL regulation of such conflicts. In a line of cases starting with the interlocutory jurisdictional appeal in *Tadić*, the ICTY refuted the long-held notion that war crimes can only be committed in international armed conflicts, and concluded that violations of Common Article 3 entailed individual criminal responsibility.[23] Another

---

[19] Statute of the International Criminal Tribunal for the Former Yugoslavia 1993, Article 2 (ICTY Statute).

[20] Protocol Additional to the Geneva Conventions of 12 August 1949, and Relating to the Protection of Victims of Non-International Armed Conflicts 1977 (1125 UNTS 609) (AP II).

[21] Statute of the International Criminal Tribunal for Rwanda 1994, Article 4 (ICTR Statute).

[22] On the definition of 'seriousness' as a criterion for construing breach of an IHL rule as a war crime, see, §4 below.

[23] ICTY—*Tadić jurisdiction* (n 1), paras 87–137, and in particular, paras 128–136. The *Tadić* interlocutory appeal concerned, amongst other things, the scope of the jurisdiction *ratione materiae* of the ICTY. The question in dispute was whether the accused could be held responsible for war crimes perpetrated in the context of an armed conflict of a non-international character (as, at that time, the conflict in Bosnia-Herzegovina was considered to be). The Appeals Chamber answered this question in the affirmative. It did so by adopting an expansive interpretation of Article 3 of the Statute of the ICTY, which conferred on the tribunal jurisdiction over 'persons violating the laws or customs of war' without referring to the international and non-international nature of the armed conflict where such violations occurred. This opened the door to the assertion by the Appeals Chamber that there were rules of customary international law governing non-international armed conflicts and that Common Article 3 of the GCs (*rectius*: the rule of customary international law derived from Common Article 3) was one of them. This, in turn, formed the basis for the significant and subsequent assertion that under

example is the decision in *Galić*, where an ICTY Trial Chamber, drawing upon the prohibition of attacks intended to induce terror amongst civilian populations in customary and conventional international law,[24] defined the war crime of terrorizing attacks.[25] Yet another example is the decision of the ICTY in *Mrkšić et al*, where the Trial Chamber interpreted the Common Article 3 proscription of cruel treatment by reference to Article 13 of GC III.[26] The latter refers to the obligation of the High Contracting Parties to ensure the humane treatment of prisoners of war at all times. In *Mrkšić et al*, the ICTY converted this obligation incumbent on states into an obligation incumbent on individuals, regardless of their ability to effect changes in their states' detention policy of prisoners of war.[27]

These are not isolated examples. Across its jurisprudence, the ICTY has had occasion to refer to a broad range of IHL norms across the GCs, AP I, AP II, and the Regulations annexed to HC IV (HC IV Regulations),[28] and construe violations of their provisions as war crimes. For instance, in *Mucić et al* alone, an ICTY Trial Chamber interpreted the grave breach of wilful killing and the Common Article 3 violation of murder by reference to Article 32 of GC IV and Article 85 of AP I;[29] it interpreted the grave breach of torture to include rape by reference to Article 27 of GC IV, Article 76(1) of AP I, Article 4 of AP II, and Article 46 of the HC IV Regulations;[30] it interpreted the grave breach of inhumane treatment by reference to Article 12 of GC I, Article 12 of GC II, Articles 13, 20, 46, and 89 of GC III, Articles 27, 32, 119, and 147 of GC IV, Article 75 of AP I, and Articles 4 and 7 of AP II;[31] it interpreted the Common Article 3 prohibition of cruel treatment by reference to Article 87 of GC III and Articles 3 and 4 of AP II;[32] it interpreted the

---

customary international law, serious violations of Common Article 3 gave rise to individual criminal responsibility for war crimes, including in non-international armed conflicts.

This was a particularly revolutionary position, since at that time (the early 1990s) the traditional wisdom was that individual criminal responsibility for war crimes was a matter 'confined' to war proper, namely, international armed conflicts. As the late Antonio Cassese (who participated, as president of the ICTY and of the Appeals Chamber, in the drafting of the decision) put it, it seemed 'crazy' to 'stick to the traditional concept that war crimes can only be committed in international armed conflict .... A rape is a rape; a murder is a murder, whether it is committed within the framework of an international armed conflict ... or a civil war': Joseph Weiler, 'Editorial: Nino—In His Own Words; In this Issue; The Last Page and Roaming Charges', *EJIL* 22, no. 4 (2011), pp. 931–947, at p. 942.

[24] AP I, Article 51(2) explicitly prohibits such attacks.

[25] *Prosecutor v Stanislav Galić (Trial Chamber)* [2003] International Criminal Tribunal for the Former Yugoslavia IT-98-29-T [86–138]. This was affirmed by *Prosecutor v Stanislav Galić (Appeals Chamber)* [2006] International Criminal Tribunal for the Former Yugoslavia IT-98-29-A [79–109].

[26] *Prosecutor v Mile Mrkšić et al (Trial Chamber)* [2007] International Criminal Tribunal for the Former Yugoslavia IT-95-13/1-T [668]; *Prosecutor v Mile Mrkšić et al (Appeals Chamber)* [2009] International Criminal Tribunal for the Former Yugoslavia IT-95-13/1-A [151].

[27] *ICTY—Mrkšić et al—AC judgment* (n 26), paras 71–74.

[28] Hague Convention (IV) Respecting the Laws and Customs of War on Land and Its Annex: Regulations Concerning the Laws and Customs of War on Land 1907 (HC IV Regulations).

[29] *ICTY—Mucić—TC judgment* (n 18), para 432.

[30] Ibid., para 476. *See also, Prosecutor v Anto Furundžija (Trial Chamber)* [1998] International Criminal Tribunal for the Former Yugoslavia IT-95-17/1-T [165–9, 175].

[31] *ICTY—Mucić—TC judgment* (n 18), paras 516–532.

[32] Ibid., para 548.

170 INDIVIDUALIZATION OF IHL RULES THROUGH CRIMINALIZATION

grave breach of unlawful confinement by reference to Articles 5, 27, 41, 42, 43, and 78 of GC IV;[33] and, it construed the war crime of plunder by reference to Article 15 of GC I, Article 18 of GC II, Article 18 of GC III, and Article 33 of GC IV.[34] Similarly, in *Naletilić and Martinović*, the ICTY identified forced labour as a war crime, by reference to Articles 49, 50, and 52 of GC III.[35]

Nor is this phenomenon restricted to the ICTY. For instance, the statutes of tribunals like the ICTR[36] and the Special Court for Sierra Leone (SCSL)[37] expressly provided for jurisdiction over violations of Common Article 3. Similarly, the expanded list of war crimes set out in Article 8 of the Rome Statute criminalizes the violation of a number of IHL provisions such as violations of the principle of distinction in relation to civilian objects,[38] denial of quarter,[39] the use of poisoned weapons and poisonous gases,[40] and the use of human shields.[41]

The increasing tendency to individualize the rules of IHL by ascribing individual criminal responsibility for war crimes for their violations may be attributed, in part, to the scope of these tribunals' jurisdiction over war crimes. In most cases, these tribunals were simply granted jurisdiction over grave breaches of the GCs or serious violations of IHL without any additional strict requirement for the identification of violations of IHL rules amounting to war crimes.[42] To define the content of these broadly defined war crimes these tribunals therefore had to rely upon IHL norms, whose content is often too vague and loose to comply with the strict

---

[33] Ibid., para 566 et seq.

[34] Ibid., para 315, fn 329.

[35] *Prosecutor v Mladen Naletilić and Vinko Martinović (Trial Chamber)* [2003] International Criminal Tribunal for the Former Yugoslavia IT-98-34-T [250–61]. *See also, Prosecutor v Simić et al (Trial Chamber)* [2003] International Criminal Tribunal for the Former Yugoslavia IT-95-9-T [86].

[36] ICTR statute, Article 4.

[37] Statute of the Special Court for Sierra Leone 2002 Article 3 (SCSL Statute).

[38] Rome Statute of the International Criminal Court 1998 (2187 UNTS 38544) Article 8(2)(b)(ii) (Rome Statute). The analogous IHL provisions include AP I, Articles 48 and 52.

[39] Rome Statute, Article 8(2)(b)(xii). The analogous IHL provisions include HC IV Regulations, Article 23(d); AP I, Article 40.

[40] Rome Statute, Articles 8(2)(b)(xvii) and (xviii). The analogous IHL provisions include HC IV Regulations, Article 23(a); Geneva Protocol for the Prohibition of the Use of Asphyxiating, Poisonous or Other Gases, and of Bacteriological Methods of Warfare 1925.

[41] Rome Statute, Article 8(2)(b)(xxiii). The analogous IHL provisions include AP I, Articles 51(7) and 58.

[42] See, e.g., ICTY statute, Articles 2 and 3: Article 2 refers to grave breaches of the Geneva Conventions, and Article 3 refers to violations of the laws or customs of war, along with an indicative list of such violations, drawn from Article 23 of the HC IV Regulations; ICTR statute, Article 4: referring to serious violations of Common Article 3 and of AP II, along with an indicative list of such violations; SCSL Statute, Articles 3 and 4: Article 3 refers to serious violations of Common Article 3 and of AP II, along with an indicative list of such violations, and Article 4 refers to three specific 'serious violations of international humanitarian law'; Law on the Establishment of Extraordinary Chambers in the Courts of Cambodia for the Prosecution of Crimes Committed During the Period of Democratic Kampuchea 2004, Article 6: referring to grave breaches of the Geneva Conventions, along with an indicative list of such breaches.

requirements of criminal law rules.[43] The Rome Statute presents an exception in this regard by setting out an exhaustive list of war crimes in Article 8, so that IHL norms have been adapted to the requirements of criminal law. However, as will be discussed below (§5), one of the consequences of individualization of IHL norms through the determination of the legal ingredients of war crimes is the misinterpretation of these norms by criminal law judges. This problem remains unresolved even in the context of the Rome Statute, as the list of war crimes set out in Article 8 refers to and implicates several IHL concepts and principles.

This increasing individualization of the rules of IHL through responsibility for war crimes also stems from the fact that the GCs, aimed as they are at the protection of the victims of war, are replete with provisions that impose on belligerents a duty to protect identified groups of people (the 'protected persons'). The GCs have, thus, offered international criminal law judges a golden opportunity to argue that, since belligerents cannot but act through individuals, the ultimate bearers of the duties of protection established by the GCs are the individuals acting on behalf of the parties to the conflict.[44]

Finally, there is the fact that IHL instruments like the GCs draw upon a scheme based on 'humanization and individualization of inter-belligerent enforcement'.[45] The GCs are the first IHL instruments expressly envisaging, even if only at the domestic level, criminal responsibility for breaches of the rules contained therein. In addition, they also ban reprisals against protected persons and property—a ban that is 'one of the great civilizing achievements of the laws of armed conflict since World War II'.[46] Arguably, the prohibition of reprisals as a means to enforce the rules of the GCs has contributed to raising expectations in the system of criminal repressions of the breaches of the Conventions. The tendency in the rules and practice of war crimes law to individualize the provisions contained in the GCs, and more generally the rules of IHL, is perhaps a response to these great expectations.

---

[43] They have also had to embark upon relevant contextual interpretations of other IHL rules that were beyond the purely criminal aspects of the case, such as the determination of the nature of an armed conflict, or the qualification of the victim of a crime as protected person under the GCs.

[44] See, e.g., *ICTY—Mucić—TC judgment* (n 18), paras 1112–1124, and particularly 1117; *ICTY—Mrkšić et al—AC judgment* (n 26), paras 71–72; *Prosecutor v Tihomir Blaškić (Trial Chamber)* [2000] International Criminal Tribunal for the Former Yugoslavia IT-95-14-T [154, 186]; *Prosecutor v Kordić & Čerkez (Trial Chamber)* [2001] International Criminal Tribunal for the Former Yugoslavia IT-95-14/2-T [168–169].

[45] Derek Jinks, 'Humanization and Individualisation in the Enforcement of International Humanitarian Law', Paper Presented at a Colloquium on *Virtue, Vices and Human Behavior and Democracy in International Law*, organized by the Institute for International Law and Justice at New York University Law School in Spring 2009. Available at http://iilj.org/courses/documents/2009Colloquium.Session1.Jinks.pdf, p. 9.

[46] Kenneth Anderson, 'The Rise of International Criminal Law: Intended and Unintended Consequences', *EJIL 20*, no. 2 (2009), pp. 331–358, at p. 340.

4. The Requirements for Criminalization

Which violations of IHL rules give rise to individual criminal responsibility for war crimes? This is a fundamental question that serves to establish the requirements whereby conduct that is unlawful under IHL can also constitute the *actus reus* of a war crime, thus 'individualizing' the IHL rule.

As early as 1944, renowned international lawyer Lauterpacht warned against the risks of penalizing by criminal prosecution 'all and sundry breaches of the law of war' since this could tend 'to blur the emphasis which must be placed on the punishment of war crimes proper in the limited sense of the term.'[47] He suggested that only offences against the laws of war 'which, on any reasonable assumption, must be regarded as condemned by the common conscience of mankind' should be considered as warranting individual criminal punishment.[48]

Arguably this view is echoed in subsequent developments according to which not every violation of the rules of IHL applicable to an armed conflict gives rise to war crimes. For instance, the approach set out by the ICTY in the seminal jurisdictional decision in the *Tadić* case allows for individual criminal responsibility for violations of IHL norms subject to two conditions, the first of which is that they must be 'serious'. The ICTY explained seriousness in the following terms:[49]

> the violation must be 'serious', that is to say, it must constitute a breach of a rule protecting important values, and the breach must involve grave consequences for the victim. Thus, for instance, the fact of a combatant simply appropriating a loaf of bread in an occupied village would not amount to a 'serious violation of international humanitarian law' although it may be regarded as falling foul of the basic principle laid down in Article 46, paragraph 1, of the Hague Regulations (and the corresponding rule of customary international law) whereby 'private property must be respected' by any army occupying an enemy territory.

While one could share the view that seriousness of the violation is an indispensable condition for criminalization,[50] this requirement is not always interpreted in the same way as the ICTY has suggested. For instance, in an explanatory note the International Committee of the Red Cross (ICRC) contends that 'serious violations of international humanitarian law are war crimes' but takes the view that:[51]

---

[47] Hersch Lauterpacht, 'The Law of Nations and the Punishment of War Crimes', in Guénaël Mettraux (ed.), *Perspectives on the Nuremberg Trial* (Oxford: OUP, 2008), p. 36.

[48] Ibid.

[49] *ICTY— Tadić—AC—jurisdiction* (n 1), para 94.

[50] Criminalizing all IHL breaches would be impractical given that all IHL rules are not addressed to, or capable of being implemented by, individuals.

[51] International Committee of the Red Cross, 'Explanatory Note: What Are "Serious Violations of International Humanitarian Law"?'. Available at: https://www.icrc.org/en/doc/assets/files/2012/att-what-are-serious-violations-of-ihl-icrc.pdf

violations are serious, and are war crimes, if they endanger protected persons (e.g. civilians, prisoners of war, the wounded and sick) or objects (e.g. civilian objects or infrastructure) or if they breach important values.

The approach of the ICRC in its interpretation of seriousness thus differs significantly from the one adopted by the ICTY. Both approaches define seriousness in terms of two elements, and both stipulate that the implication of 'important values' is one of those two elements. But they differ on the identity of the second element and the relationship between the two elements. For the ICTY, the second element is 'grave consequences for the victim', and the two elements are conjunctive. For the ICRC, the second element is 'endangering protected persons or objects', and the two elements are disjunctive. Consequently, the ICRC's definition of seriousness is far broader than that of the ICTY. More importantly, the ICRC's definition extends to crimes of conduct, while the ICTY's definition, by requiring 'grave consequences for the victim', is restricted to crimes of result.

Consequently, the requirement of 'seriousness' cannot unequivocally determine which violations of IHL rules can also be subject to criminal punishment. As Abi-Saab correctly put it:[52]

> It is not enough ... simply to use adjectives, by describing the violation as 'serious' or 'grave' or the violated norm as 'fundamental'. Such a question-begging approach is neither valid nor operational as a distinguishing criterion.

To bring the identification of violations of IHL that can amount to war crimes in conformity with the requirements of criminal law, the ICTY has thus identified an additional requirement, that 'the violation must entail, under customary or conventional law, the individual criminal responsibility of the person breaching the rule'.[53] Arguably, this additional requirement serves two objectives. First: to distinguish clearly between violations of IHL that trigger *only* the international responsibility of the state (or eventually *mutatis mutandis*, the responsibility of the relevant party to the conflict to which the violation is attributable) from the violations of IHL that *may also* trigger the individual criminal responsibility of the relevant individuals implicated in the violation. Second: to set the relevant international legal standard against which one can identify respect for the principle of legality in criminal matters as enshrined in international human rights law and international criminal law, so as to guarantee that punishment absent an

---

[52] Georges Abi-Saab, 'The Concept of "War Crimes"', in Sienho Yee and Tieya Wang (eds), *International Law in the Post-Cold War World: Essays in Memory of Li Haopei* (New York: Routledge 2001), p. 112.
[53] *ICTY—Tadić—AC—jurisdiction* (n 1), para 94.

174 INDIVIDUALIZATION OF IHL RULES THROUGH CRIMINALIZATION

applicable national criminal rule at the time of the conduct can be based instead on an applicable rule of international law.[54]

Therefore, it is no surprise that the requirement of an international rule criminalizing the serious violation of IHL, while absent in the ICRC's definition of war crimes, has generally found support in the case of law of other international criminal tribunals, besides being endorsed by academic commentators.[55] For instance, the SCSL invoked the ICTY criteria of seriousness plus international criminalization to defend its jurisdiction over a war crime expressly included in its jurisdiction. In response to a jurisdictional challenge in the *Norman* case,[56] the SCSL thus felt it necessary to demonstrate that the war crime of 'conscripting or enlisting children under the age of 15 years into armed forces or groups or using them to participate actively in hostilities', clearly envisaged in its Statute,[57] constituted a 'serious violation of IHL' and was criminalized by customary international law at the time when the alleged unlawful conduct took place. Similarly, in spite of the explicit provision of jurisdiction over violations of Common Article 3 in the Statute of the ICTR, the ICTR has had occasion to defend its jurisdiction on the basis, inter alia, of the criminalization of breaches of Common Article 3 in customary international law.[58]

However, even though the ICTY's requirement of criminalization under international law of serious violations of IHL seems to have prevailed, in practice, this assessment is conducted cursorily, particularly when it concerns criminalization under customary international law.

A prime example is the judgment of the ICTY Trial Chamber in *Galić*, concerning the criminalization of the IHL prohibition of attacks terrorizing the civilian population in Article 51(2) of AP I.[59] It discusses the criminalization of these attacks in customary international law at length, before concluding that such conduct was in fact criminalized in customary international law.[60] However, a closer analysis of the Trial Chamber's analysis severely undermines this conclusion. The practice that the Trial Chamber relied on in reaching its finding can be divided into three categories. First, is a range of practice which the Trial Chamber itself

---

[54] The ICC has had occasion to reject legality-based challenges based on prior criminalization in the Rome Statute. See, e.g., *The Prosecutor v Thomas Lubanga Dyilo (Decision on the Confirmation of Charges)* [2007] International Criminal Court ICC-01/04-01/06 [302–314].

[55] See, e.g., Oona Hathaway et al., 'What Is a War Crime?', *Yale Journal of International Law 44*, no. 1 (2019), pp. 54–112, at pp. 69–70.

[56] *Prosecutor v Moinina Fofana and Allieu Kondewa (Trial Chamber Judgment)* [2007] Special Court for Sierra Leone Case No. SCSL-04-14-T [94–95, 184–189].

[57] SCSL Statute, Article 4(c).

[58] *The Prosecutor v Jean-Paul Akayesu (Trial Chamber)* (International Criminal Tribunal for Rwanda) [617].

[59] *Supra* notes 24–25 and accompanying text.

[60] *ICTY—Galić—TC judgment* (n 25), paras 113–129.

distinguished.[61] Second, is the criminalization of terrorizing attacks under Yugoslav law.[62] Third, is the prohibition of terrorizing attacks under Article 51(2) of AP I.[63] The Trial Chamber blithely notes the criminalization of one part of Article 51(2) of AP I (the broader principle of distinction) and the unanimous acceptance of the prohibition of terrorizing attacks, and from this concludes that terrorizing attacks also constituted war crimes. In light of this questionable assessment of criminalization under customary law,[64] it seems that it is the value protected by the rule in issue and the seriousness of its violation in light of the harmful results for the victims that drove the *Galić* Trial Chamber's individualization of the prohibition of terrorizing attacks in AP I Article 51(2).[65]

The cursory assessment of criminalization under customary international law of violations of IHL in the *Galić* case is a feature that can be identified in several cases decided at international criminal courts and tribunals. Consequently, though in principle criminalization is proclaimed based on the aforementioned *Tadić* requirements, namely the seriousness of the violation and its criminalization in international law, in practice the assessment of criminalization in customary law tends to be cursory and seriousness appears the dominant factor. A clear example of this trend is, for instance, the view taken by the SCSL in the aforementioned *Norman* case. To ground the assertion that customary international law already criminalized the violation of the IHL rule prohibiting recruitment of child soldiers at the relevant tome, the Appeals Chamber of the Court argued, inter alia, as follows:[66]

> The prohibition of child recruitment constitutes a fundamental guarantee and although it is not enumerated in the ICTR and ICTY Statutes, it shares the same character and the same gravity of the violations that are explicitly listed in those Statutes. The fact that the ICTY and the ICTR have prosecuted violations of Additional Protocol II provides further evidence of the criminality of child recruitment before 1996.

---

[61] Ibid., paras 113–119.

[62] Ibid., paras 121–126.

[63] Ibid., paras 120, 127–128.

[64] In this regard, see the criticism of the majority's approach in the separate and dissenting opinion of Judge Nieto-Navia: *Prosecutor v Stanislav Galić (Trial Chamber) (Separate and Partially Dissenting Opinion of Judge Nieto-Navia)* [2003] International Criminal Tribunal for the Former Yugoslavia IT-98-29-T [108–113]. In this vein, questions might equally be raised in relation to the determination of the customary criminalization of Common Article 3 breaches in the *Tadić* interlocutory appeal, based as it was on a cursory review of the practice of seven states and of two resolutions of the UN Security Council. *See, ICTY—Tadić—AC—jurisdiction* (n 1), paras 130–134. *See also, Prosecutor v Duško Tadić, IT-94-1-A (Decision on the Defence Motion for Interlocutory Appeal on Jurisdiction) (Separate Opinion of Judge Li)* (International Criminal Tribunal for the Former Yugoslavia) [10–13], raising this criticism.

[65] The *Galić* trial chamber's assessment of the seriousness requirement is set out at *ICTY—Galić—TC judgment* (n 25), paras 106–112.

[66] *Prosecutor v Sam Hinga Norman (Decision on Preliminary Motion Based on Lack of Jurisdiction (Child Recruitment))* [2004] Special Court for Sierra Leone Case No. SCSL-2004-14-AR72(E) [39].

Conflating the seriousness of the violation of an IHL rule with its criminalization entailing individual responsibility raises concerns from the viewpoint of respect of the principle of legality in criminal matters, as many commentators have noted.[67]

However, the solution cannot be obliterating altogether the requirement of proving the criminalization under a rule of international law of the illegality of a wartime conduct and focusing instead on seriousness as the key criterion, as a recent contribution to the war crimes law literature has recommended.[68] It is notoriously difficult to ascertain the content of customary international law. And that may well be a necessary and unavoidable constraint upon the requirement of criminalization under customary law. Nonetheless, it is submitted here that relying on the seriousness of the violation of IHL as the key requirement for grounding criminal responsibility for war crimes is undesirable and the ICTY's approach, with its requirements of international criminalization, including through customary law (with its attendant practical difficulties), is preferable. As mentioned above, first, the ICTY approach would help to preserve respect for the principle of legality in criminal matters, otherwise jeopardized by relying exclusively on the seriousness requirement. Second, the approach taken by the ICTY would help to maintain the distinction between IHL rules addressing states and other collective entities parties to an armed conflict and international *criminal* rules addressing individuals when they commit certain unlawful behaviours in warfare.

Importantly, however, the criminalization requirement should be applied rigorously to avoid it becoming mere theoretical tinsel. Its removal or superficial assessment in practice would entail the risk of progressively 'conflating' IHL norms addressing the parties to an armed conflict with criminal law norms grounding war crimes charges against individuals. To some extent, this conflation has already occurred, and arguably has had an impact on the interpretation and scope of application of some corresponding IHL rules. Some of these, possibly unintended, consequences are addressed in the following section.

5. The Impact of Criminalization of IHL Violations on the Corresponding IHL Rules

Building on the foregoing analysis of the individualization of IHL through criminalization, this section will draw out two of the consequences and tensions produced by this individualization—distortion of the content of IHL rules (§ 5.1), and misplaced prioritization of IHL rules which are amenable to individualization (§ 5.2).

---

[67] See, e.g., Darryl Robinson, 'The Identity Crisis of International Criminal Law', *Leiden Journal of International Law 21*, no. 4 (2008), pp. 925–963, at pp. 946–955; Beth Van Schaack, 'Crimen Sine Lege: Judicial Lawmaking at the Intersection of Law and Morals', *Georgetown Law Journal 97*, no. 1 (2008), pp. 119–192, at pp. 149–155.

[68] *See*, Hathaway et al. (n 55).

5.1 Distortion of the Content of IHL Rules

The specific requirements of criminal law in the field of war crimes have already had the effect of distorting the content of the underlying relevant rules of IHL. One example is the IHL rule of proportionality enshrined in Article 51(5)(b) of AP I, prohibiting attacks involving expected collateral damage which is *excessive* in relation to the anticipated military advantage. Admittedly, this subjective requirement of knowledge of excessiveness is somewhat ambiguous and uncertain. Therefore, the corresponding war crime provision in the Rome Statute has replaced 'excessive' with 'clearly excessive'.[69] This makes the standard somewhat clearer and more precise by clarifying that, for the purpose of individual criminal responsibility, the excessiveness should be obvious, thus restricting the scope of the relevant war crime to particularly egregious cases of violations of the IHL rule.

However, this 'clarification' made for the purpose of the war crime provision in the Rome Statute also seems to have had impact on the interpretation of the relevant underlying IHL rule. By reference to the requirements of the Rome Statute, a number of eminent IHL commentators now postulate that the proportionality rule under IHL itself requires clear excessiveness as well.[70] The replacement of 'excessive' with 'clearly excessive' in a criminal law context is entirely reasonable, given the inherent ambiguity of the requirements of proportionality, and the requirements of legality and fairness in criminal law. But the underlying IHL norm, applicable to parties to an armed conflict, is not textually subject to any analogous constraints. In effect, then, the scope of the IHL norm has been restricted by reference to the individualized war crime.

It might plausibly be argued that this example is limited in its valency by the particular ambiguity and imprecision of the underlying proportionality rule under IHL. In other words, the defects of the underlying rule were not only unsuitable from the perspective of individual criminal responsibility, but even from the more lenient lens of the determination of transgressions by parties to the armed conflict, and above all for the purpose of establishing state responsibility. Consequently, the reverse effect of the restricted war crime on the underlying IHL rule might be restricted to similar cases of exceptional ambiguity. The problem with this line of argumentation is that the ambiguity and imprecision of the proportionality rule is far from extraordinary in the context of IHL rules on the conduct of hostilities. Reference may be made here to the difficulties in defining 'direct participation in hostilities' for the purposes of Article 51(3) of AP I, 'feasible' for the purposes of Articles 57(2)(a)(i) and (ii) of AP I, or 'effective advance warning' for the purposes

---

[69] Rome Statute, Article 8(2)(b)(iv).

[70] See, e.g., Michael N. Schmitt and John J. Merriam, 'The Tyranny of Context: Israeli Targeting Practices in Legal Perspective', *University of Pennsylvania Journal of International Law 37*, no. 1 (2015), pp. 53–139, at pp. 129–130; William H. Boothby, *The Law of Targeting* (Oxford: OUP, 2012), p. 97; Yoram Dinstein, *The Conduct of Hostilities Under the Law of International Armed Conflict* (Cambridge: CUP, 3rd ed., 2016), p. 155.

of Article 57(2)(c) of AP I. Ambiguity and imprecision are a necessary feature of the difficult balance that IHL strives to achieve between military and humanitarian values. The restriction of IHL norms through translation into war crimes, as seems to be occurring in relation to the proportionality obligation, would distort this delicate balance, usually towards the military side.

Other distortions of the content of the relevant IHL norms seem to reflect international criminal law judges' dismissal of the relevance of IHL norms for interpreting corresponding war crimes.

Consider, for instance, an extraordinary series of decisions of the ICC in the *Ntaganda* case. That case featured charges under Article 8(2)(e)(vi) of the Rome Statute, which proscribes sexual crimes in non-international armed conflicts. Unusually, however, the conduct which formed the basis of the charge was directed against the accused's own forces.[71] Ntaganda repeatedly challenged these charges, arguing that IHL does not regulate internal conduct and that the crimes proscribed by Article 8(2)(e)(vi) could not be charged on the basis of Ntaganda's conduct in relation to his own armed forces.[72] At each stage, this challenge was dismissed by various ICC chambers. These dismissals seem to rely, sometimes implicitly, sometimes explicitly, on two arguments: one is that Article 8(2)(e)(vi) does not specify the persons who fall within its protective scope; the other is that the prohibition of sexual crimes is drawn from Common Article 3 of the GCs, which applies generally to persons not actively participating in hostilities, without mention of the allegiance of the protected persons.[73] Consequently, given the humanitarian purpose of Common Article 3, there is no reason to exclude a

---

[71] Ntaganda was charged with the rape and sexual slavery of child soldier of his armed group. These charges were confirmed in *The Prosecutor v Bosco Ntaganda (Decision Pursuant to Article 61(7)(a) and (b) of the Rome Statute on the Charges of the Prosecutor Against Bosco Ntaganda)* [2014] International Criminal Court ICC-01/04-02/06 [76–82].

[72] Following the confirmation of the charges (supra note 71 and accompanying text), Ntaganda challenged the jurisdiction of the ICC in relation to these specific charges. This challenge was denied on the grounds that it did not raise a question as to the jurisdiction of the court: *The Prosecutor v Bosco Ntaganda (Decision on the Defence's Challenge to the Jurisdiction of the Court in Respect of Charges 6 and 9)* [2015] International Criminal Court ICC-01/04-02/06 [22–29]. Ntaganda then appealed this decision, and an appeals chamber concluded that the challenge did, in fact, raise questions regarding the jurisdiction of the court, and remanded the challenge to the trial chamber: *The Prosecutor v Bosco Ntaganda (Judgment on the Appeal of Mr Bosco Ntaganda Against the 'Decision on the Defence's Challenge to the Jurisdiction of the Court in Respect of Charges 6 and 9')* [2016] International Criminal Court ICC-01/04-02/06 OA 2 [40–42]. Finally, an ICC trial chamber once again rejected the jurisdictional challenge: *The Prosecutor v Bosco Ntaganda (Second Decision on the Defence's Challenge to the Jurisdiction of the Court in Respect of Charges 6 and 9)* [2017] International Criminal Court ICC-01/04-02/06 2.

[73] *ICC—Ntaganda—confirmation* (n 71), para 77; *ICC—Ntaganda—trial chamber jurisdiction 1* (n 72), para 25. The reasoning of the ICC on this question is best developed in the second decision on jurisdiction in relation to these charges: *ICC—Ntaganda—trial chamber jurisdiction 2* (n 72), paras 40–54, and especially, paras 46–52.

belligerent's own forces from its scope.[74] The humanitarian impulse which motivates this argument is laudable and understandable. However, it is at odds with the traditional understanding of the scope of IHL which is restricted to the acts of a belligerent against the persons and property of other belligerents or of third states.[75] Though there are some exceptions to this, for the most part, the regulation of a belligerent's behaviour in relation to its own persons and property falls within the remit of international human rights law, and other parts of international criminal law. The ICC's extension of the scope of IHL in the *Ntaganda* case is difficult to reconcile with the purpose and scope of IHL.

Another example of the unmooring of war crimes from the underlying IHL rules and distortion of the IHL rule in the process of interpreting war crimes, is the definition of 'attack' in the war crimes of directing attacks against, inter alia, hospitals and historical monuments in Articles 8(2)(b)(ix) and 8(2)(e)(iv) of the Rome Statute. The ICC has recognized that 'attack' is a term of art in IHL and should be interpreted in conduct of hostilities war crimes in consonance with its meaning under IHL, i.e., as defined in Article 49(1) of AP I as 'acts of violence against the adversary, whether in offence or defence'.[76] In effect, references to 'attacks' in conduct of hostilities war crimes implicate a requirement of nexus to hostilities

---

[74] A broader critique of the reasoning and sources employed in the decision is beyond the scope of this analysis. However, one point in particular demands underscoring. Arguably, a key piece of evidence relied upon in the second decision on jurisdiction was the fact that the ICRC's updated commentary to GC I extended the scope of Common Article 3 of the GCs to a belligerent's own forces: *ICC—Ntaganda—trial chamber jurisdiction 2* (n 72), para 50. That extension has a very interesting history. The second jurisdiction decision noted that the ICRC's revised commentary to GC I extended the protective scope of Common Article 3 to include a belligerent's own forces. It did not note the sources cited by the ICRC for that proposition. The relevant footnote cites three sources: Knut Dörmann et al. (eds), *Commentary on the First Geneva Convention: Convention (I) for the Amelioration of the Condition of the Wounded and Sick in Armed Forces in the Field* (Cambridge: CUP, 2016), para 547, fn 293. One is the *Sesay* trial chamber judgment of the SCSL, which is recognized as not supporting the extension of Common Article 3 to a belligerent's own forces. Another is the ICC decision on confirmation of charges in the *Katanga* case. However, in that decision the analogous charge related to the conscription of child soldiers, a crime that is explicitly extended to a party's own forces by the Rome Statute: Rome Statute, Articles 8(2)(b)(xxvi) and 8(2)(e)(vi); *The Prosecutor v Germain Katanga and Mathieu Ngudjolo Chui (Decision on the Confirmation of Charges)* [2008] International Criminal Court ICC-01/04-01/07 [248]. Consequently, this source also does not support the proposition. The third cited source was the ICC's decision on confirmation of charges in the *Ntaganda* case. In other words, in relying on the ICRC's endorsement of its position regarding the protective scope of Common Article 3 in the second jurisdiction decision in *Ntaganda*, the ICC was relying on its own previous judgment in the same case. Finally, completing the circle, in 2017, in its updated commentary on GC II, the ICRC cited the second jurisdiction decision as further support for the extension of the protective scope of Common Article 3: Dörmann et al. (n 6), para 569. It bears emphasis that what is being highlighted here is not so much the humanitarian expansion of Common Article 3 to include intra-party conduct (which enjoys broader academic support), but the manner in which that interpretive expansion has been extended to corresponding war crimes, seemingly without consideration for the difference between the two sets of norms or concerns of legality in relation to war crimes.

[75] Dinstein (n 70) 3; Antonio Cassese et al., *Cassese's International Criminal Law* (Oxford: OUP, 3rd ed., 2013), p. 67; Kai Ambos, *Treatise on International Criminal Law: Volume II: The Crimes and Sentencing* (Oxford: OUP, 2014), p. 118.

[76] See, e.g., *ICC—Katanga—confirmation* (n 74), para 266–267.

(distinct from the broader requirement of nexus to the armed conflict that applies to all war crimes)—the impugned conduct is required to have taken place during the conduct of hostilities rather than during the armed conflict more generally.[77] This narrow interpretation and the requirement of nexus to hostilities gives effect to the distinction between IHL rules governing the conduct of hostilities and IHL rules governing the protection of persons and property within the 'power' of a belligerent, i.e., between Hague and Geneva law. This distinction recognizes the qualitative difference between situations of active hostilities and other parts of armed conflicts, and that regulatory limitations which are feasible in relation to the protection of prisoners of war or the sick and wounded away from the battlefield, may not be practicable in the 'fog of war'.

Despite the provenance of this interpretation and its recognition in the ICC's jurisprudence, in the Trial Chamber judgment in *Al Mahdi*,[78] and in the decision on the confirmation of charges in *Al Hassan*,[79] the Chambers construed a special meaning for 'attack' in the context of war crimes against historical and medical buildings. In both cases, the charges related to destruction of cultural property in the context of administration of territory by armed groups after seizing control through hostilities and in both cases the possibility of charging the same conduct under Article 8(2)(e)(xii)—destruction or seizure of enemy property unless imperatively demanded by military necessity—was dismissed.[80] Both Chambers preferred charges under Article 8(2)(e)(iv), arguing that for these particular objects, in light of their broader protection under international law, 'attack' should have a broader meaning which is not restricted to the conduct of hostilities and should cover acts of destruction committed by armed groups in the course of administration and control of territory.

The same issue arose in the *Ntaganda* case, where *ratissage* operations involving the looting of churches and hospitals in areas seized and controlled by Ntaganda's forces was charged under Article 8(2)(e)(iv). The Trial Chamber's judgment skirted the issue, noting the possibility of a broader protection for cultural objects unconstrained by a requirement of nexus to hostilities, but endorsing an interpretation of 'attack' in consonance with its meaning in IHL.[81] The Prosecutor appealed against this decision, arguing that 'attack' in the Article 8(2)(e)(iv) should have a broader meaning, in line with the decisions in *Al Mahdi* and *Al Hassan*

---

[77] Yves Sandoz et al. (eds), *Commentary on the Additional Protocols* (Geneva: Martinus Nijhoff, 1987), p. 603, para 1880.

[78] *The Prosecutor v Ahmad Al Faqi Al Mahdi (Judgment and Sentence)* [2016] International Criminal Court ICC-01/12-01/15 [11–18]. For a comprehensive criticism of the Al-Mahdi conviction, see, William Schabas, 'Al Mahdi Has Been Convicted of a Crime He Did Not Commit', *Case Western Reserve Journal of International Law 49*, no.1 (2017), pp. 75–101.

[79] *Le procureur c. Al Hassan Ag Abdoul Aziz Ag Mohamed Ag Mahmoud (Décision relative à la confirmation des charges)* [2019] International Criminal Court ICC-01/12-01/18 [518–522].

[80] The corresponding war crime in international armed conflicts is set out in Article 8(2)(b)(xiii) of the Rome Statute.

[81] *The Prosecutor v Bosco Ntaganda (Judgment)* [2019] International Criminal Court ICC-01/04-02/06 [1136], fn 3147.

discussed above.[82] The Appeals Chamber dismissed the prosecution appeal,[83] but three of five judges agreed with the Prosecutor that 'attack' should be interpreted in accordance with its plain meaning, rather than in conformity with its narrow meaning under IHL, and without a requirement of nexus to hostilities.[84] Interestingly, these three judges framed their opinions so broadly that they could be interpreted as support for a broader interpretation of 'attack', devoid of a requirement of nexus to hostilities, for all war crimes rather than just the war crimes in Articles 8(2)(b)(xii) and 8(2)(e)(iv).[85]

Given the fragmented decision in the *Ntaganda* appeal, it is still possible that a more restrictive interpretation of 'attack', requiring a nexus to hostilities in conformity with its meaning under IHL, will prevail. As things stand, however, the decisions in *Al Mahdi, Al Hassan*, and *Ntaganda* provide strong support for the argument that 'attack' for the purposes of the war crimes in Articles 8(2)(b)(ix) and 8(2)(e)(iv) (and perhaps even generally) is not constrained by its meaning in IHL. The result is a dilution of the distinction between active hostilities and other situations in an armed conflict in the context of war crimes and individual criminal responsibility, even as that distinction remains fundamental to the regulatory scheme of IHL, creating a chasm between the underlying IHL rules and the corresponding war crimes.

The narrow interpretation of 'attack' and the requirement of nexus to hostilities serves to distinguish the war crime of murdering civilians (Articles 8(2)(a)/(c)(i) of the Rome Statute) from the war crime of attacking civilians (Articles 8(2)(b)/(e)(i) of the Rome Statute). The former requires a result (causing death) and knowledge of the civilian status of the victim; the latter requires conduct (directing an attack) and intent to attack civilians. If 'attack' is not interpreted narrowly in accordance with its definition under IHL, an attack that complies with

---

[82] *The Prosecutor v Bosco Ntaganda (Prosecution Appeal Brief)* [2019] International Criminal Court ICC-01/04-02/06.

[83] *The Prosecutor v Bosco Ntaganda (Appeal Judgment)* [2020] International Criminal Court ICC-01/04-02/06 [1169].

[84] *Ibid.* paras 1165–1168 (dissenting opinion of Judge Ibáñez Carranza); *The Prosecutor v Bosco Ntaganda (Appeal Judgment) (Separate Opinion of Judge Solomy Balungi Bossa)* [2020] International Criminal Court ICC-01/04-02/06; *The Prosecutor v Bosco Ntaganda (Appeal Judgment) (Partly Concurring Opinion of Judge Chile Eboe-Osuji)* [2020] International Criminal Court ICC-01/04-02/06 [103–137]. While Judges Ibáñez Carranza, Balungi Bossa and Eboe-Osuji all agreed with the Prosecutor's interpretation of attack, only Judge Ibáñez Carranza upheld the appeal. Judges Balungi Bossa and Eboe-Osuji joined Judges Morrison and Hofmański in dismissing the appeal. While Judges Morrison and Hofmański did so because they disagreed with the Prosecutor's interpretation of 'attack'—*see, The Prosecutor v Bosco Ntaganda (Appeal Judgment) (Separate Opinion of Judges Howard Morrison and Piotr Hofmański)* [2020] International Criminal Court ICC-01/04-02/06—Judges Balungi Bossa and Eboe-Osuji did so because they thought the conduct would have been better charged under Article 8(2)(e)(xii) of the Rome Statute.

[85] *See amplius,* Abhimanyu George Jain, 'The Ntaganda Appeal Judgment and the Meaning of "Attack" in Conduct of Hostilities War Crimes', *EJIL: Talk!* (2 April 2021). Available at: https://www.ejiltalk.org/the-ntaganda-appeal-judgment-and-the-meaning-of-attack-in-conduct-of-hostilities-war-crimes/

182 INDIVIDUALIZATION OF IHL RULES THROUGH CRIMINALIZATION

the rules of distinction and proportionality (it was not directed at civilians but caused proportionate civilian deaths) can still be prosecuted as murder.

In the first example of distortion of IHL norms in the process of interpreting associated war crimes discussed above—the extension of the Article 8(2)(e)(vi) war crime to cover conduct within an armed group—it could be argued that the distortion of the IHL norm was balanced by the extension of the protective scope of the ICC's jurisdiction, and the impugned conduct could not otherwise have been prosecuted. That is not necessarily adequate justification, but in this case, even that much is absent, since the impugned conduct could just as well have been charged under Article 8(2)(e)(xii).

A final example of the distortion of IHL through the process of interpretation of the corresponding war crimes is the interpretation of the proportionality rule by the ICTY in the *Gotovina* case. The rule of proportionality requires attackers to determine the collateral damage which may be expected and the military advantage which is anticipated, and to compare the two. For an attack to be proportionate, the expected collateral damage should not be excessive in relation to the anticipated military advantage. The *Gotovina* Trial Chamber applied the proportionality test in precisely this manner, estimating and comparing collateral damage and military advantage.[86] In its assessment of foreseeable collateral damage it relied on prior findings on the accuracy of the artillery employed. The Appeals Chamber vehemently disagreed with this specific finding,[87] and though it did not set out further findings on the proportionality of the attack in question,[88] it rearticulated the proportionality rule as requiring 'concrete assessment of comparative military advantage' and 'findings on resulting damages or casualties.'[89] This reframing of the proportionality test distorts and misrepresents it. The assessment of proportionality does not require the assessment of 'comparative military advantage',[90] and its prospective nature renders post facto knowledge of resulting damage or casualties irrelevant. There are contexts and circumstances in which these factors might be relevant to proportionality analyses under IHL, but the appeals chamber seems to frame these factors as necessary parts of the proportionality analysis under IHL, which is a distortion of the proportionality rule.

---

[86] *Prosecutor v Ante Gotovina, Ivan Čermak, Mladen Markač (Trial Chamber)* [2011] International Criminal Tribunal for the Former Yugoslavia IT-06-90-T [1910].

[87] *Prosecutor v Ante Gotovina and Mladen Markač (Appeals Chamber)* [2012] International Criminal Tribunal for the Former Yugoslavia IT-06-90-A [58–63, 82].

[88] Ibid., para 82.

[89] Ibid.

[90] This requirement may have been drawn from the precautionary obligation under Article 57(3) of AP I, which provides that if different military objectives provide similar military advantages, the objective to be attacked should be the one expected to cause least danger to civilians lives and objects. However, though this obligation gives effect to and extends the proportionality rule, it is not in itself a necessary part of the proportionality assessment.

5.2 Misplaced Prioritization of IHL Norms

The construction of serious IHL breaches as war crimes, driven by a desire to improve the enforcement of IHL, also risks diverting attention away from the rules of IHL that have no criminal law dimension at all. A large number of the IHL rules cover issues whose violations are not susceptible to criminal sanction.

A key example in this regard is the rules contained in GC III devoted to prisoner of war (PoW) camps. These rules are certainly important for the organization of the camps and the everyday life of PoWs, but it is hard to discern from them any content that might potentially fall within the province of criminal law.[91] An individualization-oriented perspective consequently deprioritizes these subsidiary obligations in comparison to the more prominent and more easily criminalizable obligations of humane treatment.

Another example is the detailed rules on precaution set out in AP I Article 57, which operationalize the broader principles of distinction and proportionality by imposing detailed obligations of conduct. Though these obligations of precaution are an integral component of the principles of distinction and proportionality, they are less amenable to criminalization.

The prioritization of the criminalizable rules of IHL risks propagating the idea that 'all behaviour in armed conflict is either a war crime or lawful.'[92] The potential risk is that the criminal law of war swallows the rest of the laws of war, carrying with it the loss of the idea that compliance with IHL is not really about individual liability but rather about the legitimacy built around shared values and rules for 'the social organization of conflict'.[93]

In other words, in emphasizing individual criminal responsibility as a means of enforcement of IHL rules over state responsibility or other possible collective forms of international responsibility, there is a risk of jettisoning critical parts of the broader IHL infrastructure which do not easily lend themselves to criminalization. In doing so, individualization of IHL rules through criminalization of violations ignores the greater scope of IHL which is enforceable upon states and other collective entities than upon individuals. In pursuit of greater enforceability, individualization seems to choose short-term gains over a longer-term remediation of the flaws in the collective dimension of the international responsibility system, and consequently, potentially compromises the broader enforceability of IHL.

---

[91] Anderson (n 46), p. 357.
[92] Sassòli (n 8), p. 118.
[93] Anderson (n 46), pp. 346–349.

6. Conclusion

The appeal of individualization of IHL violations through criminal punishment of war crimes is both significant and self-evident. Criminal prosecution of wartime atrocities offers a way around the impasse of state responsibility and provides a way to enforce IHL upon non-state actors; in this way it greatly enhances the enforcement of IHL. It also provides the cathartic, demonstrative, retributive, and restorative benefits of criminal justice.

However, notwithstanding these many and significant benefits, there are adverse consequences as well. It is important to highlight here that these adverse consequences are neither unavoidable nor irreversible. But they can and do occur in conjunction with individualization through criminalization. Recognizing these consequences is critical to any careful assessment of the phenomenon.

Any such careful assessment of individualization through criminal repression of war crimes must move beyond the practicalities of translating IHL rules into war crimes, to understanding and assessing these consequences. To return to *Galić* as an example, one might reasonably ask why the criminalization of terrorizing attacks is noteworthy or problematic, given that terrorizing attacks are simply a subset of attacks which breach the principle of distinction, and such attacks are already recognized as war crimes. Or, one might point to the examples of misinterpretation of IHL rules by criminal law judges and argue that this problem is quite easily remediable. However, the importance of these examples, and the others discussed in this chapter, is not in the manner in which unlawful conduct under IHL is translated into war crimes, or in the manner and mode of remedying resulting concerns. Those concerns go to the method of individualization through criminalization, and not to its substance.

The heart and substance of individualization through war crimes is the prioritization of individual criminal responsibility over state responsibility and other possible forms of collective international responsibility. It is this prioritization strategy that defines individualization, which forms the ultimate source of its desirable and undesirable consequences, and which must form the focus of any careful analysis of the phenomenon.

As discussed at the end of the previous section, the prioritization of individual criminal responsibility implies the abandonment of the project of resuscitating state responsibility, with the costs and benefits that that entails. But in closing, it is worth highlighting that this prioritization is itself potentially problematic. Increasingly, critical scrutiny of international criminal law is revealing the limitations of criminal responsibility. These include a limited perspective of justice, questionable legitimacy, false universalism, sexism, racism, and neocolonialism.[94] Indeed, as states increasingly assert sovereign immunities before foreign municipal courts,

---

[94] See, e.g., Mégret (n 9).

and as the role of these courts in furthering the individualization project expands, it is only private individuals, i.e., members of armed non-state actors, who will be brought to 'justice'. In this way, the enforcement gap of IHL in relation to armed non-state actors is turned entirely on its head.

Against this context and with all of these factors at play, entrenching the structure of international criminal law in the name of better enforcement of IHL, or even perpetuating the biases of international criminal law in order to enhance the effectiveness of IHL, demands careful consideration.

References

Abi-Saab, G. (2001) 'The Concept of "War Crimes"', in S. Yee and T. Wang (eds), *International Law in the Post-Cold War World: Essays in Memory of Li Haopei*. New York: Routledge, pp. 129–148. doi: 10.4324/9780203468975-18.

Ambos, K. (2014) *Treatise on International Criminal Law: Volume II: The Crimes and Sentencing*. Oxford, New York: Oxford University Press.

Anderson, K. (2009) 'The Rise of International Criminal Law: Intended and Unintended Consequences', *European Journal of International Law*, 20(2), pp. 331–358.

Boothby, W.H. (2012) *The Law of Targeting*. Oxford: Oxford University Press.

Cassese, A. et al. (2013) *Cassese's International Criminal Law*. Third edition. Oxford: Oxford University Press.

Dinstein, Y. (2016) *The Conduct of Hostilities under the Law of International Armed Conflict*. Third edition. Cambridge: Cambridge University Press.

Dörmann, K. et al. (2016) *Commentary on the First Geneva Convention: Convention (I) for the Amelioration of the Condition of the Wounded and Sick in Armed Forces in the Field*. Cambridge: Cambridge University Press (Commentaries on the 1949 Geneva Conventions).

Dörmann, K. et al. (2017) *Commentary on the Second Geneva Convention: Convention (II) for the Amelioration of the Condition of Wounded, Sick, and Shipwrecked Members of Armed Forces at Sea*. Cambridge: Cambridge University Press (Commentaries on the 1949 Geneva conventions).

Gaeta, P. (2015) 'Grave Breaches of the Geneva Conventions', in A. Clapham, P. Gaeta, and M. Sassòli (eds), *The 1949 Geneva Conventions: A Commentary*. Oxford: Oxford University Press, pp. 615–646.

George Jain, A. (2021) 'The Ntaganda Appeal Judgment and the Meaning of "Attack" in Conduct of Hostilities War Crimes', *EJIL: Talk!* Available at: https://www.ejiltalk.org/the-ntaganda-appeal-judgment-and-the-meaning-of-attack-in-conduct-of-hostilities-war-crimes/

Hathaway, O.A. et al. (2019) 'What Is a War Crime?', *Yale Journal of International Law*, 44(1). Available at: https://digitalcommons.law.yale.edu/yjil/vol44/iss1/3

Heller, K.J. and Simpson, G.J. (eds) (2013) *The Hidden Histories of War Crimes Trials*. Oxford: Oxford University Press.

Jenks, D. (2009) 'Humanization and Individualization in the Enforcement of International Humanitarian Law'. Available at: http://iilj.org/courses/documents/2009Colloquium.Session1.Jinks.pdf, p. 9.

Lauterpacht, H. (2008) 'The Law of Nations and the Punishment of War Crimes', in M. Guénaël (ed.), *Perspectives on the Nuremberg Trial*. Oxford: Oxford University Press, pp. 13–54.

Mégret, F. (2014) 'International Criminal Justice: A Critical Research Agenda', in C.E.J. Schwöbel (ed.), *Critical Approaches to International Criminal Law: An Introduction*. New York: Routledge, pp. 17–53.

Méron, T. (1995) 'International Criminalisation of Internal Atrocities', *The American Journal of International Law*, 89(3), pp. 554–577.

Robinson, D. (2008) 'The Identity Crisis of International Criminal Law', *Leiden Journal of International Law*, 21(4), pp. 925–963. doi: 10.1017/S0922156508005463.

Sandoz, Y. et al. (eds) (1987) *Commentary on the Additional Protocols*. Geneva: Martinus Nijhoff.

Sassòli, M. (2009) 'Humanitarian Law and International Criminal Law', in A. Cassese (ed.), *The Oxford Companion to International Criminal Justice*. Oxford: Oxford University Press, pp. 111–122.

Schabas, W. (2017) 'Al Mahdi Has Been Convicted of a Crime He Did Not Commit', *Case Western Reserve Journal of International Law*, 49(1), pp. 75–101.

Schabas, W. (2018) *The Trial of the Kaiser*. Oxford: Oxford University Press.

Schmitt, M. and Merriam, J. (2015) 'The Tyranny of Context: Israeli Targeting Practices in Legal Perspective', *University of Pennsylvania Journal of International Law*, 37(1), pp. 53–139.

Simpson, G.J. (2007) *Law, War and Crime: War Crime Trials and the Reinvention and International Law*. Cambridge: Polity.

Simpson, G.J. (2018) 'NM 68226 84912; TQ 30052 80597', in J. Hohmann and D. Joyce (eds), *International Law's Objects*. Oxford: Oxford University Press, pp. 294–304.

Tallgren, I. and Thomas, S. (eds) (2019) *The New Histories of International Criminal Law: Retrials*. Oxford: Oxford University Press.

Van Schaack, B. (2008) 'Crimen Sine Lege: Judicial Lawmaking at the Intersection of Law and Morals', *Georgetown Law Journal*, 97(1), pp. 119–192.

Weiler, J. (2011) 'Editorial: Nino—In His Own Words; In this Issue; The Last Page and Roaming Charges', *European Journal of International Law*, 22(4), pp. 931–947.

7

Tensions between the Pursuit of Criminal Accountability and Other International Policy Agendas in Situations of Armed Conflict

Sarah M.H. Nouwen

Prologue

They fell every man to get their man;
we the people are bleeding.[1]

Does the [International Criminal Court] want to use the [Uganda Peoples' Defence Forces] to arrest people?
We are moving from the frying pan to the fire.[2]

After seven months' deliberation, the judges of the international criminal court finally issued an arrest warrant for Omar al-Bashir, the Sudanese president… Their appeal for retributive justice… was solemnly echoed in European and US capitals, and universally by rights organisations and activist groups. Within hours, however, the Sudan government showed that the court and its backers were powerless to defend the millions of Darfurians in whose name justice is being sought.[3]

'They', in the first quote, referred to all those who were pursuing criminal accountability for Thomas Kwoyelo, a former member of the Lord's Resistance Army (LRA), in the Ugandan International Crimes Division. 'They' included Western

---

[1] Phone discussion with a Ugandan lawyer, November 2011. The interviews and conversations cited in this chapter were part of the research that led to the author's book *Complementarity in the Line of Fire: The Catalysing Effect of the International Criminal Court in Uganda and Sudan* (Cambridge: Cambridge University Press, 2013). See ch. 1 of that book for more background on the interviews.

[2] Interview with an attendant of a workshop on the ICC in northern Uganda in 2004, Kampala, November 2011.

[3] Julie Flint and Alex de Waal, 'To Put Justice before Peace Spells Disaster for Sudan', *The Guardian*, 6 March 2009.

Sarah M.H. Nouwen, *Tensions between the Pursuit of Criminal Accountability and Other International Policy Agendas in Situations of Armed Conflict*. In: *The Individualization of War*. Edited by: Jennifer Welsh, Dapo Akande, and David Rodin, Oxford University Press. © Sarah M.H. Nouwen (2023). DOI: 10.1093/oso/9780192872203.003.0008

188   CRIMINAL ACCOUNTABILITY AND OTHER POLICY AGENDAS

donors who wanted to see a first case before the special court that they had invested in, and the Ugandan Attorney-General's Chambers, which had adopted the argument made by donor-seconded advisors that the Ugandan Amnesty Act of 2000 was unconstitutional. 'They' were willing to put at risk the legal certainty of more than 26,000 beneficiaries of the Amnesty Act in order to prosecute one man before the International Crimes Division. 'We the people' referred to Ugandan society and included the speaker, a Ugandan lawyer. In his view, individual criminal accountability was pursued at the expense of the rule of law and self-determination.

The second quote reflects the reaction of people in Northern Uganda upon learning that the ICC did not have its own enforcement powers, and would instead rely on the same army that had failed to defeat the LRA for twenty years. A similar concern was expressed by an elder in the community: 'If you want to issue arrest warrants, then make sure that [LRA leader] Kony is within your reach. If you cannot arrest Kony, then it is the local people that will suffer.'[4] In their view, the pursuit of individual criminal accountability came at the risk of increased violence and diminished chances for peace.

The third quote is from two Sudan experts, commenting on the fact that the Sudanese government, in response to the ICC's issuing of an arrest warrant for President Bashir, expelled at least ten significant international aid agencies from Sudan and closed down Sudanese human rights organizations at gunpoint. In their view, the pursuit of individual criminal accountability had become an obstacle to the delivery of humanitarian aid and the promotion of human rights.

All three quotes illustrate the perception of tensions between the pursuit of individual criminal accountability and other international policy agendas, ranging from the promotion of peace, security, human rights, self-determination, and the rule of law to the delivery of humanitarian aid.

1. Introduction

The pursuit of individual criminal accountability in situations of armed conflict is one of the manifestations of what the editors of this volume have called 'the individualization of war':[5] 'a process in which individuals (both as agents and as subjects) increase in importance compared with collective entities for the purposes of explaining and normatively assessing the causes, conduct, and consequences of

---

[4] Interview, Gulu, September 2008.
[5] However, the pursuit of individual criminal accountability is also part of a broader 'fight against impunity', which is not limited to situations of armed conflict.

war.[6] As the editors argue in the Introduction to this volume, this process of individualization can generate a variety of tensions for the actors most actively engaged in or associated with contemporary armed conflict.[7]

The primary aim of this chapter is to illustrate tensions with other policy areas that the pursuit of individual criminal accountability can create. Elaborating on the quotes above, it identifies nine such areas: peace (in multiple meanings); humanitarian relief; humanitarian law promotion; military action to end atrocities; peacekeeping; economic cooperation; human rights promotion; rule-of-law promotion; and democratization.

The limitations of this first aim must immediately be spelled out. The aim is to illustrate; not to exhaust. Many of the examples derive from Uganda and Sudan, because they were observed there during fieldwork on related research questions.[8] The chapter identifies tensions that *can* arise; they need not always arise. Since the focus is on tensions, the chapter does not elaborate on the many synergies that can exist between the pursuit of individual criminal accountability and other policy agendas, for instance, the pursuit of individual criminal accountability (eventually) promoting positive peace or international humanitarian law. While it is recognized that pure liability as a result of the existence of (international) criminal law could already create tensions,[9] the focus is on tensions created by the *pursuit* of individual criminal *accountability*, that is, attempts to transform liability into accountability through criminal proceedings. Individual criminal accountability

---

[6] Jennifer Welsh, Dapo Akande, and David Rodin, 'Introduction: Understanding Individualization', this volume, pp. 7–8. See also Jennifer M. Welsh, 'Humanitarian Actors and International Political Theory', in Chris Brown and Robyn Eckersley, eds, *The Oxford Handbook of International Political Theory* (Oxford: Oxford University Press, 2018). The increasing attention for the individual reflects the international dominance of liberalism in the late 1990s and early 2000s. That political orientation may now seem under threat from other (re-)emerging 'isms', in particular nationalism, but law and policymaking (possibly healthily) lag behind.

[7] See Welsh et al., Introduction, above note 6.

[8] See Nouwen, *Complementarity in the Line of Fire*, above note 1.

[9] For instance, the criminalization of aggression, and the existence of jurisdiction over that crime, may discourage actors from pursuing so-called 'humanitarian intervention', that is, the use of force for humanitarian reasons without Security Council authorization. The argument that because the legality of humanitarian intervention is in a 'grey zone', it does not 'by its character, gravity and scale, ... constitute ... a manifest violation of the Charter of the United Nations' may not be sufficient to convince potential interveners. For this argument, see Claus Kreß and Leonie von Holtzendorff, 'The Kampala Compromise on the Crime of Aggression', *Journal of International Criminal Justice* 8, no. 5 (2010), pp. 1179–1217, at pp. 1192–1193. Another example is the classification of an evacuation of a civilian population from a besieged area as the war crime of forced displacement. See Emanuela-Chiara Gillard in response to Kai Ambos, 'Evacuation of Civilian Populations and Criminal Responsibility: A Critical Appraisal of the February 2017 Report of the Syria Commission of Inquiry', 24 May 2017. Available at: https://www.ejiltalk.org/evacuation-of-civilian-populations-and-criminal-complicity-a-critical-appraisal-of-the-february-2017-report-of-the-syria-commission-of-inquiry/comment-page-1/ observing 'the negative impact that labelling an evacuation as a war crime is likely to have on future endeavours to negotiate and implement evacuations or other arrangements to assist and protect civilians "trapped in conflict"'.

can be pursued for violations of domestic law and for violations of international law; by domestic actors and by international actors. Given the project's focus on tensions with other *international* policy agendas, the chapter will concentrate on international or foreign actors pursuing criminal accountability, whether in domestic courts (as in the example of the *Kwoyelo* case mentioned in the prologue) or in foreign or international courts (as in the quotes above referring to the ICC). The 'other international policy agendas' explored are dominant policy agendas of some influential international or foreign actors. These international policy agendas do not always coincide with the policy agenda of the state most directly affected and could thus lead to what we can call 'vertical tensions': tensions between the international or intervening foreign actor and the target state. The focus of this chapter, however, is on horizontal tensions:[10] tensions between policy agendas, often of one and the same international or foreign actor. The overview of the tensions is empirical, not normative. That is: it could be argued that some of these tensions *should* be there, that is to say, that they are a good thing. Indeed, when we move to trying to understand the character of the tensions, we will see that some have been created intentionally. However, the normative explanation and justification should not pre-empt the identification of the tension in the first place. Finally, the focus is on the pursuit of individual criminal accountability in times of ongoing armed conflict, whether international or non-international.

A secondary objective of this chapter is to use the overview of tensions between the pursuit of individual criminal accountability and other policy agendas to review the categories of tensions, and strategies of resolution, developed in the context of the Individualization of War project and set out in the Introduction of this book. It will show the relevance of those categories, but also some of their limitations. The chapter will add some categories for thinking through the tensions: tensions due to policy agendas having their own logics and specifically tensions produced by the logic of international criminal justice, tensions inherent in the definition of individualization and the difference between tensions due to incompatibilities in outcome and tensions as a result of incompatibilities in process. It will also speak to the idea of 'resolving' tensions, adding to the existing ideas that tensions that have been intentionally created are not meant to be resolved and that some of the purported strategies for 'resolution' in fact do not 'resolve' tensions but prioritize one policy agenda over another: the tension continues to exist. Whether

---

[10] For that reason, the chapter does not discuss the interesting potential tension between the pursuit of individual criminal accountability and self-determination: that tension mostly emanates from a vertical tension, between the imposition of a policy (the pursuit of individual criminal accountability or indeed any other international or foreign policy) and decision-making by the polity. For an exposition of the tension between self-determination and the Responsibility to Protect, see Alex de Waal and Sarah M.H. Nouwen, 'The Necessary Indeterminacy of Self-Determination: Politics, Law and Conflict in the Horn of Africa', *Nations and Nationalism 27*, no. 1 (2021) pp. 41–60, section 4.3.

through law or ad hoc, these prioritizations are ultimately determined by political choice.

The chapter will begin with some observations on categories of tensions, so that when we next turn to the overview of policy agendas with which the pursuit of individual criminal accountability can be in tension, the strengths and limitations of these categories can be illustrated.

2. Categories of Tensions

As elaborated by the editors in the Introduction to this volume, there are four main categories of tensions emerging from individualization:

(1) Tensions at the normative level where the values pursued clash among themselves;

(2) Tensions at the practical level due to intrinsic and unavoidable facts about the world;

(3) Tensions at the practical level due to contingent facts about the world; and

(4) Tensions that arise between different manifestations and domains of individualization.[11]

Let's focus on the first three categories of tensions. The fourth category definitely exists: this chapter will for instance illustrate that the pursuit of individual criminal accountability can be in tension with the promotion of international humanitarian law, which in and of itself also has features that are manifestations of the individualization of war.[12] But the reason to bracket off the fourth category is that it is qualitatively different from the first three, in that the first three categories seem to be alternatives to each other, whereas the fourth category can be a subcategory of any of the first three categories. That is, tensions that arise between different manifestations of individualization could themselves be due to tensions at the normative level, practical tensions due to intrinsic facts about the world or practical tensions due to contingent facts about the world.

As to the remaining three categories of tensions, we will see that the most fundamental challenge is identifying the boundaries between them, in particular between normative and practical and between intrinsic and contingent. These boundaries are not watertight. Normative tensions have practical consequences and practices heavily draw on normative ideas. In the words of Scott Shapiro when discussing this chapter: '[N]ormative tensions generate behaviour that is often at cross-purposes.'[13] Similarly, the line between intrinsic and contingent facts

---

[11] Welsh et al., Introduction, see above note 6.

[12] See, for instance, Part II and Chapter 6 (Gaeta and Jain) in this volume.

[13] The Individualization of War workshop on 11–13 June 2018 and email from Scott Shapiro to the author, 13 December 2018.

about the world is hard to draw because many seemingly contingent facts have strong roots, making them almost 'intrinsic' facts about the world. As Susan Marks has argued in her classic article on 'false contingency': 'things can be, and quite frequently are, contingent without being random, accidental, or arbitrary.'[14] For instance, at first sight, limitations in attention, understanding or resources seem contingent: usually, there could be more attention, better understanding or greater budget allocations, thereby reducing these tensions. However, ultimately, competition for scarce resources, including attention and understanding, is an intrinsic fact about the world.

With respect to the first category of tensions, that of tensions at the normative level, we will see that tensions between the pursuit of individual criminal accountability and other policy agendas are seldom due to the values pursued themselves being in tension with each other. For instance, peace in the sense of absence of violence and justice in the sense of criminal accountability need not be in tension; in an ideal world they go together. The ideal pursued is often one in which all objectives have been realized together: criminal accountability, peace in the sense of the absence of violence, other forms of justice, self-determination, etc. Hardly ever do the objectives fight among themselves. And yet, the tensions that arise are not purely 'practical' (whether due to intrinsic or contingent facts about the world) either.

Rather, it is frequently the *logics* of the pursuit of these objectives that create frictions with other policy agendas because the logics point in diverging directions. The logics refer to the courses of actions that are suggested by or following as a necessary consequence of, say, the pursuit of individual criminal accountability, humanitarianism or peacekeeping. Thus, it is, for instance, the *logic* of international criminal justice—one prominent way of pursuing individual criminal accountability—rather than its ultimate objective—accountability—that creates tensions with other policy agendas. The most famous warning for the logic of international criminal justice has come from the infamous Carl Schmitt: such universal norms provide a vocabulary to transform one's own enemies into enemies of mankind and in doing so places them beyond the bonds that hold international society together, which in turn leads to an intensification of conflict because those who violate international norms become enemies who must be destroyed.[15]

---

[14] Susan Marks, 'False Contingency', *Current Legal Problems* 62, no. 1 (2009), pp. 1–21, at p. 2.
[15] See Carl Schmitt, *The Nomos of the Earth in the International Law of the* Jus Publicum Europaeum. (trans. G.L. Ulmen, New York: Telos Press); Carl Schmitt, *Die Wendung zum diskriminierenden Kriegsbegriff* (Berlin: Duncker & Humblot, 2007, reprint from 1938 ed.), Carl Schmitt, *The Concept of the Political* (trans. G. Schwab, Chicago: University of Chicago Press, 1996), p. 54. Schmitt is notorious because of the centrality of National Socialist ideology to his writing and actions. See J.H.H. Weiler, 'Cancelling Carl Schmitt?' in 'Editorial', *European Journal of International Law* 32, no. 2 (2021), pp. 389–399. For an elaboration and qualification of the relevance of Schmitt's concept of the political for the field of international criminal justice, see Sarah M.H. Nouwen and Wouter G. Werner, 'Doing Justice to the Political: The International Criminal Court in Uganda and Sudan', *European Journal of International Law* 21, no. 4 (2010), pp. 941–965.

However, contrary to Schmitt's gloomy predication, as the definition of 'logic' reflects—'the course of action *suggested by or* following as a necessary consequence of'—logics need not always lead to the action that would be 'logical': sometimes, that action is merely suggested by it. And states, international organizations and other actors often do not follow logics to their conclusion. So, in practice, Schmitt's prediction is hardly ever fully realized: those accused of having committed international crimes still benefit from human rights and, under certain circumstances, international humanitarian law protections.[16] However, whilst we will not see the total destruction that Schmitt predicted, we will see *elements* of the logic of international criminal justice that he warned for manifesting themselves, still leading to the intensification of conflict. As I noted above, these consequences may be normatively defensible or even desirable—the purpose here is merely to illustrate them, in order to make the normative evaluation possible.

Apart from tensions due to the different logics of different policy agendas, there are tensions that are inherent in the definition of the phenomenon of the 'individualization of war'. The editors of this volume have defined it as 'a process in which individuals ... increase in importance, compared with collective entities'.[17] The definition thus recognizes that even prior to the process of individualization, there is competition for 'importance'. Such competition exists not just between individuals and collective entities, but also among policies associated with these categories. Tensions among policy agendas thus precede the individualization of war: there is always competition for importance. However, individualization will affect these tensions in a particular direction because individualization of war means, by definition, that one category becomes more important compared to another. This will inevitably create tensions between the policy agenda that gains in importance and those policy agendas that seem to be losing out, since the shift in importance will influence the competition for scarce resources, including money, attention, and ways in which issues are understood.

Since the pursuit of individual criminal accountability is a manifestation of the individualization of war, it, too, will produce such tensions of competition in its relationship to other policy agendas. I will give two examples, one pertaining to competition for determining how situations are understood, and one relating to competition for other scarce resources.

First, the pursuit of individual criminal accountability may lead to an understanding of a conflict that reinforces the need for that policy agenda, thereby potentially standing in the way of other understandings of the conflict and corresponding policy agendas. When individual criminal accountability is pursued in a particular situation, that is by definition done by applying the framework

---

[16] See also David Luban, 'The Enemy of all Humanity', in Kevin J. Heller et al. (eds), *The Oxford Handbook of International Criminal Law* (Oxford: OUP, 2020), pp. 558–582.

[17] See above note 6.

of criminal law to that situation. As a result, the situation gets 'framed' by criminal law. Frames 'shape what is viewed and how what is viewed is interpreted'.[18] Thus, the specific situation is described and understood in terms of criminal law, with a particular focus on the actions of some individuals, rather than those of the state, other states, international institutions, or, at least in international criminal law, corporations. Consequently, the emphasis of the explanation is on the criminal intent of a few individuals, rather than, for instance, the weakness of state institutions, inequality, or the impact of international (economic) interventions on a society.[19] The analysis of a situation through the prism of individual criminal accountability thus leads to an understanding of a conflict that in turn asks for criminal law as a response: if a conflict is understood as being due to the criminal intent of a few individuals (e.g., a President Bashir or a President Putin), the necessary response seems to be criminal accountability of those individuals. When that analysis becomes dominant, for instance as a result of efforts to muster support for the enforcement of criminal law, it can crowd out other, more structural understandings of conflict, and corresponding policy agendas.

Frames can coexist, so the existence of a criminal law frame need not rule out the existence of a geopolitical, political-economy, neocolonial, or other type of frame. However, frames by definition highlight some parts of reality over others.[20] In a world of limited capabilities to understand and diverging political preferences—thus due to inherent facts about the world, only the extent of the limitations being contingent—frames compete for dominance. Analysing the literature on frames, Séverine Autesserre has identified features of narratives that succeed in becoming dominant:

> certain stories resonate more, and thus are more effective at influencing action, when they assign the cause of the problems to 'the deliberate actions of identifiable individuals'; when they include 'bodily harm to vulnerable individuals, especially when there is a short and clear causal chain assigning responsibility'; when they suggest a simple solution; and when they can latch on to pre-existing narratives.[21]

---

[18] Sharath Srinivasan, 'The Politics of Negotiating Peace in Sudan', in Devon Curtis and Gwinyayi A. Dzinesa (eds), *Peacebuilding, Power and Politics in Africa* (Athens: Ohio University Press, 2012), pp. 195-211, p. 205. See also Sarah M.H. Nouwen, 'The Importance of Frames: The Diverging Conflict Analyses of the United Nations and the African Union', *Proceedings of the One Hundred Seventh Annual Meeting of the American Society of International Law 107* (2013), pp. 330-335.

[19] For instance, for a political economy explanation of the Balkan wars, see Susan Woodward, *Balkan Tragedy: Chaos and Dissolution after the Cold War* (Washington: The Brookings Institution, 1995).

[20] See also André Nollkaemper, 'Framing Elephant Extinction', *ESIL Reflections*, Vol. 3 (2014). Available at: https://esil-sedi.eu/fr/esil-reflection-framing-elephant-extinction/

[21] Séverine Autesserre, 'Dangerous Tales: Dominant Narratives on the Congo and Their Unintended Consequences', *African Affairs 111*, no. 443 (2012), pp. 202-222, at p. 207.

The criminal law frame scores highly on many of these indicators of success and is thus likely to do well in the competition.

Beyond competition over dominant frames, the pursuit of individual criminal accountability may create tensions with other policy agendas because resources, attention and political energy are limited. For instance, the pursuit of individual criminal accountability can, in practice, serve as an excuse not to undertake other types of action because 'we are already doing something.' Here again, international criminal law has its advantages over other policy agendas: it seems relatively clean and inexpensive compared to, for instance, peacekeeping or global redistribution.

Finally, we can differentiate among tensions as a result of incompatibilities in outcome and tensions as a result of incompatibilities in process. With respect to incompatibilities in outcome, a tension is recognized if, in the short term, outcomes are incompatible, even if in the long term they might go together.

3. Strategies for 'Resolution' of Tensions

In their Introduction, the editors consider how tensions emerging from the individualization of war with other policy agendas may be resolved. But before we move to attempts to resolve tensions, it must be recognized that some tensions have been intentionally created, by subordinating one policy agenda to another. Those who have done so may not wish the ensuing tensions to be resolved, or only once one policy agenda has been entirely fulfilled. One example is making economic integration conditional upon support for the pursuit of individual criminal accountability.[22] Similarly, some would argue that the tension that we will see below between the pursuit of individual criminal accountability and peace negotiations should not be resolved, indeed, that the purpose of the development of international criminal justice is to make peacemaking without criminal accountability impossible. In other words, tensions between policy agendas are often not a technical issue, but an emanation of political projects, sometimes given effect by law, for instance, international legal obligations to pursue individual criminal accountability.

When it comes to attempts to resolve tensions arising from individualization, the editors have conceptualized four strategies along a spectrum, ranging from principled and general to ad hoc and context specific. In summary, they are:

(1) Reconceptualization of a normative terrain, so that one value or norm is consistently prioritized over another;

---

[22] See below, §4.6.

196 CRIMINAL ACCOUNTABILITY AND OTHER POLICY AGENDAS

(2) Reconciliation: context-specific relationships between competing norms and values, for instance, through 'interpretative complementarity' of applicable legal regimes;[23]

(3) Institutional adaptation, for instance, by organizations such as the United Nations;[24]

(4) Ad hoc strategies: no systematic strategy, but paralysis (no action); sequencing (one value is pursued first and then the other) or principled inconsistency (through a case-by-case assessment of which value or objective to privilege in any given situation).[25]

These may be ways to *address* tensions, but not all are ways to 'resolve' them. In many approaches, the underlying tension does not disappear. For instance, reconceptualization involves prioritizing one value over another. Thus, in the concept of 'sovereignty as responsibility', the notion of 'sovereignty' may have been reconceptualized so that, in some circumstances, it is no longer incompatible with some forms of foreign or international intervention. The underlying tension between deciding for oneself and intervention continues to exist; it is just that, in some circumstances, intervention has been prioritized. As we will see, in the context of tensions with the pursuit of individual criminal accountability, there are similar attempts at reconceptualization. For instance, in the slogan 'no peace without justice', the argument is that peace that is not accompanied by individual criminal accountability does not amount to 'real peace'. The underlying tension between the absence of violence and the pursuit of criminal justice still exists, but the reconceptualization makes clear that criminal justice is prioritized because it is assumed to contribute to a normatively better peace. In sum, such reconceptualizations do not 'resolve' a tension, but 'deal with' a tension by prioritizing one value over another. The tensions will continue to exist but prioritization makes clear which policy agenda should prevail.

The 'reconciliation' approach comes closer to 'resolving' tensions, in that it can amount to a bit of give and take: both policy agendas can continue to exist, but have to accommodate each other in a concrete situation. The editors give as an example Nehal Bhuta's idea of 'interpretative complementarity' according to which rules of international humanitarian law and international human rights law interact in a specific case, one sometimes changing the other, without their supplementation having been fixed.[26]

---

[23] For 'interpretative complementarity', see Nehal Bhuta, 'States of Exception: Regulating Targeted Killing in a "Global Civil War"', in Philip Alston and Euan Macdonald (eds), Human Rights, Intervention, and the Use of Force (Oxford: OUP, 2008), ch. 7.

[24] I do not address this type of resolution, because it seems a category that is not independent of the other three. Rather, I imagine that organizations such as the UN also use strategies of reconceptualization, reconciliation, and ad hoc responses.

[25] Welsh et al., Introduction, above note 6.

[26] Idem, citing Bhuta, 'States of Exception'.

Two factors seem particularly important for the plausibility of the reconciliation approach and the idea of 'interpretative complementarity' more specifically. First, the availability of the approach depends on the policy agendas having been given effect in legal regimes. Bhuta's example works for interpretative complementarity precisely because both human rights and the conduct of armed conflict have been regulated in legal regimes. Interpretative complementarity is more difficult when one policy agenda has been given effect in a legal regime, and the other not, or far less so. For instance, the delivery of humanitarian aid has been given far less effect and protection in law than, say, the conduct of armed conflict.

Secondly, while most policy agendas will promote values that can find some protection in international law, the institutionalization of those legal regimes varies widely. For instance, the right to food has less of an international legal instrumentarium dedicated to its promotion than the objective of individual criminal accountability for certain international crimes. As a result of the emergence of these specialized instrumentaria, the likelihood and outcome of interpretative complementarity is likely to depend on the institution doing the interpretation.[27] Specialized international courts will have to apply first and foremost the law specified in the legal instrument by which they have been created. Thus, the European Court of Human Rights applies the European Convention on Human Rights and its Protocols; the International Criminal Court, the Rome Statute; investment tribunals, the relevant investment law. In case a term requires interpretation, they often turn to the rules on interpretation as reflected in the Vienna Convention on the Law of Treaties, which directs the interpreter to the 'ordinary meaning' to be given to the terms of the treaty in their 'context' and in light of the its 'object and purpose'.[28] The object and purpose of the treaty is usually to further precisely the values protected by that treaty: human rights, international criminal justice, investment, etc. In other words, simply because the relevant treaty's object and purpose is to further that policy agenda, and not others, the relevant adjudicators will not quickly interpret the treaty in a way to give priority to a conflicting policy agenda. For instance, even though the Rome Statute has not only a provision on the inapplicability of immunities before the Court but also an article protecting immunities in some circumstances, several of the International Criminal Court's Chambers have used purposive reasoning to say that an interpretation that would respect immunities would go against the object and purpose of the Statute.[29] There is no court specifically designed to promote the values that the law on immunity was

---

[27] See Martti Koskenniemi, 'The Politics of International Law—20 Years Later', *European Journal of International Law 20*, no. 1 (2009), pp. 7–19.

[28] Vienna Convention on the Law of Treaties (VCLT), art. 31(1).

[29] See, for instance, *Corrigendum to the Decision Pursuant to Article 87(7) of the Rome Statute on the Failure by the Republic of Malawi to Comply with the Cooperation Requests Issued by the Court with Respect to the Arrests and Surrender of Omar Hassan Ahmad Al Bashir*, Pre-Trial Chamber II Decision, ICC-02/05-01/09-139-Corr, 13 December 2011, at para. 41 and *Judgment in the Jordan Referral re Al-Bashir Appeal*, Appeals Chamber Decision, ICC-02/05-01/09-397-Corr, 6 May 2019, para. 124.

once designed to protect (for instance, protecting the functioning of the state or fostering international dialogue and the equality of states)[30] but it is to be expected that a court that applies international law more generally, such as the International Court of Justice, would have been more open to interpretative complementarity than the ICC with its sole anti-impunity agenda. As Martti Koskenniemi has argued, the institutional fragmentation that results from the creation of all these specialized courts (human rights, international criminal law, trade, investment, etc.), is not a technical issue, but political: it is the product of conscious attempts to foster specific policy agendas through specific institutions.[31] The tensions between policy agendas that exist at the political level (which policy agenda should be given priority in terms of logics, resources, attention) thus continue to exist once they have been given effect in laws and are promoted through legal institutions: the political battle among policy agendas continues, now also on the legal plane.

Still, even if a specialized court applies and interprets its own applicable law, reconciliation with other policy agendas may be possible, depending on its understanding of its own object and purpose. Take the subject of this chapter: the pursuit of individual criminal accountability. The answer to the question whether and how norms are prioritized between the pursuit of individual criminal accountability and other policy agendas, or whether context-specific accommodation is possible, depends on one's philosophy of international criminal law. One's philosophy of criminal law includes a vision on what and whom international criminal law is for. If one's philosophy is that international criminal law is primarily about promoting social order, then punishment could be less required than if one's philosophy is that international criminal law is about retribution. In a social order–oriented approach there may thus be more scope for sanctions other than incarceration, thus facilitating compromise with policy agendas such as promoting peace negotiations, than in a retributive approach. Similarly, if one's philosophy of international criminal law is that its primary constituent is the 'international community', this will limit the extent to which policy agendas focusing on the community where the crimes were committed can be taken into account.

Moreover, in some instances, specialized courts have reconciled the values they are primarily promoting with legal rules protecting the values of other policy agendas on the ground that their statutes declare such rules applicable, or because the rules on treaty interpretation provide that '[t]here shall be taken into account, together with the context: .... [a]ny relevant rules of international law applicable in the relations between the parties.'[32] Accordingly, in *Hassan v UK*, the Grand Chamber of the European Court of Human Rights interpreted the right to liberty and security 'against the background of the provisions of international humanitarian

---

[30] For a challenge to the continued relevance of these rationales, see Adil Haque, Chapter 1 in this volume.

[31] Koskenniemi, 'The Politics of International Law—20 Years Later'.

[32] VCLT, art 31(3)(c).

law', effectively giving precedence to the latter in the case at hand.[33] Note, however, that the partly dissenting opinion objected to this interpretation, arguing that:

> the powers of internment under the Third and Fourth Geneva Conventions, relied on by the Government as a permitted ground for the capture and detention of Tarek Hassan, are in direct conflict with Article 5 § 1 of the Convention. The Court does not have any legitimate tools at its disposal, as a *court of law*, to remedy this clash of norms. It must therefore give priority to the Convention, as its role is limited under Article 19 to '[ensuring] the observance of the engagements undertaken by the High Contracting Parties in the Convention and the Protocols thereto'. By attempting to *reconcile the irreconcilable*, the majority's finding today does not, with respect, reflect an accurate understanding of the scope and substance of the fundamental right to liberty under the Convention, as reflected in its purpose and its historical origins in the atrocities of the international armed conflicts of the Second World War.[34]

This case thus illustrates that it is disputed whether tensions *should be* resolved through reconciliation.

Given such disputes, an important consideration is also *who* decides on the 'resolution' of tensions. Thus far, the examples have focused on various international courts. It is not given that these do, or deem themselves obliged to, take into account the views of the societies most affected, whether local, national or regional. Moreover, many such tensions never reach an international court and are de facto decided by policymakers.

In sum, reconciliation may be a strategy to resolve tensions between policy agendas when the conflicting policy agendas have been given legal protection and when the applicable law of institutions created to promote the policy agendas allow taking into account the legal framework of other policy agendas. But it remains contested whether such reconciliation is normatively desirable and those who decide on the reconciliation are usually not those most affected by the tensions.

4. Potential Tensions between the Pursuit of Individual Criminal Accountability and Other Policy Agendas

Against this background of categories of tensions and resolutions, we can now turn to examples of potential tensions between the pursuit of individual criminal accountability and other policy agendas.

---

[33] *Case of Hassan v. The United Kingdom* [GC], no. 29750/09, ECHR 2014, para. 104.
[34] *Case of Hassan v. The United Kingdom* (Partly Dissenting Opinion Judge Spano joined by judges Nicolaou, Bianku and Kalaydjieva) [GC], no. 29750/09, ECHR 2014, para. 19 (emphasis in the original).

4.1 Peace

The tension between the pursuit of individual criminal accountability and peace is probably the most famous one, with an entire scholarly and policy debate named after it: the 'peace versus justice' debate.[35] However, the characteristics of the tension depend on the understandings of justice and peace. Justice, in this context, is usually shorthand for criminal justice, that is, the pursuit of individual criminal accountability (and not, for instance, restorative, distributive or procedural justice). Peace, in the 'peace versus justice' debate, usually refers to the absence of armed conflict, also known as 'negative peace'. In the slogan 'no peace without justice', however, peace is sometimes also interpreted to mean a condition in which structural violence is addressed, i.e., 'positive peace'.[36] Less prominent in the context of this debate is an understanding of peace as the promotion of international relations, even though the pursuit of individual criminal accountability can also be in tension with that understanding.

Peace as a Condition in Which Armed Conflict Is Absent (Negative Peace)

Whether the pursuit of individual criminal accountability is in tension with the quest for an end to armed conflict depends on how the latter objective is pursued. If the aim is to end war through total victory, the two could go smoothly hand in hand.[37] Indeed, this is what Schmitt warned for: the logic of universal norms on armed conflict leads to total warfare, because the enemy must be defeated.[38] Institutions pursuing individual criminal accountability such as international criminal courts can become instruments for such defeat: states refer their opponents, whether other states or non-state actors, to international criminal tribunals or even create such tribunals in the hope that this legal battle helps them defeat the enemy.[39] The courtroom is not an alternative to the military terrain; rather, the legal fight intensifies the military battle. We have seen this when states referred armed movements in their own countries to the International Criminal Court with a view to changing their domestic enemies into enemies of mankind, as a result of which they immunized themselves from international criticism and gained further military support.[40] We have also seen intensification of conflict when the Security Council referred a situation implicating the government of a

---

[35] This section builds on Sarah M.H. Nouwen, 'The International Criminal Court: A Peacebuilder in Africa?', in Devon Curtis and Gwinyayi Dzinesa (eds), *Peacebuilding in Africa* (Athens: Ohio University Press, 2012), p. 171.

[36] On the concepts of negative and positive peace, see Johan Galtung, 'Violence, Peace and Peace Research', *Journal of Peace Research 6*, no. 3 (1969), pp. 167–191.

[37] But tensions can emerge here, too: see below, §4.4.

[38] See above note 15.

[39] See Sarah M. H. Nouwen and Wouter G. Werner, 'Doing Justice to the Political: The International Criminal Court in Uganda and Sudan', *European Journal of International Law 21*, no. 4 (2010), pp. 941–965.

[40] Ibid.

state to the ICC.[41] And we may see it now that forty states have referred 'the situation in Ukraine' since 2013 to the International Criminal Court so that the Court can investigate alleged war crimes and crimes against humanity committed since the Russian use of force against Ukraine, while states are also discussing setting up a Special Tribunal for the Crime of Aggression in that situation.[42] In case of a military defeat, think about the situations in Germany or Japan after the Second World War or in post-genocide Rwanda, the victor can impose the terms of individual criminal accountability. There then is no tension between peace and justice because the justice meted out is on the terms of those who defined the terms of the peace (though those who are subjected to justice will often think they are because they lost).

Tensions are more likely to arise, however, when the preferred option is ending the armed conflict through negotiations, for instance because no party is strong enough to defeat the other party. In that case, the pursuit of individual criminal accountability can be in tension with the demands of both the process and the outcomes of such negotiations. With respect to the process, the pursuit of individual criminal accountability may discourage negotiations when one warring party estimates that individual criminal accountability will harm its opponent more than itself. Rather than encouraging negotiations, the pursuit of criminal justice can embolden a party to pursue an end to the conflict through a total victory, and thus intensify conflict.[43] Schmitt would see his theory that subjecting armed conflict to universal norms leads to intensification vindicated in the more contemporary observation by humanitarian Fabrice Weissman: 'In practice, the exercise of international criminal justice in wartime has a greater tendency to radicalize conflicts than to pacify them.'[44]

Even if parties do not expect to gain from the pursuit of individual criminal accountability, that pursuit may still result in a framing of a conflict that is not conducive to negotiations. Negotiations require the parties to recognize each other

---

[41] Ibid.

[42] See https://www.icc-cpi.int/ukraine (Accessed: 11 March 2022) and 'Statement calling for the Creation of a Special Tribunal for the Punishment of the Crime of Aggression against Ukraine' and 'Declaration on a Special Tribunal for the Punishment of the Crime of Aggression against Ukraine', available at: https://gordonandsarahbrown.com/2022/03/calling-for-the-creation-of-a-special-tribunal-for-the-punishment-of-the-crime-of-aggression-against-ukraine/ (Accessed: 11 March 2022).

[43] See Nouwen and Werner, 'Doing Justice', above note 39. The opposite is also possible: the pursuit of individual criminal accountability could push a party to the negotiation table. The example of the Lord's Resistance Army is often given, but the LRA's interest in peace talks was probably more driven by the loss of a safe haven after South Sudan threatened to oust it, than by ICC arrest warrants (see Ronald R. Atkinson, *The Roots of Ethnicity: Origins of the Acholi of Uganda* (Kampala: Fountain Publishers, 2nd ed., 2010), pp. 308–309.

[44] Fabrice Weissman, 'Humanitarian Aid and the International Criminal Court: Grounds for Divorce', *Centre de réflexion sur l'action et les savoirs humanitaires (CRASH)* (2009), pp. 1–11, at p. 8.

as political adversaries, rather than as criminals:[45] constituencies will often not accept negotiations with 'terrorists', *génocidaires*, or *hostes humani generis*; they can accept talks with political opponents. Dominance of the criminal law frame may make this impossible, thus impeding negotiations. Schmitt would again see his warnings about the logics of international criminal justice vindicated. But what for Schmitt is the problem of the logic of international criminal justice is for others its *raison d'être*. According to David Luban, for instance, the entire purpose of international criminal justice is that certain forms of political violence are seen as criminal,[46] and therefore, by extension, that those who commit such violence are seen as criminals, rather than as mere political opponents. In other words, for some, this tension between the pursuit of criminal accountability and the needs of a peace process should not be resolved in the favour of negotiations, but exists intentionally, precisely to ban those who have committed international crimes from political negotiations.

These conceptual frames have practical effects on peace negotiations. The pursuit of individual criminal accountability may scare mediators, funders and other supporters away from negotiations, as they are afraid of being found 'complicit' (in a legal or political sense) in the crimes by facilitating peace talks. This tension is hardly the result of the law—there is no specific international legal prohibition on facilitating peace talks with organizations whose members have been accused of committing international crimes and complicity could be established only under an extremely, indeed untenably, broad interpretation of existing modes of liability. However, the tension is the result of some influential actors' interpretation of the law and of policy agendas around the law. The previous ICC Prosecutor, for instance, has told donors that providing food aid to the Lord's Resistance Army during the peace talks with the government of Uganda amounted to a violation of the Rome Statute. Ministries of foreign affairs were indeed concerned that supporting the talks would amount to a breach of their obligations under the Rome Statute[47] (even though, the Rome Statute does not contain, in Barney Afako's words, 'a crime to talk').[48] Other foreign officials were concerned that support for those talks would go against the state's policy of promoting the International Criminal Court: even if such support would not lead to a violation of a concrete

---

[45] As Mahmood Mamdani has argued in the context of the negotiations between the African National Congress and National Party in South Africa. See Mahmood Mamdani, 'Beyond Nuremberg: The Historical Significance of the Post-Apartheid Transition in South Africa', *Politics & Society 43*, no. 1 (2015), pp. 61–88, at p. 67.

[46] See, among others, David Luban, 'After the Honeymoon: Reflections on the Current State of International Criminal Justice', *Journal of International Criminal Justice 11*, no.3 (2013), pp. 505–515, at p. 509.

[47] Speaking notes for a Minister of Development Cooperation in Europe, for a phone call with the Juba peace talks mediator, 4 August 2006: 'I am not in a position to provide support—in whatever form to the peace talks, due to our obligations towards the ICC.'

[48] Barney Afako, 'Not a Crime to Talk: Legal Aspects of Dialogue with the Lord's Resistance Army', 25 June 2006.

provision in the Statute, it would be incompatible with the purpose of the Rome Statute.[49]

If not preventing the organization of negotiations in the first place, the pursuit of individual criminal accountability, especially the issuance of arrest warrants, may result in states and international organizations that are in a position to push parties towards the negotiation table deciding to avoid contact with key belligerents. Again, this is not so much the result of the law directly, but of arguments about the logic of international criminal justice and policies to support that logic: ideally one should not talk diplomatically with someone who has been charged by an international criminal court. Yet in practice the logic is hardly ever followed to its extreme: where considered 'absolutely necessary' for other policy agendas, contacts are still maintained.[50] Much thus depends on which policy is considered 'strictly required' at any given time.

Finally, belligerents sought by criminal courts may themselves stay away from the negotiation table when they are afraid of being arrested on the spot. Their place at the table could be taken by supporters who have less to fear from the pursuit of individual criminal accountability. But the absence of leadership creates its own problems. Firstly, there is a risk that those at the table are unable to represent the positions and interests of the people truly in charge. Secondly, the absence of the leadership renders impossible one of the key ingredients for successful talks and implementation of any outcome: trust building.

In terms of incompatibilities in outcome, individual criminal accountability may be an unacceptable outcome for some of those who will have to stop fighting for the armed conflict to end. If it is predetermined that individual criminal accountability will be an outcome, the pursuit of individual criminal accountability may therefore encourage defiance of the law rather than compliance with it.[51] Lawrence Sherman has argued that defiance, in other words, more crime, is more likely than deterrence when offenders experience sanctions as illegitimate, have weak bonds to the sanctioning agent and community, and deny their shame and

---

[49] Nouwen, *Complementarity in the Line of Fire*, above note 1, pp. 355–357.

[50] See, for instance, United Nations, Interoffice memorandum relating to the United Nations position on peace and justice in post-conflict societies, 25 September 2006, United Nations Juridical Yearbook 2006, 498–500, para 4: 'Contacts between United Nations representatives and persons indicted by international criminal jurisdictions holding positions of authority in their respective countries should be limited to what is strictly required for carrying out United Nations mandated activities. The presence of United Nations representatives in any ceremonial or similar occasion with such individuals should be avoided. When contacts are absolutely necessary, an attempt should be made to interact with non-indicted individuals of the same group or party.' See also UN Doc. A/67/828-S/2013/210, 8 April 2013, 'Guidance on contacts with persons who are the subject of arrest warrants or summonses issued by the International Criminal Court'.

[51] As Julie Flint and Alex de Waal have observed, 'pressure works if the party under pressure can agree with the end point. If that is life imprisonment, pressure only generates counter-pressure'. J. Flint and A. de Waal above note 3.

become proud of their isolation from the sanctioning community.[52] If the aim is to reduce crime, this insight may counsel against involving prosecutors prior to the end of a conflict.

These specific tensions illustrate that categorizing tensions arising due to the individualization of war is not straightforward. As objectives and as outcomes, the pursuit of individual criminal accountability and the absence of armed conflict are not incompatible at the normative level. Rather, these tensions are mostly due to facts about the world. There is little contingent about the fact that people do not like to sign up for punishment. The fact that parties interpret criminal justice interventions through tactical lenses is probably also an inherent fact about the world. So is the fact that the pursuit of individual criminal accountability means that one frames people as potential criminals, whereas peace negotiations require approaching them as political opponents. These are inherent facts about the world, but the degree to which they manifest themselves is likely to vary from case to case.

More useful than the inherent-contingent facts-about-the-world spectrum may be to analyse these tensions through the lens of the logics of the types of intervention. Whereas the logics of international criminal justice and of total victory are compatible (unless the vanquished are killed; see below), the logics of international criminal justice and of peace negotiations are in some ways opposed. International criminal justice focuses on excluding people from society because of what they have done (they can return only after their punishment), whereas peace negotiations focus on inclusion of the main belligerents, irrespective of what they have done. The logic of the pursuit of individual criminal accountability is that some forms of violence are criminal and should not be seen as 'merely' political violence; the logic of peace negotiations depends on talking 'politics'.

'Resolving' these tensions requires a normative choice as to which logic should prevail, either in the specific circumstances, or in general. With the development of international criminal justice institutions, the pursuit of individual criminal accountability has become more strongly entrenched as a matter of law, than the value of negotiated peace.[53] What is more, in accordance with Koskenniemi's theory of the politics of fragmentation,[54] such institutions will often put their object and purpose over various other policy goals and accordingly actively develop the law in a way that promotes their purpose, even if the letter of the law leaves some room for accommodation. It is thus that the ICC Prosecutor has argued that governments of ICC states parties may not negotiate with people for whom the ICC

---

[52] Lawrence W. Sherman, 'Defiance, Deterrence, and Irrelevance: A Theory of the Criminal Sanction', *Journal of Research in Crime and Delinquency 30* (1993), p. 445. See also S.M.H. Nouwen, 'The International Criminal Court and Conflict Prevention in Africa', in Tony Karbo and Kudrat Virk (eds), *Palgrave Handbook of Peacebuilding in Africa* (Palgrave, Basingstoke, 2018) 83–102.

[53] But for initiatives to provide peace mediation with more legal protection, see https://ifit-transitions.org/peace-treaty-initiative/ (Accessed: 2 February 2022).

[54] See above note 27.

has issued arrest warrants. The Rome Statute contains no such provision, but from the ICC's perspective it is clear: you sign up to the Rome Statute, you sign up to the objective of individual criminal accountability, and the logic of pursuing that objective is that you must then also help the Court in obtaining the persons it seeks to try, which means politically marginalizing them. And yet, in practice, governments sometimes refuse to follow this logic when other policy agendas are considered more valuable. For instance, while many European ICC states parties initially did not want to support the peace talks between the government of Uganda and the Lord's Resistance Army because their priority was the ICC's success in the case against the leadership of the LRA, once they saw the chances of the peace process increase and the positive impact that the peace talks had on the humanitarian situation in northern Uganda, they switched reasoning and logics.[55] Similarly, international organizations supportive of the ICC's mandate keep open opportunities for dialogue and resist executing arrest warrants if, in specific cases, they do not want to pay the price.[56] The result is one of ad hoc accommodation, as well as accusations of double standards. For the same reason, Schmitt was wrong in his predictions about the logical end-point of subjecting war to international law: even though, as we have seen above, the logics of the pursuit of international criminal justice can lead to the intensification of warfare, states are seldom willing to pay the price that total war would impose. But as the war in Syria has shown, this ambivalence of on the one hand identifying who the 'good guys' and who the 'bad guys' are, while at the same time not wanting to pay the price of trying to secure a military defeat, can considerably protract the armed conflict.

Peace as a Condition in Which Structural Violence Is Addressed (Positive Peace)

While the (negative) peace versus (criminal) justice debate is well rehearsed, tensions with positive peace have not often been articulated, probably because individual criminal accountability is usually seen as a necessary component of positive peace. Formulated in Johan Galtung's terms, positive peace is the absence of structural violence, with structural violence being present whenever 'human beings are being influenced so that their actual somatic and mental realizations are below their potential realizations.'[57] The strength of the concept of positive peace, its comprehensiveness, is at the same time its weakness: it encompasses almost everything good and therefore becomes conceptually intangible. Consequently, one can see individual criminal accountability as part of positive peace, while at the same time identifying tensions with other elements of positive peace. For instance, the pursuit of individual criminal accountability could in some instances

---

[55] Nouwen, *Complementarity in the Line of Fire*, above note 1, pp. 355–356.
[56] See above note 50.
[57] See Galtung, 'Violence, Peace and Peace Research', p. 167.

be in tension with more restorative forms of justice, for instance, when the result of individual criminal accountability is exclusion, and restorative justice would have focused on inclusion through healing relationships.[58] Or, the pursuit of individual criminal accountability by international institutions may help maintain the global international order, including all its inequality[59]—an inequality that would have to be addressed for positive peace to be achieved.

Categorized in accordance with the editors' triad of normative/inherent fact/contingent fact, most of these tensions fall into the 'fact' categories; at the normative level, all good things seem to go together. A key factor in the promotion of positive peace is the inherent fact about the world that resources are limited. More contingent is the exact distribution of these resources among policies aimed at promoting specific elements of positive peace. For instance, it is possible to imagine budgets increasing so that individual criminal accountability can be pursued in combination with reparations aimed at restorative justice. However, an increase in those budgets is still likely to be to the detriment of other elements of positive peace: the concept of positive peace requires investment in so many areas of life, ranging from health care and education to distribution, that an increase in investment in one area will almost always be at the expense of another area. In terms of categories of 'resolution', these tensions are usually addressed through prioritization. The tensions emerging from budgetary competition continue to exist and are therefore not 'resolved' at a deep level, but they are temporarily decided through budget allocations.

Some of the other tensions between the pursuit of individual criminal accountability and positive peace seem inherent in the phenomenon of the individualization of war. As suggested above, the individualization of war means that processes related to the individual gain more prominence in explaining war than others. When a conflict is described and understood in the language of criminal law, and thus in terms of specific individuals having criminal intent, there may be less attention for types of injustice that have fuelled or emerged from the conflict, for instance distributive injustices.[60]

Finally, it is again the *logics* of the pursuits of the various elements of positive peace that create many of the tensions. For instance, the pursuit of individual criminal accountability becomes an obstacle to, for example, restorative justice

---

[58] Sarah Nouwen and Wouter G. Werner, 'Monopolizing Global Justice: International Criminal Law as Challenge to Human Diversity', *Journal of International Criminal Justice 13*, no. 1 (2015), pp. 157–176.

[59] On the ICC accommodating the interests of great powers, see David Bosco, *Rough Justice: The International Criminal Court in a World of Power Politics* (New York: OUP, 2014). On the ICC and (in)equality, see also Sarah Nouwen, 'Legal Equality on Trial: Sovereigns and Individuals before the International Criminal Court', *Netherlands Yearbook of International Law 43* (2012), pp. 151–181.

[60] See also Mark Kersten, *Justice in Conflict: The Effects of the International Criminal Court's Interventions on Ending Wars and Building Peace* (Oxford: OUP, 2016).

or reconciliation when the legal form of criminal trials—incentivizing perpetrators not to incriminate themselves—obstructs truth telling and acknowledgement of the truth produced during the trial.[61] Similarly, criminal justice does not promote reconciliation when that justice is understood by a (vanquished) part of the population as 'victor's justice'. The dominant 'toolbox approach' in the field of transitional justice, according to which states should apply transitional justice 'tools' such as trials, truth commissions, reparations, and vetting simultaneously is aimed at pursuing many good and complementary objectives at the same time, but insufficiently recognizes the tensions produced by logics pointing in opposite directions.

Peace as the Promotion of International Dialogue

In an understanding of peace that focuses on dialogue among states, the pursuit of individual criminal accountability may become an obstacle when a state perceives the pursuit of individual criminal accountability as an international sanction against it. For instance, the government of Sudan perceived the Security Council's referral of the situation in Darfur to the ICC as a sanction just like the other sanctions that had been imposed on it in the very same week.[62] When the head of state subsequently becomes subject to an ICC arrest warrant, states parties may find it even more difficult to develop or maintain, let alone improve relations with that state given that the state perceives the arrest warrant as a regime-change warrant.

Although at the normative level compatible (one can want to have good relations with Sudan, while wishing to see its president in court), the logics of the pursuit of these objectives often clash: international criminal justice focuses on marginalization; the promotion of dialogue on inclusion. Some diplomats have complained that policies in support of the accountability regime obstruct other policy agendas. For instance, in Sudan, the existence of an arrest warrant for the head of state meant that foreign officials were discouraged by their superiors from interacting with the person who was key to all other policy agendas, whether it was peacemaking, economic development, or refugee policies.[63] The tension they experienced was the result of a policy choice to prioritize the pursuit of individual criminal accountability over the promotion of dialogue. The tension was addressed, not resolved, by prioritizing one policy agenda over another. Such prioritization was in some instances temporary: the EU, for instance, changed its

---

[61] See, among others, Desmond Tutu, *No Future without Forgiveness* (New York: Doubleday, 2000).

[62] Cf UN Security Council resolutions 1591 (arms embargo) and 1593 (ICC referral) of 2005. See Nouwen, *Complementarity in the Line of Fire,* above note 1, p. 308.

[63] Discussion with a key ambassador in Sudan, January 2010: 'We want to change our relation with the north [as opposed to then Southern Sudan], but there is this one obstacle: the ICC. I am prevented from meeting Bashir, whereas Salva Kiir [the leader of the SPLM and president of the government of Southern Sudan] and others urge me to meet with Bashir to facilitate the peace process. In order to have influence in this country you must be able to meet with the President.'

208 CRIMINAL ACCOUNTABILITY AND OTHER POLICY AGENDAS

stance vis-à-vis Sudan generally and its leadership more specifically when Sudan became seen as a useful partner in constraining refugees on their way to Europe.

Once a policy prioritization has been cast in law, it is harder to change. As mentioned above, according to the ICC's interpretation, the Rome Statute obliges states parties to arrest persons for whom the Court has issued warrants if those persons are on their territory, even if such persons benefit from immunities under international law before foreign courts.[64] Some states parties and regional organizations had offered alternative interpretations, arguing that the objective of the promotion of dialogue among states was in fact protected in the Rome Statute. But in light of Koskenniemi's theory of the politics of fragmentation,[65] it is not surprising that a court that sees as its object and purpose the fight against impunity, prioritizes an interpretation that promotes that policy agenda, over competing interpretations.[66]

4.2 Humanitarian Relief

At the operational level, tensions between the pursuit of individual criminal accountability, particularly when pursued by international actors, and humanitarian relief can arise when the pursuit of accountability is perceived, by the belligerents or the public, as a form of political intervention (which, on the ground, it often is) and humanitarian relief gets, unwillingly, associated with that intervention.[67] Key to humanitarian relief is access to those in need in a way that is secure for both staff and beneficiaries. Humanitarian organizations try to secure that so-called 'humanitarian space' by respecting the core humanitarian principles of neutrality and independence. Intervening politically is considered a violation of those principles, and therefore as a threat to the humanitarian space. The intervention of an international criminal court is often perceived by the public as a 'political' intervention and humanitarian space can thus be endangered when belligerents or the public regard humanitarian organizations as associated with such intervention.[68] Such association can be made on the basis of allegations that the

---

[64] See *Judgment in the Jordan Referral re Al-Bashir Appeal,* Appeals Chamber Decision, ICC-02/05-01/09-397-Corr, 6 May 2019.

[65] Above note 27.

[66] See also S.M.H. Nouwen, 'Return to Sender: Let the International Court of Justice Justify or Qualify International-Criminal-Court Exceptionalism Regarding Personal Immunities', *Cambridge Law Journal 78*, no. 3 (2019), pp. 596–611.

[67] This section heavily draws on Sara Kendall and Sarah M.H. Nouwen, 'International Criminal Justice and Humanitarianism', in Heller et al. (eds), *The Oxford Handbook of International Criminal Law* (Oxford: OUP, 2020) 719-747. For tensions, and ways of addressing these, between accountability mechanisms and humanitarians, see also Emanuela-Chiara Gillard and Dapo Akande, 'Humanitarian Actors' Engagement with Accountability Mechanisms in Situations of Armed Conflict: Workshop Report', European University Institute, 21 January 2016. Available at: https://cadmus.eui.eu/handle/1814/51546

[68] See, for instance, Kate Mackintosh, 'Note for humanitarian organizations on cooperation with international tribunals', *International Review of the Red Cross 86*, no. 853 (2004), pp. 131–146, at p. 145:

humanitarian organization has spurred the intervention. Or, humanitarian space is at risk when belligerents fear that relief agencies will help enforce arrest warrants. Or, when they fear that relief agencies might provide evidence in court.[69] Even when humanitarian organizations have no such mandates, the association is quickly made, given the outward similarities of humanitarian organizations and other intervening agencies. UN humanitarian agencies may write the words 'United Nations' in blue on their vehicles, to distinguish themselves from the Security Council–authorized troops that drive around with 'United Nations' in black letters, but to observers it often seems the same UN, and for that matter, the same UN that referred a situation to the ICC. The association is even more explicit when the ICC publicly acknowledges the role of aid agencies in providing critical information or references such information.[70]

This perceived similarity with and support for international criminal justice can impede humanitarian work. In some instances, it has led to denial of access, fewer permits, physical attacks, and, as the scenario referenced in the prologue's third quote illustrates, expulsion of staff.[71]

In the editors' triad of normative/practical-intrinsic/practical-contingent factors, most of these tensions at the operational level seem the result of practical-contingent factors: as a matter of normative objectives, humanitarian relief and international criminal justice can be pursued simultaneously, but in practice there are tensions due to people making associations. The challenge is assessing how

'Public cooperation with an international court ... may compromise the organizations' abilities to provide those life-saving services.'

[69] Pursuant to rule 73(4) of its Rules of Procedure and Evidence, the ICC has to regard as privileged information coming from the ICRC, including its officials. This does not cover other humanitarian organizations. Moreover, even for the ICRC the privilege is not absolute. Rule 73(6) provides that 'If the Court determines that ICRC information, documents or other evidence are of great importance for a particular case, consultations shall be held between the Court and ICRC in order to seek to resolve the matter by cooperative means, bearing in mind the circumstances of the case, the relevance of the evidence sought, whether the evidence could be obtained from a source other than ICRC, the interests of justice and of victims, and the performance of the Court's and ICRC's functions.'

[70] Humanitarian organizations 'were appalled that the ICC publicly thanked aid organizations operating in Darfur for providing critical information and felt no surprise when Sudanese President Omar al-Bashir evicted nearly a dozen aid agencies on the grounds that they were not keeping people alive but rather helping Sudan's enemies' (Michael N. Barnett, *The Empire of Humanity: A History of Humanitarianism* (Ithaca, NY: Cornell University Press, 2011), p. 16). For examples of referencing information likely to be provided by aid agencies, see Situation in Darfur, the Sudan, Public Redacted Version of the Prosecutor's Application under Article 58, ICC-02/05-157-AnxA, OTP, 12 September 2008, pp. 53–56.

[71] With respect to Sudan, see for instance, UN Doc. S/2009/201, Report of the Secretary-General on the Deployment of the African Union-United Nations Hybrid Operation in Darfur (14 April 2009), para. 26: '[O]n 4 March, the Sudan's Humanitarian Aid Commission revoked the registrations and expelled 13 international NGOs as well as dissolved 3 national NGOs working in north Sudan with immediate effect, for allegedly collaborating with International Criminal Court investigations. As part of this process, Government officials also requested the organizations in question to hand over an inventory of assets, gathered banking details, confiscated office equipment such as laptop computers, and seized project materials .... On 5 March, during an address to the Council of Ministers and a crowd of a few thousand people in Khartoum, high-ranking officials, including President al-Bashir and the Commissioner of Humanitarian Aid, confirmed the expulsion of the NGOs on the grounds that they had acted outside their mandate.'

210 CRIMINAL ACCOUNTABILITY AND OTHER POLICY AGENDAS

contingent these associations are. The emergence of 'new humanitarianism',[72] in which 'humanitarian' work has expanded to encompass human rights promotion and even military operations in order to address presumed causes of humanitarian crises, has made differentiating between humanitarianism and the pursuit of individual criminal accountability only more difficult.

However, the tensions between international criminal justice and humanitarianism also exist due to at times opposing logics. Humanitarian relief aims at preventing suffering by protecting life and health. International criminal justice is sometimes justified as a means of preventing international crimes, and by extension of saving lives, but its direct aim is to hold individuals to account, even if this could impede saving lives. The different objectives stem from distinct animating values: empathy in the case of humanitarianism; responsibility in the case of international criminal justice. Didier Fassin, one of the foremost theorists of humanitarianism, gives an example of humanitarianism where its logic points in the opposite direction of that of the pursuit of individual criminal accountability. In the cases of Augusto Pinochet and Maurice Papon, humanitarianism was invoked to 'exempt individuals accused or convicted of crimes against humanity from facing justice or punishment'.[73]

One way in which this tension has been addressed is through law. Again, rather than resolving the tension, the law, or the interpretation of the law, has prioritized one policy agenda and its logic over the other. Generally, the pursuit of individual criminal accountability has received much more protection in international law than humanitarian aid: there is an International Criminal Court, and while there are thousands of humanitarian agencies, humanitarian relief is not protected by a specific international court.

4.3 Humanitarian Law Promotion

From one perspective, the pursuit of individual criminal accountability and the promotion of humanitarian law go hand in hand: by holding individuals to account for, among others, violations of international humanitarian law, criminal law can give international humanitarian law more teeth. However, tensions do emerge if the pursuit of individual criminal accountability interferes with other ways of promoting international humanitarian law, ways that are considered

---

[72] On 'new humanitarianism', see, inter alia, Fiona Fox, 'New Humanitarianism: Does It Provide a Moral Banner for the 21st Century?', *Disasters 25*, no. 4 (2001), pp. 275–289. The label is controversial since its newness is contested: see Barnett, *Empire*.

[73] Didier Fassin, *Humanitarian Reason: A Moral History of the Present* (trans. Rachel Gomme, Berkeley: University of California Press, 2012), p. xi.

more effective or more holistic, because they also pay attention to international humanitarian law norms the violation of which does not amount to international crimes.[74] For instance, one representative of an organization involved in the promotion of international humanitarian law in Sudan observed:

> Now with the ICC, it is over. The request for the arrest warrant against Bashir was a turning point, for Sudan, and for African states more generally. They now say: 'We cannot commit ourselves to any new convention, agreement, related to international humanitarian law.' These fields have been politicised and this will backlash on our work.[75]

In this representative's view, humanitarian law was best promoted through 'soft' norm infiltration: training, encouragement to sign up to treaties, more training, dialogue. Rather than seeing the ICC's request for an arrest warrant against President Bashir, including for charges of war crimes, as a way to promote compliance with international humanitarian law, he saw the Court as a threat to international humanitarian law: the fact that in Sudan the ICC intervention was perceived as a tool for regime change and therefore as political, tainted the whole of international humanitarian law as political.

These tensions are thus not due to tensions at the normative level, but a result of diverging ways of pursuing the objectives. They are unlikely to be resolved. Rather, they will be addressed differently, depending on the theory of change underpinning the work of a specific organization, for instance, that of an organization encouraging compliance through training, or of an international criminal court punishing those who have committed war crimes.

4.4 Military Action to End Atrocities

Military action to end atrocities and the pursuit of individual criminal accountability can go hand in hand when both are targeting the same people. However, here, too, tensions may emerge, for instance when the objectives of that targeting are different. As the case of Muammar Gaddafi illustrates, for those taking military action to end atrocities, it may be acceptable that the target is killed. For those pursuing individual accountability, such killing defeats their objective. Again, the objectives of ending atrocity and individual criminal accountability are normatively compatible, but the ways of achieving them, may not.

---

[74] On which, see Gaeta and Jain, 'The Individualization of IHL rules through Criminalization for War Crimes: Some (Un)intended Consequences', this volume, Chapter 6.

[75] Interview with a senior representative of a humanitarian organization, Khartoum, October 2008.

4.5 Peacekeeping

The pursuit of individual criminal accountability may make peacekeeping more difficult if the state or non-state armed group on whose consent the peacekeeping relies fears that the peacekeeping force might support the pursuit of individual criminal accountability that it objects to, for instance, by providing evidence or executing arrest warrants. A consequence could be that the state or armed group concerned withholds consent, restricts the number of peacekeepers that it accepts, or creates obstacles to access.[76] The peacekeeping operation's association with individual criminal accountability, particularly when enforced internationally, could also render peacekeepers more likely subjects of attacks. Finally, a tension could emerge between the pursuit of individual criminal accountability and troop contributing countries' willingness to send peacekeepers if these countries fear that this might render their nationals subject to (international) criminal jurisdiction. All these tensions are likely to intensify the moment that a peacekeeping operation in fact supports the pursuit of individual criminal accountability, whether through international or local courts.[77]

These tensions are mostly due to the different logics of the interventions. Peacekeeping is ultimately based on a form of consent from the warring parties, especially the host state; the pursuit of individual criminal accountability may require going against some members of those parties. In practice, these tensions are mostly addressed—again: not resolved—by prioritizing one agenda over the other. That could happen at the level of the mandate, but UN Security Council resolutions mandating peacekeeping operations are notorious for their lack of prioritization: the members of the Council want all good things (peacekeeping, the promotion of human rights, gender equality, HIV/Aids awareness, disarmament, rule-of-law promotion) to go together. Thus, the prioritization often happens at the practical level. Cooperation with, for instance, international criminal courts happens as long as it does not create tensions, for example, because it happens under the radar. Unsurprisingly, when tensions do arise, peacekeeping operations usually prioritize the value of protecting the existence and safety of their own mission.

---

[76] For empirical evidence of enhanced 'indirect obstruction' to UNAMID in Darfur after the issuance of the ICC arrest warrant against President Bashir, see Allard Duursma and Tanja R. Müller, 'The ICC indictment against Al-Bashir and its repercussions for peacekeeping and humanitarian operations in Darfur', *Third World Quarterly 40*, no. 5 (2019), pp. 890–907, at pp. 897–898.

[77] On which, see Tom Buitelaar and Gisela Hirschmann, 'Criminal Accountability at What Cost? Norm Conflict, UN Peace Operations and the International Criminal Court', *European Journal of International Relations 27*, no. 2 (2021) 548–571 and Emily Paddon Rhoads, *Taking Sides in Peacekeeping: Impartiality and the Future of the United Nations* (New York: OUP, 2016), pp. 79, 305–306.

4.6 Economic Cooperation

In the area of economic cooperation, we can find intentionally created tensions with the pursuit of individual criminal responsibility: economic cooperation has at times been made conditional upon a state's support for the individual criminal accountability agenda. Tensions arise when that agenda is unacceptable to the state concerned. For instance, under the amended Cotonou Agreement states could benefit from development cooperation from the European Union only if they sought 'to take steps towards ratifying and implementing the Rome Statute and related instruments'.[78] Another example of potential tension is regional integration being made conditional upon cooperation with international criminal tribunals, as happened in the former Yugoslavia.[79] Intentionally created tensions can be easily resolved by removing the conditionality. But the point of intentionally created tensions is that one policy agenda is considered normatively superior to the other.

4.7 Human Rights Promotion

While the pursuit of individual criminal accountability can be seen as promoting human rights—in a similar way as it can promote international humanitarian law—tensions can occur. Resentment against the pursuit of individual criminal accountability may cause a backlash against human rights promotion. Such a backlash can manifest itself in the denial of visas to people working in the field of human rights, the closing down of domestic human rights organizations, the fleeing of human rights activists and, more generally, the discourse of human rights becoming more politically sensitive.[80] Many of these tensions are similar in character to those between the pursuit of individual criminal accountability and the provision of humanitarian relief.

---

[78] The Cotonou Agreement 2014, signed in Cotonou on 23 June 2000, revised in Luxembourg on 25 June 2005, revised in Ouagadougou on 22 June 2010 and multiannual financial framework 2014–20, in particular art. 11(7). After the African backlash against the ICC, the negotiated text of the new agreement contains a less strong commitment to the ICC: the parties are (merely) 'encouraged to ratify and implement the Rome Statute of the International Criminal Court and related instruments, and to further enhance the effectiveness of the International Criminal Court'. See 'Partnership Agreement between [the European Union / the European Union and its Member States], of the one part, and Members of the Organisation of African, Caribbean and Pacific States, on the other', Negotiated Agreement text initialled by the EU and OACPS chief negotiations on 15 April 2021, https://ec.europa.eu/international-partnerships/system/files/negotiated-agreement-text-initialled-by-eu-oacps-chief-negotiators-20210415_en.pdf (Accessed: 11 March 2022).

[79] See, for instance, Stabilisation and Association Agreement between the European Communities and their Member States, of the one part, and Bosnia and Herzegovina, of the other part [2015] L164/2, Art. 2 and Art. 4.

[80] For an illustration of such an impact in Sudan, see Nouwen, *Complementarity in the Line of Fire,* above note 1, Chapter 4. For an illustration of such an impact of an international commission

Other tensions are similar in character to the tension between the pursuit of individual criminal accountability and the promotion of international humanitarian law. Human rights promotion may include, but is also much more encompassing than, the pursuit of individual criminal accountability. International criminal law protects only some human rights. It focuses mostly on accountability for human rights violations that are the result of physical, direct and visible violence. The eye of international criminal law, with its focus on individual attribution, does not see structural violence (other than, perhaps, as 'context' for the 'real' violence).[81] Conceptually, the pursuit of individual criminal accountability does not stand in the way of addressing human rights violations not targeted by international criminal law. In practice, however, increasing dominance of the criminal law frame can mean that other issues are not even seen as human rights issues, just like Paola Gaeta and Abhimanyu George Jain have warned that international humanitarian law not enforced through international criminal law risks losing in importance.[82] The tension is not merely one of scope, but also one of theory of change. The theory of change underpinning the pursuit of individual criminal accountability as a way to promote human rights (punishment of those who violate certain human rights) is fundamentally different from other avenues of human rights promotion, for instance, political organization around issues of social justice.[83] At a normative level, these avenues can be pursued in parallel. But here we are again confronted with an inherent fact about the world, or tension inherent in the phenomenon of the concept of individualization, namely that in a world of limited resources, including political energy, some ways crowd out others.[84]

---

of inquiry recommending the pursuit of individual criminal accountability in Israel, see Hala Khoury-Bisharat, 'The Unintended Consequences of the Goldstone Commission of Inquiry on Human Rights Organizations in Israel', *EJIL 30*, no. 3 (2019), pp. 877–901.

[81] See, more elaborately, S.M.H. Nouwen, '"As You Set Out for Ithaka": Practical, Epistemological, Ethical, and Existential Questions About Socio-Legal Empirical Research in Conflict', *Leiden Journal of International Law 27*, no. 1 (2014) pp. 227–260, at pp. 254–255.

[82] See above note 74.

[83] Public discussion with Gacheke Gachihi, coordinator of the Mathare Social Justice Centre, Cambridge, 29 May 2018, as part of the project 'Rethinking Transitional Justice from African Perspectives'. Gachihi explained that the Mathare Social Justice Centre mobilized around 'social justice' rather than 'human rights' or 'international criminal justice' because social justice allowed making connections among intersecting issues such as the environment and extrajudicial killings, whereas human rights and international criminal justice were about isolating and individualizing. Asked about the role of donors, he observed: 'For a while they bought into the ICC; that shot down debate about justice more generally.'

[84] On the impoverishing impact of the dominance of the ICC on global justice struggles, see Adam Branch, *What the ICC Review Conference Can't Fix*. Working Paper, 2010. Available at: https://www.law. ox.ac.uk/sites/files/oxlaw/adambranchicc_final1.pdf (Accessed: 10 April 2021). See also above note 58, Nouwen and Werner, 'Monopolizing'.

4.8 Rule-of-Law Promotion

The pursuit of individual criminal accountability can be a way to promote the rule of law, both at the domestic and international level. However, as the first example in the prologue illustrates, in practice it can also be pursued in ways that undermine elements of the rule of law, in particular the requirements of legal certainty and constitutionality. This tension, mostly due to contingent facts about the world, manifests itself if there is so much pressure to pursue individual criminal accountability that it is done at the cost of respect for legal guarantees and constitutional checks and balances.[85] The tension can be solved by not pursuing a policy objective at all costs.

4.9 Democratization

The pursuit of individual criminal accountability may become an obstacle to democratization. International arrest warrants can be a factor influencing political actors to stay in power. People around Sudanese President Bashir, for instance, have observed how the ICC's arrest warrant against him informed his decision to continue leading the National Congress Party despite his earlier intentions to step down.[86] In that light, some Sudanese civil society actors lamented the ICC as holding the entire country 'hostage'.[87] Another way in which the international pursuit of individual criminal accountability can obstruct democratization is when it is accompanied by financial, military, and political support for a government to suppress a rebel movement, thereby shoring up that government's power compared to that of any opposition—as it did in Uganda.[88]

5. Conclusion

This exploration of tensions between the pursuit of individual criminal accountability and other policy agendas has suggested that most of these tensions do not exist at the normative level—the objectives are not conflicting—but result from diverging logics: what is deemed necessary to pursue those objectives. Other tensions are inherent in the concept of individualization, in which the increase in

---

[85] Sarah M.H. Nouwen, 'The ICC's Intervention in Uganda: Which Rule of Law Does It Promote?', in Michael Zürn, André Nollkaemper, and Randall Peerenboom (eds), *Rule of Law Dynamics* (New York: CUP, 2012), p. 278.
[86] Nouwen, *Complementarity in the Line of Fire*, above note 1, pp. 272–273.
[87] Phone conversation with a Sudanese businessman, February 2018.
[88] Nouwen, *Complementarity in the Line of Fire*, above note 1, ch. 3.

importance of one policy agenda by definition means that other agendas receive less attention and less explanatory power. Yet again, other tensions have been intentionally created, by subjecting one policy agenda to another. That last tension is often practically the easiest to resolve (lift the conditionality) but usually normatively not desired. Other tensions are not resolved but addressed, most prominently through prioritization, either in law and legal institutions, or ad hoc. Compared to the policy agendas with which it can be in tension, the pursuit of individual criminal accountability has been relatively strongly institutionalized in legal form, among others, by virtue of the creation of the International Criminal Court. The logic of subjecting war to universal norms, and the politics of fragmentation, can in some cases give that regime influence beyond what the letter of the law stipulates. That said, contrary to what Schmitt feared, such logics are seldom pursued to their conclusion. Ultimately, states do weigh policy agendas. Whether through law or ad hoc, all these prioritizations are based on political choice.

References

Akande, D. and Gillard, E.-C. (2017) *Humanitarian Actors' Engagement with Accountability Mechanisms in Situations of Armed Conflict: Workshop Report.* Working Paper. Available at: https://cadmus.eui.eu//handle/1814/51546 (Accessed: 10 April 2021).

Ambos, K. (2017) 'Evacuation of Civilian Populations and Criminal Complicity: A Critical Appraisal of the February 2017 Report of the Syria Commission of Inquiry', *EJIL: Talk!*, 24 May. Available at: https://www.ejiltalk.org/evacuation-of-civilian-populations-and-criminal-complicity-a-critical-appraisal-of-the-february-2017-report-of-the-syria-commission-of-inquiry/

Atkinson, R. R. (1994) *The Roots of Ethnicity: The Origins of the Acholi of Uganda before 1800.* Philadelphia: University of Pennsylvania Press (The ethnohistory series).

Autesserre, S. (2012) 'Dangerous tales: Dominant narratives on the Congo and their unintended consequences', *African Affairs*, 111(443), pp. 202–222. doi: 10.1093/afraf/adr080.

Barnett, M.N. (2011) *The Empire of Humanity: A History of Humanitarianism.* Ithaca, NY: Cornell University Press.

Bhuta, N. (2008) 'States of Exception: Regulating Targeted Killing in a "Global Civil War"', in P. Alston and E. Macdonald (eds), *Human Rights, Intervention and the Use of Force.* Oxford: Oxford University Press (The collected courses of the Academy of European Law; v. 10/2).

Bosco, D. L. (2014) *Rough Justice: The International Criminal Court in a World of Power Politics.* New York: Oxford University Press.

Branch, A. (2010) *What the ICC Review Conference Can't Fix.* Working Paper. Available at: https://www.law.ox.ac.uk/sites/files/oxlaw/adambranchicc_final1.pdf (Accessed: 10 April 2021).

Buitelaar, T. and Hirschmann, G. (2020) 'Criminal Accountability at What Cost? Norm Conflict, UN Peace Operations and the International Criminal Court', *European Journal of International Relations*, 27(2), pp. 548–571.

De Waal, A. and Nouwen, S.M.H. (2021) 'The Necessary Indeterminacy of Self-Determination: Politics, Law and Conflict in the Horn of Africa', *Nations and Nationalism*, 27(1) pp. 41–60.

Duursma, A. and Müller, T.R. (2019) 'The ICC Indictment against Al-Bashir and Its Repercussions for Peacekeeping and Humanitarian Operations in Darfur', *Third World Quarterly*, 40(5), pp. 890–907. doi: 10.1080/01436597.2019.1579640.

Fassin, Didier. (2012) *Humanitarian Reason: A Moral History of the Present Times.* Translated by Rachel Gomme. Berkeley: University of California Press.

Flint, J. and de Waal, A. (2009) 'To Put Justice before Peace Spells Disaster for Sudan', *The Guardian*, 6 March. Available at: https://www.theguardian.com/commentisfree/2009/mar/06/sudan-war-crimes (Accessed: 3 April 2021).

Fox, F. (2001) 'New Humanitarianism: Does It Provide a Moral Banner for the 21st Century?', *Disasters*, 25(4), pp. 275–289. doi: https://doi.org/10.1111/1467-7717.00178.

Galtung, J. (1969) 'Violence, Peace, and Peace Research', *Journal of Peace Research*, 6(3), pp. 167–191.

Gillard, E.C. (2017) 'In Response: Evacuation of Civilian Populations and Criminal Complicity: A Critical Appraisal of the February 2017 Report of the Syria Commission of Inquiry', *EJIL: Talk!*, 24 May. Available at: https://www.ejiltalk.org/evacuation-of-civilian-populations-and-criminal-complicity-a-critical-appraisal-of-the-february-2017-report-of-the-syria-commission-of-inquiry/ (Accessed: 10 April 2021).

Kendall, S. and Nouwen, S.M.H. (2020) 'International Criminal Justice and Humanitarianism', in K. J. Heller et al. (eds), *Oxford Handbook of International Criminal Law.* Oxford: Oxford University Press (Oxford Handbooks), pp. 719–747.

Kersten, M. (2016) *Justice in Conflict: The Effects of the International Criminal Court's Interventions on Ending War and Building Peace.* Oxford: Oxford University Press.

Khoury-Bisharat, H. (2019) 'The Unintended Consequences of the Goldstone Commission of Inquiry on Human Rights Organizations in Israel', *European Journal of International Law*, 30(3), pp. 877–901. doi: 10.1093/ejil/chz044.

Koskenniemi, M. (2009) 'The Politics of International Law—20 Years Later', *European Journal of International Law*, 20(1), pp. 7–19.

Kress, C. and von Holtzendorff, L. (2010) 'The Kampala Compromise on the Crime of Aggression', *Journal of International Criminal Justice*, 8(5), pp. 1179–1217.

Luban D. (2013) 'After the Honeymoon: Reflections on the Current State of International Criminal Justice', *Journal of International Criminal Justice*, 11(3), pp. 505–515. doi: 10.1093/jicj/mqt023.

Luban, D. (2020) 'The Enemy of all Humanity', in K. J. Heller et al. (eds), *Oxford Handbook of International Criminal Law.* Oxford: Oxford University Press (Oxford Handbooks) 558-582.

Mackintosh, K. (2004) 'Note for Humanitarian Organizations on Cooperation with International Tribunals', *International Review of the Red Cross*, 86(853), pp. 131–146. doi: 10.1017/S1560775500180125.

Mamdani, M. (2015) 'Beyond Nuremberg: The Historical Significance of the Post-apartheid Transition in South Africa', *Politics and Society*, 43(1), pp. 61–88.

Marks, S. (2009) 'False Contingency', *Current Legal Problems*, 62(1), pp. 1–21. doi: 10.1093/clp/62.1.1.

Nouwen, S.M.H. (2008) 'The International Criminal Court: A Peacebuilder in Africa?', in D. Curtis and G.A. Dzinesa (eds), *Peacebuilding in Africa*. Oxford: Oxford University Press.

Nouwen, S.M.H. (2012) 'The ICC's Intervention in Uganda: Which Rule of Law Does It Promote?', in M. Zürn, A. Nollkaemper, and R. Peerenboom (eds), *Rule of Law Dynamics: In an Era of International and Transnational Governance*. Cambridge: Cambridge University Press, pp. 278–304.

Nouwen, S.M.H. (2012) 'Legal Equality on Trial: Sovereigns and Individuals Before the International Criminal Court', *Netherlands Yearbook of International Law*, 43, pp. 151–181. doi: 10.1007/978-90-6704-915-3_7.

Nouwen, S. M. H. (2013) *Complementarity in the Line of Fire: The Catalysing Effect of the International Criminal Court in Uganda and Sudan*. Cambridge: Cambridge University Press (Cambridge studies in law and society).

Nouwen, S. M. H. (2013) 'The Importance of Frames: The Diverging Conflict Analyses of the United Nations and the African Union', *Proceedings of the ASIL Annual Meeting*, 107, pp. 330–335. doi: 10.5305/procannmeetasil.107.0330.

Nouwen, S.M.H. (2014), '"As You Set Out for Ithaka": Practical, Epistemological, Ethical, and Existential Questions About Socio-Legal Empirical Research in Conflict', *Leiden Journal of International Law*, 27(1), pp. 227–260.

Nouwen, S.M.H. (2018), 'The International Criminal Court and Conflict Prevention in Africa', in T. Karbo and K. Virk (eds), *Palgrave Handbook of Peacebuilding in Africa*, Basingstoke: Palgrave, pp. 83–102.

Nouwen, S.M.H. (2019), 'Return to Sender: Let the International Court of Justice Justify or Qualify International-Criminal-Court Exceptionalism Regarding Personal Immunities', *Cambridge Law Journal*, 78(3), pp. 596–611.

Nouwen, S.M.H. and Werner, W. G. (2010) 'Doing Justice to the Political: The International Criminal Court in Uganda and Sudan', *European Journal of International Law*, 21(4), pp. 941–965.

Nouwen, S.M.H. and Werner, W.G. (2015) 'Monopolizing Global Justice: International Criminal Law as Challenge to Human Diversity', *Journal of International Criminal Justice*, 13(1), pp. 157–176.

Paddon Rhoads, E. (2016) *Taking Sides in Peacekeeping: Impartiality and the Future of the United Nations*. New York: Oxford University Press.

Schmitt, C. (1996) *The Concept of the Political*. Translated by G. Schwab. Chicago: University of Chicago Press.

Schmitt, C. (2003) *The Nomos of the Earth in the International Law of the* Jus Publicum Europaeum. Translated by G.L. Ulmen. New York: Telos Press.

Schmitt, C. (2007) *Die Wendung zum diskriminierenden Kriegsbegriff*. Reprint of 1938 Edition. Berlin: Duncker & Humblot.

Sherman, L.W., 'Defiance, Deterrence, and Irrelevance: A Theory of the Criminal Sanction', *Journal of Research in Crime and Delinquency 30* (1993), p. 445

Srinivasan, S. (2012) 'The Politics of Negotiating Peace in Sudan', in D. Curtis, G.A. Dzinesa, and A. Adebajo (eds), *Peacebuilding, Power, and Politics in Africa*. Athens: Ohio University Press, pp. 195–211.

Tutu, D. (2000) *No Future without Forgiveness*. First Image books edition. New York: Doubleday.

Weiler, J.H.H. (2021) 'Cancelling Carl Schmitt?' in 'Editorial', *European Journal of International Law*, 32(2), pp. 389–99.

Weissman, F. (2009) 'Humanitarian Aid and the International Criminal Court. Grounds for Divorce', *msf-crash.org*. Available at: https://www.msf-crash.org/en/publications/rights-and-justice/humanitarian-aid-and-international-criminal-court-grounds-divorce (Accessed: 3 April 2021).

Woodward, S.L. (1995) *Balkan Tragedy: Chaos and Dissolution after the Cold War*. Washington, D.C.: Brookings Institution.

8

Two Decades of Civilian Protection Mandates for United Nations Peacekeepers

Paul D. Williams

1. Introduction

United Nations (UN) peacekeeping operations are primarily political tools for conflict management with an admixture of military capabilities.[1] Since the 1950s, the UN's roughly seventy peacekeeping operations have been guided by three basic (but interrelated and flexible) principles, namely, operating with the consent of the main parties to the conflict, especially the host state; impartiality in their dealings with the conflict parties; and non-use of force except in self-defence—and later—in defence of the mission mandate.[2] Since the end of the Cold War, UN peacekeeping operations dramatically increased in number, increasingly sought to implement broadly liberal agendas to help stabilize war-torn territories, and frequently deployed into active theatres of armed conflict where there is no peace to keep.[3]

These developments saw UN peacekeepers increasingly expected to protect civilians trapped in those war-torn territories. This was a direct result of the individualization process in which individual agents and subjects played increasingly important roles in the conduct of warfare and conflict management. Yet UN peacekeepers were not given explicit protection of civilians (POC) mandates until 1999, starting with the mission in Sierra Leone (UNAMSIL). Since then, the Security Council has given POC mandates to sixteen of the nineteen subsequent UN peacekeeping operations. Today, over 90 per cent of UN peacekeepers are deployed in missions with POC mandates and they are often judged on how well they reduce the civilian casualties of war.

These POC mandates emerged as a direct consequence of the inability of UN peacekeepers to protect civilians from atrocity crimes, most notably during the

---

[1] For an overview, see Joachim Koops et al. (eds), *The Oxford Handbook of United Nations Peacekeeping Operations* (Oxford: Oxford University Press, 2015).

[2] *United Nations Peacekeeping Operations: Principles and Guidelines* (New York: UN DPKO/DFS, 2008).

[3] See Paul D. Williams with Alex J. Bellamy, *Understanding Peacekeeping* (Cambridge: Polity Press, 3rd ed., 2021), chs. 4–5.

Paul D. Williams, *Two Decades of Civilian Protection Mandates for United Nations Peacekeepers*. In: *The Individualization of War*. Edited by: Jennifer Welsh, Dapo Akande, and David Rodin, Oxford University Press. © Paul D. Williams (2023). DOI: 10.1093/oso/9780192872203.003.0009

1994 Rwandan genocide and the 1995 massacres at the UN's designated 'safe area' of Srebrenica in Bosnia-Herzegovina. After these atrocities, many people questioned the value of deploying peacekeepers if they were not going to protect civilians. But these mandates were also a reflection of the broader trends about the prominence of individuals in contemporary warfare and the growing concern among external actors to protect civilians from atrocities even during periods of armed conflict.[4]

The rise of POC mandates has generated various political, legal, moral and operational consequences and challenges for UN peacekeeping at its headquarters and in its field missions. That's because individualization was not the only process influencing UN peacekeeping; it existed alongside other, often more prominent principles and political realities. Most notably, reducing civilian harm has almost never been the central reason or cause for the deployment of UN peacekeepers. Rather, peacekeepers are only able to protect civilians in cases where there's a peace process to support—either a ceasefire or political agreement—and after receiving an invitation from the host state(s). These challenges and tensions have stimulated ongoing institutional adaptation and contestation within the UN. So far, however, these reforms remain incomplete and not fully effective.

This chapter analyses the evolution and consequences of POC mandates for UN peacekeepers in four parts. It starts by explaining how the individualization of war contributed to the emergence and evolution of POC mandates in UN peace-keeping operations as well as some of the ambiguities in how they have defined the core concepts of 'civilians' and 'protection'. The third section then summa-rizes some of the major practical and legal consequences for UN peacekeeping of adopting the new POC mandates. The fourth section examines the main tensions and challenges that arose from POC mandates. These arose, in part, because of the limits of the individualization process as it applied to UN peacekeeping. The final section assesses how far UN peacekeeping has overcome these tensions and sum-marizes some of the institutional adaptation undertaken by the UN to improve its record as well as institutional contestation over some of the organization's relevant decision-making processes.

Overall, I argue that POC mandates are evidence of the individualization of war and have been a useful addition despite sometimes unduly raising local and international expectations about what UN peacekeepers can achieve in the field. Ironically, growing negative perceptions about peacekeeping failures related to POC have come at a time when UN peacekeepers are generally doing a better job than before to help stop, reduce, and mitigate many threats of physical vio-lence to civilians. However, peacekeepers have generally been unable to resolve the underlying governance and political problems that generate most threats to civilians in the first place. In this sense, the individualization process as it relates to

---

[4] See, for example, Alex J. Bellamy, *Massacres and Morality* (Oxford: OUP, 2012).

222 CIVILIAN PROTECTION MANDATES FOR UN PEACEKEEPERS

UN peacekeeping has produced both operational and tactical benefits for civilians. Yet, despite the organization's significant attempts at institutional adaptation there remains a lack of strategic progress and continued institutional contestation.

2. The Emergence and Evolution of POC Mandates in UN Peacekeeping Operations

UN peacekeepers have long been confronted with the challenges and dilemmas of protecting civilians. During the early 1990s, for example, they were sometimes given mandates to protect particular narrowly defined groups of civilians, including VIPs and NGO workers.[5] But it was not until the UN's mission in Sierra Leone (UNAMSIL) was established in 1999 that explicit POC mandates were formally authorized by the Security Council. However, the first draft operational policy on civilian protection did not emerge from the UN Department of Peacekeeping Operations (DPKO) until 2010 and was not formalized until 2015. At this point, the UN policy defined protection of civilians as a whole-of-mission effort to include the military, police, and civilian components. In the interim, peacekeepers struggled to interpret and act upon the mandates handed to them by the UN Security Council while the Council sought to limit the practical impact of POC mandates by including a variety of conceptual and practical caveats.

The new POC mandates for UN peacekeepers were part of a gradual individualization process which eventually influenced the Security Council to initiate a range of thematic debates, statements and resolutions related to civilian protection. These were prompted by a variety of actors pushing distinct (but sometimes interrelated) protection agendas. In addition to the discussions in the Security Council, the POC mandates were part of a convergence of four other interconnected streams of thought and policy which developed in reaction to different aspects of civilian suffering during war.

One stream came from international lawyers calling for greater protection of civilians via the ongoing development of international humanitarian law (IHL) and human rights law, including the establishment of the International Criminal Court.[6] Then there were international NGOs and humanitarian relief agencies, some of which adopted protection agendas of their own and called for broader

---

[5] For example, UN Security Council Resolution 814 (26 March 1993) authorized UNOSOM II to 'neutralize armed elements that attack, or threaten to attack, such facilities and personnel' of the ICRC and NGOs.

[6] See, for example, Robert I. Rotberg (ed.), *Mass Atrocity Crimes* (Washington, D.C.: Brookings Institution Press, 2010); William A. Schabas, *The International Criminal Court* (Cambridge: Cambridge University Press, 5th ed., 2017), chs. 1–2.

support at the UN.[7] A third push for POC mandates came from some regional organizations, notably in Africa and Europe, which had themselves embraced various protection agendas.[8] Finally, several advocates for the emerging 'responsibility to protect' principle called for peacekeepers to play their part, a call that grew stronger with the adoption of the principle by the UN General Assembly in 2005.[9]

Although interrelated, these streams of thought reflected the particular concerns and interests of the respective actors. Unsurprisingly, they involved different definitions and emphasized distinct approaches to protection. But they all contributed to the Council's adoption of a new generation of POC mandates for its peacekeepers. On the other hand, the divergent approaches created some important gaps and tensions in the contemporary protection agenda, some of which are analysed below.

At the UN, it took some time to settle on agreed definitions of the two core terms of 'civilians' and 'protection'. The former was easier in theory if not always in practice. In IHL, civilians are persons who are not members of the armed forces, although state practice has been ambiguous as to whether members of armed opposition groups are considered members of armed forces or civilians.[10] The UN officially adopted a related definition in its 2015 POC policy, which defined a civilian as: 'Any person who is not or is no longer directly participating in hostilities or other acts of violence shall be considered a civilian, unless he or she is a member of armed forces or groups. In case of doubt whether a person is a civilian, that person shall be considered a civilian.'[11] The practical challenge was always how to make such a judgement call in the field, especially in war-torn territories where civilians including pastoralist or hunting communities might carry weapons and where armed groups didn't always wear uniforms.

In terms of defining protection, the concept's scope has long been the source of debate. For example, even after nearly a decade of operating with POC mandates, the 2008 UN's *Principles and Guidelines* document identified civilian protection as a core task of UN peacekeeping but did not elaborate on what protection entailed

---

[7] See, for example, Michael Barnett, *The Empire of Humanity: A History of Humanitarianism* (Ithaca, NY: Cornell University Press, 2011); Pierre Gentile, 'Humanitarian Organizations Involved in Protection Activities', *International Review of the Red Cross 93*, no. 884 (2011), pp. 1165–1191.

[8] See, for example, J.M. Okeke and Paul D. Williams (eds), *Protecting Civilians in African Union Peace Support Operations* (South Africa: ACCORD, 2017) and Karen Smith, *Genocide and the Europeans* (Cambridge: CUP, 2010).

[9] See, for example, Francis M. Deng et al., *Sovereignty as Responsibility* (Washington, D.C.: Brookings Institution Press, 1996); UN General Assembly, '2005 Summit Outcome', A/60/L.1, 20 September 2005, paras. 138–40; Gareth Evans, *The Responsibility to Protect* (Washington, D.C.: Brookings Institution Press, 2008); Alex J. Bellamy, *Responsibility to Protect* (Cambridge: Polity, 2009); Ramesh Thakur, *The Responsibility to Protect* (London: Routledge, 2011); Charles T. Hunt and Alex J. Bellamy, 'Mainstreaming the Responsibility to Protect in Peace Operations', *Civil Wars 13*, no. 1 (2011), pp. 1–20.

[10] Article 50 of Additional Protocol I to the Geneva Conventions (8 June 1977).

[11] *The Protection of Civilians in United Nations Peacekeeping Operations* (UN DPKO/DFS Policy, 2015.07, 1 April 2015), p. 5.

or how UN peacekeepers might achieve it in practice.[12] The document noted only that civilian protection required the promotion of IHL and coordination among disparate actors (i.e., the military, police, and civilian components of the peacekeeping operation as well as UN humanitarian agencies and NGOs).[13] Even to this day there has not always been clarity over what constitutes a threat (even in abstract terms). The UN Security Council's framing of POC centred on a nonlegalized concept of physical security, which encompassed a wide range of acts of violence directed at civilians, usually in armed conflicts or post-war settings. This approach was notable in part because it broadened the scope of POC in peacekeeping to encompass protecting people from incidents of physical violence that may be permitted under international law.[14] The Security Council's more general reference to a 'threat of physical violence' and the absence of legally defined triggers for action also introduced an element of selectivity and gave peacekeepers a great deal of discretion in interpreting what constitutes a threat.

In part because of the fuzzy scope of protection, there was also sometimes ambiguity about the actions that peacekeepers should take once a threat was identified. Put bluntly, if civilians are threatened by violence, UN peacekeepers were expected to mitigate the threat. But there has been a lack of clarity over the nature of their obligation, and specifically their legal obligations established by Council mandates.[15] Moreover, until very recently, peacekeepers received little guidance on how they should intervene in particular incidents, including whether some actions are obligatory and when and how force should be used.

Of course, many civilians on the receiving end of UN peacekeeping operations always expected some protection from peacekeepers regardless of whether there was a formal mandate to that effect. Sometimes this was down to basic but confusing issues, such as the UN peacekeeping force in Bosnia-Herzegovina being called the 'UN Protection Force' (UNPROFOR) but not having an explicit mandate to protect civilians. Some UN force commanders felt the same way; perhaps most famously General Dallaire, Force Commander of UNAMIR, who urged his peacekeepers to protect civilians when his mission found itself in the middle of the 1994 Rwandan genocide, even though his force did not have a mandate authorized under Chapter VII of the UN Charter.[16] The Council's explicit adoption of POC

---

[12] *United Nations Peacekeeping Operations: Principles and Guidelines* (New York: UN DPKO/DFS, 2008).

[13] Ibid., p. 24.

[14] See Haidi Willmot et al. (eds), *Protection of Civilians* (Oxford: OUP, 2016), Part II.

[15] It was not always clear what positive obligations a POC mandate bestowed upon UN peacekeepers in operational terms. See Siobhán Wills, *Protecting Civilians: The Obligations of Peacekeepers* (Oxford: OUP, 2009) and 'International Responsibility for Ensuring the Protection of Civilians', in Willmot et al. (eds), *Protection of Civilians*.

[16] The most prominent example is General Dallaire's role in UNAMIR. See Romeo Dallaire and Brent Beardsley, *Shake Hands with the Devil* (New York: Random House, 2003). For example, in UNAMIR, the Force Commander's Directive No.2 (1994) stated: 'There may also be ethnically or politically motivated criminal acts committed during this mandate which will morally and legally require

mandates in 1999 might therefore be understood as little more than a codification of existing realities on the ground. Moreover, even without formal POC mandates, UN peacekeepers were clearly expected to comply with IHL and human rights law in their areas of operations and to try and ensure that other actors complied too.[17]

Whatever their initial merits or demerits, POC mandates probably raised local expectations even further, but they certainly raised international expectations about what UN peacekeepers should accomplish in the field. The Council therefore developed a strategy for managing these expectations by building a series of caveats into its new POC mandates. These caveats made clear that UN peacekeepers could not be expected to protect all civilians from all threats in all places at all times. The Security Council's political, geographical, and operational caveats are summarized in Table 8.1.

Politically, POC was supposed to take place with the consent of the host state authorities and support government forces, who maintained the principal role in protecting local civilians. UN activities were therefore not supposed to prejudice the host government's responsibility to play the leading role in protection.[18] Geographically, resource constraints on UN operations meant that peacekeepers were clustered in relatively small number of locales in the theatre in question.[19] Hence the caveat that peacekeepers should only be expected to protect civilians within their areas of deployment. Operationally, civilian protection tasks were also supposed to be limited to those commensurate with the peacekeepers' capabilities. And because peacekeepers were not meant to prevent all threats to civilians they should focus on protecting people from imminent threats of physical violence (although the word 'imminent' was subsequently dropped in some mission mandates). Finally, not all POC mandates authorized peacekeepers to use 'all means necessary' to achieve their objectives.

Over time, the focus on POC in UN peacekeeping operations shifted from trying to clarify the definition of protection to concentrating more on the operational tools needed to effectively implement POC mandates in the field. The operational

---

UNAMIR to use all available means to halt them. Examples are executions, attacks on displaced persons or refugees.' Similarly, on 17 April 1994, Dallaire suggested that his force's current mandate allowed it to try to protect civilians in danger of massacre. As he told Col. Nazrul Islam, 'Our orders from New York are quite explicit; we are to conduct the evacuation of the expatriate community and to offer protection when feasible of Rwandese citizens. Within our peacekeeping rules of engagement we can use force to defend persons under UN protection and to prevent crimes against humanity. We must however balance the use of force with the requirement to protect our men.' Cited in Paul D. Williams, 'The Peacekeeping System, Britain and the 1994 Rwandan Genocide', in Zachary Kaufman and Phil Clark (eds), *After Genocide* (London: Hurst, 2009), p. 79.

[17] See, for example, Conor Foley, *UN Peacekeeping Operations and the Protection of Civilians* (New York: CUP, 2017). Although it was not always clear what positive obligations this bestowed upon UN peacekeepers in operational terms. See Wills, *Protecting Civilians*.

[18] See *United Nations Peacekeeping Operations: Principles and Guidelines* (New York: UN DPKO/DFS, 2008), pp. 31–33; Draft DPKO/DFS Operational Concept on the Protection of Civilians in United Nations Peacekeeping Operations (New York: UN DPKO/ DFS, January 2010), paras 7–8.

[19] Beatrice Pouligny, *Peace Operations Seen from Below* (London: Hurst, 2006), pp. 27–30.

226 CIVILIAN PROTECTION MANDATES FOR UN PEACEKEEPERS

Table 8.1 Caveats in UN Protection of Civilians Peacekeeping Mandates

Mission	Country	Dates	'Protect civilians under imminent threat of violence'	'Without prejudice to responsibility of host nation'	'Within capabilities and areas of deployment'	'All means necessary'
UNIFIL	Lebanon	19 March 1978–present	Yes	No	Yes	Yes
UNAMSIL	Sierra Leone	22 Oct. 1999–31 Dec. 2005	Yes	Yes	Yes	No
MONUC, MONUSCO	DRC	30 Nov. 1999–present	Yes	No	Yes	Yes
UNMIL	Liberia	19 Sept. 2003–30 Mar. 2018	Yes	Yes	Yes (partial)	No
UNOCI	Côte d'Ivoire	4 Apr. 2004–30 Jun. 2017	Yes	Yes	Yes	Yes
MINUSTAH	Haiti	30 April 2004–15 Oct. 2017	Yes	Yes	Yes	No
ONUB	Burundi	22 May 2004–1 Jan. 2007	Yes	Yes	Yes	Yes
UNMIS	Sudan	24 Mar. 2004–8 July 2011	Yes	Yes	Yes	Yes
UNAMID	Sudan	31 July 2007–2020	Yes	Yes	Yes	No
MINURCAT	Chad & Central African Republic	25 Sept. 2007–31 Dec. 2010	Yes	No	Yes	Yes
UNMISS	South Sudan	8 July 2011–present	Yes*	No	Yes	Yes
UNISFA	Abyei Area (Sudan & South Sudan)	27 June 2011–present	Yes	Yes	Yes	No
MINUSMA	Mali	25 Apr. 2013–present	Yes	Yes	Yes	Yes
MINUSCA	Central African Republic	15 Sept. 2014–present	No	Yes	Yes	Yes
Percentage of mandates with component			**93**	**81**	**100**	**64**

* The word 'imminent' was subsequently dropped from the UNMISS mandate.
Source: Adapted from Victoria K. Holt and Glyn Taylor with Max Kelly, *Protecting Civilians in the Context of UN Peacekeeping Operations* (New York: UN DPKO/OCHA, 2009), p. 45.

breakthrough came in 2009 when a detailed study commissioned by the UN's DPKO and OCHA highlighted how much work was still required to clarify the POC agenda.[20] In response, in early 2010, DPKO and the UN Department of Field Support (DFS) drafted an operational concept on the protection of civilians in UN peacekeeping operations which utilized a three-tier approach to conceptualize protection:

- Tier 1 entailed protection by promoting a political process of conflict resolution; ending the armed conflict that was a major source of threats to civilians. DPKO/DFS concluded the 'maintenance of peace through an effective peace process is perhaps the single largest contribution a mission can make to protecting civilians'.[21]
- Tier 2 entailed providing protection from physical violence. This was to be undertaken by all mission components across four broad phases: assurance and prevention; pre-emption, response, and consolidation.
- Tier 3 entailed establishing a protective environment that enhanced the safety and supported the rights of civilians. This was conceptualized as involving the promotion of legal protection (especially IHL but also relevant human rights and refugee law), the facilitation of humanitarian assistance and advocacy, and support for national institutions.[22]

The three tiers were said to be 'mutually accommodating and should be taken forward simultaneously, in accordance with mission mandates and in light of the circumstances on the ground'.[23] The interrelationship of these tiers should be emphasized, not least because research from populations suffering from armed conflict has consistently shown that locals rarely see the utility of separating out what they see as intimately connected issues.[24]

In 2015, the official DPKO/DFS policy on POC provided a much more detailed elaboration of the issues, including guiding principles, operational concept, response phases and discussion of how peacekeepers should implement POC mandates. It defined protection of civilians as a whole-of-mission effort to include the military, police and civilian components and stated that implementing POC mandates might require: 'all necessary means, up to and including the use of deadly force, aimed at preventing or responding to threats of physical violence against civilians, within capabilities and areas of operations, and without

---

[20] Victoria K. Holt and Glyn Taylor with Max Kelly, *Protecting Civilians in the Context of UN Peacekeeping Operations* (New York: UN DPKO/OCHA, 2009).

[21] *Draft DPKO/DFS Operational Concept on the Protection of Civilians* (January 2010), para.18.

[22] Ibid., para. 20.

[23] Ibid., para. 15.

[24] See, for example, Erin Baines and Emily Paddon, '"This Is How We Survived": Civilian Agency and Humanitarian Protection', *Security Dialogue* 43, no. 3 (2011), pp. 231–247; Justin Corbett, Learning from the Nuba: Civilian Resilience and Self-Protection during Conflict, October 2011, *Local to Global Protection*. Available at: www.local2global.info

prejudice to the responsibility of the host government.'[25] The new policy also clarified that 'All components of the mission have a role to play in each of the tiers.'[26] Tier 1 was rephrased as protection through dialogue and engagement, including dialogue with potential perpetrators, conflict resolution and mediation between conflict parties, persuading actors to protect civilians, and public information efforts to encourage direct engagement. Tier 2 remained the provision of physical protection, including peacekeepers threatening or using force to prevent, deter, pre-empt, and respond to threats against civilians, as well as offensive operations. Tier 3 remained focused on the establishment of a protective environment and included activities such as strengthening the rule of law, security sector reform, supporting the participation of women in peacebuilding or DDR programmes.

The tiered approach has been criticized for broadening the meaning of protection, and particularly Tier 1 and 3 activities can often involve a broader set of actors beyond peacekeepers (e.g., diplomats, mediators, NGOs, humanitarian, and development agencies). However, it remains a sensible way to conceptualize the potential activities peacekeepers might need to undertake and an abstract sketch of the relevant division of labour with other actors.

3. Consequences of POC Mandates in UN Peacekeeping Operations

POC mandates had a range of consequences for particular missions and for UN peacekeeping more generally. Most immediately, the conceptual choices made in how to define 'protection' raised some fundamental operational questions for peacekeepers and the UN Security Council. They increased the moral and legal authority of peacekeepers to prevent and stop threats against civilians but also generated a long list of potential tasks, which in turn put a premium on developing new expertise and capabilities to implement them. POC mandates also dramatically increased international expectations about what peacekeepers should be able to accomplish. In response, peacekeepers in the field developed some innovative ways to implement their new mandates, especially in the operations in DR Congo, Sudan, and South Sudan.

First of all, the way that peacekeepers understood the concepts of 'civilians' and 'protection' mattered for how the Security Council should best engage politically

---

[25] *The Protection of Civilians in United Nations Peacekeeping Operations* (New York: UN DPKO/DFS Policy, 2015.07, 1 April 2015), at p. 5. The 2018 C-34 Special Committee report on peacekeeping also concluded that POC 'is a whole-of-mission task that requires an integrated approach among military, police and civilian components, in coordination with national authorities, local communities and relevant humanitarian organizations'. *Report of the Special Committee on Peacekeeping Operations* (UN doc. A/72/19, 2018 substantive session), para. 296.

[26] *The Protection of Civilians in United Nations Peacekeeping Operations* (2015), at p. 8.

and what operational tasks peacekeepers would be expected to perform. Politically, the key issue was maintaining a unified Council that developed and then supported a viable strategy for resolving the crisis in question. Among the more operational challenges were practical issues such as what type of actors (military, police, civilian) were best placed to alleviate the identified threats, and how many of these foreign peacekeepers would be required. This quickly led to a discussion about what types of capabilities, doctrine, training, and rules of engagement UN peacekeepers would need to implement these POC mandates. And if the threat or use of force was authorized, would this entail greater risks for peacekeepers and locals alike? Moreover, what was the way out: how could a viable exit strategy be based around POC mandates? In light of these issues, in 2006, two authors asked whether civilian protection was 'mission impossible' for UN peacekeeping.[27] They concluded that POC wasn't an impossible mandate, but it was likely to prove very difficult, especially if peacekeepers didn't receive requisite capabilities and political support from the Council and host state(s).

Second, the new POC mandates imbued UN peacekeepers with a stronger moral and legal authority to protect civilians. As the Brahimi Report had noted in 2000, when faced with conflict parties aggressively targeting civilians, 'No failure did more to damage the standing and credibility of United Nations peacekeeping in the 1990s than its reluctance to distinguish victim from aggressor.'[28] The POC mandates were part of the UN's way of correcting this failure. But they would open the UN up to justifiable criticism if its peacekeepers couldn't live up to these mandated expectations. As noted above, local civilians had long expected protection, regardless of the precise vocabulary in the mission mandate. But the new POC mandates now dramatically raised international expectations. A major excuse for failure vanished, and the nuances of the Council's caveats were often lost in subsequent debates. This was particularly true of missions where POC was raised to the status of prime directive, as in DR Congo, Darfur, and South Sudan, each of which saw the host state's security forces responsible for large amounts of civilian harm.

Not surprisingly, POC mandates also lengthened the list of tasks that peacekeepers might need to perform.[29] Peacekeepers now had to understand the threats facing local civilians (including how these agendas might differ depending on the

---

[27] Victoria Holt and Tobias Berkman, *The Impossible Mandate? Military Preparedness, the Responsibility to Protect, and Modern Peace Operations* (Washington, D.C.: Henry L. Stimson Center, 2006).

[28] *Panel on United Nations Peace Operations* (UN doc. A/55/305-S/2000/809, August 2000), p. ix.

[29] For details, see Erin Weir, *The Last Line of Defense: How Peacekeepers Can Better Protect Civilians* (Washington, D.C.: Refugees International, 2010); Sarah Sewall, et al., *Mass Atrocity Response Operations: A Military Planning Handbook* (Harvard, MA: Harvard Kennedy School and PKSOI, 2010); Max Kelly with Alison Giffen, *Military Planning to Protect Civilians: Proposed Guidance for United Nations Peacekeeping Operations* (Washington, D.C.: Henry L. Stimson Center, 2011); Dwight Raymond, *Protection of Civilians Military Reference Guide* (Carlisle, PA: US Army War College, PKSOI, 2013).

sex, age, location, livelihood, and socio-economic status of individuals). They had to ascertain which threats could be alleviated by peacekeepers and which could be left to the host state authorities or the local communities themselves. To do this well, peacekeeping forces would need to pay attention to local sources of knowledge and hence would need to develop better relationships with local populations. Once the relevant threats had been identified and prioritized, peacekeepers had to prepare for the relevant tasks accordingly.

To deliver on these tasks in the field, UN peacekeepers would require additional capabilities. First, they needed relevant doctrinal guidance and training.[30] As the UN's C-34 Special Committee put it, 'effective training, pre- and post-deployment, is essential and critical for military and police forces in order to identify the proper response against perpetrators of civilian attacks.'[31] This was initially in short supply. It took about a decade before such guidelines and training packages were available as standard to UN peacekeepers, including both senior mission leadership and rank-and-file personnel. It was not until 2011 that the UN Secretariat completed a series of POC training modules and 2012 when it finished the resource and capabilities matrix for implementation of protection mandates in UN peacekeeping operations, a mechanism to help missions match available resources and capabilities with the protection tasks they intend to undertake. It was also difficult to train large numbers of peacekeepers in various conflict management skills required to implement POC mandates.[32] Second, peacekeepers would require some new expertise. This, in turn generated greater need for more diverse and specialized personnel across several dimensions, such as more police and other civilians and more women peacekeepers. Specialized skills were also necessary, particularly to enable peacekeepers to effectively engage with local communities, discern the nature of threats to civilians and understand how best to respond, not least by learning from local sources of resilience.[33] Third, UN peacekeepers required a range of military and civilian enablers. Perhaps most notably, POC mandates put greater emphasis on the need for rapid mobility (e.g.,

---

[30] Alison Giffen, *Addressing the Doctrinal Deficit: Developing Guidance to Prevent and Respond to Widespread or Systematic Attacks Against Civilians* (Washington, D.C.: Henry L. Stimson Center, 2010).

[31] *Report of the Special Committee on Peacekeeping Operations* (UN doc. A/72/19, 2018 substantive session), para. 387.

[32] See Alison Milofsky et al., *Conflict Management Training for Peacekeepers* (Washington, D.C.: USIP Special Report, August 2017). There is also a need for greater clarity about how POC might change peacekeepers' rules of engagement (ROE). Of course, ROE have long emphasized that UN personnel must uphold IHL by requiring them, among other things, not to intentionally target civilians, not to take unnecessary actions that might harm civilians, not to abuse civilians, protect civilians from the effects of combat where possible, and provide support to wounded civilians. But it is less clear in what circumstances POC mandates generate more proactive legal obligations for peacekeepers to rescue civilians or intervene in impending disputes. See Wills, *Protecting Civilians*; Foley, *UN Peacekeeping Operations and the Protection of Civilians*, ch. 5.

[33] Paul D. Williams, 'Protection, Resilience and Empowerment: United Nations Peacekeeping and Violence against Civilians in Contemporary War Zones', *Politics* 33, no. 4 (2013), pp. 287–298, esp. at pp. 291–294.

through aviation assets); protected mobility (e.g., through armoured vehicles); information gathering (e.g., through intelligence, surveillance, and reconnaissance capabilities as well as civilian casualty tracking); medical support (e.g., rapid casualty evacuation and sufficient level-II hospital facilities); engineering (e.g., for infrastructure repair, runway maintenance, and base construction); strategic communications (e.g., radio and internet communications and experts who could develop communications strategies); and even special operations forces (e.g., commando and psyops units).

Over time, UN peacekeepers developed innovative techniques, especially in contemporary Africa where POC mandates have been most sorely tested, including in DR Congo, Sudan, South Sudan, Mali, and Central African Republic. A few salient examples will suffice to illustrate the point. One key improvement was using the DPKO/DFS framework as a guide to develop 'mission-wide protection strategies', which identified the respective threats to civilians in each peacekeeping theatre and set out the roles and responsibilities of the different components of the peacekeeping operation as well as their interaction with relevant external actors. However, the UN Secretariat only completed a framework for drafting such mission-wide strategies in early 2011. Some missions, such as UNMISS in South Sudan, went a step further and developed distinct regional protection strategies to account for the unique local circumstances in each of the country's provinces. Other examples of POC-related innovation in UN field missions include the creation of multidimensional Joint Protection Teams, Community Alert Networks, the Must-Could-Should POC Matrix, and Community Liaison Officers/Assistants employed to good effect in DR Congo.[34]

Another notable example is the Protection of Civilians Sites established by UNMISS in South Sudan.[35] Following the outbreak of civil war in December 2013, multiple armed groups deliberately targeted civilians across the country, including the capital city Juba.[36] As an emergency measure to provide physical protection to civilians fleeing for their lives towards UN bases, UNMISS leadership 'opened the gates' and created POC sites. Sometimes comprising of little more than a cleared patch of land near a UN base with a berm or basic fence, UNMISS maintained up to eight different POC sites.[37] By the end of 2014, 102,000 civilians were sheltering

---

[34] See MONUSCO, 'Protection of Civilians and Protection Tools'. Available at: https://monusco.unmissions.org/en/protection-civilians-and-protection-tools

[35] See Ray Murphy, 'The United Nations Mission in South Sudan and the Protection of Civilians', *Journal of Conflict and Security Law 22*, no. 3 (2017), pp. 367–394; and Hilde F. Johnson, 'Protection of Civilians in the United Nations: A Peacekeeping Illusion?', in Cedric de Coning and Mateja Peter (eds), *United Nations Peace Operations in a Changing Global Order* (Basingstoke: Palgrave Macmillan, 2018), pp. 133–151.

[36] For details see, *Final Report of the African Union Commission of Inquiry on South Sudan* (Addis Ababa: 14 October 2015). Available at: http://www.peaceau.org/uploads/auciss.final.report.pdf

[37] The mission was clear from the outset that these were not meant to be ordinary IDP camps, which are supposed to meet a range of legal standards in order to function.

in them, and by mid-August 2015 the number was over 200,000 (by way of comparison, as of May 2016, the number of conflict-affected civilians in South Sudan stood at over 2.3 million internally displaced persons (IDPs) and refugees).[38] The principal objective of the POC sites was to provide emergency protection to civilians who were under immediate threat of physical violence. The rationale was to use the UNMISS Status of Forces Agreement (SOFA) with the government of South Sudan as a protection tool since UN premises are inviolable and subject to the exclusive control of the mission.[39] UNMISS described this policy as 'a pragmatic reaction to the need to save lives, given that limited capabilities and restrictions of movement exhausted the Mission's capacity to protect civilians outside UNMISS bases at such a scale. The POC sites are thus a form of physical protection of last resort, tailored to the circumstances in South Sudan.'[40]

Most recently, the UN has started pilot projects on what it calls 'protection through projection', 'which requires both military and civilian staff to be highly mobile and be able to, at the first signs of a deteriorating security situation, deploy temporarily to prevent violence.'[41] First developed in MONUSCO since 2016, this model was designed as an alternative to relying primarily on 'protection by presence'.[42]

4. Tensions and Challenges Raised by POC Mandates in UN Peacekeeping Operations

The POC mandates have generated important tensions with other aspects of the UN's peacekeeping project and how civilian protection relates to other mandated tasks. This section briefly analyses what I consider to be the five most important, and they reflect the normative, practical, and cross-cutting tensions in the individualization process identified in this book's Introduction. They are the tensions between POC and the principle of impartiality, the principle of consent, and the importance of promoting a peace process to settle the war in question; and a tension between using proactive military power to protect civilians and ensuring reasonable levels of force protection. There was also the additional practical challenge of ensuring peacekeepers were prepared to implement them because of a lack of adequate doctrinal guidance and training packages.

---

[38] UN DPKO, *Challenges, lessons learned and implications of the protection of civilian sites in South Sudan* (Internal document, 17 June 2016), para. 4.
[39] *The Status of Forces Agreement between UNMISS and the Government of the Republic of South Sudan*, 8 August 2011, para. 16.
[40] UN DPKO, *Challenges, lessons learned and implications*, para. 3.
[41] *Report of the Special Committee on Peacekeeping Operations* (UN doc. A/72/19, 2018 substantive session), para. 300.
[42] See Lauren Spink, *Protection with Less Presence* (Washington, D.C.: CIVIC, 2018), pp. 10–20.

4.1 POC and Impartiality

Impartiality is one of the three basic principles of UN peacekeeping.[43] A normative tension emerged in some theatres because the increasing prominence of POC mandates has undermined the UN's claims to impartial authority. Specifically, the increasing centrality of POC mandates has both reflected and helped to drive a shift in the UN's traditional, consensual approach to impartiality towards the more forceful imposition of claims to authority based on acceptance of liberal values. As Emily Paddon Rhoads has argued, at the same time as the UN has adopted this new generation of POC mandates, it has promoted a rather partisan notion of impartiality based on the principles of 'assertive liberal internationalism'. In her words, 'Claims to impartial authority [in UN peace operations] are no longer based exclusively on terms to which all parties consent. Instead, they are premised on a more ambitious and expansive set of human-rights-related norms, around which consensus is presumed but not always secured.'[44] She notes that this more assertive approach to impartiality was institutionalized at the UN 'since 2000'—almost precisely when POC mandates were adopted—and that protection of civilians is 'at the core of the new understanding of impartiality and robust peacekeeping'.[45] The tension is most clearly seen where UN peacekeepers operate in civil wars and where their mandate to protect civilians is perceived to favour the host state and target non-state actors. Even in situations where the host state's forces are responsible for attacks on civilians, it is only certain non-state groups that are defined as illegal actors or spoilers. Although this dynamic is not solely the result of introducing POC mandates, where the UN's claims to impartiality are not accepted by all parties, this undermines the UN's traditional position of not being considered a party to the conflict. This, in turn, can undermine the UN's ability to be an effective peacemaker in the conflict zone in question (see below).

4.2 POC and Consent

A second normative tension revolves around the relationship between POC and consent, another of UN peacekeeping's basic principles. The tension here flows in almost the opposite political direction as that regarding impartiality. In relation to consent, the problem is that the implementation of POC mandates in UN peacekeeping operations relies on maintaining the consent of the host state's *de jure* government. While UN peacekeepers can operate without the consent of all non-state parties to the conflict, they are only legally able to deploy on the host

---

[43] *United Nations Peacekeeping Operations: Principles and Guidelines*, ch. 3.
[44] Emily Paddon Rhoads, *Taking Sides in Peacekeeping* (Oxford: OUP, 2016), p. 2.
[45] Ibid., p. 65, 68ff.

state's territory with the consent of its government. This highlights one of the severe limits of the individualization process as it relates to UN peacekeeping. As a result, in cases where the host government's forces are major perpetrators of atrocities or harm against local civilians, UN peacekeepers are put at a distinct political disadvantage. This has happened in several recent UN missions but perhaps most notably in Darfur (UNAMID), DR Congo (MONUC/MONUSCO), and South Sudan (UNMISS). Legally, UN peacekeepers retain the authority to use force against host government forces that attack civilians. As Mona Khalil, former Senior Legal Officer in the UN Office of the Legal Counsel noted, 'While the POC mandate includes assisting host governments to fulfill their responsibility, it also requires UNPKOs to act independently when the host Government is unable or unwilling, and even to take action against the host Government forces where and when they pose a threat to civilians. The POC mandate therefore applies "irrespective of the source of the threat"'.[46] Politically, however, this legal authority raises a practical challenge: it is very difficult to use force regularly against host government forces without placing UN peacekeepers in severe risk—because a host government can invariably muster considerably more firepower than even a robust UN peacekeeping force—or jeopardizing the host government's consent for the UN mission. If that consent was withdrawn, the UN's blue helmets must leave.

4.3 POC and Peace Processes

A third, more practical tension arises between the implementation of POC mandates and the political imperative of the UN to develop a political solution to the crisis in question. UN peacekeeping operations have always been principally political instruments with limited military power. Their principal political role is to support the creation and/or implementation of a peace process, usually through some form of confidence-building and deterrence function. As such, UN peacekeepers are not traditionally regarded as having designated enemies but instead use their military power impartially in the service of peace. In 2015, this imperative was captured in the idea that the UN must ensure 'the primacy of politics' when designing and implementing its peace operations.[47] Most recently, the C-34 Special Committee on Peacekeeping reiterated that 'The implementation of such [POC] mandates should be an integral part of a comprehensive peace process,

---

[46] Mona Khalil, 'Why are UN Peacekeepers Failing to Protect Civilians?', 6 September 2015, *Opinio Juris*. Available at: http://opiniojuris.org/2016/09/06/protection-of-civilians-symposium-why-are-un-peacekeepers-failing-to-protect-civilians/

[47] The phrase was coined by the report of the High-Level Independent Panel on Peace Operations (HIPPO), *Uniting Our Strengths for Peace: Politics, Partnership, and People* (A/70/95–S/2015/446, 17 June 2015).

underpinned by national ownership and involving relevant stakeholders, as well as the support of the international community.'[48] In this instance, the tension arises between the need to ensure physical protection of civilians and promoting a political process to end the crisis in question. It is most likely to occur in situations where UN operations have been deployed in conflict zones without a viable political process—such as Darfur, eastern DR Congo, and South Sudan—and consequently represent band-aids rather than one of the strategic steps toward a political solution. In such circumstances, activities carried out by peacekeepers in order to protect civilians might undermine the immediate prospects of finding a viable political solution by targeting one of the conflict parties. As Ralph Mamiya, a former team leader of the POC team in UN DPKO, noted, this tension stems from at least three dynamics.[49] First, 'the "ripe" moment for political dialogue versus the urgent need for protection'. Where belligerents become predatory towards the local population, protecting civilians jeopardizes their war aims and perhaps their very survival. Second, 'the focus on elites in political processes versus the interests and voices of the wider civilian population'. In this case, ignoring localized civil society representatives and focusing on elite pacts at the national level incentivizes the emergence of rent-seeking militias. And, third, using the 'military as a tool to further a political strategy versus as the driver of a political strategy'. This produces a tendency to focus on achieving military solutions when no such solutions exist and they, in turn, may limit the mission's political room for manoeuvre.

4.4 POC and Force Protection

A fourth, practical tension emerges when the implementation of POC mandates might entail what the contributing countries consider to be unacceptable levels of risk to their peacekeepers. In other words, an ethical dilemma is generated over finding the right balance between conducting proactive POC activities that might involve fighting armed groups—potentially even host government forces—and force protection. In theory, undertaking proactive and sometimes offensive military operations to protect vulnerable civilians would be likely to raise the risk to UN personnel. This would be particularly true if the mission lacked adequate medical support facilities and effective casualty evacuation capabilities.[50] In practice, UN peacekeepers have generally been very reluctant to use force to directly protect civilians even when they have been present or nearby when threats were made

---

[48] *Report of the Special Committee on Peacekeeping Operations* (A/72/19, 2018 substantive session), para. 293.

[49] Ralph Mamiya, *Protection of Civilians and Political Strategies* (New York: IPI, May 2018), p. 2.

[50] On the importance of medical support in UN peacekeeping operations see Lesley Connolly and Havard Johansen, *Medical Support for UN Peace Operations in High-Risk Environments* (New York: IPI, April 2017).

against civilians.[51] This tension matters because if the governments contributing UN peacekeepers believe that their contingents are facing unacceptably high levels of risk—especially in the absence of a viable political strategy to resolve the crisis— they are more likely to withdraw them or not deploy them to missions in the first place.[52] It was therefore particularly notable that in December 2017, Brazilian Lt-General Dos Santos Cruz published a major report for the UN on improving the safety and security of UN peacekeepers. Its starting point was the fact that two-thirds of UN peacekeepers are deployed in high-risk environments, and more were killed by acts of violence between 2013 and 2017 than any other five-year period in UN history.[53] These figures were not all due to POC-related activities but they were a significant part of the reason why UN forces had been targeted in multiple theatres. His solution was for UN peacekeepers to wield greater levels of military power more effectively, which he argued would enable them to simultaneously implement POC more effectively and ensure higher levels of force protection.

4.5 POC and (Lack of) Preparedness

These tensions are all potentially exacerbated by a very practical challenge facing UN peacekeepers: should they be expected to achieve POC mandates without sufficient doctrinal guidance, training programmes and capabilities? As discussed above, the vast majority of UN peacekeepers lacked all of these elements until the 2010s. One notable area of persistent deficiency was military doctrine for POC. To this day, very few militaries worldwide have doctrinal guidance on how to protect civilians through the pursuit of military tasks.[54] Second, although police forces had more experience in the area of protecting civilians from violence than their military counterparts they were deployed in much smaller numbers than troops on UN peacekeeping operations and were not usually experienced in operating in zones of armed conflict. As discussed below, in recent years there is evidence that they have responded to far fewer POC incidents than their military and civilian counterparts. Third, although training regimes on POC have

---

[51] For details see Report of the Office of Internal Oversight Services (OIOS), *Evaluation of the implementation and results of protection of civilians mandates in United Nations peacekeeping operations* (UN doc. A/68/787, 7 March 2014).

[52] It is debatable how often contributing countries make this calculation. See Steffi Raes, Cind du Bois, and Caroline Buts, 'Supplying UN Peacekeepers: An Assessment of the Body Bag Syndrome among OECD Nations', *International Peacekeeping 26*, no. 1 (2019), pp. 111–136; and Andrew Levin, 'Peacekeeper Fatalities and Force Commitments to UN Operations', *Conflict Management and Peace Science 38*, no. 3 (2021), pp. 292-315.

[53] Lt-Gen. Carlos Alberto Dos Santos Cruz et al., *Improving Security of United Nations Peacekeepers* (New York: UN, 17 December 2017).

[54] To my knowledge, the US military was the first to officially adopt doctrine on POC. But this was not until 2015, and during the twenty-first century it has not deployed a single military contingent in a UN peacekeeping operation. See US Army, *Protection of Civilians* (ATP 3-07.6, October 2015). Available at: https://fas.org/irp/doddir/army/atp3-07-6.pdf

improved significantly over the last decade there is still comparatively little guidance for civilian personnel and the UN remains unable to evaluate how successful these programmes have been or track whether they are reaching all peacekeepers. Fourth, the UN's persistent capabilities gaps continue to undermine the potential for effective implementation of POC mandates, especially a lack of aviation assets, armoured mobile units, and special forces.[55] Finally, there are still no performance evaluation standards for POC. In its 2018 substantive session the C-34 Special Committee at long last requested 'the Secretariat to develop performance evaluation standards for all relevant civilian and uniformed personnel for the implementation of protection-of-civilians mandates, in consultation with Member States.'[56] The passing of Security Council resolution 2436 (2018) calling for a performance policy framework for UN peacekeepers is a mark of significant progress on this issue.

5. Overcoming the Tensions in the UN's Approach to POC?

How should we evaluate the UN's performance in trying to implement POC mandates over the last two decades? Various academic studies have pronounced on the effectiveness of POC mandates; so too has the UN's Office of Internal Oversight (OIOS). The academic literature has drawn several interrelated conclusions that point to a variety of benefits for civilians trapped in war-torn or post-war territories of giving UN peacekeepers POC mandates. First, UN peacekeepers tend to deploy to crises where other international actors are reluctant to lead.[57] Second, they can reduce the length of local conflict episodes in host countries, even protracted civil wars, and have a good record of stopping the recurrence of major violence.[58] UN peacekeeping operations also reduce the geographic scope of violence and the risk of armed conflicts spreading across international borders.[59] Moreover, the presence of UN troops is associated with a reduction in ongoing

---

[55] Since their release during 2009, the various iterations of the UN's peacekeeping capabilities gaps lists (military, police and civilian) have succeeded in identifying numerous important thematic and mission-specific gaps.

[56] *Report of the Special Committee on Peacekeeping Operations* (A/72/19, 2018 substantive session), para. 304. See also para. 102.

[57] Virginia Page Fortna, *Does Peacekeeping Work? Shaping Belligerents' Choices after Civil War* (Princeton: Princeton University Press, 2008) and Alex J. Bellamy and Paul D. Williams, 'Trends in Peace Operations, 1947–2013', in Koops et al. (eds), *The Oxford Handbook of United Nations Peacekeeping Operations* (Oxford: Oxford University Press, 2015), pp. 13–42.

[58] Andrea Ruggeri, Han Dorussen, and Theodora-Ismene Gizelis, 'Winning the Peace Locally: UN Peacekeeping and Local Conflict', *International Organization 71*, no. 1 (2017), pp. 163–185; Michael W. Doyle and Nicolas Sambanis, *Making War and Building Peace: United Nations Peace Operations* (Princeton: Princeton University Press, 2006); Anke Hoeffler, 'Can International Interventions Secure the Peace?' *International Area Studies Review 17*, no. 1 (2014), pp. 75–94.

[59] Kyle Beardsley and Kristian S. Gleditsch, 'Peacekeeping as Conflict Containment', *International Studies Review 17*, no. 1 (2015), pp. 67–89; and Kyle Beardsley, 'Peacekeeping and the Contagion of Armed Conflict', *The Journal of Politics 73*, no. 4 (2011), pp. 1051–1064.

violence in war-torn territories; the more UN peacekeeping troops deployed, the lower the number of battlefield deaths.[60] At the operational level, UN peacekeepers also help protect civilians in war zones by deploying to locations where non-combatants are particularly at risk.[61] Finally, it is also notable that the peacekeepers are usually successful in enhancing the overall level of protection for civilians, and the extent of protection increases the more UN troops and police are deployed.[62] Importantly, all of these benefits have come despite the fact that peacekeepers have regularly faced intimidation and obstruction by local armed actors—including host governments—explicitly designed to stop them protecting civilians.[63]

This is not to say there haven't been numerous failures where UN peacekeepers have stood by or failed to stop major attacks on civilians. Arguably two of the most infamous recent cases came in South Sudan when UNMISS peacekeepers failed to stop major violence against civilians in the POC site in Malakal in February 2016, and in the capital city, Juba in July.[64] These were two episodes that illustrated a conclusion drawn earlier by the 2014 OIOS report, which noted a persistent pattern of UN peacekeeping operations not using force when civilians were under attack.[65] Although the report noted that 'peacekeeping missions have successfully prevented and mitigated harm to civilians', it concluded that, although the 'use of force is legally authorized and consistent with the intent of the Security Council and the expectations of civilians', it has 'been routinely avoided as an option by peacekeeping operations. The reasons include different views in the Security Council and among troop-contributing countries and, importantly, a de facto dual line of command involving mission leadership and troop-contributing countries that regulates the use of force by missions.'[66]

In 2018, another OIOS report examined POC incidents and responses in four of the five largest UN peacekeeping operations—MINUSCA, UNAMID,

---

[60] Lisa Hultman, Jacob Kathman, and Megan Shannon, 'Beyond Keeping Peace: United Nations Effectiveness in the Midst of Fighting', *American Political Science Review 108*, no. 4 (2014), pp. 737–753.

[61] Lisa Hultman, 'UN Peace Operations and Protection of Civilians: Cheap Talk or Norm Implementation?' *Journal of Peace Research 50*, no. 1 (2013), pp. 59–73; Lisa Hultman, Jacob Kathman and Megan Shannon, 'United Nations Peacekeeping and Civilian Protection in Civil War', *American Journal of Political Science 57*, no. 4 (2013), pp. 875–891.

[62] Lisa Hultman, Jacob Kathman, and Megan Shannon, *Peacekeeping in the Midst of War* (Oxford: OUP, 2019); Hanne Fjelde, Lisa Hultman, and Desirée Nilsson, 'Protection through Presence: UN Peacekeeping and the Costs of Targeting Civilians', *International Organization 73*, no. 1 (2019), pp. 103–131.

[63] See, Allard Duursma, 'Obstruction and Intimidation of Peacekeepers: How Armed Actors Undermine Civilian Protection Efforts', *Journal of Peace Research 56*, no. 2 (2019), pp. 234–248.

[64] Center for Civilians in Conflict, *A Refuge in Flames: The February 17–18 Violence in Malakal POC* (CIVIC Report, April 2016) and *Under Fire: The July 2016 Violence in Juba and UN Response* (CIVIC Report, October 2016).

[65] Report of the Office of Internal Oversight Services (OIOS), *Evaluation of the Implementation and Results of Protection of Civilians Mandates in United Nations Peacekeeping Operations* (UN doc. A/68/787, 7 March 2014).

[66] Ibid., pp. 1–2.

MINUSMA, MONUSCO—between March 2014 and July 2017.[67] During that period, it concluded peacekeepers in those four missions responded to 62 per cent of the 138 reported POC incidents that had a clearly identifiable location and date. The 38 per cent of incidents with no reported response had led to 247 civilian deaths. Interestingly, 64 per cent of those operational responses were conducted after the POC incident had occurred (within seven days); 24 per cent were conducted on the day of the incident, and 12 per cent were carried out pre-emptively.[68] Examples of pre-emptive POC activities were patrols, reinforcing positions, preventing armed groups entering a location, enforcing a weapons-free zone, liaising with local authorities, firing warning shots, and dismantling illegal barricades. Examples of responses during POC incidents were engaging armed actors to stop looting, dispatching reinforcements, urging immediate intervention by state authorities, returning fire to protect civilians, intensifying patrols, and maintaining a dissuasive presence. While examples of operational responses after POC incidents were clashing with armed actors to stop looting, conducting military assessments, reinforcing positions, intensifying patrolling, urging armed actors to de-escalate tensions, offensive operations, and urging the host state to intervene.

In line with the tiered approach, the military component was the primary responder in 52 per cent of incidents, followed by the civilian component in 30 per cent of cases. Significantly, the civilian component in these four operations had more relevance before and after violence against civilians had occurred. The police component was involved in the fewest responses, accounting for just 18 per cent. The report's regression analysis of the response rate for military contingents from twenty-five troop-contributing countries concluded that prior knowledge about the incident and the number of fatalities were the main factors that affected missions' operational responses (not capability in terms of troops and equipment or proximity to the incident).

Despite the benefits illustrated in these assessments, continued institutional adaptation is necessary to further improve implementation of the UN's POC mandates. The UN has engaged in various examples of operational adaptation to improve its effectiveness. This includes developing clearer standards of performance for peacekeepers, better training and principles/guidelines on POC, and providing UN missions with the required capabilities. In addition to the Human Rights Due Diligence Policy mentioned in the book's Introduction, two other examples are the Kigali Principles on the Protection of Civilians, launched

---

[67] OIOS Report, Inspection of the performance of missions' operational responses to Protection of Civilians (POC) related incidents (UN OIOS Report IED-18-010, 30 July 2018).

[68] Ibid. Response/Non-Response rates by mission were MINUSCA (27 no responses; 73 responses); MINUSMA (46:54); MONUSCO (44:56) and UNAMID (44:56) p. 16. The vast majority of responses were classified as falling under Tier 1 or Tier 2 activities and use of force constituted 38 per cent of all the Tier 2 operational responses.

in 2015, and the Dos Santos Cruz report on ensuring the safety and security of UN peacekeepers, published in December 2017. The Kigali principles are a non-binding set of pledges to implement certain best practices related to POC in UN peacekeeping.[69] These eighteen principles are understood by the C-34 Special Committee 'as non-United Nations voluntary principles'.[70] They address the most relevant operational aspects of peacekeeping, including assessment and planning, force generation, training and equipping personnel, performance and accountability. The principles have now been endorsed by nearly fifty UN member states. Although the Dos Santos Cruz report is not focused on POC per se its recommendations for improving the safety and security of peacekeepers are relevant. In particular, Cruz's overriding recommendation is that UN peacekeeping operations must become better suited to wielding military power and using military force much more effectively. This would have significant impact on the UN's ability to implement POC mandates, although the recommendations are also controversial in terms of their likely political consequences.[71]

In terms of more political adaptation, there have also been efforts to strengthen support for UN peace operations amongst the Security Council and UN membership more broadly. Arguably the four most notable reform efforts linked to POC issues are as follows: first, the broadening-the-base initiative. Developed in the 2010s, this plan aimed to increase the number of UN member states that contributed personnel and/or capabilities to UN peacekeeping operations.[72] Since, 2015, this has been complemented by a related initiative known as the Peacekeeping Leaders' summits and subsequent defence ministerials to generate concrete pledges of personnel, units, and capabilities to UN peacekeeping missions and get them officially logged into the UN's new Peacekeeping Capabilities Readiness System. Judged by the increased number of troop- and police-contributing countries to UN peacekeeping operations, these efforts have been broadly successful.

A second important initiative has focused on ensuring more effective triangular consultation between those contributing countries, the states on the Security Council that take the key decisions to design and authorize mandates, and those countries that pay the majority of the peacekeeping bill.[73] These three groups clearly continue to exhibit significant disagreements but at the very least the

---

[69] The principles were launched at the High-level International Conference on the Protection of Civilians held in Kigali, Rwanda, 28–29 May 2015.

[70] *Report of the Special Committee on Peacekeeping Operations* (A/72/19, 2018 substantive session), para. 308.

[71] See, for example, the collection of articles about the Dos Santos Cruz report published by IPI's Global Observatory during February and March 2018. Available at: https://theglobalobservatory.org/tag/cruz-report/

[72] See Alex J. Bellamy and Paul D. Williams, *Broadening the Base of United Nations Troop- and Police-Contributing Countries* (New York: IPI Providing for Peacekeeping No.1, August 2012).

[73] Alexandra Novosseloff, 'Triangular Cooperation: Key to All', *Global Peace Operations Review*, 10 November 2015. Available at: https://peaceoperationsreview.org/thematic-essays/triangular-cooperation-key-to-all/

contours of the most controversial issues have become clearer. This represents an example of ongoing institutional contestation over the way in which strategic-level decisions about POC are institutionalized.

A third, and related initiative has involved another form of institutional contestation, namely, the use of compacts in what might be called 'quadrilateral' consultation because it involves an effort to reform the relationship between UN peacekeeping operations and the host government. Specifically, the Secretary-General has attempted to iron out some of the tensions generated between POC mandates and host state consent through compacts to bolster both national ownership and consent for the presence of a peacekeeping operation.[74] Following the High-Level Independent Panel on Peace Operations (HIPPO) report, these have focused on the areas of strengthening mutual accountability; serving as a platform for coherence of international support; and leveraging the political influence of the Security Council and/or Peacebuilding Commission.

Finally, the HIPPO report's emphasis on ensuring the 'primacy of politics' as one of the four essential shifts it identified for UN peace operations is directly related to implementing Tier 1 POC activities. The report's main argument was that stable peace is achieved through political solutions and not through military and technical engagements alone. Consequently, all UN peace operations must be guided by and part of political solutions to the crisis in question. The HIPPO report stimulated a useful debate within both UN headquarters and its field missions and helped generate a restructuring of the UN's bureaucracy for managing peace operations and other conflict management initiatives. However, evidence from several UN missions, notably those in DR Congo, Darfur, and South Sudan, suggests there is still a long way to go to translate this recommendation into reality. This highlights a key point: institutional adaptation at the operational level spurred in large part by the individualization of war is not sufficient to resolve the fundamentally political and strategic tensions that confront the UN's civilian protection agenda.

References

Baines, E. and Paddon, E. (2012) '"This Is How We Survived": Civilian Agency and Humanitarian Protection', *Security Dialogue*, 43(3), pp. 231–247.

Barnett, M.N. (1960/2011) *The Empire of Humanity: A History of Humanitarianism*. Ithaca, NY: Cornell University Press.

Beardsley, K. (2011) 'Peacekeeping and the Contagion of Armed Conflict', *The Journal of Politics*, 73(4), pp. 1051–1064. doi: 10.1017/s0022381611000764.

---

[74] See Herve Ladsous, speech to the 4th Committee, 30 October 2015. Available at: https://peacekeeping.un.org/sites/default/files/hl_statement_to_4th_committeeas_delivered30oct2015.pdf, at pp. 5–6.

Beardsley, K. and Gleditsch, K. (2015) 'Peacekeeping as Conflict Containment', *International Studies Review*, 17(1), pp. 67–89. doi: 10.1111/misr.12205.

Bellamy, A.J. (2009) *Responsibility to Protect: The Global Effort to End Mass Atrocities.* Cambridge: Polity.

Bellamy, A.J. (2012) *Massacres and Morality: Mass Atrocities in an Age of Civilian Immunity.* Oxford: Oxford University Press.

Bellamy, A.J. and Williams, P.D. (2012) *Broadening the Base of United Nations Troop- and Police-Contributing Countries.* No. 1. New York: International Peace Institute.

Center for Civilians in Conflict. (2016) *A Refuge in Flames: The February 17–18* Violence in Malakal POC. Center for Civilians in Conflict. Available at: https://civiliansinconflict.org/publications/research/refuge-flames-february-17-18-violence-malakal-poc/

Center for Civilians in Conflict. (2016) *Under Fire: The July 2016 Violence in Juba and UN Response.* Center for Civilians in Conflict. Available at: https://civiliansinconflict.org/publications/research/fire-july-2016-violence-juba-un-response/

Connolly, L. and Johansen, H. (2017) *Medical Support for UN Peace Operations in High-Risk Environments.* New York: International Peace Institute.

Lt-Gen. Cruz, A.D.S., Phillips, W.R., and Cusimano, S. (2017) *Improving Security of United Nations Peacekeeper.* New York: United Nations.

Dallaire, R. and Beardsley, B. (2003) *Shake Hands with the Devil: The Failure of Humanity in Rwanda.* New York: Random House.

Deng, F.M. (1996) *Sovereignty as Responsibility: Conflict Management in Africa.* Washington, D.C.: Brookings Institution Press.

Doyle, M.W. and Sambanis, N. (2006) *Making War and Building Peace: United Nations Peace Operations.* Princeton: Princeton University Press.

Duursma, A. (2019) 'Obstruction and intimidation of peacekeepers: How armed actors undermine civilian protection efforts', *Journal of Peace Research*, 56(2), pp. 234–248. doi: 10.1177/0022343318800522.

Evans, G.J. (2008) *The Responsibility to Protect: Ending Mass Atrocity Crimes Once and for All.* Washington, D.C.: Brookings Institution Press.

Fjelde, H., Hultman, L. and Nilsson, D. (2019) 'Protection Through Presence: UN Peacekeeping and the Costs of Targeting Civilians', *International Organization*, 73(1), pp. 103–131. doi: 10.1017/S0020818318000346.

Foley, C. (2017) *UN Peacekeeping Operations and the Protection of Civilians: Saving Succeeding Generations.* New York: Cambridge University Press.

Fortna, V.P. (2008) *Does Peacekeeping Work?: Shaping Belligerents' Choices after Civil War.* Princeton: Princeton University Press.

Gentile, P. (2011) 'Humanitarian Organizations Involved in Protection Activities: A Story of Soul-Searching and Professionalization', *International Review of the Red Cross*, 93(884), pp. 1165–1191. doi: 10.1017/S1816383112000343.

Giffen, A. (2010) *Addressing the Doctrinal Deficit: Developing Guidance to Prevent and Respond to Widespread or Systematic Attacks Against Civilians.* Washington, D.C.: Henry L. Stimson Center.

Hoeffler, A. (2014) 'Can international interventions secure the peace?', *International Area Studies Review*, 17(1), pp. 75–94. doi: 10.1177/2233865914525380.

Holt, V. and Berkman, T. (2006) *The Impossible Mandate? Military Preparedness, the Responsibility to Protect, and Modern Peace Operations.* Washington, D.C.: Henry L. Stimson Center.

Holt, V.K., Taylor, G., and Kelly, M. (2009) *Protecting Civilians in the Context of UN Peacekeeping Operations: Successes, Setbacks and Remaining Challenges.* New York: UN Department of Peace Operations and Office for the Coordination of Humanitarian Affairs.

Hultman, L. (2013) 'UN Peace Operations and Protection of Civilians: Cheap Talk or Norm Implementation?', *Journal of Peace Research*, 50(1), pp. 59–73. doi: 10.1177/0022343312461662.

Hultman, L., Kathman, J., and Shannon, M. (2013) 'United Nations Peacekeeping and Civilian Protection in Civil War', *American Journal of Political Science*, 57(4), pp. 875–891.

Hultman, L., Kathman, J., and Shannon, M. (2014) 'Beyond Keeping Peace: United Nations Effectiveness in the Midst of Fighting', *American Political Science Review*, 108(4), pp. 737–753. doi: 10.1017/S0003055414000446.

Hultman, L. Kathman, J., and Shannon, M. (2019) *Peacekeeping in the Midst of War.* Oxford: Oxford University Press.

Hunt, C.T. and Bellamy, A.J. (2011) 'Mainstreaming the Responsibility to Protect in Peace Operations', *Civil Wars*, 13(1), pp. 1–20. doi: 10.1080/13698249.2011.555688.

Johnson, H.F. (2018) 'Protection of Civilians in the United Nations: A Peacekeeping Illusion?', in C. De Coning and M. Peter (eds), *United Nations Peace Operations in a Changing Global Order.* Basingstoke: Palgrave Macmillan, pp. 133–151.

Kelly, M. and Giffen, A. (2011) *Military Planning to Protect Civilians: Proposed Guidance for United Nations Peacekeeping Operations.* Washington, D.C.: Henry L. Stimson Center.

Khalil, M. (2016) 'Protection of Civilians Symposium: Why are UN Peacekeepers Failing to Protect Civilians?', *Opinio Juris*, 6 September. Available at: http://opiniojuris.org/2016/09/06/protection-of-civilians-symposium-why-are-un-peacekeepers-failing-to-protect-civilians/ (Accessed: 11 April 2021).

Koops, J.A. et al. (2015) *The Oxford Handbook of United Nations Peacekeeping Operations.* First edition. Oxford: Oxford University Press (Oxford Handbooks).

Levin, A. (2021) 'Peacekeeper Fatalities and Force Commitments to UN Operations', *Conflict Management and Peace Science*, 38(3), pp. 292-315. doi: 10.1177/0738894218818815.

Mamiya, R. (2018) *Protection of Civilians and Political Strategies.* New York: International Peace Institute.

Milofsky, A., Sany, J., and Lancaster, I.M. (2017) *Conflict Management Training for Peacekeepers.* Washington, D.C.: United States Institute for Peace.

Murphy, R. (2017) 'The United Nations Mission in South Sudan and the Protection of Civilians', *Journal of Conflict and Security Law*, 22(3), pp. 367–394. doi: 10.1093/jcsl/krx016.

Novosseloff, A. (2015) 'Triangular Cooperation—Key to All', *Global Peace Operations*, 10 November. Available at: https://peaceoperationsreview.org/thematic-essays/triangular-cooperation-key-to-all/ (Accessed: 12 April 2021).

Okeke, J.M. and Williams, P.D. (2017) *Protecting Civilians in African Union Peace Support Operations.* South Africa: ACCORD. Available at: https://www.accord.org.za/publication/protecting-civilians-african-union-peace-support-operations/ (Accessed: 5 April 2021).

Paddon Rhoads, E. (2016) *Taking Sides in Peacekeeping: Impartiality and the Future of the United Nations.* New York: Oxford University Press.

Pouligny, B. (2006) *Peace Operations Seen from Below: Un Missions and Local People.* London: Hurst.

Raes, S., Bois, C.D., and Buts, C. (2019) 'Supplying UN Peacekeepers: An Assessment of the Body Bag Syndrome among OECD Nations', *International Peacekeeping*, 26(1), pp. 111–136. doi: 10.1080/13533312.2018.1512858.

Raymond, D. (2013) *Protection of Civilians Military Reference Guide.* Carlisle, PA: US Army War College and Peacekeeping and Stability Operations Institute.

Rotberg, R.I. (ed.) (2010) *Mass Atrocity Crimes: Preventing Future Outrages.* Cambridge, MA: World Peace Foundation.

Ruggeri, A., Dorussen, H., and Gizelis, T.-I. (2017) 'Winning the Peace Locally: UN Peacekeeping and Local Conflict', *International Organization*, 71(1), pp. 163–185.

Schabas, W.A. (2016) *The International Criminal Court: A Commentary on the Rome Statute.* 5th edition. Oxford: Oxford University Press (Oxford Commentaries on International Law).

Sewall, S., Raymond, D., and Chin, S. (2010) *Mass Atrocity Response Operations: A Military Planning Handbook.* Harvard, MA: Harvard Kennedy School and Peacekeeping and Stability Operations Institute.

Smith, K.E. (2010) *Genocide and the Europeans.* New York: Cambridge University Press.

Spink, L. (2018) *Protection with Less Presence.* Washington, D.C.: Center for Civilians in Conflict.

Thakur, R. (2011) *The Responsibility to Protect: Norms, Laws and the Use of Force in International Politics.* London: Routledge.

Weir, E. (2010) *The Last Line of Defense: How Peacekeepers Can Better Protect Civilians.* Washington, D.C.: Refugees International.

Williams, P.D. (2009) 'The Peacekeeping System, Britain and the 1994 Rwandan Genocide', in Clark, P. and Kaufman, Z. (eds), *After Genocide: Transitional Justice, Post-conflict Reconstruction and Reconciliation in Rwanda and Beyond.* London: Hurst, pp. 43–63.

Williams, P.D. (2013) 'Protection, Resilience and Empowerment: United Nations Peacekeeping and Violence against Civilians in Contemporary War Zones', *Politics*, 33(4), pp. 287–298. doi: 10.1111/1467-9256.12014.

Williams, P.D. with Bellamy, A.J. (2021) *Understanding Peacekeeping.* Third edition. Cambridge: Polity Press.

Willmot, H. et al. (eds) (2016) *Protection of Civilians.* Oxford: Oxford University Press.

Wills, S. (2009) *Protecting Civilians: The Obligations of Peacekeepers.* Oxford: Oxford University Press.

PART IV
BEYOND FORMAL ARMED CONFLICT

9

Individualization and Collectivization in Contexts of Organized Criminal Violence

The Case of Mexico's War on Organized Crime

Pablo Kalmanovitz and Miriam Bradley

In 2018, 78,667 people were killed violently in Brazil and 43,089 in Mexico, compared with 29,584 in Afghanistan and 16,905 in Syria—yet only the latter two countries were widely classified as armed conflicts.[1] Most contemporary lethal violence does not occur in war zones, and the levels of lethal violence in non-war settings are often higher than in war zones.[2] Rates of lethal violence are especially high in Latin America, a region with 8 per cent of the world's population and 33 per cent of the world's homicides.[3] A significant proportion of these homicides—estimated to be between a third and a half in the case of Mexico, and two-thirds in El Salvador—are linked to organized crime.[4] And homicide is only the most visible manifestation of criminal violence, which also has many other repertoires and effects, including sexual violence, forced displacement, extortion, as well as restrictions on access to basic health care and education.[5]

---

[1] Data from the Global Violent Death database by the Small Arms Survey.

[2] Nicholas Barnes, 'Criminal Politics: An Integrated Approach to the Study of Organized Crime, Politics, and Violence', *Perspectives on Politics 15*, no. 4 (2017), pp. 967–987, at pp. 970–971; Dennis Rodgers and Robert Muggah, 'Gangs as Non-State Armed Groups: The Central American Case', *Contemporary Security Policy 30*, no. 2 (2009), pp. 301–317, at p. 301; Guillermo Trejo and Sandra Ley, *Votes, Drugs, and Violence: The Political Logic of Criminal Wars in Mexico* (Cambridge: Cambridge University Press, 2020).

[3] Caroline O.N. Moser and Cathy McIlwaine, 'Latin American Urban Violence as a Development Concern: Towards a Framework for Violence Reduction', *World Development 34*, no. 1 (2006), pp. 89–112; Robert Muggah and Katherine Aguirre Tobón, *Citizen Security in Latin America: Facts and Figures* (Rio de Janeiro: Igarapé Institute, 2018), p. 2.

[4] Ana Balcazar Moreno et al., *The War Report 2017: Gang Violence in Colombia, Mexico and El Salvador* (Geneva: Geneva Academy of International Humanitarian Law and Human Rights, 2017), pp. 7, 11.

[5] Tristan Clavel, 'Extorsión y violencia sexual: el padecimiento oculto de las mujeres', *Insight Crime 8* (January 2020); IDMC, *New Humanitarian Frontiers: Addressing Criminal Violence in Mexico and Central America* (Geneva: Internal Displacement Monitoring Centre, 2015); Eduardo Ubierna, 'Violencia armada en Latinoamérica: ¿cuáles son los nuevos retos humanitarios?' (Lima: Universidad del Pacífico, 2018).

Pablo Kalmanovitz and Miriam Bradley, *Individualization and Collectivization in Contexts of Organized Criminal Violence*. In: *The Individualization of War*. Edited by: Jennifer Welsh, Dapo Akande, and David Rodin, Oxford University Press. © Pablo Kalmanovitz and Miriam Bradley (2023). DOI: 10.1093/oso/9780192872203.003.0010

The use of military force or militarized police has become widespread in such contexts.[6] Governments in Colombia, Peru, Mexico, El Salvador, and Brazil have essentially treated highly armed organized criminal groups as enemies of the state, and deployed against them levels and means of force more commonly associated with non-international armed conflicts (NIACs). War vocabularies have been used widely by commentators and public authorities to describe and operate in these contexts—'war on drugs', 'cartel wars', 'national security threats', etc.—if often rhetorically and not necessarily to denote the technical category of NIAC. And yet the capacity for coordinated action of non-state armed groups, and the humanitarian toll resulting from either state 'wars on crime' or 'turf wars' among criminal groups, appears to be at the level or above situations of violence that have been widely classified as NIAC.

In international law, the distinction between NIAC and other forms of organized violence is made on the basis of legal thresholds relating to the intensity of violence and the level of organization of participating non-state armed groups.[7] When these thresholds are met, at least common Article 3 of the four Geneva Conventions and customary international humanitarian law (IHL) come into effect, as well as the possibility to investigate and prosecute for war crimes. Centrally for our purposes, the threshold for qualification of organized violence as NIAC does not include reference to the motives or proximate goals of non-state armed actors. In principle, situations of violence with unclear or outright pecuniary motives can be qualified as NIAC, which means that militarized criminal organizations can be non-state parties to NIAC.[8]

In the case of Colombia, the International Committee of the Red Cross (ICRC) identified six overlapping NIACs in 2021, five of which involve non-state groups with unclear or inexistent political motives, and only half of which involve state forces.[9] Aerial bombardment of organized criminal camps has been official policy of Colombian forces since 2016.[10] Less plausibly, the Peruvian government has issued legislation and emergency decrees since 2007 declaring drug trafficking organizations in the VRAEM region (Valley of the rivers Apurímac, Ene and

---

[6] Gustavo Flores-Macías and Jessica Zarkin, 'The Militarization of Law Enforcement: Evidence from Latin America', *Perspectives on Politics* 19, no. 2 (2019), pp. 519–538; Juan Albarracín and Nicholas Barnes, 'Criminal Violence in Latin America', *Latin American Research Review* 55, no. 2 (2020).

[7] ICRC, *How Is the Term 'Armed Conflict' Defined in International Humanitarian Law?* Opinion Paper, March 2008 (Geneva: ICRC, 2008).

[8] Sandesh Sivakumaran, *The Law of Non-international Armed Conflict* (Oxford: Oxford University Press, 2012), pp. 164–182; Anthony Cullen, *The Concept of Non-International Armed Conflict in International Humanitarian Law* (Cambridge: CUP, 2010), pp. 117–158.

[9] CICR, *Retos humanitarios 2022: Colombia*, CICR (Bogotá, 2022), p. 3.

[10] Ibid., p. 3; Revista Semana, 'Bombardean campamento del "Clan Úsuga" en Chocó', *Revista Semana* (Bogotá), 3 November 2015; Ana Balcazar Moreno et al., *The War Report 2017: Gang Violence in Colombia, Mexico, and El Salvador* (Geneva: Geneva Academy, 2018), pp. 2–6.

Mantaro) as 'hostile groups' and as such lawful military targets in a context of hostilities.[11]

In the case of Mexico, legal scholars and international think tanks have been divided as to whether organized violence can be characterized as NIAC for some or all of the time since the 'war on drugs' began in 2006. While many experts have argued that it can be, both Mexican authorities and the ICRC are working on the basis of Mexico being a situation of violence that is 'below the threshold of armed conflict', and as such regulated not by the 'hostilities paradigm' of IHL but rather by the 'law enforcement paradigm' of international human rights law (IHRL) in peacetime.[12]

Through a case of study of Mexico's ongoing war on organized crime in this chapter we show how the qualification of a situation of organized violence as NIAC or as below the NIAC threshold has major implications for how individualization processes operate. Our study serves both to elucidate the normative structure of situations of violence below the NIAC threshold, and to shed light on the assumptions and conditions that enable individualization processes in contexts of armed conflict.

As is well known, when a situation of violence is treated as NIAC, the relatively more permissive IHL norms on the use of force apply, whereas if treated as below the NIAC threshold, the more restrictive norms of IHRL in peacetime apply. As the ICRC has put it, 'the conduct of hostilities does not prohibit the killing of legitimate targets, provided that, among others, the IHL principles of proportionality and precautions are fulfilled. Under law enforcement, by contrast, lethal force may be used only as a last resort in order to protect life' at imminent risk.[13] Under the IHL principle of proportionality, more 'incidental loss of life' is permitted than under law enforcement proportionality, which makes lethal force proportional only to unlawful lethal threats.[14]

Differences between the two 'paradigms' extend beyond the regulation of lethal force. In situations of violence falling below the NIAC threshold, the ICRC protection mandate includes a 'right of initiative' which was set out in the Statutes of the International Red Cross and Red Crescent Movement and adopted in 1986 by

---

[11] Alonso Gurmendi, *Conflicto Armado en el Perú* (Universidad del Pacífico, 2019), pp. 149–52. At the end of 2020, the leader of one prominent group in the area was killed in aerial bombardments, along with three others. See Parker Asmann and Laura Ávila, 'Shining Path Commander's Death Strikes Blow to Peru Rebel Group', *Insight Crime*, 31 March, 2021.

[12] Pablo Kalmanovitz and Alejandro Anaya-Muñoz, 'To Invoke or Not to Invoke: International Humanitarian Law and the "War on Drugs" in Mexico', 2022, unpublished manuscript; ICRC, 'ICRC's Role in Situations of Violence below the Threshold of Armed Conflict', *International Review of the Red Cross 96*, no. 893 (2014); ICRC and Gloria Gaggioli, *The Use of Force in Armed Conflicts: Interplay between the Conduct of Hostilities and Law Enforcement Paradigms* (Geneva: International Committee of the Red Cross, 2013).

[13] Ibid., p. iv.

[14] ICRC, *The Use of Force in Law Enforcement Operations* (Geneva: International Committee of the Red Cross, 2022).

states parties to the Geneva Conventions.[15] While such a right of initiative allows the ICRC to propose responses to all kinds of collective violence, the obligation on the ICRC to do so, and the obligation on the relevant authorities to accept any proposal from the ICRC, are both weaker in contexts that do not meet the NIAC thresholds.[16] In fact, 'in this type of situation, the ICRC ensures that it has the consent of the State for its work.'[17] Under IHL, by contrast, states are not free to arbitrarily withhold consent to international humanitarian relief operations, and their consent may in some situations be unnecessary.[18]

Underpinning these and other differences in applicable norms are contrasting basic assumptions about the context of the use of force. Whereas hostilities presuppose at least two enemy groups seeking to overcome each other's resistance through large-scale armed force, law enforcement is governed by human rights norms that were conceived to protect individuals from state abuse or negligence. While IHL regulates resort to force among belligerents with the purpose of minimizing the humanitarian toll of their armed confrontation, IHRL regulates resort to force by state authorities narrowly conceived, 'in order to maintain or restore public security, law and order' in mostly peaceful times.[19] IHL implicitly accepts the use of lethal force as a legitimate means to broader ends, while under IHRL the intentional use of lethal force is only a legitimate means to preventing the use of unlawful lethal force.

Organized criminal violence appears to fit neither paradigm. While its intensity and level of organization can potentially meet NIAC qualification thresholds, it is typically not among the objectives of organized crime to develop large-scale armed forces capable of state capture or regional displacement. Instead of armed confrontation with state forces, organized crime prefers to lay low and bribe or co-opt state officials in order to carry on illicit profit-making undisturbed by law enforcement.[20] Although in this way essentially different from political insurgencies, the military capabilities of some criminal organizations and the level of violence they

---

[15] ICRC, 'The International Committee of the Red Cross's (ICRC's) Role in Situations of Violence below the Threshold of Armed Conflict: Policy document, February 2014', *International Review of the Red Cross 96*, no. 893 (2014), pp. 276, 303.

[16] Miriam Bradley, 'Protecting Civilians in War: The ICRC, UNHCR, and Their Limitations in Internal Armed Conflicts' (Oxford: Oxford University Press, 2016) pp. 79–92.

[17] ICRC, 'The International Committee of the Red Cross's (ICRC's) Role in Situations of Violence below the Threshold of Armed Conflict: Policy Document, February 2014' (Geneva), p. 304.

[18] Dapo Akande and Emanuela-Chiara Gillard, 'Arbitrary Withholding of Consent to Humanitarian Relief Operations in Armed Conflict', *International Law Studies 92* (2016), pp. 483–511.

[19] ICRC and Gaggioli, *The Use of Force in Armed Conflicts: Interplay between the Conduct of Hostilities and Law Enforcement Paradigms*, p. 7.

[20] Diego Gambetta, *The Sicilian Mafia* (Cambridge: Harvard University Press, 1993);Benjamin Lessing, 'Logics of Violence in Criminal War', *Journal of Conflict Resolution 59*, no. 8 (2015), pp. 1486–1516; Benjamin Lessing, *Making Peace in Drug Wars* (Cambridge: CUP, 2018); Nicholas Barnes, 'Criminal Politics: An Integrated Approach to the Study of Organized Crime, Politics, and Violence', *Perspectives on Politics 15*, no. 4 (2017), pp. 967–987; Gustavo Duncan, '*Más que plata o plomo: El poder político del narcotráfico en Colombia y México*. Bogotá: Debate, 2014', *OPERA 16*, no. 16 (2015), pp. 153–158.

can unleash frequently lead to state responses that defy clear-cut categorizations as either law enforcement or hostilities.[21]

As the editors of this volume note in the Introduction, processes of individualization can be conceptualized as moving away from a collective baseline. In armed conflict, individualization refers to normative trajectories in which collectives become less central and individuals more prominent in state practice, international law, and the ethics of war. The Individualisation of War Project has shown how, relative to the baseline of hostilities prior to the development of the individualization norm complex, norms governing resort to and the conduct of war, as well as accountability for wrongs, have become more individualized. As the volume editors also note, this does not mean that contemporary practices of armed conflict have substituted all collective elements by individualized standards. On the contrary, relative to the more individualized standards of law enforcement in peacetime, contemporary armed conflicts still retain significant collective elements.

In this chapter we take as our baseline the law enforcement paradigm, rather than hostilities in a pre-individualized era. Our goal is to identify and analyse processes of *collectivization* in contexts of large-scale organized criminal violence that are not qualified as NIAC, even though they have comparable intensity and humanitarian protection needs.[22] They are, as it were, situations that fall *just below* the NIAC threshold. Its distinctive agents are non-state armed groups that operate in very lucrative illicit markets and seek to protect their business against non-state rivals and state law enforcement—rather than insurgencies driven by political projects and aiming at state capture.[23]

By starting from an IHRL baseline, we identify and analyse processes of collectivization through reverse analogy with processes of individualization in armed conflicts. Specifically, we show that when law enforcement tasks are militarized in contexts of organized criminal violence, collective designations tend to become more prominent and normatively important in the domains of protection and liability to harm. We additionally make the normative argument that this kind of collectivization generates problematic legal gaps which leave individuals without

---

[21] For further discussion, and an argument for a presumption *against* NIAC qualifications in these contexts, see Pablo Kalmanovitz, 'Can criminal organizations be non-State parties to armed conflict?', *International Review of the Red Cross* No. 923, June 2023.

[22] The UN Convention against Transnational Organized Crime defines organized criminal organization as 'a structured group of three or more persons, existing for a period of time and acting in concert with the aim of committing one or more serious crimes ... in order to obtain a financial or other material benefit'. See Pierre Hauck and Sven Peterke, 'Organized Crime and Gang Violence in National and International Law', *International Review of the Red Cross* 92, no. 878 (2010), pp. 407–436. We are interested in more robust forms of organization, which contain considerable coercive arms and are capable of engaging in high-intensity violence, i.e., which come close to meeting the NIAC threshold.

[23] For a characterization of organized crime and its distinctive violent groups, see Kalmanovitz, Can criminal organizations be non-State parties to armed conflict?

adequate protection. While much of what we say may be applicable to other cases in Latin America and beyond, our analysis was generated through a case study of Mexico's war on organized crime, which is precisely a situation of intense collective violence with dire humanitarian needs, which is ostensibly understood by state agents and humanitarian actors to fall below the NIAC threshold.

The chapter proceeds as follows. The first section provides a general discussion of collectivization processes in situations of violence below the NIAC threshold, looking specifically at the domains of protection and liability to harm. The second section discusses collectivization in the Mexican case, with focused discussions on protection and liability. We believe there are also complex and important contrasts in the domain of accountability, but they deserve separate discussion. The third and final section concludes.

1. Collectivization in Contexts of Organized Criminal Violence

In its policy document on situations of violence below the threshold of armed conflict, the ICRC explained that such situations came within its field of action in virtue of three features: violence of considerable intensity, which is 'the work of one or several groups made of a large number of people', and which has 'significant humanitarian consequences'.[24] Violence is collective in the sense that it is perpetrated by groups, the members of which 'feel that they belong to the group (shared identity, collective purpose, activities carried out jointly, etc)'.[25] Humanitarian consequences result from attacks and threats on the life and physical integrity of populations deserving protection, particularly in cases of 'people in a hostile environment who are not protected from the acts perpetrated against them' by de facto powers.[26]

Consequences to be addressed by humanitarian actors in areas controlled or disputed by non-state armed groups include physical harm, human trafficking, sexual violence, forced disappearance, forced displacement and migration, torture, arbitrary detention, and more.[27] Even though governed by IHRL and domestic law rather than IHL, these 'other situations of violence' can have humanitarian consequences 'even more far-reaching than those of armed conflicts' and as such activate the ICRC's mandate of humanitarian protection.[28]

---

[24] ICRC, 'ICRC's Role in Situations of Violence below the Threshold of Armed Conflict', pp. 275–277.
[25] Ibid., p. 281.
[26] Ibid., p. 291.
[27] Ibid., p. 290.
[28] Ibid., at pp. 288–289.

The militarization of law enforcement in situations of collective violence below the NIAC threshold triggers an important process of collectivization, which is militarization itself. Typically, governments justify resort to their armed forces in law enforcement tasks in terms of collective, even national, security threats, which are said to require exceptional levels of force and social control. Collective threats typically receive collective designations of agency—cartel, gang, organized crime, *mara*—the members of which can in practice come to be treated as state enemies who are liable to attack in virtue of their membership status rather than of posing imminent unlawful threats.

Furthermore, the armed forces have more capacity for coordinated action than any other security body in the state. Military authority has stricter requirements of due obedience, more rigid chain of command structures, and more demanding discipline and training. This rigid construction of authority is meant to diminish individual judgment and agency, to create *esprit de corps*, i.e., a sense of collective agency and unity. In this way, military forces can deploy 'tactical units' that coordinate action on a larger scale, for a longer time, and potentially with larger destructive impact than police forces. This higher capacity can have protective effects, as when it deters organized crime from preying on populations, but it can also exacerbate violence and multiply humanitarian needs.

On the other hand, organized criminal violence by definition involves organizations with the capacity to act collectively and deploy violence on a large scale. They can use their considerable resources—violence in particular—to persuade or intimidate populations and public authorities into joining the organization, providing labour or information, not cooperating with other public authorities or rival criminal groups, etc.

Large-scale criminal enterprises are known to seek territorial control in ways instrumental to their illicit business, which includes securing geographic areas for the production, transportation, and distribution of illicit goods or persons. In order to secure territorial control, criminal organizations engage in forms of legitimization that enable them to recruit informants and other forms of local support, exclude rival groups, and rule illicit economies more efficiently. Some criminal organizations have developed forms of governance and public service provision comparable to those provided by political insurgencies and even state authorities, including provision of security, dispute settlement mechanisms, and basic forms of social assistance.[29] Conquering and managing territory through the strategic use of coercion and legitimization are of course eminently collective enterprises.

---

[29] Barnes, 'Criminal Politics: An Integrated Approach to the Study of Organized Crime, Politics, and Violence'; Enrique Desmond Arias, 'The Impacts of Differential Armed Dominance of Politics in Rio de Janeiro, Brazil', *Studies in Comparative Development 48* (2013), pp. 263–284; Vanda Felbab-Brown, 'Conceptualizing Crime as Competition in State-Making and Designing an Effective Response', *Brookings* (2010).

1.1 Collective Protection in Contexts of Organized Criminal Violence

In contexts of organized criminal violence, and relative to the law enforcement baseline, we can also identify several processes of collectivization in the domain of protection. Notably, there is the collectivization of the objects of protection. Threats from organized criminal violence can serve to create collectives, as when people flee their homes in response to threats, becoming internally displaced persons (IDPs) or, if they cross an international border, migrants. Furthermore, criminal organizations often target particular collectives. It is widely known that criminal organizations engaged in human trafficking systematically prey on migrants moving from Central America to the United States through Mexico. Migrants are collectives on the move, sometimes moving together as self-designated 'caravans' seeking collective self-protection, and in urgent need of humanitarian protection that state authorities do not always provide.

Membership of particular collectives can also determine the rights and international protections to which individuals are entitled. For example, the status of migrant, displaced person, or more broadly 'victim of human rights violation', are administrative categories in Mexico and many other Latin American countries. However, some countries restrict their definition of IDPs to those fleeing conflict-related violence, and international law offers migrants who do not qualify for refugee status few special rights or protections beyond basic human rights standards.

Consideration of international responses and responsibilities highlights important ways in which collectivization from an IHRL baseline in contexts of organized criminal violence differs from IHL regulation of NIAC. Despite the urgent humanitarian needs and intensity of threat prevalent in these 'other situations of violence', the status of sovereignty remains largely intact. Whereas armed conflicts and international crimes are understood to be grave international concerns, in which the international community has a responsibility to protect civilian populations,[30] no equivalent category or responsibility exists in contexts of organized criminal violence. Violence below the threshold of NIAC is in this sense a domestic rather than international issue. This gap has led to a paradoxical legal state of affairs, in which the right to life is nearly absolute de jure under IHRL, but there is more scope both for coercive foreign military action and for civilian international humanitarian response to protect the population in contexts regulated by IHL.

Debates about the legitimacy of humanitarian intervention and the 'responsibility to protect' principle have mostly focused on armed conflicts and, to a lesser degree, the commission of international crimes. As is well known, the bar

---

[30] Bradley, 'Protecting Civilians in War'; ICISS, *The Responsibility to Protect* (Ottawa: IDRC, 2001); Jennifer Welsh, 'Norm Contestation and the Responsibility to Protect', *Global Responsibility to Protect* 5, no. 4 (2013), pp. 365–396.

for crimes against humanity is set higher than that for war crimes (which by definition can only occur in contexts of armed conflict), because to constitute a crime against humanity, the acts in question must be committed as part of a widespread and systematic attack. Thus, while forced disappearances, extrajudicial killings, and forced displacement can occur in connection with organized criminal violence and militarized state responses without any implication for the 'responsibility to protect', if the same acts constituted war crimes, they could trigger the 'responsibility to protect'.

In humanitarian emergencies outside of armed conflict, there is also no clearcut obligation for states to accept external humanitarian assistance. Under IHL, states must not arbitrarily withhold consent to an offer from an impartial humanitarian body to assist the population with relief actions to provide such necessities as food, water, medical supplies, clothing, and means of shelter.[31] Under IHRL, it could be argued that not only the right to life, but also the rights to adequate food, housing, and health imply that where people cannot realize these rights due to a humanitarian crisis, the state must either meet their basic needs or allow humanitarian agencies to do so. However, the obligation is not as explicit as it is in IHL. Even where a state consents to humanitarian operations in non-IHL contexts, the fact that it does so at its own discretion and not as a matter of obligation means the state has greater latitude to limit the scope of the operations. For the ICRC specifically, working outside of armed conflicts implies significant adaptations from its core mandate, which can generate tensions between the institutional mission to protect individuals from violence and the institutional commitment to neutrality, a principle which for the ICRC is delineated by IHL.[32]

Where IHL applies, the ICRC has an obligation to respond, and maintains a commitment to dialogue with all state and non-state parties to conflict, regardless of their motives. Through that dialogue, the ICRC seeks to increase compliance with IHL and hence to reduce the impact of violence on protected persons.[33]

By contrast, working in contexts of organized criminal violence where IHL does not apply, the ICRC lacks a normative framework that is applicable to both state and non-state actors, and with which to structure its dialogue. Thus while the ICRC engages in dialogue with the police and other public forces, working to get them to comply with international human rights law or domestic legislation on the use of force, it has begun to distinguish non-state armed groups according to their motives, and to restrict dialogue with those it deems to be economically

---

[31] Akande and Gillard, 'Arbitrary Withholding of Consent to Humanitarian Relief Operations in Armed Conflict'.

[32] Miriam Bradley, 'From Armed Conflict to Urban Violence: Transformations in the International Committee of the Red Cross, International Humanitarianism, and the Laws of War', *European Journal of International Relations* 26, no. 4 (2020), pp. 1061–1083.

[33] Bradley, 'Protecting Civilians in War', pp. 162–166.

motivated or criminal.[34] At the same time, it has expanded the scope of its work to include efforts to prevent young people from joining armed groups and to promote the socio-economic rehabilitation of offenders, goals that would be non-neutral in conflict contexts. In short, when dealing with at least some criminal organizations, the ICRC appears to be implicitly taking the side of the state.[35]

1.2 Liability to Harm in Contexts of Organized Criminal Violence

The emergence of practices of organized criminal violence has contributed to an outpouring of doctrinal analysis of the conditions under which force, in particular lethal force, can be used in law enforcement operations. This doctrine is grounded on IHRL and on two soft-law instruments which have been widely used by UN human rights bodies: the UN Code of Conduct for Law Enforcement Officials of 1979 and the UN Basic Principles on the Use of Force and Firearms by Law Enforcement Officials of 1990.

On this basis, the ICRC itself has spelled out conditions under which individuals could be liable to harm, in particular lethal force, in the context of law enforcement operations.[36] Firearms are permissible 'only where necessary to counter an imminent or grave threat to life or physical integrity, and when less violent means are not or would not be effective.'[37] The lowest amount of force necessary to achieve a law enforcement objective is to be applied. Law enforcement proportionality is much narrower than IHL proportionality—the level of force must be weighed directly against the gravity of the unlawful threat, and the anticipated benefit of force should outweigh the anticipated harm, including to the attacker.[38]

The ICRC has identified several further principles governing the use of force in law enforcement operations, which include the obligation in states to adopt and implement regulations on the use of force by state officials—'legality'—and the obligation to carefully plan operations in order to avoid the use of force and minimize the risk to bystanders—'precaution.'[39]

However, as the following section on Mexico shows, while these principles are restrictive and highly individualized, in the context of militarized law enforcement against organized crime, violent agents do often identify and distinguish between collectives in quasi-IHL ways. Public authorities are widely documented to target

---

[34] Bradley, 'From Armed Conflict to Urban Violence', p. 1074.
[35] Ibid., pp. 1073–1074.
[36] ICRC, *The Use of Force in Law Enforcement Operations*.
[37] Ibid., p. 4.
[38] Ibid.
[39] ICRC, *The Use of Force in Law Enforcement Operations*, pp. 3–4.

(alleged) members of collectively designated groups—gangs, *maras*, *bandas criminales*, cartels—on the basis of group membership. Either by state forces or rival non-state groups, alleged members of these groups become de facto if not de jure liable to harm in virtue of their status, rather than of their posing imminent threats.

2. The War on Organized Crime in Mexico

Military involvement in law enforcement is not a recent phenomenon in Mexico. The military has participated for decades in interdiction operations and the eradication of illicit crops. At least since the late 1970s, active or retired military officers have been appointed to high command positions in state and municipal police forces, as well as in civilian prosecutorial roles.[40]

But drug-related violence was rare in Mexico before the late 1990s. For decades, illicit business operated peacefully under the supervision of 'informal government protection networks' that operated at all levels of government. These networks began to collapse in the early stages of the Mexican transition to democracy, particularly after the 1996 election, when the hegemony of the *Partido Revolucionario Institucional* (PRI) began to fracture in several important states. The dissolution of informal protection networks led first to inter-cartel 'turf wars', which led cartels to fund standing militia, and later to the 'war on drugs', in which these militias were confronted by the Mexican armed forces.[41]

Violence escalated to historically unprecedented levels when President Felipe Calderón (2006–12) put the army and navy at the forefront of his government's declared objective of 'direct combat to drug trafficking and other expressions of organized crime'.[42] Military confrontation of organized crime unleashed a virulent escalation of collective violence that has yet to recede.[43] Since the mid-2000s, criminal organizations have fought each other and state forces in ways that have

---

[40] Jesús López-González, 'Civil-Military Relations and the Militarization of Public Security in Mexico, 1989–2010: Challenges to Democracy', in George Philip and Susana Berruecos (eds), *Mexico's Struggle for Public Security* (New York: Palgrave Macmillan, 2012).

[41] Guillermo Trejo and Sandra Ley, 'Why Did Drug Cartels Go to War in Mexico? Subnational Party Alternation, the Breakdown of Criminal Protection, and the Onset of Large-Scale Violence', *Comparative Political Studies* 51, no. 7 (2018), pp. 900–937. Trejo and Ley estimate conservatively there were 4275 murders perpetrated by drug cartels and their criminal associates between 1995 and 2006, mostly in the context of turf wars (at p. 906).

[42] Objective 8 of the National Development Plan DOF, *PLAN Nacional de Desarrollo 2013–2018*, Presidency of Mexico (Mexico, 2007).

[43] Several security experts have attributed the sharp increase of lethal violence in Mexico after 2006 to Calderon's aggressive military response to organized criminal violence. See among others Javier Osorio, 'The Contagion of Drug Violence: Spatiotemporal Dynamics of the Mexican War on Drugs', *Journal of Conflict Resolution* 59, no. 8 (2015), pp. 202–238; Guillermo Trejo and Sandra Ley, *Votes, Drugs, and Violence* (Cambridge: CUP, 2020), pp. 143–179; Lessing, *Making Peace in Drug Wars*, pp. 202–237.

258   THE CASE OF MEXICO'S WAR ON ORGANIZED CRIME

caused unprecedented numbers of violent deaths, forced disappearance, internal displacement, and other gross human rights violations.

After Calderón, President Enrique Peña Nieto (2012–18) de-escalated the war rhetoric but continued the militarized approach; homicide rates continued to rise, and militarization was gradually normalized in law and practice.[44] President Andrés Manuel López Obrador (2018–24) gave further powers and tasks to the armed forces—in security and beyond—which he has even called 'the people in uniform'.[45] The army and navy continue to be on the streets to this day, if with a less confrontational mandate and often acting through a formally civilian but organically military National Guard.

The humanitarian toll of this violence is above that of many NIACs. Between 2006 and 2020, an estimated 260,000 violent deaths occurred as a consequence of the war on organized crime. At the 2011 peak of lethal violence carried out by the Mexican army, over 1400 yearly killings of 'aggressors' were reported by the army itself, which resulted from over one thousand 'clashes' (*confrontaciones*) with (alleged) members of organized crime.[46] The year 2011 also saw a peak in soldier deployment, with over 52,000 troops on the streets, but troop deployment has been above 30,000 every year since the 'war on drugs' began in earnest in 2006.[47] While there is no official IDP count in the country, according to the best available monitoring system, from 2006 to 2020, over 350,000 individuals were and remain internally displaced as a consequence of collective violence in Mexico.[48] In a country visit in early 2022, the UN Committee against Enforced Disappearance noted that the official registry of cases of disappearance had reached over 95,000 missing persons, over 98 per cent of whom were reported disappeared after 2006.[49]

---

[44] Alejandro Anaya-Muñoz and Natalia Saltalamacchia, 'Factors Blocking the Compliance with International Human Rights Norms in Mexico', in Alejandro Anaya-Muñoz and Barbara Frey (eds), *Mexico's Human Rights Crisis* (Philadelphia: University of Pennsylvania Press, 2019), pp. 220–224; Kalmanovitz and Anaya-Muñoz, 'To Invoke or Not to Invoke: International Humanitarian Law and the "War on Drugs" in Mexico'.

[45] The expression appears in López-Obrador's National Peace and Security Plan 2018–2024, and often in his morning conferences and media declarations. 'In substance', the Plan states, 'Mexican soldiers and marines were and continue to be people in uniform.' It is because of their 'popular character' that they can be trusted to provide public security Andrés Manuel López-Obrador, *Plan Nacional de Paz y Seguridad 2018–2024*, Partido Morena (Mexico City, 2018).Animal Político, 'No militarizamos al país, soldados son pueblo uniformado', *Animal Político* (Mexico), 1 December 2020.

[46] Javier Trevino-Rangel et al., 'Deadly Force and Denial: The Military's Legacy in Mexico's "War on Drugs"', *The International Journal of Human Rights* (2021), pp. 567–590, at pp. 4, 9.

[47] Catalina Pérez Correa, Carlos Silva Forné, and Rodrigo Gutiérrez Rivas, 'Deadly Forces: Use of Lethal Force by Mexican Security Forces 2007–2015', in Alejandro Anaya-Muñoz and Barbara Frey (eds), *Mexico's Human Rights Crisis* (Philadelphia: University of Pennsylvania Press, 2019), pp. 28–29.

[48] CMDPDH, *Episodios de Desplazamiento Interno Forzado Masivo en México: Informe 2020*, Comisión Mexicana de Defensa y Promoción de los Derechos Humanos (Mexico City, 2021). IDMC uses CMDPDH data for its reports on Mexico. According to its latest report, the number at the end of 2021 was 379,000, see https://www.internal-displacement.org/countries/mexico

[49] CED, *Informe del Comité contra la Desaparición Forzada sobre su Visita a México en virtud del artículo 33 de la Convención* (Geneva: Committee against Enforced Disappearance, 2022).

With these staggering levels of collective violence, it is unsurprising that many have found Mexico's 'war on drugs' to be a case of NIAC, although this conclusion remains contested. Some of the NIAC *indicia* are clearly present, others clearly absent; some have appeared intermittently in time and space, others remain unclear. Multiple law review articles and reports by international think tanks have concluded that Mexico has had a NIAC since the beginning of its 'war on drugs' in 2006, at least in certain areas, for certain periods, and for certain non-state armed groups; others have forcefully challenged these conclusions.[50] Mexican authorities themselves have taken the negative view and throughout the war on organized crime have formally invoked the law enforcement paradigm. In practice, however, organized crime has been treated as a legal grey zone, regulated neither as war nor as peace, and with collective elements prominent both in practice and normatively in the domains of protection and liability to harm.

2.1 Collective Protection

Despite the massive humanitarian consequences resulting from organized criminal violence in Mexico, and from the militarized response of the state, the efforts of international and national actors to protect those subject to violence have been extremely limited. Many collectives have sought to protect themselves, and local- rather than national- or international-level organizations have led the humanitarian response.

Mexico does not feature in international debates on the use of force for protective purposes. Since 1999, the Security Council has issued seventeen thematic resolutions on the protection of civilians, and the Secretary-General has submitted twenty-three reports on the protection of civilians, but not one of these mentions Mexico.[51] While the protection needs in Mexico are enormous, the category of civilian is not strictly relevant, and the protection of civilians agenda within the

---

[50] In favour of a NIAC qualification, see, e.g., Carina Bergal, 'The Mexican Drug War: The Case for a Non-international Armed Conflict Classification', *Fordham International Law Journal 34* (2011), pp. 1042–1088; Callin Kerr, 'Mexico's Drug War: Is It Really a War?', *Texas Law Review 54* (2012); Craig Bloom, 'Square Pegs and Round Holes: Mexico, Drugs, and International Law', *Houston Journal of International Law 34*, no. 2 (2012); Leiden University Human Rights Clinic, *The Situation of Drug Related Violence in Mexico from 200 to 2017: A Non-International Armed Conflict?*; Ana Gabriela Rojo Fierro, 'La Guerra contra el Narcotráfico en México ¿Un Conflicto Armado No Internacional no Reconocido?', *Foro Internacional 60* (2020), pp. 1415–1462. For the negative position, see Patrick Gallahue, 'Mexico's "War on Drugs"—Real or Rhetorical Armed Conflict?', *Journal of International Law of Peace and Armed Conflict 24*, no. 1 (2011), pp. 39–45; Andrea Nill Sánchez, 'Mexico's Drug "War": Drawing a Line between Rhetoric and Reality', *The Yale Journal of International Law 38* (2013), pp. 467–509; Alejandro Rodiles, 'Law and Violence in the Global South: The Legal Framing of Mexico's "Narco War"', *Journal of Conflict & Security Law 23*, no. 2 (2018), pp. 269–281.

[51] See respectively: 'UN documents for protection of civilians: Security Council resolutions' (Accessed: 8 June 2022), https://www.securitycouncilreport.org/un_documents_type/security-council-resolutions/?ctype=Protection%20of%20Civilians&cbtype=protection-of-civilians; 'UN documents for protection of civilians: Secretary-General's reports' (Accessed: 8 June 2022), https://www.

260   THE CASE OF MEXICO'S WAR ON ORGANIZED CRIME

UN is explicitly focused on the protection of civilians *in armed conflict*. Nearly every peacekeeping mandate since 1999 has included protection language, but mandating peacekeepers to operate in Mexico seems unthinkable. Implementing the 'responsibility to protect' principle in Mexico appears equally unlikely.

While the Mexican state is under no clear obligation to consent to international humanitarian agencies operating on its territory, many are operational there, assisting migrants and refugees, and sometimes also providing support to victims of criminality and violence more broadly. The United Nations Refugee Agency (UNHCR) and the International Organization for Migration (IOM) have particular mandates for protecting displaced persons and managing migration, respectively, and both are working in Mexico. The regional delegation of the ICRC, covering Central America and Mexico, is based in Mexico City, and from there the ICRC manages activities focused on Mexico itself. These activities include training for the Mexican police and armed forces, and confidential bilateral dialogue to persuade the security forces to comply with international law.[52] For the most part, however, the efforts of international humanitarian agencies do not match the level of humanitarian need and have only a limited focus on protection from violence. Indeed, in some parts of Mexico characterized by high levels of violence, including some border areas where large numbers of migrants gather or transit through, international actors are most conspicuous by their absence.[53]

The Calderón and Peña Nieto administrations were reluctant to accept the very existence of IDPs, or to acknowledge that applicability of the UN Guiding Principles on Internal Displacement. Neither government took steps towards developing a coordinated and comprehensive inter-agency response to internal displacement, and in 2015, the Ministry of the Interior argued that displacement as a consequence of violence, insofar as it occurred, was not generalized.[54]

The 2014–18 Program for the Attention of Victims of the Executive Commission for the Support of Victims (CEAV for its initials in Spanish) included among its objectives providing adequate support to IDPs. Remarkably, however, the CEAV reported that individuals could not be registered as victims of human rights violations solely by virtue of being internally displaced. The National Human Rights Commission (CNDH) also found that while some key government agencies implicitly recognized the existence of internal displacement in the country,

securitycouncilreport.org/un_documents_type/secretary-generals-reports/?ctype=Protection%20of
%20Civilians&cbtype=protection-of-civilians

[52] CICR, *Balance humanitario 2021/2022: Mexico* (Mexico City: CICR, 2022), p. 6.

[53] Katrina Burgess and Alba Loureiro, 'Comparing Humanitarian Responses at the US-Mexico Border' (Barcelona, Spain: VI Congreso Internacional de Estudios del Desarrollo, 2022).

[54] Laura Rubio Díaz-Leal, 'Violence-Induced Internal Displacement in Mexico, the Inter-American Commission on Human Rights, and Official State Responses', in Alejandro Anaya-Muñoz and Barbara Frey (eds), *Mexico's Human Rights Crisis* (Philadelphia: University of Pennsylvania Press, 2019), pp. 55–56.

others explicitly claimed there were not internally displaced populations in Mexico. While the López Obrador government has publicly acknowledged internal displacement as a problem, little appears to have changed in practice.

Given the inadequacy of international and national support, responding to the needs of migrants and the displaced has largely fallen to local-level actors. In some parts of the country, local government authorities have mounted a limited response. However, most state and municipal governments have not recognized internal displacement and therefore have not implemented specific policy responses.[55] More commonly, local civil society actors, including Church-based organizations, have been the main or only provider of humanitarian support. For example, throughout Mexico, migrant shelters have emerged through a bottom-up process, offering services and solidarity.[56]

With only limited assistance and protection from authorities and official organizations, most of those subject to violence in Mexico must depend primarily on their own protective strategies, and these very often rely on collective action. As already mentioned, since 2018, migrants have often sought safety in numbers by travelling in large caravans. The hope is that this will not only limit harassment and violence, but also that it will give maximum visibility to their situation, with the ultimate goal of pressuring the authorities to offer a better public policy response.[57]

Communal self-defence groups have also been created in response to threats from organized crime directed at local populations, and the failure of the state to protect those populations from organized criminal violence. These groups also highlight a distinction widely made in public discourse between members of organized crime and those who are 'civilian' members of the wider population, whether or not they resort to violence. Despite taking up arms, these self-defence groups are not considered liable to harm, and were even briefly legitimized from 2014 to 2016, with the creation by the government of a 'Rural Defence Force', which allowed vigilantes to operate lawfully.[58] They are referred to as *civilian* vigilantes, or armed *civilians*, and as such distinguished from cartels and organized crime.[59]

---

[55] Ibid., p. 50.

[56] Burgess and Loureiro, 'Comparing Humanitarian Responses at the US-Mexico Border'; Alejandro Olayo Mendez, 'Humanitarianism from the Ground: Humanitarian Aid to Migrants and Refugees in Mexico' (ed. Oxford Department of International Development, 27 March 2017). https://www.qeh.ox.ac.uk/blog/humanitarianism-ground-humanitarian-aid-migrants-and-refugees-mexico

[57] Valentina Benincasa and Almudena Cortés, 'Humanitarizando la movilidad en México: la migración centroamericana como problema humanitario', *Oñati Socio-Legal Series 11*, no. 3 (2021), pp. 809–832.

[58] Juan Del Rio, 'Do Vigilante Groups Reduce Cartel-Related Violence? An Empirical Assessment of Crime Trends in Michoacán, Mexico', *Studies in Conflict & Terrorism* (2020), pp. 1–25, at p. 2.

[59] Irene María Álvarez-Rodríguez, 'The Moral Economy of Drug Trafficking: Armed Civilians and Mexico's Violence and Crime', *Latin American Perspectives 48*, no. 1 (2021), pp. 231–244.

262 THE CASE OF MEXICO'S WAR ON ORGANIZED CRIME

2.2 Collective Liability to Harm

Calderón's National Development Plan—the master policy document for his presidency—made public security the government's top priority and set organized crime as the most serious national security threat. As the Plan put it, it was necessary to 'recover the strength of the State and security' through 'direct combat to drug trafficking and other expressions of organized crime', which made involvement of the armed forces necessary 'as keepers of the internal security of the country'.[60] Throughout his presidency, Calderón mobilized politically the rhetoric of war and widely publicized military victories over drug cartels.

While not equally keen on aggressive militarization, Presidents Peña Nieto and López Obrador continued to use war vocabularies in their master security policy documents. Peña Nieto's Plan claims that large illicit economies have threatened Mexico's national stability, and that a central cause of its 'public security crisis' was the creation of militias linked to organized criminal groups and specialized in the use of violence. The document recognizes that criminal groups have territorial control over large areas in the country, where they have imposed 'social orders' around illicit economies, and sets as one of its goals to regain state control over all national territory.[61]

During his presidential campaign, López-Obrador announced a U-turn in security policy, in which instead of a war against drugs, transitional justice mechanisms and 'peacebuilding' (*pacificación*) would be at the heart of security. The campaign proposal included the creation of a high-level Peacebuilding Council as well as the implementation of a Demobilization, Disarmament, and Reintegration (DDR) programme as a response to the 'organizational level, firepower and territorial control' of organized criminal groups, which are understood to be at the level of political insurgencies. Neither of these initiatives has been actually implemented, but President López-Obrador's master security policy document continues to emphasize peacebuilding and the recovery of national territory from criminal control.[62]

The use of this type of language in such high-level policy documents reflects generalized perceptions of threat from organized criminal organizations. Mexican criminal organizations are known to have the capacity to procure and use large arsenals of high-calibre weapons, including drones, grenade launchers, anti-tank rockets, armour-piercing ammunition, and industrial explosives. In many

---

[60] Cited in Anaya-Muñoz and Saltalamacchia, 'Factors Blocking the Compliance with International Human Rights Norms in Mexico', p. 220.

[61] DOF, *PROGRAMA Nacional de Seguridad Pública 2014–2018*, Secretaría de Gobernación (Mexico City, 2014).

[62] López-Obrador, *Plan Nacional de Paz y Seguridad 2018–2024* (Mexico City, 2018); DOF, *PROGRAMA Sectorial de Seguridad y Protección Ciudadana 2020–2024*, Secretaría de Gobernación (Mexico City, 2020).

areas, their armed capacity surpasses that of local, state, and federal police forces.[63] Some of them—notably the Zetas, Sinaloa, and *Jalisco Nueva Generación* cartels—have standing militias at their disposal with weaponry, levels of organization, and command structures that arguably allow them to pursue military objectives in sustained ways.[64] Mexican cartels are known to compete and fight for territorial control, which has caused forced displacement and created pressing humanitarian needs in populations living in territories under criminal control.[65]

On the other hand, the Mexican armed forces are known to have used armed conflict categories to refer to non-state groups in internal operational documents. A leaked official database recording homicides and casualties connected to organized criminal violence uses the categories of 'aggressor' to denote members of organized criminal groups that have (allegedly) attacked public authorities (and been killed as a result); 'clashes' to refer to events in which public forces detain, injure, or kill 'civilians' (public forces need not first have been under fire themselves); and 'killed' or 'wounded civilian' to denote non-aggressors who come under state fire.[66]

According to this same database, the use of military lethal force during the first five years of the 'war on drugs' (2006–11) followed a logic of state enmity rather than criminal suspicion and capture. Fewer than 3 per cent of recorded 'clashes' resulted from operations based on pre-existing military intelligence or criminal investigations; over 30 per cent took place in the context of area patrols without pre-established objectives, and for over 25 per cent there is no information on the context in which lethal force was used.[67]

Most troublingly, military clashes showed a very high rate of killed relative to wounded non-military individuals. In years 2011 and 2012, at the peak of killings reported by the military, there were on average nine and fourteen times more killed than wounded individuals respectively. In the state of Zacatecas in year 2013, the lethality rate was fifty-eight—'clashes' left nearly no 'civilian' survivors.[68]

---

[63] Bergal, 'The Mexican Drug War: The Case for a Non-international Armed Conflict Classification'; Carrie Comer and Daniel Mburu, 'Humanitarian Law at Wits' End: Does the Violence Arising from the "War on Drugs" in Mexico Meet the International Criminal Court's Non-International Armed Conflict Threshold?', in *Yearbook of International Humanitarian Law 2015* (The Hague: T.M.C. Asser Press, 2015).

[64] Leiden University Human Rights Clinic, *The Situation of Drug Related Violence in Mexico from 200 to 2017: A Non-International Armed Conflict?*; Bergal, 'The Mexican Drug War: The Case for a Non-international Armed Conflict Classification'.

[65] Ibid.

[66] Trevino-Rangel et al., 'Deadly Force and Denial: The Military's Legacy in Mexico's "War on Drugs"', pp. 6–7. On the history and composition of the database, see Laura Atuesta, Oscar Siordia, and Alejandro Madrazo, 'The "War on Drugs" in Mexico: (Official) Database of Events between December 2006 and November 2011', *Journal of Conflict Resolution 63*, no. 7 (2019), pp. 1765–1789.

[67] Alejandro Madrazo, Calzada Olvera, Rebeca, and Romero Vadillo, 'La "guerra contra las drogas": Análisis de los combates de las fuerzas públicas 2006–2011', *Política y Gobierno XXV*, no. 2 (2018), pp. 379–402, at p. 390.

[68] Pérez Correa, Silva Forné, and Gutiérrez Rivas, 'Deadly Forces: Use of Lethal Force by Mexican Security Forces 2007–2015', pp. 32–38.

264 THE CASE OF MEXICO'S WAR ON ORGANIZED CRIME

Such lethality is hardly to be expected in operations that comply with the strict regulations on the use of lethal force under the law enforcement paradigm. A survey made in 2013 revealed little sympathy in public opinion for those harmed in the context of the 'war on drugs', a lack of sympathy that may be related to the generalized perception that those killed were liable to harm.[69]

Liability to harm based on membership status operates not only in public discourse and military procedures, but also in national criminal legislation. An exceptional criminal law regime has been built in Mexico around the crime of collectively organizing to commit a crime, in a way that in effect enlists domestic criminal law in the 'war' efforts. In a particular version of what criminal legal theorists have called 'enemy criminal law' (derecho penal del enemigo, Feindstrafrecht), Mexican law permits the preventive detention of alleged members of criminal organizations in virtue of their presumed collective dangerousness.[70] No specific wrongful act allegedly committed or attempted is necessary for indictment. Furthermore, alleged members of organized criminal groups are liable to 'administrative detention' without judicial order, which is inconsistent with basic human rights but entrenched in Mexico's Constitution. In effect, sheer membership in a criminal organization is a crime under Mexican criminal law. As has happened in the case of global counter-terror efforts, due process protections aimed at individualizing responsibility have been weakened for the sake of 'effectiveness' in the combat of organized criminal groups.

3. Conclusions

Our discussion has identified and analysed collectivization patterns in situations of violence that fall below the NIAC threshold. Very little research has been done on the normative structure of these other forms of violence, and there is still a great deal to understand about Mexico and the Latin American region more broadly. But one finding of our research so far is that, while organized criminal violence can create humanitarian needs comparable to those of NIAC, there is no international legal framework to underpin it, and consequently not the same level of protection mandate. Much of the international legal and institutional apparatus for the protection of individuals or collectives is linked to IHL and restricted to contexts of armed conflict. Sovereignty is more conditional in armed conflict than in contexts of criminal violence. This makes coercive international military action

---

[69] Andreas Schedler, 'The Criminal Community of Victims and Perpetrators: Cognitive Foundations of Citizen Detachment From Organized Violence in Mexico', Human Rights Quarterly 38 (2016), pp. 1038–1069.

[70] Günther Jakobs, 'On the Theory of Enemy Criminal Law', in Markus Dubber (ed.), Foundational Texts in Modern Criminal Law (Oxford: OUP, 2014); Oscar Gutiérrez Santos, 'La delincuencia organizada a la luz del derecho penal del enemigo', Díkê: Revista de Investigación en Derecho, Criminología y Consultoría Jurídica 26 (2019), pp. 367–393.

to protect populations unlikely, and reduces the obligations on states to consent to humanitarian relief operations.

Relatedly, our analysis has shed light on the structure of processes of individualization in armed conflict. Individualization in armed conflict is not a move from regulating hostilities under IHL towards regulating peacetime under IHRL, but something distinct. The NIAC threshold creates a discontinuity in international legal regulation, with a glaring gap in international protection mechanisms. Key dimensions of individualization processes in war, particularly the erosion of the condition of state consent for humanitarian operations, are largely absent from peacetime under IHRL.

While our analysis may initially have appeared to be framed in terms of two opposite baselines—and pointing to two processes moving in opposite directions—in reality the continuum between individualization and collectivization is not linear. Much of the individualization process in armed conflicts is not a move towards peacetime regulation of violence under IHRL; conversely, the collectivization and intensification of violence need not lead to NIAC. And while humanitarian needs may be equally or more severe in situations below the NIAC threshold, only NIACs contain strong international legal mechanism for protection.

Lastly, there is a striking substantive match between the law enforcement paradigm and revisionist just war theory. The case of Mexico illustrates just how difficult in practice it is for military forces to operate under the demanding criteria of revisionist just war theory, even in conditions that may fall below the threshold of NIAC. While the law enforcement paradigm has been formally applicable in Mexico throughout the 'war on drugs', the armed forces have shown little will or ability to operate under its restrictive rules. There are deep institutional and political reasons for that, which may also be reasons to be sceptical of the compatibility between the military ethos and the law enforcement paradigm.[71]

References

Akande, D. and Gillard, E.-C. (2016) 'Arbitrary Withholding of Consent to Humanitarian Relief Operations in Armed Conflict', *International Law Studies*, 92, pp. 483–511.

Albarracín, J. and Barnes, N. (2020) 'Criminal Violence in Latin America', *Latin American Research Review*, 55(2), pp. 397–406.

---

[71] This work was supported by the European Research Council under the European Union's Seventh Framework Programme (FP/2007–2013) ERC Grant Agreement 340956 IOW and the Spanish Ministry of Science and Innovation (Ministerio de Ciencia e Innovación) through its Generation of Knowledge initiative (Grant Number PID2020-115145GA-I00).

Álvarez-Rodrígez, I. M. (2021) 'The Moral Economy of Drug Trafficking: Armed Civilians and Mexico's Violence and Crime', *Latin American Perspectives*, 48(1), pp. 231–244. https://doi.org/10.1177/0094582X20982941.

Anaya-Muñoz, A. and Saltalamacchia., N. (2019) 'Factors Blocking the Compliance with International Human Rights Norms in Mexico', in A. Anaya-Muñoz and B. Frey (eds) *Mexico's Human Rights Crisis*. Philadelphia: University of Pennsylvania Press, pp. 207–226.

Animal Político. (2021) 'No militarizamos al país, soldados son pueblo uniformado', *Animal Político*, Mexico, 1 December, 2021.

Arias, E. D. (2013) 'The Impacts of Differential Armed Dominance of Politics in Rio De Janeiro, Brazil', *Studies in Comparative Development*, 48, pp. 263–284.

Asmann, P. and Ávila, L. (2021) 'Shining Path Commander's Death Strikes Blow to Peru Rebel Group', *Insight Crime*, 31 March, 2021.

Atuesta, L., Siordia, O., and Madrazo, A. (2019) 'The "War on Drugs" in Mexico: (Official) Database of Events between December 2006 and November 2011', *Journal of Conflict Resolution*, 63(7), pp. 1765–1789.

Balcazar Moreno, A., Galvez Lima, X., Lambin, J., and Rodriguez, L. (2018) *The War Report 2017: Gang Violence in Colombia, Mexico, and El Salvador*. Geneva: Geneva Academy of International Humanitarian Law and Human Rights.

Balcazar Moreno, A., Mercedes Galvez Lima, X., Lambin, J., and Rodriguez, L. (2017) *The War Report 2017: Gang Violence in Colombia, Mexico and El Salvador*. Geneva: Geneva Academy of International Humanitarian Law and Human Rights.

Barnes, N. (2017) 'Criminal Politics: An Integrated Approach to the Study of Organized Crime, Politics, and Violence', *Perspectives on Politics*, 15(4), pp. 967–987. https://doi.org/10.1017/S1537592717002110.

Benincasa, V. and Cortés, A. (2021) 'Humanitarizando la movilidad en México: la migración centroamericana como problema humanitario', *Oñati Socio-Legal Series*, 11(3), pp. 809–832.

Bloom, C. (2012) 'Square Pegs and Round Holes: Mexico, Drugs, and International Law', *Houston Journal of International Law*, 34(2), pp. 246–414.

Bradley, M. (2016) 'Protecting Civilians in War: The ICRC, UNHCR, and Their Limitations in Internal Armed Conflicts', Oxford: Oxford University Press.

Bradley, M. (2020) 'From Armed Conflict to Urban Violence: transformations in the International Committee of the Red Cross, International Humanitarianism, and the Laws of War', *European Journal of International Relations*, 26(4), pp. 1061–1083. https://doi.org/10.1177/1354066120908637.

Burgess, K., and Loureiro, A. (2022) *Comparing Humanitarian Responses at the US-Mexico Border*. Barcelona, Spain: VI Congreso Internacional de Estudios del Desarrollo.

Carina, B. (2011) 'The Mexican Drug War: The Case for a Non-International Armed Conflict Classification', *Fordham International Law Journal*, 34, pp. 1042–1088.

CED. (2022) *Informe del Comité contra la Desaparición Forzada sobre su Visita a México en virtud del Artículo 33 de la Convención*. Geneva: Committee against Enforced Disappearance.

CICR. (2022) *Balance Humanitario 2021/2022: Mexico*. Mexico City: CICR.

CICR. (2022) *Retos Humanitarios 2022: Colombia*. Bogotá: CICR.

CMDPDH. (2021) *Episodios De Desplazamiento Interno Forzado Masivo En México: Informe 2020*. Mexico City: Comisión Mexicana de Defensa y Promoción de los Derechos Humanos.

Comer, C. and Mburu, D. (2015) 'Humanitarian Law at Wits' End: Does the Violence Arising from the "War on Drugs" in Mexico Meet the International Criminal Court's Non-International Armed Conflict Threshold?', in T. D. Gill (ed.), *Yearbook of International Humanitarian Law 2015*. The Hague: T.M.C. Asser Press.

Cullen, A. (2010) *The Concept of Non-International Armed Conflict in International Humanitarian Law*. Cambridge: Cambridge University Press.

Del Rio, J. (2020) 'Do Vigilante Groups Reduce Cartel-Related Violence? An Empirical Assessment of Crime Trends in Michoacán, Mexico', *Studies in Conflict & Terrorism*, pp. 1–25. https://doi.org/10.1080/1057610X.2020.1816683.

DOF. (2007) *Plan Nacional De Desarrollo 2013–2018*. Mexico: Presidency of Mexico.

DOF. (2014) *Programa Nacional De Seguridad Pública 2014–2018*. Mexico City: Secretaría de Gobernación.

DOF. (2020) *Programa Sectorial De Seguridad Y Protección Ciudadana 2020–2024*. Mexico City: Secretaría de Gobernación.

Felbab-Brown, V. (2010) 'Conceptualizing Crime as Competition in State-Making and Designing an Effective Response'. *Brookings*.

Flores-Macías, G. and Zarkin, J. (2019) 'The Militarization of Law Enforcement: Evidence from Latin America', *Perspectives on Politics*, 19(2), pp. 519–538.

Gallahue, P. (2011) 'Mexico's "War on Drugs"—Real or Rhetorical Armed Conflict?', *Journal of International Law of Peace and Armed Conflict*, 24(1), pp. 39–45.

Gambetta, D. (1993) *The Sicilian Mafia*. Cambridge, MA: Harvard University Press.

Gurmendi, A. (2019) *Conflicto Armado En El Perú*. Lima: Fondo Editorial Universidad del Pacífico.

Gustavo, D. (2015) '*Más que plata o plomo: El poder político del narcotráfico en Colombia y México*. Bogotá: Debate, 2014', *OPERA*, 16(16), pp. 153–158.

Gutiérrez Santos, O. (2019) 'La delincuencia organizada a la luz del derecho penal del enemigo', *Díkê: Revista de Investigación en Derecho, Criminología y Consultoría Jurídica*, 26, pp. 367–393.

Hauck, P. and Peterke, S. (2010) 'Organized Crime and Gang Violence in National and International Law', *International Review of the Red Cross*, 92(878), pp. 407–436.

ICISS. (2001) *The Responsibility to Protect*. Ottawa: IDRC.

ICRC. (2008) *How Is the Term 'Armed Conflict' Defined in International Humanitarian Law?* Opinion Paper, March 2008, ICRC.

ICRC. (2014) 'ICRC's Role in Situations of Violence below the Threshold of Armed Conflict', *International Review of the Red Cross*, 96(893).

ICRC. (2014) 'The International Committee of the Red Cross's (ICRC's) Role in Situations of Violence below the Threshold of Armed Conflict: Policy Document, February 2014', *International Review of the Red Cross*, 96(893), pp. 275–304. https://doi.org/10.1017/S1816383114000113.

ICRC. (2022) *Retos Humanitarios 2022: Colombia*. Bogotá: Comité Internacional de la Cruz Roja.

ICRC. (2022) *The Use of Force in Law Enforcement Operations*. Geneva: International Committee of the Red Cross.

ICRC, and Gaggioli, G. (2013) *The Use of Force in Armed Conflicts: Interplay between the Conduct of Hostilities and Law Enforcement Paradigms*. Geneva: International Committee of the Red Cross.

IDMC. (2015) *New Humanitarian Frontiers: Addressing Criminal Violence in Mexico and Central America*. Geneva: Internal Displacement Monitoring Centre.

Jakobs, G. (2014) 'On the Theory of Enemy Criminal Law', in M. Dubber (ed.), *Foundational Texts in Modern Criminal Law*. Oxford: Oxford University Press.

Kalmanovitz, P. (2023) 'Can Criminal Organizations be Non-State Parties to Armed Conflict?', *International Review of the Red Cross*, No. 923.

Kalmanovitz, P. and Anaya-Muñoz, A. (unpublished manuscript) 'To Invoke or Not to Invoke: International Humanitarian Law and the "War on Drugs" in Mexico'.

Kerr, C. (2018) 'Mexico's Drug War: Is It Really a War?', *South Texas Law Review*, 54(1), pp. 193–224.

Leiden University Human Rights Clinic. (2018) *The Situation of Drug Related Violence in Mexico from 2006 to 2017: A Non-International Armed Conflict?*. Grotius Centre for International Legal Studies. University of Leiden.

Lessing, B. (2015) 'Logics of Violence in Criminal War', *Journal of Conflict Resolution*, 59(8), pp. 1486–1516.

Lessing B. (2018) *Making Peace in Drug Wars*. Cambridge: Cambridge University Press.

López-González, J. (2012) 'Civil-Military Relations and the Militarization of Public Security in Mexico, 1989–2010: Challenges to Democracy', in G. Philip and S. Berruecos (eds), *Mexico's Struggle for Public Security: Organized Crime and State Responses*. New York: Palgrave Macmillan.

López-Obrador, A. M. (2018) *Plan Nacional De Paz Y Seguridad 2018–2024*. Mexico City: Partido Morena.

Madrazo, A., Olvera, C., Vadillo, R., and Vadillo, R. (2018) 'La "guerra contra las drogas": Análisis de los combates de las fuerzas públicas 2006–2011', *Política y Gobierno*, XXV(2), pp. 379–402.

Moser, C.O.N. and McIlwaine, C. (2006) 'Latin American Urban Violence as a Development Concern: Towards a Framework for Violence Reduction', *World Development*, 34(1), pp. 89–112.

Muggah, R. and Aguirre Tobón, K. (2018) *Citizen Security in Latin America: Facts and Figures*. Rio de Janeiro: Igarapé Institute.

Nill Sánchez, A. (2013) 'Mexico's Drug "War": Drawing a Line between Rhetoric and Reality', *The Yale Journal of International Law*, 38, pp. 467–509.

Olayo Mendez, A. (2017) 'Humanitarianism from the Ground: Humanitarian Aid to Migrants and Refugees in Mexico' (ed. Oxford Department of International Development). https://www.qeh.ox.ac.uk/blog/humanitarianism-ground-humanitarian-aid-migrants-and-refugees-mexico

Osorio, J. (2015) 'The Contagion of Drug Violence: Spatiotemporal Dynamics of the Mexican War on Drugs', *Journal of Conflict Resolution*, 59(8), pp. 202–238.

Pérez Correa, C., Silva Forné, C., and Gutiérrez Rivas, R. (2019) 'Deadly Forces: Use of Lethal Force by Mexican Security Forces 2007–2015', in A. Anaya-Muñoz and B. Frey (eds), *Mexico's Human Rights Crisis*. Philadelphia: University of Pennsylvania Press, pp. 23–42.

Revista S. (2015) Bombardean campamento del "Clan Úsuga" en Chocó', *Revista Semana* (Bogotá), 3 November 2015.

Rodgers, D. and Muggah, R. (2009) 'Gangs as Non-State Armed Groups: The Central American Case', *Contemporary Security Policy*, 30(2), pp. 301–317. https://doi.org/10.1080/13523260903059948.

Rodiles, A. (2018) 'Law and Violence in the Global South: The Legal Framing of Mexico's "Narco War"', *Journal of Conflict & Security Law*, 23(2), pp. 269–281.

Rojo F. and Gabriela, A. (2020) La Guerra contra el Narcotráfico en México ¿Un Conflicto Armado No Internacional no Reconocido?', *Foro Internacional*, 60, pp. 1415–1462.

Rubio Díaz-Leal, L. (2019) 'Violence-Induced Internal Displacement in Mexico, the Inter-American Commission on Human Rights, and Official State Responses', in A. Anaya-Muñoz and B. Frey (eds), *Mexico's Human Rights Crisis*. Philadelphia: University of Pennsylvania Press, pp. 43–62.

Schedler, A. (2016) 'The Criminal Community of Victims and Perpetrators: Cognitive Foundations of Citizen Detachment from Organized Violence in Mexico', *Human Rights Quarterly*, 38, pp. 1038–1069.

Sivakumaran, S. (2012) *The Law of Non-International Armed Conflict*. Oxford: Oxford University Press.

Trejo, G. (2018) 'Why Did Drug Cartels Go to War in Mexico? Subnational Party Alternation, the Breakdown of Criminal Protection, and the Onset of Large-Scale Violence', *Comparative Political Studies*, 51(7), pp. 900–937.

Trejo, G. and Ley, S. (2020) *Votes, Drugs, and Violence: The Political Logic of Criminal Wars in Mexico*. Cambridge: Cambridge University Press.

Trevino-Rangel, J., Bejarano-Romerob, R., Atuesta, L.H., and Velázquez-Moreno, S. (2021) 'Deadly Force and Denial: The Military's Legacy in Mexico's "War on Drugs"', *The International Journal of Human Rights*, 26(4), pp. 567–590.

Tristan, C. (2019) Extorsión y violencia sexual: el padecimiento oculto de las mujeres', *Insight Crime* no. 8 (January 2020). https://es.insightcrime.org/investigaciones/extorsion-y-violencia-sexual-el-padecimiento-oculto-de-las-mujeres/

Ubierna, E. (2018) 'Violencia armada en Latinoamérica: ¿cuáles son los nuevos retos humanitarios?' Nuevos retos en materia de seguridad: conflicto urbano y crimen organizado en el continente americano. Lima: Universidad del Pacífico.

'UN Documents for Protection of Civilians: Secretary-General's Reports'. Available at: https://www.securitycouncilreport.org/un_documents_type/secretary-generals-reports/?ctype=Protection%20of%20Civilians&cbtype=protection-of-civilians (Accessed: 8 June 2022).

'UN Documents for Protection of Civilians: Security Council Resolutions'. Available at: https://www.securitycouncilreport.org/un_documents_type/security-council-resolutions/?ctype=Protection%20of%20Civilians&cbtype=protection-of-civilians (Accessed: 8 June 2022).

Welsh, J.M. (2013) 'Norm Contestation and the Responsibility to Protect', *Global Responsibility to Protect*, 5(4), pp. 365–396.

Index

For the benefit of digital users, indexed terms that span two pages (e.g., 52–53) may, on occasion, appear on only one of those pages.

accountability *See also* liability
  author's analytical approach to 31, 189–191
  consent and 18–19
  democratization and 215
  economic cooperation and humanitarian
    aid 188, 208, 213
  human rights, and 188, 213
  individualization and 2–5
  individuals, of 16–17
  international humanitarian law, and 210
  introduction to 188
  liability and 31
  military actions against atrocities, and 211
  peace and 188, 200
  peacekeeping and 212
  potential tensions with other international
    policy agendas 199
  pursuit of 187–188
  rule of law, and 187–188, 215
  self-determination, and 187–188
  states, of 14
  tensions arising from individualization 21,
    191
  tensions resolution strategies 195
  tensions with other international policy
    agendas 187, 215
  transformation of liability into 31
Additional Protocols *See* international
    humanitarian law
agents
  individualization and 7
  subjects, and 7
aggression, prohibition of 11–12, 44, 47, 56 *See
    also* crime of aggression; deadly force; use
    of force
arbitrary killings *See* prohibition
armed conflict *See also* Just War theory; use of
    force; war
  human rights, and 9
  human rights in 44
  individualization and 2, 4–5, 7–8
  law of (LOAC) *See* customs and laws
    of war

  levels of lethal violence 247
  parties 16
  peace as condition where armed conflict
    absent (negative peace) 200
armed forces *See also* deadly force; military
    service; military technology; service
    personnel; use of force
  actions against atrocity crimes 211
  individualization and 1
  peacekeeping actions *See* peacekeeping
armed groups
  assertion of IHL rights against 79
  conflict parties, as 16
  individualization and 6
armed services *See* armed forces; military
    service; military technology; service
    personnel
atrocity crimes
  accountability 31
  accountability and 211
  military actions against 211
Atwood, Margaret 91–92

Baxter, Richard 48
Bohrer, Ziv 65

civilian protection *See* peacekeeping; protection
    of civilians (POC) mandates; protection of
    individuals
civilians
  crime of aggression 12–13
  crime of aggression, and 12–13
  immunity 83–84
  individualization and 15
  liability 15–16, 30, 41, 43, 44
  protected status 9–10
collectivism *See* groups
combatants *See* service personnel
combat immunity *See* service
    personnel
conflict parties *See* armed conflict
conscientious objection *See* selective
    conscientious objection

conscription
  Noble Risk Argument, and 29–30, 93, 96, 98
  Noble Risk Argument and 113
consent
  accountability and 18–19
  states' 17
Council of Europe, individualization and 15
crime of aggression
  civilians and 12–13
  deadly force and 12–13
  human rights and 12–13
  individualization and 11–13
  Just War theory and 12–13
  service personnel and 12–13
  states and 12–13
crimes against humanity
  individualization and 2, 12, 16–17
  protection of civilians (POC) mandates,
    and 200–201, 210
  responsibility to protect (RTP) and 254–255
criminal law See international criminal law
customs and laws of war
  critique of philosophical approaches to 41
  differences in application to states and to
    armed groups 45
  human rights, and 45–47
  individualization and 6, 9, 12–13
  prohibition of aggression 11–12, 44, 47, 56
  'war rights' or 'right to fight,' existence of 47

deadly force See also organized criminal
    violence; victims
  crime of aggression 12–13
  crime of aggression, and 12–13
  individualization and 2, 9, 12–13
  liability 9–10, 13–14, 256, 262
democracy, criminal accountability enforcement
    as obstacle to democratization 215
developing countries
  individualization and 4–5
  international criminal law and 4–5
  intervention and 4–5
dirty hands problem 96
duties See powers, rights and duties

Ečer, Bohuslav 54–55
economic cooperation, criminal accountability
    enforcement as obstacle to 213
ethics See also morality
  critique of philosophical approaches to laws
    of war 41
  individualization and 2, 4–5, 9, 15–16
  situationism and 146–154

European Court of Human Rights,
    individualization and 15
European Research Council research
    project 1–2

Finkelstein, Claire 110–111
force See deadly force; use of force

Geneva Conventions See international
    humanitarian law
genocide
  individual criminal accountability
    for 200–201
  individualization and 20
  motivation for 144–145
  protection of civilians (POC) mandates,
    and 220, 224–225
  study of 136
  Genocide Convention 20
globalization, individualization and 5–6
Global South See developing countries
governments See states
groups See also armed groups; organized
    criminal violence
  authors' analytical approach to 30
  collectivist approach to individualization 30,
    117
  customs and laws of war, and 45
  decisions to fight internally just wars 30, 129
  decisions to fight internally unjust wars 30,
    131, 133
  duties 30, 118–119, 133
  immunity 9
  implications of membership for member's
    duties and obligations 30, 129
  individualization and 8, 14
  international humanitarian law, and 15
  Just War theory, and 15–16
  liability 17–18, 30, 118–119, 123, 133
  moral responsibility of members 15–16,
    30–31
  obligations 127
  reductive individualism, and 30, 118–119,
    133–134
  relational grounds for duties and
    obligations 30, 128, 133
  relationship to individuals 117–119
  states, of 17–18

Hampson, Françoise 64
harm See deadly force
heads of state
  immunity 14, 53–55
  liability 54

272 INDEX

homicide *See* organized criminal violence
humanitarian aid, criminal accountability
    enforcement as obstacle to 188, 208
humanitarian organizations *See* international
    organizations
human rights *See also* victims
  applicability to non-NIAC level
    violence 249–250
  armed conflict, and 9
  armed conflict, in 44
  crime of aggression and 12–13
  criminal accountability enforcement as
    obstacle to promotion of 188, 213
  customs and laws of war, and 45–47
  individualization and 1–2, 5–6, 9–10, 15
  logical differences to IHL 62, 85
  states and 12–13

ICC *See* International Criminal Court
ICRC *See* Red Cross
IHL *See* international humanitarian law
IHRL *See* human rights
immunity *See also* liability
  civilian immunity from attack 83–84
  combat immunity 44, 48–52, 55, 61 *See also*
    service personnel
  groups 9
  heads of state 14, 53–55
  ICC override 208
  Just War theory and 9
  protection of 197–198
  states 184–185
individualization 30 *See also* individuals
  ad hoc responses to 25
  applicatory contestation of 26
  authors' analytical approach to 2, 4–7, 22
  challenge of 1, 10–12
  collectivist approach to *See* groups;
    situationism
  concept of 7
  consequences of *See* crime of aggression
  content and structure of current volume 28
  contestation of 26
  criminalization as origin of 166
  criticisms of 4
  'cross-cutting' tensions 21–22
  definition of 7–8
  drivers of 1
  individualist approach to *See* individuals
  institutional adaptation approach to 24
  institutional contestation of 26
  normative tensions 21
  potential tensions with international policy
    agendas 187

practical tensions 21
process of 1, 13
reconceptualization approach to 23
reconciliation approach to 24
research on 1–2
resolution of tensions from 22
situationism and *See* situationism
tensions arising from 21, 191
tensions resolution strategies 195
tensions with international policy
  agendas 187
validity contestation of 26
war and *See* war
individuals *See also* victims
  accountability 16–17
  assertion of IHL rights against 82
  concept of IHL rights 84
  deadly force against 13–14
  individualist approach to
    individualization 117
  reductive individualism 118–119
  relationship to groups 117–119
  rights under UHL *See* international
    humanitarian law
International Committee of the Red Cross
  (ICRC) *See* Red Cross
international crimes *See also* crime of aggression;
  victims
  individualization and 1, 3
  liability 14
International Criminal Court (ICC)
  accountability, and 11–12
  deterrency power 11
  enforcement powers 188
  individualization and 3–5, 10–12
  override of immunity from prosecution 208
  participation by victims 14
  permanence 11
  state consent and 18–19
international criminal law *See also* accountability; crime of aggression; crimes
  against humanity; genocide; International
  Criminal Court; liability; organized
  criminal violence; war crimes
  criminalization as origin of
    individualization 166
  developing countries and 4–6
  immunity from prosecution *See* immunity
  impact of criminalization 176'
  individualization and 3, 10–11
  progressive criminalization of IHL
    violations 168
  requirements for criminalization 172
  state consent and 18–19

'war on organized crime' *See* organized criminal violenceinternational disputes *See* armed conflict; peacekeeping; use of force; war
international humanitarian law (IHL) *See also* intervention; responsibility to protect
  assertion against armed groups 79
  assertion against individuals 82
  assertion against states 79
  assertion of obligations 79
  crime of aggression, and 12–13
  criminal accountability enforcement as obstacle to promotion of 210
  direct rights of individuals 58
  drafting of 61, 84–85
  duty-based approach to 64
  emancipation/empowerment effect of rights 68
  'humanization' of 62
  human rights, and 62
  impact of criminalization of violations 176
  individualization and 3–5, 10, 12–13, 15, 84
  individual rights under 58
  logical differences to human rights law 62, 85
  NIACS, applicability to 249–250
  non-renunciation of Geneva Convention rights 74–75
  objections to IHL-based rights 65
  prioritization of norms 183
  priority of rights over duties 66
  progressive criminalization of violations 168
  protection enhancement effect of rights 69
  purpose of 63, 84
  reparation rights 72
  requirements for criminalization 172
  'righting'/'rightsification' of 62
  rights-based remedies 70
  rights/duties debate, assessment of 67
  rights under Geneva Conventions and Additional Protocols 59
  right to life, and 83–84, 254, 255
  saving clauses, prohibition of 75–76
  utility of IHL-based rights 68, 84
  waiver of rights 74, 76–78
  war crimes and *See* war crimes
international human rights law (IHRL) *See* human rights
internationalism, individualization and 5–6
international law, individualization and 2 *See also* international criminal law; international humanitarian law; intervention; peacekeeping; protection of individuals; responsibility to protect; use of force
international organizations, individualization and 2–3

international security strategy
interstate force *See* use of force
intervention *See also* peacekeeping; protection of individuals; responsibility to protect
  developing countries and 4–5
  individualization and 4–5
  state consent and 17–18

jus ad bellum See Just War theory
jus in bello See customs and laws of war
Just War theory
  collectivist approach 30, 117
  crime of aggression and 12–13
  groups and 129–131
  immunity and 9
  individualist approach 28–30, 117
  individualization and 8–9, 12–13
  liability and 9
  Noble Risk Argument and 93
  Revisionist (individualist) approach 9–10, 29–30
  'situationism' 30

Kelsen, Hans 47–48, 53
killing *See* deadly force; prohibition

Latin America
  levels of lethal violence 247
  Mexico's 'war on organized crime' *See* organized criminal violence
Lauterpacht, Hersch 42
law *See* international law
law of armed conflict (LOAC) *See* customs and laws of war
laws of war *See* customs and laws of war
Lazar, Seth 96–97
lesser developed countries *See* developing countries
lethal force *See* deadly force
liability *See also* immunity
  accountability and 31
  civilians 15–16, 30, 41, 43, 44
  combat immunity *See* service personnel
  deadly force 9–10, 13–14, 256, 262
  groups 17–18, 30, 118–119, 133
  heads of state 54
  individualization and 1–2, 4, 6–10
  Just War theory and 9
  non-international armed conflict (NIAC) 32–33
  organized criminal violence 256, 262
  service personnel 15–16, 28–29, 52, 55–56
  states 13–14
  transformation into accountability 31

274 INDEX

liberalism *See* internationalism
life
    arbitrary taking of *See* prohibition
    right to *See* right to life
LOAC *See* customs and laws of war

McMahan, Jeff 28–30, 41– 42, 44, 89, 108–109,
    117, 119
Meron, Theodor 62–63
Mexico's 'war on organized crime' *See* organized
    criminal violence
military actions *See* armed forces
military personnel *See* service personnel
military service *See also* armed services
    moral risks of 89, 112–113
    Noble Risk Argument *See* Noble Risk
        Argument
    risks of 89
    supererogatory act of 89, 106
military technology, individualization and 1,
    9–10
'moral equality of soldiers' 9, 15–16
morality *See also* ethics; Just War theory; Noble
    Risk Argument; protection of individuals
    empirical uncertainty as to moral risk 101
    individualization and 3–4, 9, 15–16
    military service, of *See* military service
    'moral equality of soldiers' 9, 15–16
    moral risk as harm and distribution 110
    moral risk of military service 112–113
    optional morally praiseworthy acts 106,
        112–113
    sovereignty and 3–4
    uncertainty as to moral realities 103
    war and 41

national organizations *See* states
negative peace 200
NGOs *See* non-governmental organizations
NIAC *See* non-international armed conflict
Noble Risk Argument
    authors' analytical approach to 29–30, 93
    boundaries of 93
    commensurate risk calculation 97
    conscription and 29–30, 93, 96, 98, 113
    dirty hands problem and 96
    duty to not fight in unjust war 100, 112–113
    empirical uncertainty as to moral risk 101
    introduction to 89
    Just War theory and 93
    limits of 93
    literary example of 91–92
    moral courage, and 97
    moral risk, and 101

moral risk as harm and distribution 110
moral risk of military service 105, 112–113
moral risk of military service as
    supererogatory 108
optional morally praiseworthy acts 106,
    112–113
scope of 93
selective conscientious objection,
    and 108–109
supererogation and 106, 112
uncertainty as to moral realities 103
wrongful acts, and 96
non-combatants *See* service personnel
non-governmental organizations (NGOs),
    individualization and 2
non-international armed conflict (NIAC)
    IHL applicability 249–250
    liability 32–33
    organized criminal violence as 247–252
    other forms of organized violence, distinction
        from 248
non-intervention *See* intervention

obligations *See* powers, rights and duties
organized armed groups *See* armed groups
organized criminal violence
    authors' analytical approach to 249, 251–252
    collective protection against 254, 259
    collectivist approach to 252
    governments' miltarized responses
        to 248–249
    IHL or IHRL applicability 249–251
    key issues summarized 264
    levels of lethal violence 247
    liability to harm 256, 262
    Mexico's situation is NIAC, whether 249
    Mexico's 'War on Organized Crime' 257
    military force or militarized police, use of 248
    NIAC, as 247–252
    NIAC classification, whether
        applicable 247–252

parties (conflict) *See* armed conflict
peace *See also* peacekeeping
    accountability and 200
    criminal accountability enforcement as
        obstacle to promotion of 188
    negative peace (armed conflict is absent) 200
    positive peace (structural violence is
        addressed) 205
    promotion of international dialogue, as 207
peaceful settlement of disputes, individualization
    and 4–5 *See also* peacekeeping

peacekeeping *See also* protection of civilians
  (POC) mandates
  accountability and 212
  individualization and 1–2, 8
  state consent and 17–18
philosophy *See* ethics; Just War theory; morality;
  situationism
POC *See* protection of civilians (POC) mandates
powers, rights and duties
  duty to not fight in unjust war 112–113
  groups, duties of *See* groups
  priority of rights over duties 66
  rights/duties debate, assessment of 67
  waiver of rights 74, 76–78
prohibition
  aggression 11–12, 44, 47, 56
  arbitrary killings 45–47
  interstate force *See* use of force
protection of civilians (POC) mandates
  author's analytical approach to 31–32
  caveats in 225–227 (C8T1)
  challenges arising from 232
  consent and 233
  effects of 228
  emergence and evolution of 222
  impartiality and 233
  introduction to 220
  peacekeeping forces protection and 235
  peace processes and 234
  preparedness for 236
  tension resolution strategies 237
protection of individuals *See also* responsibility
  to protect
  individualization and 2, 4–5, 8, 9–10, 15
  protected status 9–10
psychology
  groups, of *See* groups
  situationism *See* situationism

rebel groups *See* armed groups
Red Cross, individualization and 6
reductive individualism, groups and 30,
  118–119, 133–134
remedies, rights-based 70
research, European Research Council research
  project 1–2
responsibility, customs and laws of war as to 47
responsibility to protect (RTP), individualization
  and 4–5, 8
Revisionism *See* Just War theory
rights *See* human rights; international
  humanitarian law; powers, rights and duties
'right to fight,' existence of 47

right to life
  individualization and 7–9
  international humanitarian law, and 83–84,
    254, 255
  violation of 12
risk (moral) *See* Noble Risk Argument
RTP *See* responsibility to protect
rule of law, criminal accountability enforcement
  as obstacle to 187–188, 215

saving clauses, prohibition of 75–76
science *See* military technology
security *See* state security
Security Council *See* United Nations
selective conscientious objection
  (SCO) 108–109
self-determination, criminal accountability
  enforcement as obstacle to 187–188, 215
service personnel *See also* military service
  combat immunity *See* prohibition
  crime of aggression 12–13
  crime of aggression, and 12–13
  individualization and 9, 15
  Just War theory and 9
  liability 15–16, 28–29, 52, 55–56
  'moral equality of soldiers' 9, 15–16
  targeting of 9
  'war rights' or 'right to fight,' existence of 47
Shakespeare, William 94
situationism
  authors' analytical approach to 30, 136–137
  individualization and 30, 136–137, 146–154
  introduction to 135
  psychology and 137
  war studies and 141
  wartime atrocities, application to 141
soldiers *See* service personnel
sovereignty
  individualization and 1, 3–6
  morality and 3–4
state responsibility 19
states *See also* armed forces; deadly force;
    developing countries; heads of state; use of
    force
  accountability 14
  assertion of IHL rights against 79
  conflict parties 16
  consent 17
  crime of aggression 12–13
  crime of aggression, and 12–13
  human rights, and 12–13
  immunity 184–185
  individualization and 2, 13
  liability 13–14

276 INDEX

state security, individualization and 1 *See also* international security strategy
state sovereignty *See* sovereignty
strategy *See* international security strategy
subjects *See* agents
supererogation *See* Noble Risk Argument

targeted killing *See* deadly force
Third World *See* developing countries
Trump, Donald 5–6

underdeveloped countries *See* developing countries
United Nations (UN) *See also* International Criminal Court; protection of civilians (POC) mandates; responsibility to protect
    conflict parties and 16–17
    individualization and 2, 8
    peacekeeping *See* peacekeeping
    state consent and 17–18
unjust wars *See* Just War theory; war
use of force
    actions against atrocity crimes 211
    IHL or IHRL applicability 249–250
    individualization and 2, 8, 12
    justification of *See* Just War theory
    prohibition of interstate force 42, 45

victims
    participation in ICC proceedings 14
    reparation rights 72
    'The Victim' concept 14

waiver of rights 74, 76–78
Walzer, Michael 15–16, 30, 41–45, 93–94, 96, 117, 119
war *See also* armed conflict; Just War theory; use of force
    capacities of individualization 1–2
    duty to not fight in unjust war 112–113
    explanations of 7
    individualization and 1, 7
    normative assessments of 7
    outlawing of 42
    'war rights' or 'right to fight,' existence of 47
war crimes
    accountability 18–19
    authors' analytical approach to 31
    criminalization as origin of individualization 166
    criminal responsibility for 163
    deterrency 52
    heads of state immunity 53
    IHL-based rights, and 79
    immunity from prosecution 50
    impact of criminalization of violations 176
    individualization and 17–19, 21–22
    key issues summarized 184
    prioritization of IHL norms 183
    progressive criminalization of IHL violations 168
    reparation for victims 72
    requirements for criminalization 172
    situationism and 136–137, 144–145, 151
'war on organized crime' *See* organized criminal violence